Herbarium of
the Lewis & Clark
Expedition

Sponsored by the Center for
Great Plains Studies,
University of Nebraska–Lincoln
and the American
Philosophical Society, Philadelphia

A Project of the Center for
Great Plains Studies,
University of Nebraska–Lincoln
Gary E. Moulton, Editor

Herbarium of the Lewis & Clark Expedition

*The Journals of the
Lewis & Clark Expedition*
Volume 12

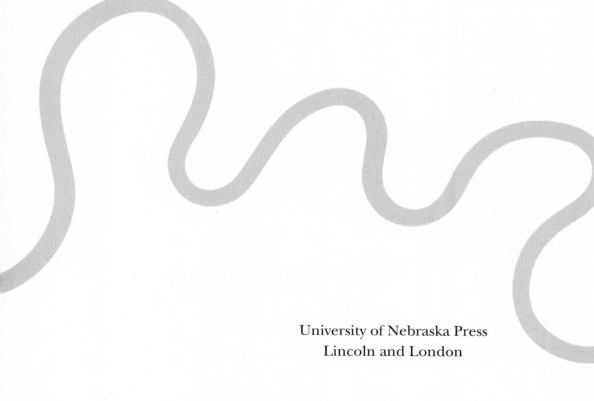

University of Nebraska Press
Lincoln and London

Publication of this book has been assisted by a grant
from the National Endowment for the Humanities, an
independent federal agency.

⊗ The paper in this book meets the minimum require-
ments of American National Standard for Information
Sciences – Permanence of Paper for Printed Library
Materials, ANSI z39.48-1984.

Library of Congress Cataloging-in-Publication Data
(Revised for volume 8)
The Journals of the Lewis and Clark Expedition.
Vol.2 - Gary E. Moulton, editor; Thomas W. Dunlay,
Assistant editor.
Vol.2 - has title: The Journals of the Lewis & Clark
Expedition.
"Sponsored by the Center for Great Plains Studies,
University of Nebraska–Lincoln, and the American
Philosophical Society, Philadelphia" – vol.1, t.p.
Includes bibliographies and indexes.
Contents: v.1. Atlas of the Lewis & Clark Expedition –
v.2. August 30, 1803-August 24, 1804 – [etc.] – vol.8.
June 10-September 26, 1806.
1. Lewis and Clark Expedition – (1804-1806).
2. West (U.S.) – Description and travel – To 1848.
3. United States – Exploring expeditions.   4. Lewis,
Meriwether, 1774-1809 – Diaries.   5. Clark,
William, 1770-1838 – Diaries.   6. Explorers – West
(U.S.)– Diaries.   I. Lewis, Meriwether, 1774-1809.
II. Clark, William, 1770-1838.   III. Moulton,
Gary E.   IV. Dunlay, Thomas W., 1944-.   V. Univer-
sity of Nebraska–Lincoln. Center for Great Plains
Studies.   VI. American Philosophical Society.
VII. Journals of the Lewis & Clark Expedition.
F592.4   1983   917.8'042   82-8510
ISBN 0-8032-2931-3 (vol.12)

Contents

Preface

This project, like the other volumes in this edition, has been favored with the assistance of numerous capable persons. Being largely ignorant of botanical matters, the editor was especially fortunate to find so many helpful people. At the institutions where Lewis and Clark botanical specimens are deposited and at locations where I searched for missing items, I found a legion of gracious curators and hosts. They not only opened their doors to a nonspecialist, but they also displayed great patience in leading me through the botanical labyrinth in their buildings. I also had to learn something about the twists and turns of scientific language. Here again, these patient people demonstrated the utmost professional courtesy and considerable tolerance. They saved me several times from serious mistakes. Errors that remain are solely of my own doing. Listing their names does not adequately do justice to their efforts.

ACADEMY OF NATURAL SCIENCES, Philadelphia: Alfred E. Schuyler, curator of botany; Janet Barber; Mary Garback; Tanya Livshultz; Rick McCourt; G. Christine Manville.
ROYAL BOTANIC GARDENS, Kew, England: Simon J. Owens, keeper of the herbarium; Sandy Atkins; Sally Bidgood; Jill Cowley; Sally Dawson; David Frodin; Nicholas Hind; Eve Lucas; Brian Schrire; Sarah Smith.
NATURAL HISTORY MUSEUM, London: Stephen Blackmore, keeper of botany; Mary Chorley.
CHARLESTON MUSEUM: Albert E. Sanders, curator of natural history.
NEW YORK BOTANICAL GARDEN: Susan Fraser; Jacquelyn Kallunki; Rosemary Lawlor; Muriel Weinerman.

CONSERVATOIRE ET JARDIN BOTANIQUES, Ville de Genève, Geneva, Switzerland: Hervé M. Burdet, conservateur.

I also had the help of a number of botanists and other professionals in addition to those at the above-mentioned institutions. They, too, gave advice unselfishly and saved me great time and effort: Joseph A. Ewan, Missouri Botanical Garden, St. Louis; Nesta Dunn Ewan, Missouri Botanical Garden, St. Louis; A. T. Harrison, Westminster College, Salt Lake City, Utah; Robert B. Kaul, University of Nebraska–Lincoln; Sarah Leroy, Hunt Institute for Botanical Documentation, Carnegie-Mellon, Pittsburgh; Wayne Phillips, Lewis and Clark National Forest, Great Falls, Montana; James L. Reveal, University of Maryland; George A. Rogers, Statesboro, Georgia; Michael Silverstein, University of Chicago (Chinookan language).

The project received financial support from a number of individuals and institutions. These people were as generous with their words of encouragement as they were with their money: Samuel H. Douglas III, Whittier, California; Jenny Levis Sadow, University City, Missouri; Robert R. Shattuck, Grass Valley, California; William P. Sherman, Portland, Oregon; Nelson S. Weller, Healdsburg, California; Aileen E. Woodcock, St. Louis, Missouri; California Chapter, Lewis and Clark Trail Heritage Foundation; Lewis and Clark Trail Heritage Foundation; National Endowment for the Humanities, an independent federal agency.

Finally, I had the support of persons closer to home: John R. Wunder, James Stubbendieck, Linda Ratcliffe, and Gretchen Walker of the Center for Great Plains Studies, and Lisa K. Roberts and Stephen Witte of the project.

The Botanical Collections of the Academy of Natural Sciences

The vast majority of extant plants from the Lewis and Clark expedition are in the herbarium of the Academy of Natural Sciences of Philadelphia. The herbarium, in the Academy's Botany Department, houses over one and a half million dried plant specimens with a sizable number dating from the eighteenth and early nineteenth centuries. The Academy has more specimens from this time period than any other institution in the Western Hemisphere. It is a unique collection strength that gives the Academy a position of eminence recognized by botanists and historians the world over.

Philadelphia's rich botanical heritage begins with John Bartram, who established the first botanical garden in the colonies and who was a founder of the American Philosophical Society. The Academy's history is closely linked with that institution, founded in 1743, and with the University of Pennsylvania, also established in the eighteenth century. The activities of these institutions and the Academy, founded in 1812, made Philadelphia the locus for botanical exploration in the Americas until the mid–nineteenth century. The botanical collections of all three institutions are now housed in the Academy's Botany Department. They include numerous specimens collected by renowned botanists, including Henry Muhlenberg, Lewis David von Schweinitz, Frederick Pursh, and Thomas Nuttall. The work and collections of these botanists are the foundation of North American botany. Benjamin Smith Barton of the University of Pennsylvania and John Bartram's son William also had active roles in early Philadelphia botany. Barton wrote the first North American textbook in botany, *Elements of Botany* (1803), while the younger Bartram produced many of the illustrations. Barton also tutored Lewis in botanical procedures prior to the expedition and was the patron of Frederick Pursh, who published the initial botanical results of the expedition. Dr. Moulton discusses the relationships among Barton, Pursh, Lewis, and the extant specimens in the introduction to this volume.

Although the materials presented here represent only a small part of the total holdings of the Academy, it is a very significant part. No other collection of North American plants has so much importance from the standpoint of both history and science. The collections are particularly valued as types of new names published by Pursh in his classic *Flora Americae Septentrionalis* (1813). Pursh acknowledges his debt to Lewis in the preface and further demonstrates it by adding in the book a significant number of illustrations based on expedition collections. Another important aspect of this collection, particularly appreciated by present-day scientists, is that collecting sites can be determined with remarkable accuracy. With the publication of this volume, scientists can correlate data from specimen labels with entries from the journals and narrow the area of collecting. Very few collections of this vintage have such a degree of verifiable data.

The Academy of Natural Sciences is pleased to be associated with the publication of the Lewis and Clark herbarium. Believing the publication of these materials to be an important historic and scientific contribution, the Academy has fully cooperated with the project. Dr. Moulton has extensively utilized the Academy's herbarium and library facilities and the Academy has provided financial support to the project. Academy staff worked closely with the American Philosophical Society in getting the specimens photographed, and the Academy now manages the original negatives and color transparencies of the collection. This volume continues the important botanical work of the Academy begun at its inception—work that the Academy intends to carry into the next century and beyond.

Map of Expedition's
Route, May 14, 1804–
September 23, 1806

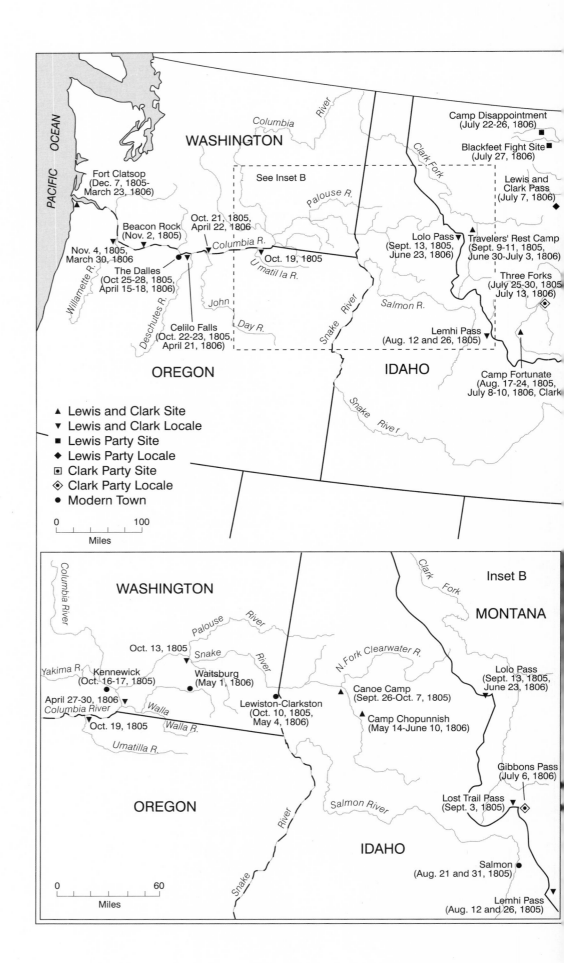

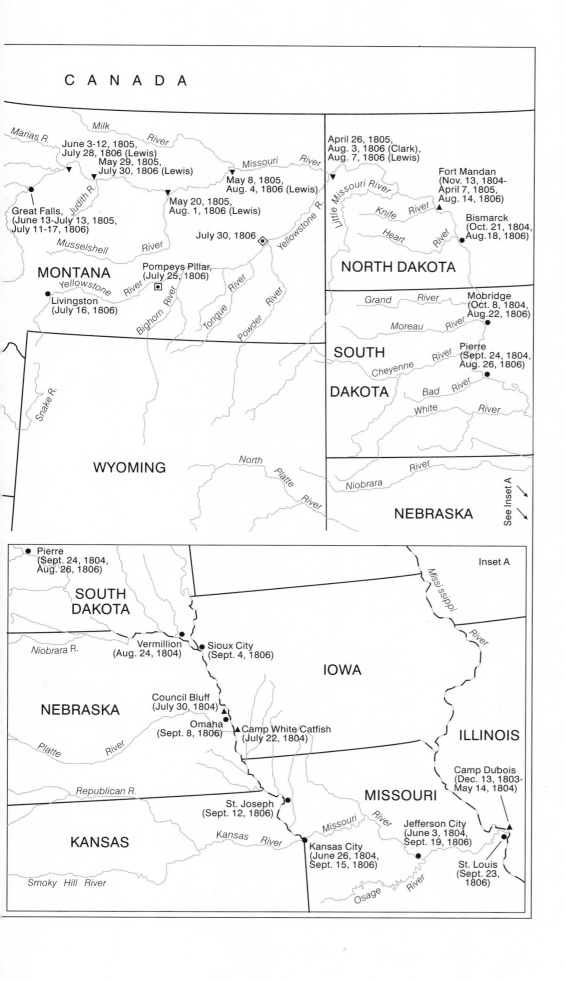

CANADA

Marias R.

Milk

River

June 3-12, 1805,
July 28, 1806 (Lewis)
May 29, 1805,
July 30, 1806 (Lewis)

Missouri   River

May 8, 1805,
Aug. 4, 1806 (Lewis)

May 20, 1805,
Aug. 1, 1806 (Lewis)

Judith R.

Great Falls,
(June 13-July 13, 1805,
July 11-17, 1806)

Musselshell   River

July 30, 1806

Yellowstone R.

April 26, 1805,
Aug. 3, 1806 (Clark),
Aug. 7, 1806 (Lewis)

Little Missouri River

Knife   River

Fort Mandan
(Nov. 13, 1804-
April 7, 1805,
Aug. 14, 1806)

Heart   River

Bismarck
(Oct. 21, 1804,
Aug.18, 1806)

MONTANA

Yellowstone   River

Pompeys Pillar,
(July 25, 1806)

Livingston
(July 16, 1806)

Bighorn River

Tongue   River

Powder   River

NORTH DAKOTA

Grand   River

Mobridge
(Oct. 8, 1804,
Aug.22, 1806)

Moreau   River

SOUTH

Cheyenne   River

Pierre
(Sept. 24, 1804,
Aug. 26, 1806)

DAKOTA

Bad   River

White   River

Snake R.

WYOMING

North

Platte   River

Niobrara   River

NEBRASKA

See Inset A

Pierre
(Sept. 24, 1804,
Aug. 26, 1806)

Inset A

Mississippi   River

SOUTH
DAKOTA

Niobrara R.

Vermillion
(Aug. 24, 1804)

Sioux City
(Sept. 4, 1806)

IOWA

NEBRASKA

Council Bluff
(July 30, 1804)

Omaha
(Sept. 8, 1806)

Camp White Catfish
(July 22, 1804)

ILLINOIS

Platte   River

Republican R.

Camp Dubois
(Dec. 13, 1803-
May 14, 1804)

KANSAS

St. Joseph
(Sept. 12, 1806)

Kansas   River

MISSOURI

Missouri   River

Jefferson City
(June 3, 1804,
Sept. 19, 1806)

Kansas City
(June 26, 1804,
Sept. 15, 1806)

St. Louis
(Sept. 23,
1806)

Smoky Hill River

Osage   River

Herbarium of
the Lewis & Clark
Expedition

[roman}	Word or phrase supplied or corrected.
[roman?]	Conjectural reading of the original.
[*italics*]	Editor's remarks within a document.
\<roman\>	Word or phrase deleted by the writer and restored by the editor

Introduction to Volume 12

Meriwether Lewis was a natural. He was blessed with those qualities most important in a naturalist: an unquenchable curiosity, keen observational powers, and a systematic approach to understanding and describing the natural world. Simply put, Thomas Jefferson could not have chosen a better person as naturalist of the expedition. One has only to look at his protégé's discourses on the environment of the West to understand that he did not err. Lewis's botanical writings are especially impressive, particularly his precise ecological distinctions. During the expedition Lewis and Clark divided their labors. For the most part William Clark became the cartographer. Nearly all the maps from the expedition are his, but Lewis shared in some of the work. On the other hand, Lewis was the naturalist. Only one plant in the herbarium (no.67) seems to have been collected by Clark: the specimen was taken on the Yellowstone River in 1806, when the two men were separated. Otherwise, Lewis did nearly all of the observing, describing, collecting, and preserving of plant specimens. Impressive as the herbarium that Lewis amassed is, here displayed for the first time as it exists today, one has to turn to his journals to appreciate the full range of his work as a naturalist.[1]

Even a born naturalist must have instruction. Given his botanical bent, Lewis was fortunate to have a parent with similar interests. His mother, Lucy Meriwether Lewis (later Lucy Marks), was a recognized herbalist in Albemarle County, Virginia, who used her knowledge of plants to prescribe and dispense simple vegetable drugs to ailing friends, family, and neighbors. From her he learned the medicinal properties of plants, and he used this knowledge in treating party members and native peoples during the expedition. Moreover, as a young outdoorsman, he became well acquainted with the vegetation of Virginia, a trait that Jefferson acknowledged when he wrote that Lewis had "a talent for observation which had led him to an accurate knowledge of plants and animals of his own country." The captain's diaries are filled with references to

eastern plants and wildlife and to the region's natural forms, which served as a basis for comparing similar western sights and species.[2]

When Lewis became Jefferson's private secretary in 1801 he had an opportunity to expand his learning and to study closely with the president, one of the best naturalists in the country. Jefferson, the American pragmatist, was primarily interested in the practical benefits of nature and not in obscure scientific theories that served a narrow audience. Jefferson displayed his own extensive knowledge of Virginia's vegetation in his *Notes on Virginia* but was not content to limit himself to local plants. Lewis would become his investigator in lands to the distant west and would carry with him Jefferson's prejudices to some extent. Lewis was a descriptive gatherer, not a botanical theorist. Jefferson found his "supreme delight" in science, and he gave highest regard to botany because plants provided "the principal subsistence of life to man and beast." He passed this love to his young friend.

In 1766, at the age of twenty-three, Jefferson began recording systematic observations of nature in his *Garden Book* and continued the practice intermittently until 1824, two years before his death. Jefferson added other notebooks to his nature writing and carried on correspondence with the leading naturalists of the day, both in the United States and in Europe. Noticing the president's careful and orderly observations of the natural world, Lewis might well want to emulate his mentor. He undoubtedly had access to these *Garden Book* writings while at Monticello, or at least he observed Jefferson jotting down his notes, because his remarks in his expedition Weather Diary nearly duplicate Jefferson's phenological procedures. Furthermore, the president had adopted the Linnaean classification system and must have recommended it to Lewis, who made some limited use of Latin terminology during the expedition. Jefferson's influence is only hinted at in these and many other instances of the captain's scientific work. His instructions and advice were critical to Lewis's success in the scientific undertakings of the expedition.[3]

Neither the president nor his protégé considered their time together a sufficient education in the sciences, so prior to the expedition Lewis spent an ambitious six weeks in the Philadelphia area in May and June 1803 getting a crash course in scientific skills. There he learned to shoot the stars and make astronomical calculations. He also extended his vocabulary of botanical Latin and gained some training in pressing plants. In Philadelphia his botany teacher was Benjamin Smith Barton, a professor of botany at the University of Pennsylvania. Jefferson had sent ahead a confidential letter to Barton apprising the scientist of Lewis's arrival and revealing the reasons for his training. In the letter the president provides what may be the most realistic assessment of Lewis's scientific abilities prior to the expedition. He wrote, "It was impossible to find a character who to a compleat science in botany, natural history, mineralogy & astronomy, joined the firmness of constitution & character, prudence, habits adapted to the woods, & a familiarity with the Indian manners & character, requisite for this undertaking. All the latter qualifications Capt. Lewis has. Altho' no regular botanist &c. he possesses a remarkable store of accurate observation on all the subjects of the three kingdoms, & will therefore readily single out whatever presents itself new to him in either." For Jefferson no perfect person for the task existed, but Lewis came as close to fulfilling his expectations as anyone in the country.[4]

It is not clear what criteria Lewis employed in his collecting. He left no written statement describing his rules of collecting, and Jefferson was equally vague in his instructions to the captain in this area. We can gain some understanding of his method by examining the plants that he collected during the first phase of the expedition to Fort Mandan in modern North Dakota. Many of the species that he collected had showy flowers or other outstanding visual display. More important, a great many had folk medicinal or native ceremonial and medicinal uses or were of potential horticultural or agricultural value. Indeed, Jefferson instructed Lewis to take special note of utilitarian plants that he encountered. This perspective is clearly reflected in Lewis's journal entries as the party proceeded upriver, as well as in the plant descriptions in his natural history notebook (Codex R). For example, of the more than sixty species Lewis collected during this phase of the

trip, eighteen have striking floral displays or have potential horticultural value as garden flowers or landscaping shrubs; thirteen have reputed medicinal or ethnobotanical value; ten have edible fruits or leaves or have other agricultural or utilitarian characteristics; and fifteen were apparently gathered because of their new or unique value as indicators of climate, animal feed, fire, or some significant ecological aspect of the locale. In addition, in present South Dakota Lewis collected a number of semi-arid species not because of their floral or horticultural properties, but because they were new to him. These plants are especially ecologically interesting and scientifically important since the expedition was entering a distinctly new floral zone of the arid high plains. Such a diverse botanical collection illustrates broad criteria for collecting plant specimens during this initial phase of the expedition, and it may reflect his overall strategy.[5]

If Lewis's collecting criteria can be characterized only generally, even less can be ascertained about his plant preservation methods. Plant collecting and preserving techniques of the time are known, and we can surmise other information based on the expedition collection. Botanists of the day carried bound books of unmarked sheets interspersed with blotting paper. Between the sheet and blotting paper they would lay the botanical specimen and weigh it down or strap it tight. We have no such books from the expedition and Lewis never spoke of using one, but some evidence points in that direction. A botanical collecting book of this type is among Barton's papers at the Academy of Natural Sciences in Philadelphia. It is probable that Barton suggested this method to Lewis, because the paper in Barton's book is quite similar to material Lewis used to preserve his plants on the expedition. None of the botanical specimens from the expedition, however, are now mounted on such paper—all the plants have been remounted over the years.[6]

What we have from Lewis are his botanical tags or labels, cut from his original paper and pasted to the new sheets. These tags contain brief notes about the plant probably made at the time of collecting—notes that would serve later as reminders. Generally, the labels give the date and place of collecting and a short description of the plant or information relative to its native use. Lewis probably intended to sort out the scientific terminology later with his botanical advisers in Philadelphia. Apparently, his tags were written on the blotting paper on which the specimen rested or sometimes on the opposing sheet. Only a few of the original tags remain. Of the 239 botanical sheets in the Lewis and Clark herbarium, only 34 have Lewis's labels attached to them today.

Jefferson and Lewis probably hoped that Barton would do more for the enterprise than simply provide pre-expeditionary training for the captain. In fact, Barton became one of the first recipients of expedition plant specimens. In August 1805 Jefferson received a shipment of expedition goods from Fort Mandan. In several boxes the captains had carefully packed their journals to that date, tables of observations, letters, maps, and a large number of natural history specimens. Selected items of the material culture of plains Indians were also included for the president's inspection. The captains had even caged up living animals; one magpie and a prairie dog survived the long journey to the capital city. The shipment provided an incredible array of information about the new lands of the Louisiana Purchase. Most important to this discussion was a stash of somewhat more than sixty plant specimens from the prairies and plains of the trans-Mississippi West. Jefferson turned over these items to the American Philosophical Society in November, and they were then consigned to Barton's care. From this point begins the disassembling of the collection. There are two lists of the Fort Mandan collection, one a sender's list in Lewis's Codex R dating from April 1805, and another that nearly duplicates it, prepared by John Vaughan of the American Philosophical Society in November 1805 as a receiving list. Sometime after receipt of the items, about thirty plants were lost. In volume 3 of this edition we applied tentative names to the lost plants based on Lewis's descriptions in Codex R and Vaughan's supporting notes. Extensive searches through the collections at the Academy of Natural Sciences have failed to locate these plants. We may suppose that these items from the lower Missouri River held little interest to eastern botanists at the time since they duplicated plants in the East. Perhaps Barton discarded familiar items, or Lewis may have disposed of them himself after he returned. Whatever happened, they are not available to us today. The earliest specimen from the herbarium (no.61, *Equisetum arvense*) comes from the area of Burt County, Nebraska, or Monona County, Iowa, and was collected on August 10, 1804. It is number 31 on both Lewis's and Vaughan's lists.[7]

When Lewis returned from the expedition he sought specialists to help him with the mass of scientific data he had collected. He turned to Barton for botanical assistance, because of his previous help. Both Jefferson and Lewis hoped that Barton would be the author of or at least a collaborator on Lewis's anticipated natural history volume. But Barton grew too ill or unwilling to assist. Fortunately, Lewis learned of a young botanist residing in Philadelphia who could help him. Frederick Pursh came to the United States in 1799 at the age of twenty-five and worked for Barton for a time as a curator and collector. While Lewis was in Philadelphia in 1807, he employed Pursh to prepare drawings of his plants and to assist him in arranging the collection. In fact, Lewis turned over his entire collection to the German botanist when he left for Washington and St. Louis. Pursh spent the next year working on the collection but apparently never had contact with Lewis again. By mid-1809 he left Philadelphia for New York and new employment. At that time he turned Lewis's botanical collection over to Bernard McMahon, a Philadelphia seed merchant and gardener who had employed him for a time. By late 1809 Lewis was dead, and Pursh had lost contact with the expedition's book enterprise. Pursh had gone his own way, first to New York and in 1811 to England and to a position with one of the world's leading botanical collectors, Aylmer Bourke Lambert.[8]

Meanwhile, Clark accepted the unwanted task of bringing the expedition's literary and scientific materials together and preparing for publication. He located the plant specimens in the hands of McMahon, regained possession of them, and then sent them to Barton for study. He tried to get Pursh's botanical drawings but apparently was unsuccessful. Pursh later said that he turned over all the drawings that he had prepared for Lewis, but Clark never acknowledged as much. Lewis had paid Pursh for work in 1807, but Pursh may have wanted compensation for work done subsequently. It is not known if Clark gave him more money or ever received any of the sketches. Some drawings of expedition specimens may have gone directly to Barton and were never seen by Clark. A number of Pursh's ink sketches are now catalogued in the Barton collection at the American Philosophical Society, and some of them may have been made for Lewis. The most likely possibilities are published for the first time in this volume (see Appendix C). In time, Nicholas Biddle completed his ghostwriting work, and his two-volume edition of the journals was published in 1814. Barton was never able to give attention to the botany (he died in 1815), and Pursh was dropped from the enterprise altogether, so a planned third volume on expedition science never appeared. In 1818 Biddle placed the expedition's journals with the American Philosophical Society, and either he, Jefferson, or Barton's heirs also gave the society the plant specimens; some of Pursh's drawings came there as well. Now we return to Pursh in London.[9]

A. B. Lambert was an English country gentleman who devoted his life and fortune to the interests of botany. By the time of his death in 1842, he may have had as many as fifty thousand herbarium specimens, ranging over decades of ardent collecting and coming from all parts of the world. He trained at Oxford but never took a degree. He seems to have been more interested in sponsoring botanists and building his collection than in systematic study or publishing his findings. Nonetheless, he was well respected by the English botanical community, and he was elected vice-president of the Linnaean Society of London. As avid as he was in acquiring specimens, he was equally active in sharing his materials. At least one of Pursh's specimens from Lewis that fell under Lambert's care went to Geneva, Switzerland, but it is not to be found today.[10]

During 1812 and 1813 Pursh worked in Lambert's herbarium. It seems he had few curatorial duties, so he concentrated on writing a book on American flora. There is a story that Lambert had to shut Pursh away and provide him with quantities of beer to get him to finish his work; another version has Lambert depriving him of alcoholic beverages altogether. By the end of 1813 Pursh completed the book, and it was published in 1814 as *Flora Americae Septentrionalis*, that is, the Flora of North America. In it Pursh identified 130 plants from the Lewis and Clark expedition, noting them usually with the label, "*in Herb. Lewis.*" Pursh also included twenty-four engravings of twenty-seven plants in the book, thirteen of which are associated with the Lewis and Clark expedition. The artist for the drawings is not always identified, but seven unsigned ones are probably Pursh's handiwork.[11]

It is ironic that the hoped-for botany volume that never got added to Biddle's edition came to be published in England while the United States and Great Britain were at war, by a German who had barely been west of the Alleghenies. Published just prior to Biddle's 1814 work, it might be considered the intended botany book from the expedition. But it was certainly not the book that Jefferson wanted, nor was it the kind of book that Lewis probably would have written. It is a catalog of specimens without a narrative to report the ranges, habitats, or native uses of the plants. Dates and places of collecting are vague and frequently misleading. In short paragraphs in the preface, Pursh does acknowledge his use of Lewis's collection but disparages the captain by declaring that Lewis "had but little practical knowledge of the Flora of North America." Nonetheless, it was a milestone publication, a significant early flora to name and describe western North American plants. Pursh accounted for more western plants in this book than anyone before him, but Lewis's contributions were not adequately recognized. Pursh also slighted the captain in another way.

What Pursh failed to mention in his book was that he had carried off a good deal of Lewis's herbarium to England. Here one gets into the murky waters of ethics. Did Pursh steal Lewis's plants? The kindest judgment is that he did not. He may have considered it his privilege to take the specimens with which he had worked, apparently for what he considered inadequate compensation. In fact, in most instances he seems to have taken a large part of most specimens rather than whole plants, thus establishing duplicates of existing specimens. We can thank him today for doing so since, of the nearly fifty items we presently have that came through Pursh, seven are not represented by any other Lewis item. The question is: did Pursh take whole specimens in these seven instances or have the other portions of each been lost? We do not know and probably never will. This question leads to the more severe criticism of the man. Even if he did leave fragments in Philadelphia, what he took to England was without Lewis's knowledge, and he never sought the approval of Clark, Barton, or Jefferson in the matter after Lewis's death. Moreover, he never attempted to return the specimens.[12]

Not long after completing his *Flora* Pursh left Lambert and traveled back to North America, this time to Canada. There he died in 1820 in Montreal, destitute and largely unknown. Some of his North American plants, which he had collected on excursions for Barton and others, stayed in Philadelphia. Others, including specimens from his personal herbarium of North American plants and those items that he had from Lewis, remained with Lambert. Lambert then integrated the Pursh items into his larger collection, which during his later years fell into disarray. When Lambert died in 1842 his finances were also in chaos, so his house, library, paintings, and prints were sold. His botanical collection was auctioned by Sotheby's. He had spent his fortune on botany.[13]

In June 1842, botanists, collectors, and the curious crowded into the Lambert house on Grosvenor Street in London for a three-day sale. The botanical collection was broken into lots to be sold to the highest bidder. Two of the lots have connections to Lewis and Clark, lot numbers 256 and 262. From detailed eyewitness accounts we know who acquired these specimens.

Edward Tuckerman was a young American graduate on his first trip to Europe. Despite degrees in law and divinity his chief interest was lichenology, and in time he became a professor of botany. He was at Lambert's auction and purchased two large lots of botanical materials and other miscellaneous items. One of the two major purchases is of slight interest to us; it was a small anonymous lot, number 284. This was a batch of Pursh's personal specimens that Tuckerman got for £1; there were no expedition items in this lot. The other lot was number 256, the jewel in the crown for Lewis and Clark enthusiasts. It contained the items that Pursh had carried off from Philadelphia. In the catalog it was listed as "a small Collection of North American Plants . . . [of] about 150 [items]." According to folklore, it was sold late in the day when many persons had already left. Tuckerman paid £5 10s for it.

Tuckerman took the Lewis/Pursh/Lambert materials back to the United States and eventually settled into a professorial career at Amherst in Massachusetts. Through the years he corresponded with fellow botanists about his Lambert items and lent some out to associates. Tuckerman realized that he had the Lewis specimens but apparently attached no special importance to them. In May 1856 he presented the materials to the Academy of Natural Sciences in Philadelphia. Today there are forty-seven sheets from the Lewis/Pursh/Lambert/Tuckerman line in the Lewis and Clark Herbarium at the academy; seven of them are singular, that is, items that have no comparable Lewis duplicate specimen.[14]

Back at the auction, William Pamphlin, a botanical bookseller and publisher in Soho Square, was making purchases, some for himself for resale and others as an agent for absentee buyers. The purchase that connects to Lewis and Clark is lot number 262, labeled in the catalog as "Pursh's very extensive Herbarium of chiefly North American Plants . . . about 750 or 1000 species." Pamphlin bought it for £25 10s. In 1970 a specialist tried to track Lambert's auction materials, but she declared the location of this lot unknown. Another researcher thought the items might be at Kew Gardens in London.[15]

Kew Gardens, or the Royal Botanic Gardens as it is officially known, is located a few miles west of London on the Thames River. The grounds became royal property in 1730, and in 1759 the mother of George III started a small garden there. Sir Joseph Banks, who accompanied Captain James Cook in the *Endeavour* on his voyage around the world (1768–71), helped make Kew an important botanical center. But by the 1840s Kew was still no more than a small garden of about eleven acres and had no library or herbarium. Today the gardens cover nearly three hundred acres, and the herbarium numbers over 7 million dried specimens. Kew is considered the premier botanical institution in the world.

It is now clear that the eventual recipient of lot number 262 was William Jackson Hooker, a close friend of Lambert's who became director of Kew the year before Lambert's death. We do not know if Pamphlin was acting as Hooker's agent at the time or whether Hooker decided to buy the specimens later, but at some point they came into his possession. In any case, he was an inveterate collector, and when he died in 1865, his extensive botanical holdings went to Kew. The sheets from his collection there have a distinctive seal that bears his name.[16]

In the 1950s Professor Joseph Ewan, then a botanist at Tulane University, was doing a study of Pursh and attempted to locate his specimens in repositories throughout the world. At Kew he discovered a number of Pursh items and annotated them, indicating the authorship of writings on the sheets. In fact, he labeled eleven specimens at Kew as coming from the Lewis collection and noted the handwriting of Pursh, Lambert, and Pamphlin on the sheets. Each sheet also carries the Hooker seal. Apparently, Ewan never made the connection (nor did it matter for his work) between Lewis, Pursh, Lambert, Pamphlin, and Hooker to lot number 262 of the auction. Pursh must have mingled the Lewis items with his general collection, and Lambert never made the separation. There have been hints of Lewis items in London over the years; now the provenance of the specimens at Kew seems evident.[17]

Another item in London has also been identified as an expedition specimen, but it seems very unlikely and is not included in this work. Ewan studied this plant (*Lonicera ciliosa*) at the Natural History Museum while in London in 1955, noticed that it had Pursh's label, and declared it to be a Lewis item; but it looks doubtful for several reasons. Most important, the date is questionable. Pursh wrote "Jul. 17, 1816" on the label, rather than an expedition date. Even if the designated year is an error for 1806, which is what Ewan thought, the date July 17 is not credible to the expedition. There are two other examples of this plant (no. 100) at Philadelphia. Lewis's label on one gives a date of September 2, 1805, when he was in the vicinity of Gibbonsville, Lemhi County, Idaho, then Pursh supplies two more dates on the Philadelphia sheets, June 5, 1806, at Camp Chopunnish, and June 16, 1806, on the Lolo Trail, both in Idaho. Moreover, on July 17, 1806 (the supposed date for the London plant), Lewis was at the Three Forks of the Missouri River, Gallatin County, Montana, and out of range of this plant, which is found in the Rocky Mountains and to the west. There is nothing else about the sheet at the Natural History Museum that links it to Lewis and Clark. A. E. Schuyler of the Academy of Natural Sciences, Philadelphia, recently examined the specimen and determined that it is *Lonicera hirsuta* Eaton, an eastern species that Pursh himself may have collected, rather than Lewis or Clark during the expedition.[18]

Ewan also acknowledged that there was a "reported fragment of type" of *Philadelpus lewisii* at the New York Botanical Garden, Bronx. This writer's examination of that specimen and its label, with the concurrence of Schuyler at the Academy of Natural Sciences, confirms that the plant is one collected by Thomas Nuttall, probably in the 1830s. That specimen is not included here, but the expedition items are shown as number 129.[19]

Finally, one other plant was once identified as a Lewis and Clark specimen but is now discredited. James A. Mears, formerly of the Academy of Natural Sciences, tentatively declared a specimen in the academy's Muhlenberg Collection to be an expedition item. Gotthilf Heinrich Ernst (Henry) Muhlenberg was a Lutheran minister in Philadelphia who was active in North American botanical circles from the 1780s until his death in 1815. It is clear that he received seeds from Lewis in 1809, and perhaps the plant in question, *Mahonia repens*, was not collected by Lewis but was grown from expedition seeds. It is not considered a part of the expedition's herbarium.[20]

There is, however, a recently discovered specimen from the expedition at the Charleston Museum, Charleston, South Carolina. While cataloguing the

botanical collection of Stephen Elliott in the last few years, Albert E. Sanders, curator of natural history at the museum, working with George A. Rogers, a scholar studying Elliott, found on one sheet a reference to Meriwether Lewis. Incredibly, at about the same time, Sanders had become interested in the expedition and had been reading portions of Lewis's and Clark's journals. Realizing the potential significance of the find, he called it to the attention of interested botanists, including the curator of the Lewis and Clark Herbarium at the academy in Philadelphia. This specimen, *Symphoricarpos albus* (no. 165), is one of the missing Pursh plants. Pursh notes that he had seen Lewis's dried specimen of this plant and that Lewis had collected it "on the banks of the Missouri." But how did it come to be at Charleston?[21]

Stephen Elliott was born in Beaufort, South Carolina, graduated from Yale in 1791, and either there or earlier developed an enduring passion for natural history. He was an avid collector of minerals, insects, birds, and plants. In time, he became acquainted with the Philadelphia circle of naturalists and exchanged items with them. In 1808 Elliott made a long-delayed botanizing trip to the north, collecting plants and visiting fellow naturalists along the way. In Lancaster, Pennsylvania, he met Muhlenberg, and in Philadelphia he was a dinner guest of Charles Willson Peale. Peale's other guests included Benjamin Smith Barton, Zaccheus Collins, and John Vaughan, all with connections to Pursh or to Lewis. It could have been at this time that Elliott received the Lewis specimen, or perhaps Collins sent it along later in one of the men's exchanges. Nonetheless, the specimen today is mounted on a sheet with Elliott's note that it came from Collins and a label that it is "Symphoricarpos missouri—N. S. [new species] Lewis."[22]

Back in Philadelphia Lewis's botanical items—the specimens that Barton acquired after Lewis's death and the ones that went to the American Philosophical Society—lay unused and largely forgotten amid the society's voluminous collections. In 1896 Thomas Meehan, a botanist at the Academy of Natural Sciences, decided to follow the suggestion of a colleague and look for expedition specimens at the American Philosophical Society. There he found Lewis's plants stored away, probably untouched for three-quarters of a century and somewhat decimated by beetles. He quickly identified Pursh's labels and convinced the society to send the specimens to the academy for safekeeping. There he joined them with the Lewis/Pursh/Lambert/Tuckerman items so that the collection stood nearly as Lewis had given it to Pursh. Pursh had, however, apparently copied Lewis's labels onto new tags and discarded most of the original explanatory tickets. Meehan mounted the specimens, perhaps for the first time, and stored them in the academy.

Having brought the collection together, Meehan published the first list of the Lewis and Clark Herbarium in 1898. Since that time other researchers have investigated the collection and collateral materials at the academy and have added to the list. Paul Russell Cutright surveyed the collection in the summer of 1966 and created his own list, published as summations of expedition discoveries at the end of chapters in his *Lewis and Clark: Pioneering Naturalists.* Cutright also pulled some expedition items from separate collections and convinced the academy to maintain the Lewis and Clark Herbarium as a discrete collection. As late as the 1980s other Lewis items were discovered in the academy's general collection and transferred to the expedition herbarium that is now maintained separately. In 1995 while investigating collateral collections, this editor discovered two additional items (nos. 118b, 146b) that had not previously been linked to Lewis and Clark. The connection of the specimens with the expedition was easily apparent: who else was collecting plants on the Columbia River in March 1806 or at the head of Clark's River (now the Bitterroot) in July of the same year?[23]

Given so many discoveries of expedition items, including journal notebooks, loose diary pages, maps, and herbarium items, no one would be willing to say with any certainty that the whole corpus of Lewis's botanical collection is now in place. What follows is an overview of the herbarium today. Although any two investigators might arrive at a different count from the one that follows and might organize the items in a different way, this summary provides a starting point for understanding the scope of the Lewis and Clark Herbarium.

At present there is a total of 239 herbarium specimens in the Lewis and Clark Herbarium at three different repositories. Most, of course, are at the Academy of Natural Sciences, which has 227 specimens. Kew Gardens has 11 items, and there is 1 specimen at the Charleston Museum. Of this number, the present list constitutes 177 distinct species names. Many items have more than one representative: 3 species are represented by quadruplicate specimens (nos. 17, 39, and 83); 4 species have triplicates (nos. 19, 49, 76, and 119); and there are numerous duplicates.[24]

Of the 227 specimens at the Academy of Natural Sciences, 179 are on permanent loan from the American Philosophical Society. There is one sheet fewer than there are plants since one sheet carries two different plants (nos. 120 and 121). Thirty-four of these items have Lewis's botanical tags.[25] Forty-seven of the 227 come from the Lambert herbarium, that is, those that traveled to Britain and were brought back by Tuckerman. One specimen (no.30b) comes from the collection of Zaccheus Collins and was placed with expedition materials at an unknown date. How it came to be in Collins's possession is also not known.

Pursh listed a total of 130 Lewis plants in his *Flora.*[26] Of these, 107 are presently available; unfortunately, 23 are missing. Perhaps the most regrettable of these is one named for Lewis, *Mimulus lewisii,* Lewis's monkey flower. According to Pursh, Lewis collected the plant at "the head springs of the Missouri, at the foot of Portage hill."[27] This would have been in the area of Lemhi Pass on the Montana-Idaho border in August 1805. As was so often the case, Lewis makes no mention in his journals of collecting the plant. Pursh must have been impressed by it since it was one of the thirteen Lewis plants illustrated in his book.

The entries for the calendar are arranged alphabetically by scientific name. These names were determined from nomenclature provided on the specimen sheets, by authorities who have examined the specimens over the years, and through consultations with botanists. Differences in synonymy were resolved by reference to John T. Kartesz, *A Synonymized Checklist of the Vascular Flora of the United States, Canada, and Greenland,* 2d ed., 2 vols. (Portland, Oreg.: Timber Press, 1994). The nomenclature was also checked against regional flora, including T. M. Barkley, ed., *Flora of the Great Plains* (Lawrence: University Press of Kansas, 1986), and C. Leo Hitchcock and Arthur Cronquist, *Flora of the Pacific Northwest: An Illustrated Manual* (Seattle: University of Washington Press, 1973). These last were also useful in providing the most appropriate vernacular name for the plants.

Each entry also gives the repository for each plant, in most cases, the Academy of Natural Sciences, Philadelphia (ANS), where the specimens are now gathered in a discrete collection, the Lewis and Clark Herbarium. The abbreviation ANS-A represents those specimens on permanent loan to the academy from the American Philosophical Society (APS) since the 1890s; ANS-C, the specimen (no.30b) that was formerly in the academy's Collins Collection; and ANS-L, items from the Pursh/Lambert/Tuckerman deposit, including two (nos. 118b and 146b) that were moved from a separate Lambert Collection at the academy in 1995. The abbreviation CM stands for the Charleston Museum; Kew is the accepted short name for the Royal Botanic Gardens at Kew.

Following the designation for repository comes the reference to Pursh's *Flora*, when applicable. Finally, the entry gives the place and date of collection, determined by Lewis's or Pursh's label on the specimen sheet or by inference from Pursh's *Flora*. For example, Pursh's label for specimen number 1 gives the place of collecting as "great rapids of Columbia." By this Pursh (or Lewis, by extension) means the modern Cascades of the Columbia River in the present states of Washington and Oregon. Since it is not clear on which side of the river Lewis collected the specimen, it is necessary to give the full range of possibilities, in this case Skamania County, Washington, and Hood River County, Oregon. The date for this specimen is equally unspecific, "Octbr: 1805." Because Lewis and Clark were in the area at the end of October, I give a date of October [31?], 1805. In some instances, the place and date are more precise; in others, much less so; and in a few, there is either the place or the date, and sometimes neither.

The remainder of the entry is a transcription of the annotation on each sheet. Over the years specialists have added their remarks to the annotations of Lewis, Pursh, and Lambert, Meehan being one of the most frequent. I transcribe the notations reading top to bottom and left to right. Within that framework I make some adjustments. The ANS or APS printed labels normally pasted in the bottom righthand corner but sometimes in other spots appear last in the transcription. So too, the transcription of the ANS 1994 label (done that year by Erica Armstrong of the academy) comes just before the APS or ANS printed labels no matter where it is pasted on the sheet. In this and a few other ways I have regularized the transcriptions. I attempt to supply the name of the author of the annotation when it is not given, and Appendix E lists the annotators.

Lewis's work as collector and preserver of plants on the expedition is only part of his accomplishments as naturalist during the expedition. To grasp the full extent of his abilities one has to read his journals and appreciate the keen interest and incredible insights he brought to the task. Jefferson made a wise choice in selecting him for the position, and we are the beneficiaries of the lasting legacy displayed in Lewis's botanical writings and preserved plants. Volume 1 in this edition, the *Atlas*, gave recognition to Clark's skill as a cartographer. This final regular volume in the edition now joins it as bookend to the captains' journals and confirms Lewis's great scientific contributrion to the nation's exploring effort.

NOTES

1. Paul Russell Cutright provides the best estimation of Lewis's skills as a naturalist. His consumate work on Lewis's botanical abilities, from which I draw heavily, is *Lewis and Clark: Pioneering Naturalists* (Urbana: University of Illinois Press, 1969). Also useful is his essay that looks solely at Lewis as a botanist: "Meriwether Lewis: Botanist," *Oregon Historical Quarterly* 69 (June 1968): 148–70.

2. Cutright, *Pioneering Naturalists*, 14–15.

3. Ibid., 8–9; John C. Greene, *American Science in the Age of Jefferson* (Ames: Iowa State University Press, 1984), 32–33; Edwin Morris Betts, *Thomas Jefferson's Garden Book* (Philadelphia: American Philosophical Society, 1944), vii.

4. Paul Russell Cutright, "Meriwether Lewis Prepares for a Trip West," *Bulletin of the Missouri Historical Society* 23 (October 1966): 13–16; Thomas Jefferson to Benjamin Smith Barton, February 27, 1803, in Donald Jackson, ed., *Letters of the Lewis and Clark Expedition with Related Documents, 1783–1854*, 2d ed., 2 vols. (Urbana: University of Illinois Press, 1978), 1:17. Lewis carried Barton's *Elements of Botany* (Philadelphia, 1803) on the expedition as well as John Miller's *Illustration of the Sexual System of Linnaeus: An Illustration of the Termini Botanici of Linnaeus*, 2 vols. (London, 1779 and 1789). The captain appears to have made extensive use of the latter in his scientific descriptions of plants. Donald D. Jackson, "Some Books Carried by Lewis and Clark," *Bulletin of the Missouri Historical Society* 16 (October 1959): 5–6.

5. Personal communication, A. T. Harrison, Sandy, Utah, October 8, 1984. Cutright also discusses Lewis's collecting strategy and notes these criteria: Lewis selected ornamental and edible plants and those with medicinal properties and general utilitarian value. Cutright, "Meriwether Lewis: Botanist," 153–56. Elliott Coues notes what quickly becomes apparent to those who compare Lewis's botanical observations in his journals with his collection of plants: "Their botany, it may be said, runs in two parallel courses. One of these is represented by the specimens which they *collected*, and which became so many of Pursh's types; the other, by the herbs, shrubs, and trees which they *observed*, and noted in their narrative, but did not actually collect." Coues, "Notes on Mr.

Thomas Meehan's Paper on the Plants of Lewis and Clark's Expedition Across the Continent, 1804–06," *Proceedings of the Academy of Natural Sciences of Philadelphia* 50 (1898): 292.

6. Cutright provides a fair description of Lewis's difficult job of pressing and preserving plants under field conditions. Cutright, "Meriwether Lewis: Botanist," 159.

7. Jackson, *Letters*, 1:235, 239–40 n.21; Clark's entry, April 3, 1805; Cutright, *Pioneering Naturalists*, 358. That not one of the thirty missing plants is listed in Frederick Pursh's *Flora* (see the discussion of Pursh below) leads to the belief that the plants may have been lost even as early as 1807, before Lewis turned the collection over to Pursh. On his botanical tag Pursh gave one plant (no.161) an 1804 date, but it seems unlikely to have been one of the specimens sent back from Fort Mandan. Pursh may have erred, and an 1806 date is possible. The species is not on either Lewis's or Vaughn's lists, and based on its time of collection, it could not be one of the unidentified missing plants. Lewis makes no mention of it in his journals on either the outbound or return trip. I supply both an 1804 and an 1806 place of collecting in the Calendar. On one occasion Lewis incorrectly posted a collection date of 1805 on a plant (no.39a) sent back from Fort Mandan, indicating that he may have been making tags well after the actual date of collecting and perhaps as late as the spring of 1805.

8. Lewis was in Philadelphia from April to July 1807. Cutright, *Pioneering Naturalists*, 358–60; Bernard McMahon to Lewis, April 5, 1807, in Jackson, *Letters*, 2:398–99; Joseph Ewan, "Frederick Pursh, 1774–1820, and His Botanical Associates," *Proceedings of the American Philosophical Society* 96 (October 1952): 601–16. Rodney H. True discusses the use that Philadelphia botanists made of the seeds, living plants, and cuttings that Lewis brought back. "Some Neglected Botanical Results of the Lewis and Clark Expedition," *Proceedings of the American Philosophical Society* 67 (1928): 1–19.

9. Cutright, *Pioneering Naturalists*, 361–63, 362 n.31; Lewis and Clark: Settlement of Account, [August 21, 1809], McMahon to Jefferson, December 24, 1809, Clark to William D. Meriwether, January 26, 1810, in Jackson, *Letters*, 2:462, 463 n.5, 484–86, 490–91; Frederick Pursh, *Flora Americae Septentrionalis* (1814; rpt. Braunschweig, Germany: Strauss and Cramer, 1979), x; Ewan, "Pursh and His Botanical Associates," 612; Ewan, "Chronology," in Pursh, *Flora*, 42–43, 53 n.59. See also Clark's recollection of the materials from the expedition, Clark to Albert Gallatin, March 31, 1826, in Jackson, *Letters*, 2:643–45.

10. Hortense S. Miller, "The Herbarium of Aylmer Bourke Lambert: Notes on Its Acquisition, Dispersal, and Present Whereabouts," *Taxon* 19 (August 1970): 492–97; A. P. de Condolle, "Remarks on two Genera of Plants . . . ," *Transactions of the Linnaean Society* 12 (1818): 152–58; personal communications, Conservatoire et Jardin botaniques de la Ville de Genève, Geneva, Switzerland, June 5 and 14, 1996.

11. Two other Pursh items may be from the expedition, but the *Flora* makes no mention of Lewis in the entries. In describing *Arctostaphylos uva-ursi*, Pursh uses language similar to that found on number 15 in the Calendar. Pursh also allows that his *Amelanchier alnifolia* may be found "on the banks of the Columbia," information that he obviously obtained from Lewis. Pursh, *Flora*, 283, 340. Ewan thinks that Pursh may have drawn his pictures while living with McMahon. If so, Pursh may not have yielded all his drawings to Clark or Barton and then created new ones in London. Therefore, some of the pictures in his book may be those done for Lewis. Ewan, "Pursh and His Botanical Associates," 610–11, 616–19; Cutright, *Pioneering Naturalists*, 362–63; Ewan, "Publication of the *Flora*," in Pursh, *Flora*, 33–34; Linda Rossi and Alfred E. Schuyler, "The Iconography of Plants Collected on the Lewis and Clark Expedition," *Great Plains Research* 3 (February 1993): 39–60.

12. Cutright, *Pioneering Naturalists*, 363–64; Ewan, "Pursh and His Botanical Associates," 610–11, 618; Ewan, "Publication of the *Flora*," in Pursh, *Flora*, 34–36.

13. Miller, "The Herbarium of Aylmer Bourke Lambert," 497, 506; Ewan, "Pursh and His Botanical Associates," 616–17, 621–24; Cutright, *Pioneering Naturalists*, 364.

14. Miller, "The Herbarium of Aylmer Bourke Lambert," 506–9, 530, 536–37, 546–47; Ewan, "Pursh and His Botanical Associates," 599–600, 599–600 n.1, 624–26; Cutright, *Pioneering Naturalists*, 364–65. The seven specimens are found under the following item numbers in this volume: 36, 62, 108, 109, 123, 124, 143.

15. Miller, "The Herbarium of Aylmer Bourke Lambert," 546–47; Ewan, "Pursh and His Botanical Associates," 625–26; Cutright, *Pioneering Naturalists*, 365 n.37.

16. Edward P. Alexander, *Museum Masters: Their Museums and Their Influence* (Nashville, Tenn.: American Association for State and Local History, 1983), 114–40.

17. Cutright, *Pioneering Naturalists*, 365 n.37; Cutright, "Well-traveled Plants of Lewis and Clark," *We Proceeded On* 4 (February 1978): 6–9. Ewan lists all of the Lewis/Pursh items at Kew in his prefatory material to Pursh's *Flora*. See, for example, Ewan, "Sertum Purshianum," in Pursh, *Flora*, 59 (*Amorpha fruticosa*), 74 (*Elaeagnus commutata*). The eleven items at Kew are represented in this volume as numbers 8b, 60b, 77b, 102b, 103, 104b, 119b, 130b, 149b, 152b, and 175b.

18. Ewan, "Sertum Purshianum," in Pursh, *Flora*, 66.

19. Ibid., 90; Shiu-ying Hu, "A Monograph of the Genus Philadelphus," *Journal of the Arnold Arboretum* 36 (January 1955), 74–75.

20. James A. Mears, "Some Sources of the Herbarium of Henry Muhlenberg (1753–1815)," *Proceedings of the American Philosophical Society* 122 (June 1978): 164–65; Cutright, *Pioneering Naturalists*, 370 n.43, 398. In his essay Mears also calls attention to another plant connected to the expedition. Apparently Muhlenberg received a specimen from McMahon's

garden, grown from seeds or roots that Lewis brought back. The plant, *Matricaria discoidea*, is in the Muhlenberg Collection at the academy. It is not included in the Lewis and Clark Herbarium, but specimens of the plant from the expedition are shown in this volume as items 110a and 110b. Mears, "Some Sources of the Herbarium of Henry Muhlenberg (1753–1815)," 164–65.

21. Personal communications, George A. Rogers, Statesboro, Georgia, June 27 and 28, 1997, and Albert E. Sanders, Charleston, South Carolina, September 25, 1996, and September 8, 1997; Pursh, *Flora*, 162.

22. Personal communications, Rogers, June 27 and 28, 1997, and Sanders, September 25, 1996, and September 8, 1997; George A. Rogers and Albert E. Sanders, "Stephen Elliott's Northward Journey, June–November 1808," unpublished MS (private collection), 1995. There is another specimen of *Symphoricarpos albus* on this sheet that was grown from seeds brought back by Lewis. The accompanying tag reads: "Symphoria racemosa MX. Raised in Mr. Prince's garden Flushing from seeds brought from the Rocky Mts. by Gov. Lewis."

23. Meehan found the Fort Mandan plants in a separate package, but these had also been examined by Pursh, at least the ones that are not now missing (see n. 7 above). Thomas Meehan, "The Plants of Lewis and Clark's Expedition Across the Continent, 1804–1806," *Proceedings of the Academy of Natural Sciences of Philadelphia* 50 (1898): 13–15; Cutright, *Pioneering Naturalists*, 365–67; Francis W. Pennell, "Historic Botanical Collections of the American Philosophical Society and the Academy of Natural Sciences of Philadelphia," *Proceedings of the American Philosophical Society* 94 (April 1950): 142–45; Cutright, "*Cleome integrifolia* the Third," *We Proceeded On* 9 (May–

June 1983): 4–7. The specimens discovered in 1995 were found in the Lambert Herbarium at the academy.

24. Cutright gives his own summary of the Lewis and Clark Herbarium as he arranged it in 1966. He mentions earlier counts of the collection that differ from his own. Cutright, *Pioneering Naturalists*, 366–69. The present one also differs from his, partly because of new discoveries and partly because of some rearrangement of the collection.

25. The following 34 items have Lewis's tags: 3a, 15, 17a, 17b, 18, 19a, 19c, 20, 24, 25, 26, 39a, 39c, 40b, 49a, 55, 61a, 66, 71a, 76a, 77a, 83a, 85, 90, 91, 100a, 114, 122a, 147a, 148, 153, 160a, 162, and 177. Lewis's tag on *Cleome serrulata* (no.49a) could also go with *Polanisia dodecandra* (no.134). The tag is applicable to either plant, and the specimens were mixed at one time. See Jesse M. Greenman's label comments on sheet 134, and Meehan, "The Plants of Lewis and Clark's Expedition Across the Continent, 1804–1806," 18. Attached to item 49b, another *Cleome serrulata*, is Clark's receipt to Toussaint Charbonneau for $408.33⅓. Not counted here as an expedition botanical label, it is apparently what an unknown writer considered a piece of scrap paper and used to identify the plant, but it was subsequently attached to the specimen sheet in reverse order. See Cutright, "*Cleome integrifolia* the Third," 6–7. On item 71a, *Fritillaria lanceolata*, Lewis provides a Chinookan name for the plant, "tel-lak-thil-pah," which is the descriptive term, *[i]t-lha-lhil-ma(xh)*, "those [which] have spots; variegated ones." Personal communications, Michael Silverstein, University of Chicago, August 30 and September 16, 1996.

26. Cutright counts 124; I cannot explain the discrepancy. Cutright, *Pioneering Naturalists*, 363. See Appendix D for a table of the expedition plants noted in Pursh.

27. Pursh, *Flora*, 427.

Calendar of Botanical Specimens

1a *Acer circinatum* Pursh, vine maple; ANS-A; Pursh, 267; collected at the Cascades (Great Rapids) of the Columbia River, Skamania County, Washington, or Hood River County, Oregon, October [31?], 1805

Deposited by American Philosophical Society [stamped]

Acer circinatum Pursh (T. M) [Meehan]

A very handsome Species of Maple. On the great rapids of Columbia. Octbr: 1805. [Pursh] Pursh's Copy of Lewis label [Meehan?]

Type collection [stamped]

Vidi, E. M. [Murray?]

ANS 1994 label: *Acer circinatum* Pursh

APS printed label: Acer circinatum Pursh

1b *Acer circinatum* Pursh, vine maple; ANS-L; Pursh, 267; collected at the Cascades (Great Rapids) of the Columbia River, Skamania County, Washington, or Hood River County, Oregon, October [31?], 1805

Acer circinatum Great rapids of Columbia Octbr. 1805. [Pursh]

Ex. Herb. A. B. Lambert [stamped]

Pursh's specimen! [Meehan?]

[Am]erica The Columbia Herb: Lewis & Clarke F. [Lambert] Pursh [Lambert] [reverse]

Type Collection [stamped]

As written above [unknown]

From Acer circinatum folder No. 7720 [unknown] [reverse]

ANS 1994 label: *Acer circinatum* Pursh

ANS printed label: Acer circinatum Pursh

2a *Acer macrophyllum* Pursh, big-leaf maple; ANS-A; Pursh, 267; collected at the Cascades (Grand Rapids) of the Columbia River, Skamania County, Washington, or Hood River County, Oregon, April 10, 1806

Deposited by American Philosophical Society [stamped]

Acer macrophyllum Pursh (T. M) [Meehan]

A large timber tree from the grand rapids of Columbia. Aprl. 10th 1806. [Pursh] Pursh's copy of Lewis label [Meehan?]

Type Collection [stamped]

ANS 1994 label: *Acer macrophyllym* Pursh

APS printed label: Acer macrophyllum Pursh

2b *Acer macrophyllum* Pursh, big-leaf maple; ANS-L; Pursh, 267; collected at the Cascades (Grand Rapids) of the Columbia River, Skamania County, Washington, or Hood River County, Oregon, April 10, 1806

Acer macrophyllus. Grand rapids of Columbia. Aprl. 10, 1806. [Pursh]

Ex. Herb. A. B. Lambert [stamped]

Pursh's specimen! [Meehan?]

As written above [unknown]

[Am]erica on the Columbia. Herb: Lewis & Clarke. [F] Pursh [Lambert] [reverse]

ANS PHILA [perforated initials]

ANS 1994 label: *Acer macrophyllym* Pursh

ANS printed label: Acer macrophyllum Pursh

3a *Achillea millefolium* L., yarrow; ANS-A; Pursh, 563; collected at Camp Chopunnish (Camp on Kooskooske), Kamiah, Idaho County, Idaho, May 20, 1806

Deposited by American Philosophical Society [stamped]

Achillea millefolium & A. tomentosum Pursh [Meehan?]

Ca[m]p on Kooskooske May 20th 1806. [Lewis]

ANS 1994 label: *Achillea millefolium* L.

APS printed label: Achillea millefolium L A. tomentosum Pursh

3b *Achillea millefolium* L., yarrow; ANS-L; Pursh, 563; collected at Camp Chopunnish (Camp on Kooskoosee), Kamiah, Idaho County, Idaho, May 20, 1806

Achillea tomentosa? L. Cape on Kooskoosee May 20th 1806. [Pursh]

Herb: Lewis & Clarcke [Lambert] Pursh [Meehan?] (3)

This specimen removed from sheet containing 3 other specimens with these labels. [unknown]

Achillea *lancelosa [Nuttall?] (Nutt. fm. Wyeth) [unknown] valleys of the Rocky Mountains July 9th from the west of Columbia [Nuttall?] (1) Nutt. Journ. Acad. Nat. Sci. Phila 7 : 36. 1834. Type. L H Shinners 1/9/1946 [Shinners] A. lancelosa Nutt. [unknown]

Ex. Herb. A. B. Lambert [stamped]

No. 57 (4) p. Achillea Millefolium L. Bloomfield, San Juan Co. New Mexico Miss M. G. Waring 1892

(2) Camp No. 18 Laguna Enematio N. M. Oct 15th 1851 Dr. Woodhouse in Sitgreaves Exped.

002543 [stamped]

ANS PHILA [perforated initials]

ANS printed label: Achillea Millefolium L.

4 *Allium textile* A. Nels. & J. F. Macbr., textile onion; ANS-A; Pursh, 223; collected at the mouth of the Walla Walla River, Walla Walla County, Washington, and not on the Clearwater (Kookooske) River, which they did not reach for several days, April 30, 1806

Deposited by American Philosophical Society [stamped]

Pursh [Meehan?] Allium Kuskuskiense. On the waters of Kookooskee Aprl. 30th 1806. [Pursh] Pursh's copy from Lewis [Meehan?]

A. reticulatum does not occur on the Kooskooskie C. V. P. [Piper]

ANS 1994 label: *Allium textile* A. Nels. & J. F. Macbr.

APS printed label: Allium reticulatum Fraser

5 *Alnus rubra* Bong., red alder; ANS-A; collected in Cowlitz County, Washington, or Columbia County, Oregon, March 26, 1806

Deposited by American Philosophical Society [stamped]

Black alder of the Pacific Ocean, grows to a large Size March 26th 1806. [Pursh]

ANS 1994 label: *Alnus rubra* Bong.

APS printed label: Alnus rubra Bong.?

6 *Amelanchier alnifolia* (Nutt.) Nutt. *ex* M. Roemer, western serviceberry; ANS-A; collected at The Dalles (Narrows) of the Columbia River, Klickitat County, Washington, or Wasco County, Oregon, April 15, 1806

Deposited by American Philosophical Society [stamped]

Amelanchier alnifolia Nutt. T. M [Meehan]

Service berry A Small bush the Narrows of Columbia R. Apr. 15th 1806. [Pursh] Pursh's Copy of Lewis label [Meehan?]

ANS 1994 label: *Amelanchier alnifolia* (Nutt.) Nutt.

APS printed label: Amelanchier alnifolia Nutt.

7 *Amelanchier* sp.?, serviceberry; ANS-A; collected on the Clearwater (Kooskooskee) River, Nez Perce County, Idaho, May 7, 1806, and between Bald Mountain and Spring Hill, Lolo Trail, Idaho County, Idaho, if June 27, 1806, is correct, and some distance from Lolo (Collins's) Creek, Clearwater and Idaho counties, which the party passed several days earlier

Deposited by American Philosophical Society [stamped]

These two appear alike—seem near Prunus T. M [Meehan]

A Shrub about 6 feet high from the Kooskooskee May 7th 1806. [Pursh]

Near the base of the Rocky mount. on the west side, near Collin's creek. The Shrub about 6—or 7 f. high Jun: 27th 1806. [Pursh]

I think this is Amelanchier sp. C. V. P. [Piper]

APS printed label: Prunus?

8a *Amorpha fruticosa* L., false indigo; ANS-A; Pursh, 466; collected at the Big Bend of the Missouri River, Lyman County, South Dakota, August 27, 1806

Deposited by American Philosophical Society [stamped]

Amorpha fruticosa L γ angustifolia T. M [Meehan]

[fruticosa?] On the great bend of the Missouri. Augst. 27th 1806. [Pursh] Pursh's copy of Lewis [unknown]

ANS 1994 label: *Amorpha fruticosa* L.

APS printed label: Amorpha fruticosa L.

8b *Amorpha fruticosa* L., false indigo; Kew; Pursh, 466; collected at the Big Bend of the Missouri River, Lyman County, South Dakota, August 27, 1806

Amorpha fruticosa? L. Great bend of Missouri Augst. 27, 1806. [Pursh] (Pursh scripsit) [Ewan]

Herbarium Hookerianum 1867 [stamped]

Loose material from this sheet [unknown]

Royal Gardens Kew H1426/55 [stamped and handwritten, unknown]

"1" Lewis and Clark coll. = *Type* Amorpha fruticosa var. angustifolia Pursh Determinavit J. Ewan [handwritten and printed label]

Herbarium Hookerianum 1867 [stamped]

Herb. Pursh propr. [Pamphlin] Amorpha fruticosa var: Fl: Amer: Pursh* [Lambert] *Lambert scripsit also on back [Ewan]

1 America Sept: Fred: Pursh. 2 Banks of the Missouri, Nuttall. [Lambert] [reverse]

9 *Ampelopsis cordata* Michx., raccoon grape; ANS-A; collection place and date unclear, if at the party's Council Bluff, Washington County, Nebraska, then September 8, 1806, if September 14, 1806, then in Leavenworth County, Kansas

Deposited by American Philosophical Society [stamped]

near Counsel Bluffs Missouri. Septb. 14th 1806. [Pursh]

ANS PHILA [perforated initials]

ANS 1994 label: *Ampelopsis cordata* Michx.

APS printed label: Cissus Ampelopsis Pers. (Vitis indivisa Willd.[)]

10 *Amsinckia intermedia* Fisch. & C. A. Mey., ranchers fiddleneck; ANS-A; collected at Rock Fort (Rocky) Camp, The Dalles, Wasco County, Oregon, April 17, 1806

Deposited by American Philosophical Society [stamped]

This is doubtful, but material scarcely sufficient for definite determination. It may be Plagiobothrys [unknown] Greenman [Meehan?]

Krynitskia Crassisepela Gray T. Meehan [Meehan]

Rocky Camp April 17th 1806. [Pursh]

Amsinckia! intermedia? C. V. P. [Piper]

ANS PHILA [perforated initials]

ANS 1994 label: *Amsinkia intermedia* Fisch. & Mey.

APS printed label: [*blank*]

11 *Anemone canadensis* L., meadow anemone; ANS-A; collected near the Omaha Indian village Tonwontonga (old Maha village), Dakota County, Nebraska, August 17, 1804

Deposited by American Philosophical Society [stamped]

Anemone dichotoma L. A. Pennsylanica L. T. M [Meehan]

Anemone Canadensis L. [Greenman] Greenman [Meehan?]

Prairies; in the camp near the old Maha village Augst. 17, 1804 [Pursh] (Lewis) [Meehan?]

ANS 1994 label: *Anemone canadensis* L.

APS printed label: Anemone canadensis L.

12 *Anemone quinquefolia* L., wood anemone; ANS-A; collected on an affluent of the Clearwater (Kooskooskee) River, Lolo Trail, Clearwater or Idaho County, Idaho, June 15, 1806

Deposited by American Philosophical Society [stamped]

Anemone nemorosa T. M. [Meehan]

Anemone quinquefolia, L. (A. nemorosa of Amer. authors) [Greenman] (Greenman) [Meehan?]

On the waters of Kooskooskee Jun: 15th 1806. [Pursh] Pursh's copy of Lewis' Label [Meehan?]

ANS 1994 label: *Anemone quinquifolia* L.

APS printed label: Anemone quinquefolia L.

13 *Angelica* sp.?, angelica; ANS-A; collected in the vicinity of Lost Trail Pass, Ravalli County, Montana, September 3, 1805, and on Hungery Creek, Lolo Trail, Idaho County, Idaho, June 25, 1806

Deposited by American Philosophical Society [stamped]

All gone! [unknown]

Angelica within the Rocky mountains in moist places Jun: 25th 1806? The flowering one taken in Septb. 3d 1805. [Pursh]

APS printed label: Angelica?

14 *Arbutus menziesii* Pursh, Pacific madrone; ANS-A; collected at the Cascades of the Columbia River, Skamania County, Washington, or Hood River County, Oregon, November 1, 1805

Deposited by American Philosophical Society [stamped]

Arbutus menziesii Pursh (T. M) [Meehan]

A middle size tree with a remarkable smooth bark which Scales off in the manner of the birch; & red berries in clusters. Columbia R. Novbr: 1st 1805. [Pursh] (Pursh's copy) [Meehan?]

ANS 1994 label: *Arbutus menzisii* Pursh

APS printed label: Arbutus Menziesii Pursh

15 *Arctostaphylos uva-ursi* (L.) Spreng., bearberry; ANS-A; collected at Fort Mandan, McLean County, North Dakota, during the winter of 1804–5

Deposited by American Philosophical Society [stamped]

Fort Mandan, open plains, Evergreen, called Sacacommis, natives Smoke its leaves. [Pursh]

No. 33 An evergreen <A> plant which grows in the open plains usually. the natives smoke it's leaves, <and> mixed with tobacco Called by the French Engages *Sacacommis*— obtained at Fort Mandan [Lewis] (Lewis) [Meehan?]

Arctostaphylos Uva-ursi, Spreng. (J. M. G.) [Greenman]

ANS 1994 label: *Arctostaphylos uva-ursi* Spreng.

APS printed label: Arctostaphylos Uva-ursi Spr.

16 *Argentina anserina* (L.) Rydb., silverweed; ANS-A; collected at Fort Clatsop, Clatsop County, Oregon, March 13, 1806

Deposited by American Philosophical Society [stamped]

Potentilla anserina, L. T. M [Meehan]

The roots are eat by the natives, & taste like Sweet Potatoes, grows in marshy ground. Fort Clatsop March 13th 1806. [Pursh] Pursh's copy of Lewis ticket [Meehan?]

ANS PHILA [perforated initials]

ANS 1994 label: *Potentilla anserina* L.

APS printed label: Potentilla Anserina L.

17a *Artemisia cana* Pursh, dwarf sagebrush; ANS-A; Pursh, 521; collected near the mouth of the Cheyenne River, Dewey, Sully, or Stanley County, South Dakota, October 1, 1804

Deposited by American Philosophical Society [stamped]

Artemisia cana Pursh (J. M. G.) [Greenman]

Type of: Artemisia cana Pursh, Fl. Am Sept. 521. 1814. (Holotype originally in Herb. Lewis) det. L. Shultz 1982 Intermountain Herbarium (UTC)—Rancho Santa Ana Botanic Garden (RSA) [printed and typed label]

"In Lookout Bend of the Missouri . . . now called Little Bend, passing mouth of Big Cheyenne River." (Coues, Proc. Phila. Acad. 1890:304.) [Shinners?]

No. 60 1804 October 1st another variety of wild sage growth of high and bottom prairies [Lewis] (Lewis) [Meehan?]

On the bluffs, Octbr 1, 1804. [Pursh] Pursh [Meehan?]

Type Artemisia cana Pursh Fl. Am. Sept 2:521. 1814. (lectotype) L H Shinners 1/9/1946

ANS PHILA [perforated initials]

ANS 1994 label: *Artemisia cana* Pursh

APS printed label: Artemisia cana Pursh

17b *Artemisia cana* Pursh, dwarf sagebrush; ANS-A; Pursh, 521; collected above the mouth of the Cheyenne River, Dewey or Sully County, South Dakota, October 2, 1804

Deposited by American Philosophical Society [stamped]

Artemisia cana Pursh [Meehan?]

No. 5[5?] October 2ed 1804 growth of the high Bluffs. [Lewis] Lewis ticket [Meehan?]

Original material (cotype) Artemisia cana Pursh Fl. Am. Sept. 2:521. 1814. L H Shinners 1/9/1946

ANS PHILA [perforated initials]

APS printed label: Artemisia cana Pursh

17c *Artemisia cana* Pursh, dwarf sagebrush; ANS-A; Pursh, 521; collected above the mouth of the Cheyenne River, Dewey or Sully County, South Dakota, October 2, 1804

Deposited by American Philosophical Society [stamped]

On the bluffs, Octr: 2, 1804. [Pursh] Pursh's copy of Lewis [Meehan?]

Artemisia cana, Pursh [Greenman] Greenman [Meehan?]

Original material (cotype). Artemisia cana Pursh Fl. Am. Sept. 2:251. 1814. L H Shinners 1/9/1946

ANS 1994 label: *Artemisia cana* Pursh

APS printed label: Artemisia cana Pursh

17d *Artemisia cana* Pursh, dwarf sagebrush; ANS-L; Pursh, 521; collected above the mouth of the Cheyenne River, Dewey or Sully County, South Dakota, October 2, 1804

Artemisia cana. On the bluffs, Octbr: 2, 1804 [Pursh]

Ex. Herb. A. B. Lambert [stamped]

A. cana, Pursh A. Columbianus Nutt. A. Gr. [Gray]

1 Herb: Lewis & Clark. 2 upper Louisiana Nuttall. [Lambert]

ANS PHILA [perforated initials]

ANS 1994 label: *Artemisia cana* Pursh

ANS printed label: Artemisia cana Pursh

18 *Artemisia dracunculus* L., silky wormwood; ANS-A; Pursh, 521; collected above the mouth of the White River, Lyman or Brule County, South Dakota, September 15, 1804

Deposited by American Philosophical Society [stamped]

Artemisia Dracunculoides, Pursh [Meehan?] (A. Dracunculus Pursh) [unknown]

On the bluffs, Septb 15 1804 [Pursh] Pursh's copy [Meehan?]

No. 52 Sept. 15th 1804. growth of the open Plains [Lewis] (Lewis) [Meehan?]

ANS 1994 label: *Artemisia dracunculus* L.

APS printed label: Artemisia Dracunculus Pursh

19a *Artemisia frigida* Willd., pasture sagewort; ANS-A; Pursh, 521; collected in Bon Homme County, South Dakota, or Knox County, Nebraska, September 2, 1804

Deposited by American Philosophical Society [stamped]

Artemisia frigida <L.> Willd. T. M [Meehan]

On the bluffs, Septb: 2, 1804. [Pursh] Purshs copy [Meehan?]

No. 41 found on the <open> Bluffs the 2ed of Sept. 1804. is the growth of open high situations [Lewis] Lewis's ticket [Meehan?]

ANS 1994 label: *Artemisia frigida* Willd.

APS printed label: Artemisia frigida Willd.

19b *Artemisia frigida* Willd., pasture sagewort; ANS-L; Pursh, 521; collected in Bon Homme County, South Dakota, or Knox County, Nebraska, September 2, 1804

Artemisia frigida! Willd. On the bluffs, Septb: 2, 1804 [Pursh]

Herb: Lewis & Clarke. [Lambert]

Pursh! [Meehan?]

From Artemisia frigida folder No. 9358 [unknown] [reverse]

ANS 1994 label: *Artemisia frigida* Willd.

ANS printed label: Artemisia frigida Willd.

19c *Artemisia frigida* Willd., pasture sagewort; ANS-A; Pursh, 521; collected near the Potter-Sully county line, South Dakota, October 3, 1804

Deposited by American Philosophical Society [stamped]

No. 51 1804—October 3rd Radix perennial [*illegible words, crossed out*] 3 to 8 stalks as high as the specimen growth of the high sides of the Bluff [Lewis] Lewis ticket [Meehan?]

Artemisia frigida Willd. T. M [Meehan]

ANS 1994 label: *Artemisia frigida* Willd.

APS printed label: Artemisia frigida Willd.

20 *Artemisia longifolia* Nutt., long-leaved sage; ANS-A; collected near the Potter-Sully county line, South Dakota, October 3, 1804

Deposited by American Philosophical Society [stamped]

Artemisia longifolia, Nutt. (A. integrifolia, Pursh) [Greenman?]

Artemisia integrifolia Pursh [Meehan?]

No. 53 October 3rd flavor like the camomile radix <prennal?> perennial growth of the high bluffs [Lewis] Lewis [Meehan?]

Wild Sage on the bluffs. Octbr: 1, 1804 [Pursh] Pursh's copy [Meehan?]

ANS 1994 label: *Artemisia longifolia* Nutt.

APS printed label: Artemisia longifolia Nutt. A. longifolium Pursh

21a *Artemisia ludoviciana* Nutt., white sage; ANS-A; Pursh, 520; collected in Skamania County, Washington, or Multnomah County, Oregon, if April 10, 1806, is correct, otherwise Rock Fort Camp, The Dalles, Wasco County, Oregon, a few days later if "Rockford Camp" is correct

Deposited by American Philosophical Society [stamped]

Artemisia Rockford Camp—[Pursh]

Artemisia Ludoviciana <leaves pinnately lobed> T. M [Meehan]

Artemisia Species Columbia R. Aprl. 10th 1806. [Pursh] Pursh's copy [Meehan?]

ANS 1994 label: *Artemisia ludoviciana* Nutt.

APS printed label: Artemisia Ludoviciana

21b *Artemisia ludoviciana* Nutt., white sage; ANS-L; Pursh, 520; collected near the mouth of the Cheyenne River, Dewey, Sully, or Stanley County, South Dakota, October 1, 1804

Artemisia integrifolia? L. Wild Sage, on the bluffs Octr: 1, 1804 [Pursh]

Ex. Herb. A. B. Lambert [stamped]

1 Herb: Lewis & Clarcke. 2 upper Louisiana. Nuttall [Lambert]

A. Ludoviciana Herb. Pursh A. Gr. [Gray]

ANS 1994 label: *Artemisia ludoviciana* Nutt.

ANS printed label: Artemisia Ludoviciana Nutt.

22 *Aster oblongifolius* Nutt., aromatic aster; ANS-A; collected at the Big Bend of the Missouri River, Lyman County, South Dakota, September 21, 1804

Deposited by American Philosophical Society [stamped]

Lasallea oblongifolia (Nutt.) Semple & Brouillet Determinavit John C. Semple 1980 Herbarium WAT University of Waterloo [typed label]

Big bend of the Missouri Septbr. 21, 1804 [Pursh] Lewis. Pursh's label [Meehan?]

Aster oblongifolius, Nutt. [Greenman] Greenman [Meehan?]

ANS PHILA [perforated initials]

APS printed label: Aster oblongifolius Nutt.

23 *Aster oregonensis* (Nutt.) Cronq., Oregon white-topped aster; ANS-A; collected on the Snake (Lewis's) River, Washington, October 1805

Deposited by American Philosophical Society [stamped]

On Lewis's River Octbr: 1805. [Pursh]

Aster subspicatus Nees (perhaps) Determined by Kenton L. Chambers July 30, 1973 [typed and printed label]

Aster Oregonus, Nutt. [Greenman] Greenman [Meehan?]

ANS PHILA [perforated initials]

ANS 1994 label: *Aster oregonensis* (Nutt.) Cronq.

APS printed label: Aster oregonus Nutt

24 *Astragalus canadensis* L., Canada milk-vetch; ANS-A; collected above the mouth of the White River, Lyman or Brule County, South Dakota, September 15, 1804

Deposited by American Philosophical Society [stamped]

Astragalus mortonii Nutt. [Meehan?]

Astragalus Nov: Speci. Open prairies Septb: 5, 1804. May be A. uralensis ? L. [Pursh]

No. 46 The growth of the open praries taken 15th of Septr. 1804. [Lewis] (Lewis) [Meehan?]

ANS 1994 label: *Astragalus canadensis* var. *mortonii* (Nutt.) Wats.

APS printed label: Astragalus Mortonii Nutt.

25 *Astragalus missouriensis* Nutt., Missouri milk-vetch; ANS-A; collected above the mouth of the White River, Lyman or Brule County, South Dakota, September 18, 1804

Deposited by American Philosophical Society [stamped]

Astragulus missouriensis Nutt. T. M [Meehan]

<No.> [*illegible numbers, crossed out*] No. 36 18th of Septr. the growth of the high Prarie—[Lewis] (Lewis) [Meehan?]

ANS 1994 label: *Astragalus missouriensis* Nutt.

APS printed label: Astragalus missouriensis Nutt.

26 *Atriplex canescens* (Pursh) Nutt., four-wing saltbush; ANS-A; Pursh, 370; collected at the Big Bend of the Missouri River, Lyman County, South Dakota, September 21, 1804

Deposited by American Philosophical Society [stamped]

Dept. of Agriculture Ottawa Canada (DAO) Photo 3986 [printed ruler label]

Atriplex canescens James Calligonum canescens Pursh [Meehan?]

Agriculture Canada Right-hand specimen designated as lectotype by McNeill et al. Taken 32 (1983) Annotated by *Annoté par* J. McNeill July 1 1981 [handwritten and printed label]

Sept. 21st [Lewis] Lewis [Meehan?]

Big Bend of the Missouri Septbr 21, 1804 [Pursh] Pursh's copy of Lewis [Meehan?]

Type Collection [stamped]

ANS PHILA [perforated initials]

APS printed label: Atriplex canescens Calligonum canescens Pursh

27 *Atriplex gardneri* (Moq.) D. Dietr., moundscale; ANS-A; collected on the Marias River, Toole County, Montana, July 20, 1806

Deposited by American Philosophical Society [stamped]

Atriplex Nuttallii Watson T. M [Meehan]

A half Shrub from the high plains of Missouri Jul. 20th 1806. [Pursh] Lewis Pursh's label [Meehan?]

ANS PHILA [perforated initials]

APS printed label: Atriplex Nuttallii Wats.

28 *Balsamorhiza sagittata* (Pursh) Nutt., arrowleaf balsamroot; ANS-A; Pursh, 564; collected in Skamania or Klickitat County, Washington, or Hood River or Wasco County, Oregon, April 14, 1806, and in the vicinity of Lewis and Clark Pass, Lewis and Clark County, Montana, July 7, 1806

Deposited by American Philosophical Society [stamped]

Rocky mountains. Dry hills Jul. 7th 1806. [Pursh] Pursh's copy [Meehan?]

"On the Columbia, one day below Rock Fort Camp." (Coues, Proc. Phila. Acad. 1898: 305.) [Shinners?]

The stem is eaten by the natives, without any preparation. On the Columbia. Apr 14th 1806. [Pursh]

Type. Buphthalmum sagittatum Pursh Fl. Am. Sept. 2: 564. 1814. 1. Lectotype 2. Authentic specimen L H Shinners 1/9/1946

Balsamorrhiza sagittata Nutt. Bupthalmum sagittatum Pursh T. M. [Meehan]

ANS PHILA [perforated initials]

ANS 1994 label: *Balsamorrhiza sagittata* (Pursh) Nutt.

APS printed label: Balsamorrhiza sagittata Nutt. Bupthalmum sagittatum Pursh

29 *Bazzania trilobata* (L.) S. F. Gray, liverwort; ANS-A; collected at Travelers' Rest, near Missoula, Missoula County, Montana, July 1, 1806

Deposited by American Philosophical Society [stamped]

A moss used by the natives as a yellow dye. Grows on the Pines of the Rocky mountain. Jul. 1st 1806 [Pursh]

ANS PHILA [perforated initials]

APS printed label: Bazzania trilobata

[*Ed.: This specimen is* Bazzania trilobata, *but Lewis's note as copied by Pursh refers probably to* Letharia vulpina *(L.) Hue, wolf's lichen or moss.*]

30a *Blechnum spicant* (L.) Roth, deer-fern; ANS-A; Pursh, 669; collected at Fort Clatsop, Clatsop County, Oregon, January 20, 1806

Deposited by American Philosophical Society [stamped]

Blechnum Spicant (T. M.) [Meehan] Lomaria spicant, Desv. [Greenman] (Greenman) [Meehan?]

Fort Clatsop. Jan: 20th 1806. [Pursh] Pursh's copy [Meehan?]

ANS PHILA [perforated initials]

ANS 1994 label: *Blechnum spicant* (L.) Sm.

APS printed label: Lomaria Spicant Desv.

30b *Blechnum spicant* (L.) Roth, deer-fern; ANS-C; Pursh, 669; collected at an unknown place and date, perhaps Fort Clatsop, Clatsop County, Oregon, January 20, 1806

Am. Lewis Herbar. com Collins [unknown]

Ex. Herb. Schweinetz [unknown] No! hand of Pick[er]ing! [Mears?]

Blechnum* elatum. Columbia wood [Nuttall] Nuttall [unknown]

ANS PHILA [perforated initials]

ANS 1994 label: *Blechnum spicant* (L.) Sm.

ANS printed label: Lomaria Spicant (L.) Desv.

31 *Calochortus elegans* Pursh, northwest mariposa; ANS-A; Pursh, 240; collected on the Clearwater (Kooskooske) River, Camp Chopunnish, Kamiah, Idaho County, Idaho, May 17, 1806

Deposited by American Philosophical Society [stamped]

Calochortus elegans Pursh T. M [Meehan]

Type collection [stamped]

Pursh—Fl. Am. Sept. i:240. [Pennell?]

A Small bulb of a pleasant flavour, eat by the natives. On the Kooskooske. May 17th 1806. [Pursh]

ANS PHILA [perforated initials]

ANS 1994 label: *Calochortus elegans* Pursh

APS printed label: Calochortus elegans Pursh

32 *Calypso bulbosa* (L.) Oakes, fairy-slipper; ANS-A; Pursh, 593; collected on Hungery Creek, Lolo Trail, Idaho County, Idaho, June 16, 1806

Deposited by American Philosophical Society [stamped]

Calypso borealis, Salisb. [Greenman] (Greenman) [Meehan?]

waters of *hungry creek*. Rocky mountain. June 16th 1806. [Pursh] (Pursh's copy of Lewis) [Meehan?]

ANS PHILA [perforated initials]

ANS 1994 label: *Calypso bulbosa* (L.) Oakes

APS printed label: Calypso borealis Salisb.

33 *Camassia quamash* (Pursh) Greene, camas; ANS-A; Pursh, 226; collected on Weippe Prairie (Quamash Flats), Clearwater County, Idaho, June 23, 1806

Deposited by American Philosophical Society [stamped]

Type collection [stamped]

Herbarium of the University of California Camassia Quamash (Pursh) Greene subsp. typica Gould Type Det. F. W. Gould Date 1940 [printed and typed label]

The Academy of Natural Sciences of Philadelphia According to Glenn Ray Downing of Pocatello, Idaho, the locality is: Weippe Prairie in Clearwater County, Idaho. See letter from Downing in files. Det. Benjamin C. Stone Date: 2, 1986 [printed and typed label]

Camassia esculentium Lindl Phalangium Quamash Pursh T. M [Meehan]

Near the foot of the Rocky mountain on the Quamash flats—June 23d 1806 [Pursh]

ANS PHILA [perforated initials]

ANS 1994 label: *Camassia quamash* (Pursh) Greene

APS printed label: Camassia esculentum Lindl.

34 *Camissonia subacaulis* (Pursh) Raven, long-leaf evening primrose; ANS-A; Pursh, 304; collected on Weippe Prairie (Squamash Flats), Clearwater County, Idaho, June 14, 1806

Deposited by American Philosophical Society [stamped]

pub as Jussieua subacaulis Pursh J A M 5/83 [Mears]

Oenothera heterantha, Nutt. [Greenman] (Greenman) [Meehan?]

Part of type of Camissonia subacaulis (Pursh) Raven [Raven?]

In moist ground on the Squamash flats. June 14th 1806 [Pursh] Pursh copy of Lewis [Meehan?]

ANS PHILA [perforated initials]

ANS 1994 label: *Camissonia subacaulis* (Pursh) Raven

APS printed label: Oenothera heterantha Nutt.

35a *Cardamine nuttallii* Greene, slender toothwort; ANS-A; Pursh, 439; collected near the mouth of Sandy (Quicksand) River, Multnomah County, Oregon, April 1, 1806

Deposited by American Philosophical Society [stamped]

Dentaria tenella Pursh T. M. [Meehan]

Columbia near Quicksand R. Aprl. 1st 1806. [Pursh]

ANS PHILA [perforated initials]

ANS 1994 label: *Cardamine nuttallii* Greene var. *nuttallii*

APS printed label: Dentaria tenella Pursh

35b *Cardamine nuttallii* Greene, slender toothwort; ANS-L; Pursh, 439; collected near the mouth of Sandy (Quicksand) River, Multnomah County, Oregon, April 1, 1806

3321 [unknown]

Pursh's specimen! [Meehan?]

Dentaria tenella Columbia near Quicksand River Aprl. 1, 1806 [Pursh]

Lewis & Clarck [Lambert]

Dentaria tenella ph. Columbia R. [Nuttall?] "Nuttall" [unknown]

Herbarium of the University of Notre Dame, Indiana Quantitative Studies in the Brassicaceae Cardamine pulcherrima (Robbins.) Greene Determined by Theodore J. Crovello 1975 Collection label data and State of the Specimen information have been captured for computer retrieval. Address inquiries to the above. [printed and typed label]

ANS PHILA [perforated initials]

ANS 1994 label: *Cardamine nuttallii* Greene var. *nuttallii*

ANS printed label: Dentaria tenella Pursh

36 *Ceanothus sanguineus* Pursh, redstem ceanothus; ANS-L; Pursh, 167; collected between Bald Mountain and Spring Hill, Lolo Trail, Idaho County, Idaho, if June 27, 1806, is correct, and some distance from Lolo (Collins's) Creek, Clearwater and Idaho counties, which the party passed several days earlier; in his *Flora* Pursh says "near the Rocky mountains on the banks of the Missouri"

Ex. Herb. A. B. Lambert [stamped]

Ceanothus atropurpureus. Near the foot of the Rocky mountain, on Collins Creek. Jun. 27, 1806. [Pursh]

Herb: Lewis & Clarck. [Lambert]

Pursh's specimen [Meehan?]

Ceanothus sanguineus Pursh Examined for dissertation research: Nancy Craft Coile 1988 University of Georgia, Athens, GA lectotype *Ceanothus sanguineus* Pursh Flora Americae Sept. I:167. 1814. Nancy Craft Coile 1988 University of Georgia Athens, GA [printed label]

ANS PHILA [perforated initials]

ANS printed label: Ceanothus sanguineus Pursh

37 *Ceanothus velutinus* Dougl. *ex* Hook., mountain balm; ANS-A; collected on an affluent of the Clearwater (Kooskooskee) River, date unknown

Deposited by American Philosophical Society [stamped]

Ceanothus velutinus Dougl T. M [Meehan]

An Evergreen A Shrub about 8 or 9 f. high. On the Rocky mountains Waters of the Kooskooskee [Pursh] Pursh copy of Lewis [Meehan?]

ANS PHILA [perforated initials]

ANS 1994 label: *Ceanothus velutinus* Dougl.

APS printed label: Ceanothus velutinus Doug.

38 *Cerastium arvense* L., field chickweed; ANS-A; Pursh, 321; collected in Klickitat County, Washington, or Wasco or Sherman County, Oregon, April 22, 1806

Deposited by American Philosophical Society [stamped]

The glandular viscidity is not found in any other of the many we have [unknown]

Plains of Columbia. Aprl. 22th 1806. [Pursh]

ANS PHILA [perforated initials]

ANS 1994 label: *Cerastium arvense* L.

APS printed label: Cerastium arvense L. C. elongatum Pursh

39a *Chrysothamnus nauseosus* (Pallas *ex* Pursh) Britt. ssp. *graveolens* (Nutt.) Piper, rabbit brush; ANS-A; Pursh,

517; collected at the Big Bend of the Missouri River, Lyman County, South Dakota, September 21, 1804

Deposited by American Philosophical Society [stamped]

The Academy of Natural Sciences of Philadelphia Chrysothamnus nauseosus ssp. graveolens Det. Harvey M. Hall Date: 1924. [printed and handwritten]

The Academy of Natural Sciences of Philadelphia H.s M. Halls det. should be taken as authoritative Det. A. T. Harrison L & C Journal Proj. Univ. of Neb Date: 9-5-84 [printed and handwritten]

Chrysothamnus [unknown] Yes! probably C. nauseosus graveolens (Tometose twigs keep it out of Gutierrezia) H M Hall 1924

Gutierrezia Euthamia, Torr. & Gray (Solidago Sarothrae, Pursh) [Greenman] Greenman [Meehan?]

Gutierrezia Euthamia T G [Meehan?]

No. 32. Specimens of aromatic plants on which the a[n]telope feeds—these were obtained 21st of Sept. 1805 [1804]. at the upper part of the bigg bend of the Missouri.—[Lewis]

Upper part of the big bend of the Missouri. Septbr: 21, 1804. [Pursh]

ANS PHILA [perforated initials]

APS printed label: Gutierrezia Euthamia T. & G. Solidago sarothrae Pursh

39b *Chrysothamnus nauseosus* (Pallas *ex* Pursh) Britt. ssp. *graveolens* (Nutt.) Piper, rabbit brush; ANS-L; Pursh, 517; collected at the Big Bend of the Missouri River, Lyman County, South Dakota, September 21, 1804

Baccharis linearis N Sp. Big bend of the Missouri Septb: 21 1804 [Pursh]

= Linosyris viscidiflora Torr. & Gr.! [Gray?]

N. America. Lewis & Clarck. [Lambert]

not viscidifloris but one of the subspp. of *C. nauseosus*, probably graveleus H M H. [Hall]

Chrysothamnus nauseosus (Pallas) Britt. subsp. *graveolens* (Nutt.) Piper (fragment, but probably this) Det. L. C. Anderson Dec 1985

0928499 [stamped]

Ex. Herb. A. B. Lambert [stamped]

From Chrysothamnus viscidiflorus folder No. 8856 [unknown] [reverse]

ANS PHILA [perforated initials]

ANS printed label: Bigelovia Douglasii Gr

39c *Chrysothamnus nauseosus* (Pallas *ex* Pursh) Britt. ssp. *graveolens* (Nutt.) Piper, rabbit brush; ANS-A; Pursh,

517; collected above the mouth of the Cheyenne River, Dewey or Sully County, South Dakota, October 2, 1804

Deposited by American Philosophical Society [stamped]

Chrysothamnus nauseosus (Pallas) Britt. subsp. *graveolens* (Nutt.) Piper (occurs in western Dakotas & eastern Montana, not in Columbia River region as suggested by Shinners) Det. L. C. Anderson Dec 1985

0928492 [stamped]

Bigelowia gravolens, Gray [Greenman] Greenman [Meehan?]

This label probably belongs to the isotype of Chrysothamnus nauseosus, q. v. [Shinners]

(Lewis' original label) [Pennell?]

No. 54. October 2ed—grows from 18 inches to 2½ feet, many stalks from the same root, from which they issue near the groun[d]—the radix [*illegible word crossed out*] perennial. The goat or antelope feed on it in the winter. it is the growth of the high bluffs. [Lewis] (Lewis) [Meehan?]

High bluffs, goats feed upon, 18 inches high. Octb: 2, 1804. [Pursh]

Chrysothamnus nauseosus ssp. graveolens (Nutt.) Hall & Clements. Most likely from the Columbia R. region. See isotype of Chrysthamnus nauseosus. L H Shinners 1/10/1946

(Oct. 2, 1804 —"Just above Little or Lookout Bend of the Missouri," near mouth of Big Cheyenne River acc. to E. Coues, 1898) Now in South Dakota. [Pennell?]

ANS PHILA [perforated initials]

APS printed label: Bigelovia graveolens Gr.

39d *Chrysothamnus nauseosus* (Pallas *ex* Pursh) Britt. ssp. *graveolens* (Nutt.) Piper, rabbit brush; ANS-L; Pursh, 517; collected above the mouth of the Cheyenne River, Dewey or Sully County, South Dakota, October 2, 1804

Chrysocoma elongata High bluffs; goats feed upon 18 inch high Oct: 2, 1804 [Pursh]

Chrysothamnus nauseosus (Pallas) Britt. subsp. *graveolens* (Nutt.) Piper Det. L. C. Anderson Dec 1985

Pursh's spec [Meehan?]

N. America Lewis & Clarck. [Lambert]

0928494 [stamped]

Ex. Herb. A. B. Lambert [stamped]

ANS PHILA [perforated initials]

ANS printed label: Bigelovia graveolens Gr. (Chrysocoma Nutt.)

40a *Chrysothamnus nauseosus* (Pallas *ex* Pursh) Britt. ssp. *nauseosus*, rabbit brush; ANS-L; Pursh, 517; collected on the Missouri River, October 1804

Chrysocoma nauseosa Pall. Missouri Octbr. [Pursh]

Pursh's spec. [Meehan?]

Herb: <Nuttall.> Lewis & Clarck. [Lambert]

Holotype: *Chrysocoma nauseosa* Pallas in Pursh, Fl. Amer. Sept. 2:517, 1814. (= *Chrysothamnus nauseosus* (Pallas) Britton) Det. L. C. Anderson Dec 1985

Probably the type of Chrysocoma nauseosa Pallas ex Pursh? Velva E. Rudd, U. S. National Museum

0928495 [stamped]

Ex. Herb. A. B. Lambert [stamped]

ANS PHILA [perforated initials]

ANS printed label: Bigelovia graveolens Gr. var. (albicaulis T. & G.) Chrysocoma Nutt.

40b *Chrysothamnus nauseosus* (Pallas *ex* Pursh) Britt. ssp. *nauseosus*, rabbit brush; ANS-A; Pursh, 517; collected at an unknown place and date but not October 15, 1805, perhaps on the Missouri River, October 1804

Deposited by American Philosophical Society [stamped]

Isotype: *Chrysocoma nauseosa* Pallas in Pursh, Fl. Amer. Sept. 2:517, 1814. (isotype on right; left is ssp. *graveolens*) Det. L. C. Anderson Dec 1985

0928491 [stamped]

This fragment does not belong with the one at right. It is apparently part of the collection of C. nauceosus ssp. graveolens (Lewis #54, by mix-up of label). [Shinners]

(1) "Calycibus pedunculis foliisque sublanato-pubescentibus" indicate this as the plant intended. See remarks by Hall & Clements, Phylog. Method in Tax. (Carn. Inst. Wash. Publ. 326) p. 219. This fragment hardly from the Columbia-Snake River region. Pursh gives the locality as "banks of the Missouri" (p. 518). See notes on sheet of *Chrysothamnus nauseosus* ssp. *graveolens*, Lewis No. 54, the tag for which has probably been interchanged with this one. [Shinners]

= Chrysothamnus nauseosus ssp. typicus Hall & Clements [Shinners]

(1) Authentic specimen. Isotype? <Type.> Chrysocoma nauseosa Pallas ex Pursh, Fl. Am. Sept. 2:517–18. 1814. Type "in Herb. Lambert." L H Shinners 1/9/1946

Actually on Snake River near the Columbia. (Coues, Proc. Phila. Acad. 1898:305.) [Shinners]

Pursh has placed two with B. douglasii which is considerably different. It might have been left here by mis-

take. [Meehan?] 15th October 1805 on the Columbia river [Lewis] [*illegible writing in pencil*]

<Chryso> <Lam?> Bigelovia graveolens var. albicaulis Gray <T & G> Chrysoma nauseosa <Pursh> "Pall. in herb" Pursh T. M. [Meehan]

ANS PHILA [perforated initials]

APS printed label: Bigelovia graveolens <Gray> var. albicaulis Gr. Chrysocoma nauseosa Pursh

41 *Chrysothamnus viscidiflorus* (Hook.) Nutt., green rabbit brush; ANS-A; collected on the Clearwater (Kooskooskee) River, Nez Perce County, Idaho, May 6, 1806

Deposited by American Philosophical Society [stamped]

Bigelovia graveolens Gray T. M [Meehan]

092893 [stamped]

Chrysothamnus viscidiflorus Nutt (= Bigelovia Douglasii Gray) H M Hall, 1924.

A low Shrub growing in the rocky dry hills on the Kooskooskee May 6th 1806. [Pursh] Pursh's copy [Meehan?]

Chrysothamnus viscidiflorus (Hook.) Nutt. ssp. *viscidiflorus* Det. by Loran C. Anderson 1977

ANS PHILA [perforated initials]

APS printed label: Bigelovia graveolens Gr.

42 *Cirsium edule* Nutt., edible thistle; ANS-A; collected at Fort Clatsop, Clatsop County, Oregon, March 13, 1806

Deposited by American Philosophical Society [stamped]

Cnicus edulis gray T. M [Meehan]

Carduus <Leafs of the Shappellel> or Thistel—Roots eatable Fort Clatsop. March 13th 1806. [Pursh] Pursh's copy of Lewis [Meehan?]

ANS PHILA [perforated initials]

ANS 1994 label: *Cirisum edule* Nutt.

APS printed label: Cnicus edulis gr.

43 *Clarkia pulchella* Pursh, ragged robin; ANS-A; Pursh, 260; collected on the Clearwater (Kooskooskee) River, Camp Chopunnish, Kamiah, Idaho County, Idaho, June 1, 1806

Deposited by American Philosophical Society [stamped]

Type collection [stamped]

Clarkia pulchella Pursh T. M. [Meehan]

A beautifull herbaceous plant from the Kooskooskee & Clarks R. Jun. 1st 1806. [6?] [Pursh]

ANS PHILA [perforated initials]

ANS 1994 label: *Clarkia pulchella* Pursh

APS printed label: Clarkia pulchella Pursh

44   *Claytonia lanceolata* Pursh, western springbeauty; ANS-A; Pursh, 175; collected between Bald Mountain and Spring Hill, Lolo Trail, Idaho County, Idaho, on an affluent of the Clearwater (Kooskooski) River, June 27, 1806

Deposited by American Philosophical Society [stamped]

Claytonia lanceolata Pursh T. M. [Meehan]

Monographic Studies of *Claytonia* BioSystems Analysis, Inc. & Oregon State University Holotype *Claytonia lanceolata* Pursh Fl. Am. Sept. 1 : 175. 1814. John M. Miller & Kenton L. Chambers September 3, 1993 [printed label]

Head waters of Kooskooski June 27th 1806. [Pursh] Pursh's copy of Lewis [Meehan?]

Type collection [stamped]

Pursh, Fl. Am. Sept. 1 : 175 t 3 [Pennell?]

ANS PHILA [perforated initials]

APS printed label: Claytonia lanceolata Pursh

45   *Claytonia parviflora* Dougl. *ex* Hook., littleleaf montia; ANS-A; collected in Cowlitz County, Washington, or Columbia County, Oregon, March 26, 1806

Deposited by American Philosophical Society [stamped]

BioSystems Analysis, Inc. *Claytonia parviflora* Hook. subsp. *parviflora* John M. Miller February 24, 1993 [printed]

Montia parviflora, Howell forma? [Greenman] (Greenman) [Meehan?]

Claytonia perfoliata Don (T. M) [Meehan]

On the Columbia in moist ground. March 26 1806. [Pursh]

ANS PHILA [perforated initials]

APS printed label: Claytonia perfoliata Donn.

46   *Claytonia perfoliata* Donn *ex* Willd. ssp. *perfoliata*, miner's lettuce; ANS-A; Pursh, 176; collected at Rock Fort (Rocky) Camp, The Dalles, Wasco County, Oregon, April 17, 1806

Deposited by American Philosophical Society [stamped]

Claytonia peroliata Don (T. M) [Meehan]

Rocky camp. Aprl. 17th 1806 [Pursh]

Montia parviflora, Howell Claytonia perfoliata, Pursh. Fl. i.176 non Don [Greenman] (Greenman) [Meehan?]

Oregon State University Herbarium *Claytonia perfoliata* ssp. *perfoliata* Donn ex Willdenow John M. Miller May-July 1991 [printed]

ANS PHILA [perforated initials]

APS printed label: Claytonia perfoliata Pursh

47   *Claytonia sibirica* L., Siberian montia; ANS-A; Pursh, 175; collected above the mouth of the Sandy River, Multnomah County, Oregon, or Skamania County, Washington, April 8, 1806

Deposited by American Philosophical Society [stamped]

BioSystems Analysis, Inc. *Claytonia sibirica* Linnaeus John M. Miller August 25, 1993 [printed]

Columbia R. Aprl. 8th 1806. [Pursh]

Montia Sibirica, Howell (Claytonia Sibrica, L.) [Greenman] (Claytonia alsinoides, Pursh) [unknown]

ANS PHILA [perforated initials]

APS printed label: Claytonia Sibirica L.

48   *Clematis hirsutissima* Pursh, Douglas's clematis; ANS-A; Pursh, 385; collected in the vicinity of Camp Chopunnish, Kamiah, Idaho County, Idaho, May 27, 1806

Clematis Douglasii Hook T. M [Meehan]

Clematis Douglasii H no ticket with the specimen (T. M) <no doubt> probably Kooskooskee—It has been collected on the Clearwater by Spalding [Meehan]

APS printed label: Clematis douglasii Hook.

This flower and stem, mounted by Meehan on separate sheets, are undoubtedly parts of the same plant; if the flower were turned over, the broken ends of the peduncle could be fitted together. On May 27, 1806, Lewis was at Camp Chopunnish, "the position [of which] is in Shoshone Co., across the river from, and nearly opposite, that of present Kamai or Kamiah, in Nez Perces Co., Idaho." (See Coues, 1898) Ralph O. Erickson 11-Mr-42 [typed and handwritten]

Monograph of Clematis, section Viorna Type of Clematis hirsutissima Pursh Determined by Ralph O. Erickson 11-Mr-42 [printed, typed, and handwritten]

One of the most common plants of the plains of Columbia May 27th 1806. [Pursh]

Clematis Douglasii? P. A. R. 1905 [Rydberg]

Certainly C. Douglasii C. V. P. [Piper]

ANS PHILA [perforated initials]

ANS 1994 label: *Clematis hirsutissima* Pursh

APS printed label: Compositae?

49a *Cleome serrulata* Pursh, Rocky Mountain bee plant; ANS-A; Pursh, 441; collected above the mouth of the Vermillion River, Clay County, South Dakota, or Cedar or Dixon County, Nebraska, August 25, 1804

Deposited by American Philsophical Society [stamped]

[Nov: Spec.?] Open prairies, Augst. 25, 1804. [Pursh]

Cleome serrulata, Pursh [Greenman?]

Type collection [stamped]

No. 43. August 25th growth of the open Praries [Lewis] Cleome [unknown]

ANS PHILA [perforated initials]

ANS 1994 label: *Cleome serrulata* Pursh

APS printed label: Cleome serrutala Pursh

49b *Cleome serrulata* Pursh, Rocky Mountain bee plant; ANS-A; Pursh, 441; collected above the mouth of the Vermillion River, Clay County, South Dakota, or Cedar or Dixon County, Nebraska, August 25, 1804

Deposited by American Philosophical Society [stamped]

Cleome Serrulata var rosea Nova Species [Pursh]

Probably a copy of Charbonneau's receipt. He was paid off (approx. this sum, as I recall) at Mandan ±, since he did not wish to go on to St. Louis, or Washington with Lewis. Rudd

Received of Captain Meriwether Lewis four hundred and Eight Dollars Thirty three and ⅓ cents in full of my monthly pay as an Indian enterpreter from the Seventh of April 180 five until the Sixteenth of August 180 six inclusive at 25 $ pr month having Signed duplicate receipts of the same Rec. & [blank] for one horse Par pd. <sold> by him of me on Dec. 1805 for Public sum R. Lodge on [Clark] [reverse: "Specimen from the White River, Cleome, a new species" *and other illegible words by an unknown writer*]

Cleome integrifolia T. & G. T. M. [Meehan]

ANS PHILA [perforated initials]

ANS 1994 label: *Cleome serrulata* Pursh

APS printed label: Cleome integrifolia T. & G. *Locality*, White River—Lewis Date Aug. 29, 1806

49c *Cleome serrulata* Pursh, Rocky Mountain bee plant; ANS-L; Pursh, 441; collected above the mouth of the Vermillion River, Clay County, South Dakota, or Cedar or Dixon County, Nebraska, August 25, 1804

Cleome Serrulata alba Open prairies, Augst. 25, 1804 [Pursh]

Ex. Herb. A. B. Lambert [stamped]

Pursh's specimen! [Meehan?]

[Amer]ica. Herb: Lewis & Clarke. Fred: Pursh. [Lambert]

ANS PHILA [perforated initials]

ANS 1994 label: *Cleome serrulata* Pursh

ANS printed label: Cleome integrifolia Torr. & Gr.

50 *Collinsia parviflora* Lindl. var. *grandiflora* (Lindl.) Ganders & Krause, small-flowered blue-eyed Mary; ANS-A; Pursh, 421; collected at Rock Fort (Rocky) Camp, The Dalles, Wasco County, Oregon, April 17, 1806

Deposited by American Philosophical Society [stamped]

Collinsia parviflora, Dougl. [envelope] [Greenman?]

Collinsia parviflora, Dougl. (J. M. G.) [Greenman]

Rockford Camp—Aprl: 17th 1806. [Pursh] Pursh's copy of Lewis herb [Meehan?]

C. p. F W P 1942 C. grandiflora Doug. F W P 1943 [Pennell] (acc. to comment on large flowers in Pursh's original description of Antirrhinum tenellum, Fl. Amer. Sept. 421, 1814, of which the present specimen would presumably be Type. But Pursh claims to have seen his species living, and I suppose that his comments were likely based on material grown from seeds of this at the Hosack Garden in 1808.) [Pennell?]

Type collection [stamped]

Antirrhinum tenellum Pursh Type (or source of type) [Pennell?]

ANS 1994 label: *Collinsia grandiflora* Lindl.

APS printed label: Collinsia parviflora Doug.

51 *Collomia linearis* Nutt., narrow-leaf collomia; ANS-A; collected at Rock Fort (Rockford) Camp, The Dalles, Wasco County, Oregon, April 17, 1806

Deposited by American Philosophical Society [stamped]

Collomia linearis Nutt. (T. M) [Meehan]

Rockford camp. Aprl: 17th 1806. [Pursh] Lewis—Pursh's copy [Meehan?]

ANS PHILA [perforated initials]

ANS 1994 label: *Collomia linearis* Nutt.

APS printed label: Collomia linearis Nutt.

52 *Coreopsis tinctoria* Nutt. var. *atkinsoniana* (Dougl. *ex* Lindl.) H. M. Parker, calliopsis; ANS-A; collected on the Snake (Lewis's) River, Washington, October 1805

Deposited by American Philosophical Society [stamped]

On Lewis's R. Octbr: 1805. [Pursh]

Apparently near Bidens or Cosmos [Greenman] Greenman [Meehan?]

Probably Coreopsis atkinsoniana C. V. P. [Piper]

ANS PHILA [perforated initials]

ANS 1994 label: *Coreopsis tinctoria* Nutt. var. *atkinsoniana* (Dougl. ex Lindl.) Parker

APS printed label: Bidens?

53 *Cornus canadensis* L., bunchberry; ANS-A; collected on the Lolo Trail, Idaho County, Idaho, but probably not on Lolo (Collins's) Creek, which the party passed a few days earlier, June 16, 1806

Deposited by American Philosophical Society [stamped]

Cornus canadensis <Willd.> Linn. T. M. [Meehan]

Root horizontal Jun. 16th 1806. Collins's creek. [Pursh] Pursh's label, copy of Lewis [Meehan?]

ANS PHILA [perforated initials]

ANS 1994 label: *Cornus canadensis* L.

APS printed label: Cornus canadensis L.

54 *Crataegus douglasii* Lindl., black hawthorn; ANS-A; Pursh, 337; collected at the mouth of the Walla Walla River, Walla Walla County, Washington, April 29, 1806

Deposited by American Philosophical Society [stamped]

Crataegus Douglasii Lindl T. M [Meehan]

Deep purple Haw. Columbia R. Aprl. 29th 1806. [Pursh] Pursh's copy of Lewis Label [Meehan?]

Probably C. Piperi C. V. P. [Piper]

ANS PHILA [perforated initials]

ANS 1994 label: *Crataegus douglasii* Lindl.

APS printed label: Crataegus Douglasii Lindl.

55 *Dalea purpurea* Vent., purple prairie clover; ANS-A; collected in Bon Homme County, South Dakota, or Knox County, Nebraska, September 2, 1804, and in the vicinity of Camp Disappointment, Cut Bank Creek, Glacier County, Montana, July 22, 1806

Deposited by American Philosophical Society [stamped]

Petalostemum violaceus Mx. T. M [Meehan]

Petalostemon violaceus, Michx.? (J. M. G.) [Greenman]

On the Missouri Jul. 22d 1806. [Pursh] Pursh copy of Lewis [Meehan?]

found September 2ed the Indians use it as an application to fresh wounds. they bruise the leaves adding a little water and apply it.— [Lewis]

ANS PHILA [perforated initials]

ANS 1994 label: *Dalea purpureum* Vent.

APS printed label: Petalostemum violaceus Mx.

56 *Delphinium menziesii* DC., Menzies' larkspur; ANS-A; collected in Skamania or Klickitat County, Washington, or Hood River or Wasco County, Oregon, April 14, 1806

Deposited by American Philosophical Society [stamped]

Root of the specimen of D. menziesii [envelope] [Meehan?]

Delphinium Menziesii, DC. [Greenman] (Greenman) [Meehan?]

A Sort of Larkspur with 3 styles; On the Columbia Aprl. 14th 1806. [Pursh] Pursh's copy of Lewis ticket [Meehan?]

ANS PHILA [perforated initials]

ANS 1994 label: *Delphinium menziesii* DC.

APS printed label: Delphinium Menziesii DC.

57 *Dodecatheon jeffreyi* Van Houtte, Jeffrey's shooting star; ANS-A; collected near The Dalles (Narrows) of the Columbia River, Klickitat County, Washington, or Wasco County, Oregon, April 16, 1806

Deposited by American Philosophical Society [stamped]

Collected by Meriwether Lewis on Lewis and Clark expedition, the original label having been copied by Pursh. Deposited by the American Philosophical Society. [typed]

Dodecatheon meadia L T. M [Meehan]

Near the narrows of Columbia R. Aprl. 16th 1806. [Pursh]

D. campestae Howell C. V. P. [Piper]

ANS PHILA [perforated initials]

ANS 1994 label: *Dodecatheon meadia* L.

APS printed label: Dodecatheon Meadia L.

58 *Dryopteris expansa* (K. Presl) Fraser-Jenkins & Jermy, mountain wood-fern; ANS-A; collected at Fort Clatsop, Clatsop County, Oregon, January 20, 1806

Deposited by American Philosophical Society [stamped]

Aspidium spinulosum, Sw. (J. M. G.) [Greenman]

Polypodium Species. Fort Clatsop Jan: 20th 1806. [Pursh] Pursh's Copy [Meehan?]

ANS 1994 label: *Dryopteris spinulosa* (Muell) Watt.

APS printed label: Aspidium spinulosum Sw.

59 *Egregia menziesii* (Turn.) Aresch., Menzies' rockweed; ANS-A; collected in Pacific County, Washington, November 17, 1805

Deposited by American Philosophical Society [stamped]

Egregia Menziesii (Turn.) Aresch. (Phyllospora Menziesii) [Farlow?] (Determined at Cambridge) [Meehan?]

Fucus From the mouth of the Columbia River on the Pacific Ocean. Novb: 17th 1805. [Pursh]

ANS PHILA [perforated initials]

ANS 1994 label: *Egrigia menziesii* (Turn.) Aresch.

APS printed label: Egregia menziesii Aresch.

60a *Elaeagnus commutata* Bernh. *ex* Rydb., silverberry; ANS-A; Pursh, 114; collected at Nevada Valley (Prairie of the Knobs), Blackfoot River, Powell County, Montana, July 6, 1806

Deposited by American Philosophical Society [stamped]

Elaeagnus argentea, Pursh (J. M. G.) type [Greenman]

Silver tree of the Missouri From the prairi of the Knobs. Jul. 6th 1806. [Pursh]

Type collection [stamped]

ANS PHILA [perforated initials]

ANS 1994 label: *Elaeagnus commutata* Bernh. ex Rydb.

APS printed label: Elaeagnus argentea Pursh

60b *Elaeagnus commutata* Bernh. *ex* Rydb., silverberry; Kew; Pursh, 114; probably collected at Nevada Valley, Blackfoot River, Powell County, Montana, July 6, 1806

*Elaeagnus argentea. Fl: Amer: Pursh [Lambert] Herb. Pursh propr. [Pamphlin]

*A. B. Lambert scripsit J. Ewan

Elaeagneae [unknown]

Herbarium Hookerianum 1867 [stamped]

1 America Herb. Lewis & Clarke. Fred: Pursh 2 Lousiana Bradbury. [Lambert] (A. B. Lambert scripsit) [Ewan] [reverse]

61a *Equisetum arvense* L., field horsetail; ANS-A; collected in Burt County, Nebraska, or Monona County, Iowa, August 10, 1804

Deposited by American Philosophical Society [stamped]

Sandbanks on the Missouri. Augst: 10, 1804 [Pursh]

No. 31. growth of the sand bars near the banks of the river—taken the 10th of August 1804 [Lewis] (Lewis) [Meehan?]

Equisetum arvense L. (T. M.) [Meehan]

ANS PHILA [perforated initials]

ANS 1994 label: *Equisetum arvense* L.

APS printed label: Equisetum arvense L.

61b *Equisetum arvense* L., field horsetail; ANS-L; collected in Burt County, Nebraska, or Monona County, Iowa, August 10, 1804

Equisetum Sylvaticum L. laevigatum P [Pursh] B. D. 128. [unknown] Pursh's writing [Meehan?] Pursh label [Mears?]

Equisetum arvense L. A E Schuyler 1996

Equisetum Sylvaticum? L. Sandbanks on the Missouri. Augst. 10, 1804 NB. A side branch only. [Pursh] Lewis label coll. [Mears?]

Equisetum sylvaticum "Read." [unknown] non Lambert [Mears?]

ANS PHILA [perforated initials]

ANS 1994 label: *Equisetum sylvaticum* L.

ANS printed label: Equisetum sylvaticum L.

62 *Erigeron compositus* Pursh, cut-leaved daisy; ANS-L; Pursh, 535; collected on the Clearwater (Kooskoosky) River, Idaho, date unknown

Ex. Herb. A. B. Lambert [stamped]

Erigeron compositus Pursh subsp. *compositus* Det. John H. Beaman 1961 Holotype Michigan State University Herbarium [printed, typed, and handwritten label]

Herb. Lewis & Clarcke. [Lambert]

From Pursh Herbarium [Meehan?]

Type collection [stamped]

Erigeron compositum Kooskoosky. M. Lewis [Pursh?]

ANS PHILA [perforated initials]

ANS 1994 label: *Erigeron compositus* Pursh var. *compositus*

ANS printed label: Erigeron compositus Pursh

63a *Eriophyllum lanatum* (Pursh) Forbes var. *lanatum*, common eriophyllum; ANS-A; Pursh, 560; collected on the Clearwater (Kooskooskee) River, Camp Chopunnish, Kamiah, Idaho County, Idaho, June 6, 1806

Deposited by American Philosophical Society [stamped]

Eriophyllum caespitosum Dougl. Actinella lanata Pursh—[Meehan?]

Negative of type photograph on file at the Herbarium of the University of California [printed label]

"Camp Chopunnish." (v. Coues, Proc. Phila. Acad. 1898: 306.) [Shinners?]

On the uplands on the Kooskooskee R. Jun: 6th 1806. [Pursh] Pursh, copy of Lewis [Meehan?]

Herbarium of the University of California, Berkeley Eriophyllum lanatum (Pursh) J. Forbes var. lanatum Isotype of Actinella lanata Pursh Kooskooskee R. = Clearwater R., Idaho coll: M. Lewis Det. Dale E. Johnson Date 1978 [printed and handwritten label]

0929842 [stamped]

Type. Actinella lanata Pursh, Fl. Am. Sept. 2:560. 1814. L H Shinners 1/9/1946

Type collection [stamped]

ANS PHILA [perforated initials]

ANS 1994 label: *Eriophyllum lanatum* (Pursh) Forbes var. *lanatum*

APS printed label: Eriophyllum caespitosum Doug. Actinella lanata Pursh

63b *Eriophyllum lanatum* (Pursh) Forbes var. *lanatum*, common eriophyllum; ANS-L; Pursh, 560; collected on the Clearwater (Kooskooskee) River, Camp Chopunnish, Kamiah, Idaho County, Idaho, June 6, 1806

Actinea lanata N. Spec. Uplands of Kooskooskee Jun. 6 1806. [Pursh]

Herb: Lewis & Clarke [Lambert]

Bahia [*words lost, page cut*] Oregon, [*words lost, page cut*] [unknown]

Ex. Herb. A. B. Lambert [stamped]

Pursh Herbarium [Meehan?]

Negative of type photograph on file at the Herbarium of the University of California [printed label]

Herbarium of the University of California, Berkeley Eriophyllum lanatum (Pursh) J. Forbes var. lanatum

Holotype of Actinella lanata Pursh Kooskooskee R. = Clearwater R., Idaho (this is specimen Pursh took with him to London) coll: M. Lewis Det. Dale E. Johnson Date 1978 [printed and handwritten label]

0929843 [stamped]

Bahia lanata [unknown]

(Actinella of Pursh's Flora) [Pennell?]

From Eriophyllum caespitosum folder No. 9273 [unknown] [reverse]

ANS 1994 label: *Eriophyllum lanatum* (Pursh) Forbes var. *lanatum*

ANS printed label: Eriophyllum caspitosum Dgl. (Bahia lanata DC.)

64 *Erysimum asperum* (Nutt.) DC., rough wallflower; ANS-A; collected on the Clearwater (Kooskooskee) River, Camp Chopunnish, Kamiah, Idaho County, Idaho, June 1, 1806

Deposited by American Philosophical Society [stamped]

Erysimum asperum, DC. (E. lanceolatum Pursh not R. Br.) [Greenman] Greenman [Meehan?]

On the Kooskooskee Jun. 1st 1806. [Pursh] Pursh's copy [Meehan?]

ANS PHILA [perforated initials]

ANS 1994 label: *Erysimum asperum* (Nutt.) DC.

APS printed label: Erysimum asperum D.C. E. lanceolatum Pursh

65a *Erythronium grandiflorum* Pursh, pale fawn-lily; ANS-A; Pursh, 231; collected near the Clearwater (Kooskooskee) River, Nez Perce or Clearwater County, Idaho, May 8, 1806

Deposited by American Philosophical Society [stamped]

Erythronium grandiflorum, Pursh var. parviflorum, Watson [Robinson?]

this label information corresponds with Pursh's description of E. grandiflorum P. J A M 5/83 different date from type [Mears]

From the plains of Columbia near Kooskooskee R. May 8th 1806. the natives reckon this root as unfitt for food. [Pursh]

ANS PHILA [perforated initials]

ANS 1994 label: *Erythronium grandiflorum* Pursh

APS printed label: Erythronium grandiflorum Pursh var. parviflorum Watson

65b *Erythronium grandiflorum* Pursh, pale fawn-lily; ANS-A; Pursh, 231; collected on an affluent of the Clearwater (Kooskoosky) River, Lolo Trail, Clearwater or Idaho County, Idaho, June 15, 1806

Deposited by American Philosophical Society [stamped]

Erythronium grandiflorum Pursh T. M. [Meehan]

Type collection [stamped]

Pursh, Fl. Am. Sept. i:230 [Pennell?]

A Squamous bulb; On the waters of Kooskoosky Jun: 15th 1806. [Pursh]

ANS PHILA [perforated initials]

ANS 1994 label: *Erythronium grandiflorum* Pursh

APS printed label: Erythronium grandiflorum Pursh

66 *Euphorbia cyathophora* Murr., fire-on-the-mountain; ANS-A; collected in Dewey or Potter County, South Dakota, if October 4, 1804, is correct, or in Sioux or Emmons County, North Dakota, if October 15, 1804, is correct

Deposited by American Philosophical Society [stamped]

Euphorbia heterophylla L. E. cyathophora Mx. T. M. [Meehan]

High prairies & plains. Octb. 4, 1804. [Pursh]

No. 38. 1804 [15th?] October. the growth of the high Prairies or plain [Lewis] (Lewis) [Meehan?]

ANS PHILA [perforated initials]

ANS 1994 label: *Poinsettia cyathophora* (Murr.) Klutzsch & Gacke

APS printed label: Euphorbia heterophylla L.

67 *Euphorbia marginata* Pursh, snow-on-the-mountain; ANS-A; Pursh, 607; collected in Rosebud County, Montana, July 28, 1806

Deposited by American Philosophical Society [stamped]

Euphorbia marginata Pursh T. M. [Meehan]

Type Euphorbia marginata Pursh, Fl. Amer. Sept. 2: 607. 1814. Louis C. Wheeler 1938 [typed label]

On the Yellowstone River. July 28th 1806. [Pursh] (Pursh's copy) [Meehan?]

Annotation Label Revision of New World Euphorbieae Euphorbia marginata Pursh Det.: Louis C. Wheeler 1938 Gray Herbarium [printed and typed label]

ANS PHILA [perforated initials]

ANS 1994 label: *Euphorbia marginata* Pursh

APS printed label: Euphorbia marginata Pursh

68 *Festuca idahoensis* Elmer, Idaho fescue; ANS-A; collected in the vicinity of Camp Chopunnish, Kamiah, Idaho County, Idaho, June 10, 1806

Deposited by American Philosophical Society [stamped]

On the plains of Columbia Jun: 10th 1806. [Pursh]

Festuca duriuscula Smith. Festuca ovina, L. [Meehan?]

Festuca ovina ingrata Hack. C. V. P. (= F. idahoensis Elmer) a b [unknown symbol] 5-31-32 [Piper]

ANS PHILA [perforated initials]

ANS 1994 label: *Festuca ovina* L.

APS printed label: Festuca ovina L.

69a *Frangula purshiana* (DC.) Cooper, cascara; ANS-A; Pursh, 166; collected on the Clearwater (Kooskooskee) River, Camp Chopunnish, Kamiah, Idaho County, Idaho, May 29, 1806

Deposited by American Philosophical Society [stamped]

Rhamnus Purshiana, DC. Prodr. ii. 25. (J. M. G.) [Greenman]

A Shrub apparently a Species of Rhamnus [Pursh] (Pursh) [Meehan?] About 12 feet high, in Clumps. fruit a 5-valved purple berry which the natives eat & esteen highly; the berry depressed globous. On the waters of the Kooskooskee May 29th 1806. [Pursh] Lewis ticket [Meehan?]

ANS PHILA [perforated initials]

ANS 1994 label: *Rhamnus purshiana* DC.

APS printed label: Rhamnus Purshianus DC.

69b *Frangula purshiana* (DC.) Cooper, cascara; ANS-L; Pursh, 166; collected on the Clearwater (Kooskooskee) River, Camp Chopunnish, Kamiah, Idaho County, Idaho, May 29, 1806

Ex. Herb. A. B. Lambert [stamped]

(*See over*) [unknown]

1 Lewis [Mears?]

Pursh's specimen [Meehan?]

2 Menzies [Mears?]

Rhamnus ovali folius. Fruit a 5-valved depressed globous purple berry, esteem'd highly. Waters of Kooskooskee May 29, 1806. [Pursh]

R. Purshianus DC. T & G. [Meehan?]

Herb: Lewis & Clarke. Fred: Pursh America N W Coast. Arch: Menzies. Vancouver [Lambert] [reverse]

ANS PHILA [perforated initials]

ANS 1994 label: *Rhamnus purshiana* DC.

ANS printed label: Rhamnus Purshiana DC.

70 *Frasera fastigiata* (Pursh) Heller, clustered frasera; ANS-A; Pursh, 101; collected at Weippe Prairie (Squamash Flats), Clearwater County, Idaho, June 14, 1806

Deposited by American Philosophical Society [stamped]

In moist & wet places. On the Squamash flats. Jun: 14th 1806. [Pursh]

Frasera thyrsiflora, Hook. (Swertia fastigiata, Pursh) [Greenman]

Type collection [stamped]

ANS PHILA [perforated initials]

ANS 1994 label: *Frasera fastigiata* (Pursh) Heller

APS printed label: Frasera thyrsiflora, Hook. Swertia fastigiata Pursh

71a *Fritillaria lanceolata* Pursh, checker lily; ANS-A; Pursh, 230; collected on Bradford (Brant) Island, Multnomah County, Oregon, April 10, 1806

Deposited by American Philosophical Society [stamped]

Pursh states "On the headwaters of the Missouri and Columbia. M. Lewis["] July (Fl. Am. Sept. 1:230 1814) Brant Is not at headwaters, Not type! Examined in a revisionary study of Fritillaria L. (Liliaceae) at the University of California, Davis. Donald O. Santana Dec. 1977 [printed and typed label]

Type collection [stamped]

Fritillaria lanceolata Pursh T. M. [Meehan]

Brand island Aprl. 10, 1806. Bulb squamous, eaten by the natives, who call it tel-lak-thil-pah. [Pursh] Pursh's copy [Meehan?]

0927824 [stamped]

Specemin of lilliacious plant obtained on Brant Island 10th of apl 1806. the root of this plant is a squawmus bulb and is eaten by the natives. the Clah-clel-lar opposite this Island call it tel-lak-thil-pah [Lewis] Lewis label [Meehan?]

ANS PHILA [perforated initials]

ANS 1994 label: *Fritillaria lanceolata* Pursh

APS printed label: Fritillaria lanceolata Pursh

71b *Fritillaria lanceolata* Pursh, checker lily; ANS-L; Pursh, 230; collected on Bradford (Brand) Island, Multnomah County, Oregon, April 10, 1806

Fritillaria occidentalis. Brand islans. April. 10, 1806. Bulb squamous, eaten by the natives, who call it tel-lak-thil-pah. [Pursh] Lewis & Clark. [unknown]

Pursh's specimen! [Meehan?]

Type collection [stamped]

Pursh Fl. Am. Sept. i:230 [Pennell?]

N America. Herb: Lewis & Clarke. [Lambert] [reverse]

ANS PHILA [perforated initials]

ANS 1994 label: *Fritillaria lanceolata* Pursh

ANS printed label: Fritillaria lanceolata Pursh

72a *Fritillaria pudica* (Pursh) Spreng., yellow bell; ANS-A; Pursh, 228; collected near the Clearwater (Kooskooskee) River, Nez Perce or Clearwater County, Idaho, May 8, 1806

Deposited by American Philosophical Society [stamped]

Fritillaria pudica Sprengl. Lilium? pudicum Pursh [Meehan?]

Plains of Columbia near the Kooskooskee May 8th 1806. the bulb in the Shape of a bisquit, which the natives eat. [Pursh]

ANS PHILA [perforated initials]

ANS 1994 label: *Fritillaria pudica* (Pursh) Spreng.

APS printed label: Frittilaria pudica Spreg.

72b *Fritillaria pudica* (Pursh) Spreng., yellow bell; ANS-L; Pursh, 228; collected near the Clearwater (Kooskooskee) River, Nez Perce or Clearwater County, Idaho, May 8, 1806

Fritillaria? lutea Plains of Columbia near the Kooskooskee. May 8, 1806. Bulb bisquit-shaped eatable. [Pursh]

"Lewis & Clark." [unknown]

Pursh's specimen! [Meehan?]

Ex. Herb. Lambert [unknown]

N. America. Herb. Lewis & Clarck. F. Pursh. [Lambert] [reverse]

ANS PHILA [perforated initials]

ANS 1994 label: *Fritillaria pudica* (Pursh) Spreng.

ANS printed label: Fritillaria pudica Nutt

73 *Gaillardia aristata* Pursh, blanket flower; ANS-A; Pursh, 573; collected in the vicinity of Lewis and Clark Pass, Lewis and Clark County, Montana, July 7, 1806

Deposited by American Philosophical Society [stamped]

Gaillardia aristata, Pursh (J. M. G.) type [Greenman]

Gaillardia aristata, Pursh (J. M. G.) *type* [Greenman]

"Lewis & Clark's Pass of the Continental Divide, near head of Big Blackfoot River, in Deer Lodge Co., Montana." (Coues, Proc. Phila. Acad. 1898: 305–306.) [Shinners?]

Rocky mountains Dry hills. Jul. 7th 1806. [Pursh] Copy of Lewis [Meehan?]

Type. Gaillardia ("Galardia") aristata Pursh, Fl. Am. Sept. 2:573. 1814. L H Shinners 1/9/1946

ANS PHILA [perforated initials]

ANS 1994 label: *Gaillardia aristata* Pursh

APS printed label: Gaillardia aristata Pursh

74 *Gaultheria shallon* Pursh, salal; ANS-A; Pursh, 283; collected in the vicinity of Fort Clatsop, Clatsop County, Oregon, January 20, 1806

Deposited by American Philosophical Society [stamped]

Gaultheria Shallon Pursh T. M. [Meehan]

The Shallon; Supposed to be a Species of Vaccinium. On the Coast of the Pacific Ocean. Jan: 20th 1806 [Pursh] Pursh Lewis—Pursh's copy of Lewis [Meehan?]

ANS PHILA [perforated initials]

ANS 1994 label: *Gaultheria shallon* Pursh

APS printed label: Gaultheria Shallon Pursh

75 *Geum triflorum* Pursh, old man's whiskers; ANS-A; Pursh, 352, 736; collected in the vicinity of Weippe Prairie, Clearwater County, Idaho, on an affluent of the Clearwater (Kooskooskee) River, June 12, 1806

Deposited by American Philosophical Society [stamped]

Geum triflorum Pursh T. M [Meehan] (Geum ciliatum, Pursh) Fl. 352. [Greenman] Greenman [Meehan?]

On open ground comon on the waters of the Kooskooskee Jun: 12th 1806. No: 2. [Pursh] Pursh's copy of Lewis label [Meehan?]

ANS PHILA [perforated initials]

ANS 1994 label: *Geum triflorum* Pursh

APS printed label: Geum triflorum Pursh

76a *Grindelia squarrosa* (Pursh) Dunal, curly-top gumweed; ANS-A; Pursh, 559; collected near the Omaha Indian (Old Maha) village Tonwontonga, Dakota County, Nebraska, August 17, 1804

Deposited by American Philosophical Society [stamped]

Grindelia squarrosa Dunal Donia squarrosa Pursh T. M. [Meehan]

Lewis Pursh's Label [Meehan?] Anonymus balsamifera New genus? Prairies: in the camp near the old Maha village. Augst. 17, 1804 [Pursh]

probable Isotype of: Donia squarrosa Pursh Flora Americae Septentrionalis 2:559. 1814 ver. M. A. Wetter IV/1983 [printed and typed label]

NY Negative No. 11053 [printed label]

No. 40. taken on the 17th of August 1804. at our camp near the Old Maha village & is the growth of the Praries—[Lewis] (Lewis) [Meehan?]

ANS PHILA [perforated initials]

ANS 1994 label: *Grindelia squarrosa* (Pursh) Dunal.

APS printed label: Grindelia squarrosa Dunal Donia squarrosa Pursh

76b *Grindelia squarrosa* (Pursh) Dunal, curly-top gumweed; ANS-L; Pursh, 559; collected near the Omaha Indian (old Maha) village Tonwontonga, Dakota County, Nebraska, August 17, 1804

Anonymus balsamifera Prairies; in the camp near the old Maha village Augt. 17, 1804 [Pursh]

Ex. Herb A. B. Lambert [stamped]

written below [unknown]

No. Grindelia squarrosa (Pursh) Dunal Determination by J. A. Steyermark 3/19/33 [printed and handwritten label]

probable Isotype of: Donia squarrosa Pursh Flora Americae Septentrionalis 2:559. 1814. ver. M. A. Wetter IV/1983 [printed and typed label]

N America Lewis & Clarck. [Lambert]

Herb Pursh [Meehan?]

[*words illegible*]

ANS PHILA [perforated initials]

ANS 1994 label: *Grindelia squarrosa* (Pursh) Dunal.

ANS printed label: Grindelia squarrosa Dunal (Donia Pursh)

76c *Grindelia squarrosa* (Pursh) Dunal, curly-top gumweed; ANS-L; Pursh, 559; collected at an unknown place and date, probably near the Omaha Indian village Tonwontonga, Dakota County, Nebraska, August 17, 1804

Thuraria herbacea [*unknown symbol*] Fl. yellow, and the calyx resiniferous. A shrubby species of this genus, *In-*

ula glutinosa of *Persoon*, is called in Mexico, the Incense Plant: collected on the Missourie, and stands the open ground. [printed label]

Thuraria herbacea Nutt Fras Cat 1813 [Meares?]

Ex. Herb. A. B. Lambert [stamped]

Type of: Donia squarrosa Pursh Flora Americae Septentrionalis 2 : 559. 1814. "From Pursh's Herb" ver. M. A. Wetter IV/1983 [typed and printed label]

No. Type collection of Donia squarrosa Pursh (specimen on right) Grindelia squarrosa Pursh Dunal Determination by J. A. Steyermark 6/5/33 [printed and handwritten label]

N. America Lewis & Clarcke. [Lambert]

Type collection [stamped]

From Pursh Herbarium [Meehan?]

ANS PHILA [perforated initials]

ANS 1994 label: *Grindelia squarrosa* (Pursh) Dunal.

ANS printed label: Grindelia squarrosa Dunal (Donia Pursh)

77a *Gutierrezia sarothrae* (Pursh) Britt. & Rusby, snakeweed; ANS-A; Pursh, 540; collected below the Big Bend of the Missouri River, Lyman or Buffalo County, South Dakota, September 19, 1804

Deposited by American Philosophical Society [stamped]

Gutierrezia Euthamiae T. & G. [envelope] [Greenman?]

Guttierrezia Euthamia T. & G. (Solidago [Meehan?] sarothrae Pursh) [unknown]

Holotype Solidago sarothrae Pursh Fl. Amer. Sept. 2 : 540, 1814 M. A. Lane 20 Aug 1980

The University of Texas Herbarium Gutierrezia sarothrae (Pursh) Britt. & Rusby Meredith A. Lane Aug 1980 [typed and printed label]

High bear prairies mineral earth with very little grass. Septbr. 19, 1804 [Pursh]

Type Solidago Sarothrae Pursh Fl. Am. Sept. 2 : 540. 1814. (= Gutierrezia Sarothrae) L H Shinners 1/9/1946

No. <4> 59. 1804. 19th Septbr—the growth of high and bear praries which produce little grass, generally mineral with earth. [Lewis] (Lewis) [Meehan?]

ANS PHILA [perforated initials]

APS printed label: Gutierrezia Euthamia T. & G. Solidago Sarothrae Pursh

77b *Gutierrezia sarothrae* (Pursh) Britt. & Rusby, snakeweed; Kew; Pursh, 540; collected below the Big Bend of the Missouri River, Lyman or Buffalo County, South Dakota, September 19, 1804

Solidago <tenuifolia> Sarothrae High bear prairies with little grass Septb: 19, 1804 [Pursh] F. Pursh scripsit! J. Ewan

Herbarium Hookerianum 1867 [stamped]

Herb. Pursh propr. [Pamphlin] *Solidago Sarothrae Fl. Amer: Pursh [Lambert] *A. B. Lambert scripsit and also verso [Ewan]

Herbarium Hookerianum 1867 [stamped]

America Herb: Lewis & Clarke F. Pursh [Lambert] (A. B. Lambert scripsit) [Ewan] [reverse]

78a *Holodiscus discolor* (Pursh) Maxim., creambush oceanspray; ANS-A; Pursh, 342; collected on the Clearwater (Kooskooske) River, Camp Chopunnish, Kamiah, Idaho County, Idaho, May 29, 1806

Deposited by American Philosophical Society [stamped]

Spiraea discolor Pursh T. M [Meehan]

A Shrub growing much in the manner of Nine bark On the waters of Kooskooskee May 29th 1806. [Pursh] Pursh's copy of Lewis [Meehan?]

Holodiscus discolor (Pursh) Maxim. A E Schuyler 1996

ANS PHILA [perforated initials]

APS printed label: Spiraea discolor Pursh

78b *Holodiscus discolor* (Pursh) Maxim., creambush oceanspray; ANS-L; Pursh, 342; collected on the Clearwater (Kooskooske) River, Camp Chopunnish, Kamiah, Idaho County, Idaho, May 29, 1806

Holodiscus dumosus (Hook.) Heller A E Schuyler 1996

Lieut. Wheeler's Expedition, 1873. No. 401. Spiraea dumosus Upper Arkansas Valley Colorado Terr., Professors John Wolf & J. T. Rothrock. [printed and handwritten label]

Spiraea <betulifolia> <paniculata> discolor Kooskooskee. May 29th 1806. [Pursh]

2. Lambert [Mears?]

Lewis & Clark specimen S B. [Brown?]

Holodiscus discolor (Pursh) Maxim. A E Schuyler 1996

ANS PHILA [perforated initials]

ANS printed label: Spiraea discolor Pursh var. dumosa (Nutt) Wats

79a *Hordeum jubatum* L., foxtail barley; ANS-A; Pursh, 89; collected in the vicinity of Fort Clatsop, Clatsop County, Oregon, March 13, 1806

Deposited by American Philosophical Society [stamped]

Hordeum jubatum <Willd.> [Meehan?] Linn. [unknown]

Grass common to the open grounds near Fort Clatsop. March 13th 1806. [Pursh]

ANS PHILA [perforated initials]

ANS 1994 label: *Hordeum jubatum* L.

APS printed label: Hordeum jubatum L.

79b *Hordeum jubatum* L., foxtail barley; ANS-A; Pursh, 89; collected on White Bear Islands, Cascade County, Montana, July 12, 1806

Deposited by American Philosophical Society [stamped]

Hordeum jubatum <Willd.> [Meehan?] Linn. [unknown]

Calld the golden or Silken Rye. On the white bear Islands on the Missouri. Jul. 12th 1806. [Pursh]

ANS PHILA [perforated initials]

ANS 1994 label: *Hordeum jubatum* L.

APS printed label: Hordeum jubatum L.

80 *Hypnum oreganum* Sull., moss; ANS-A; collected at Fort Clatsop, Clatsop County, Oregon, January 20, 1806

Deposited by American Philosophical Society [stamped]

H. organum Sulliv [unknown]

Hypnum A Species of moss from Fort Clatsop. Jan: 20th 1806 [Pursh]

ANS PHILA [perforated initials]

APS printed label: Hypnum organum Sull.

81 *Ipomopsis aggregata* (Pursh) V. Grant ssp. *aggregata*, scarlet gilia; ANS-A; Pursh, 147; collected on Hungery Creek, Lolo Trail, Idaho County, Idaho, June 26, 1806

Deposited by American Philosophical Society [stamped]

Gilia aggregata Spengl. (T. M) [Meehan]

On hungry creek June: 26th 1806. [Pursh]

No. Lewis in 1806 Holotype! *Cantua aggregata* Pursh determined by Dieter H. Wilken, 1980 [typed and printed label]

Type collection [stamped]

Type of Cantua aggregata Pursh, Fl. Amer. Sept. 147, 1814. [Pennell?]

ANS PHILA [perforated initials]

ANS 1994 label: *Ipomopsis aggregata* (Pursh) V. Grant ssp. *aggregata*

APS printed label: Gilia aggregata Spreng.

82 *Iris missouriensis* Nutt., western blue flag; ANS-A; Pursh, 30; collected at Nevada Valley (Prairie of the Knobs), Blackfoot River, Powell County, Montana, July 5, 1806

Deposited by American Philosophical Society [stamped]

Iris missouriensis Nutt. T. M. [Meehan]

A pale blue Species of Flag. Prairi of the Knobs Jul. 5th 1806. [Pursh] Pursh's label, copy of Lewis [Meehan?]

ANS PHILA [perforated initials]

ANS 1994 label: *Iris missouriensis* Nutt.

APS printed label: Iris Missouriensis Nutt.

83a *Juniperus communis* L. var. *depressa* Pursh, common juniper; ANS-A; collected below the mouth of the Cannonball River, Sioux or Emmons County, North Dakota, October 17, 1804

Deposited by American Philosophical Society [stamped]

Common to the bluffs. Octbr. 17, 1804. [Pursh] Pursh's copy [Meehan?]

No. <46> 47 a species of Juniper, common to the bluffs— October 17th [Lewis] (Lewis) [Meehan?]

Juniperus Communis L T. M. [Meehan]

ANS PHILA [perforated initials]

ANS 1994 label: *Juniperus communis* L.

APS printed label: Juniperus communis L.

83b *Juniperus communis* L. var. *depressa* Pursh, common juniper; ANS-L; collected below the mouth of the Cannonball River, Sioux or Emmons County, North Dakota, October 17, 1804

Juniperus communis L Common to the bluffs. Octbr. 17, 1804 [Pursh] Pursh—Lewis & Clark [Meehan?]

Juniperus communis Glens falls. [New York] [Pursh] Pursh [Meehan?]

ANS PHILA [perforated initials]

ANS 1994 label: *Juniperus communis* L.

ANS printed label: Juniperus communis L.

83c *Juniperus communis* L. var. *depressa* Pursh, common juniper; ANS-A; collected in the vicinity of Lewis and Clark Pass, Lewis and Clark County, Montana, July 7, 1806

Deposited by American Philosophical Society [stamped]

Juniperus communis depressa Pursh [Meehan?]

Dwarf Juniper. Rocky mountain. July 7th 1806. [Pursh] Pursh copy of Lewis [Meehan?]

ANS PHILA [perforated initials]

ANS 1994 label: *Juniperus communis* L.

APS printed label: Juniperus communis L. var depressa Pursh

83d *Juniperus communis* L. var. *depressa* Pursh, common juniper; ANS-L; collected in the vicinity of Lewis and Clark Pass, Lewis and Clark County, Montana, July 7, 1806

Natural History Survey of Russia America Juniperus nana Aleutian Islands. Ft. Simpson [printed and handwritten label]

Tenth Census of the United States. Department of Forestry Journey to the Pacific Coast, 1880 Juniperus communis, L. v. alpina, Gaud. Mt. Shasta, Cal. Aug 24. Alt. 8,000' Coll. G. Engelmann and C. S. Sargent.

Juniperus communis nana Dwarf Juniper Rocky Mountains. Jul. 7th 1806. [Pursh]

Pursh Lewis & Clark specimen [Meehan?]

Expedition to Alaska, 1867. U. S. Coast Survey, Geo. Davidson. 134 Name Juniperus nana Willd. Locality Alaska Collector Dr. A. Kellogg [printed and handwritten label]

ANS PHILA [perforated initials]

ANS 1994 label: *Juniperus communis* L.

ANS printed label: Juniperus communis L. var.

84a *Juniperus horizontalis* Moench, creeping juniper; ANS-A; Pursh, 647; collected in Sioux or Emmons County, North Dakota, October 16, 1804

Deposited by American Philosophical Society

Juniperus Sabina L. Procumbens Pursh [Meehan?]

[procumbens?] Dwarf Cedar, never more than 6 inches high, open prairies. Octbr: 16, 1804. [Pursh] Lewis label [Meehan?]

ANS PHILA [perforated initials]

ANS 1994 label: *Juniperus horizontalis* Moench.

APS printed label: Juniperus Sabina L. J. procumbens Pursh

84b *Juniperus horizontalis* Moench, creeping juniper; ANS-L; Pursh, 647; collected in Sioux or Emmons County, North Dakota, October 16, 1804

Juniperus Sabina procumb. L. Dwarf cedar, never more than 6 inches high, Octb: 16, 1804 [Pursh] Pursh!!! [Meehan?]

This label next sheet [unknown]

The two forms of leaf [unknown]

Ex Herb. J. H. Redfield Plantae Americae Septentrionalis. No. Juniperus Sabinae L. var. procumbens Pursh. Hab. Clement's Pt. Mt. Desert, Maine Legit John H. Redfield, Sept 11, 1885 [printed and handwritten label]

ANS PHILA [perforated initials]

ANS 1994 label: *Juniperus horizontalis* Moench.

ANS printed label: Juniperus Sabinae L. var. procumbens Pursh

85 *Juniperus scopulorum* Sarg., Rocky Mountain juniper; ANS-A; Pursh, 647; collected above the mouth of the Cheyenne River, Dewey or Sully County, South Dakota, October 2, 1804

Deposited by American Philosophical Society [stamped]

Herbarium of the New York Botanical Garden Plants of = J. excelsa Pall. not J. occidentalis Hook. No. Probably eccentric or impure material of J. Scopulorum Sgt. differing from typical Scopulorum By much overlap of lvs and variable relative length of glands. Fruit very immature. P. J. Van Melle Dec. 14, '50.

Juniperus occidentalis, Hook. (J. excelsa, Pursh) [Greenman] Greenman [Meehan?]

No. 58 found 2nd October 1804. A species of Cedar <on the> found on the Blufs. the trees of which are large some of them 6 feet in the girth—. [Lewis] (Lewis) [Meehan?]

M. Lewis' handwriting [Pennell?]

On the bluffs, some trees 6 feet in girth. Octbr. 2, 1804 [Pursh]

Pursh's copy of Lewis' data. [Pennell?]

ANS PHILA [perforated initials]

ANS 1994 label: *Juniperus occidentalis* var. *occidentalis* (Hook.)

APS printed label: Juniperus occidentalis Hook. J. excelsa Pursh

86 *Koeleria macrantha* (Ledeb.) J. A. Schultes, prairie Junegrass; ANS-A; Pursh, 85; collected in the vicinity of

Camp Chopunnish, Kamiah, Idaho County, Idaho, June 10, 1806

Deposited by American Philosophical Society [stamped]

Koeleria cristata Pers. [Meehan?]

On the plains of Columbia &c. Jun: 10th 1806. [Pursh]

ANS PHILA [perforated initials]

ANS 1994 label: *Koeleria cristata* (L.) Pers.

APS printed label: Koeleria cristata Pers.

87 *Lewisia rediviva* Pursh, bitterroot; ANS-A; Pursh, 368; collected near the Bitterroot (Clark's) River, Travelers' Rest, Missoula County, Montana, July 1, 1806

Deposited by American Philosophical Society [stamped]

Lewisia rediviva Pursh (T. M) [Meehan]

The Indians eat the root of this Near Clark's R. Jul. 1st 1806 [Pursh] Lewis [Meehan?] The Calyx consist of 6 or 7 leaves the Corolla many pedals and Tamina many. [TyS. P.?] Capsula. [Pursh] Pursh—[Meehan?]

Type collection [stamped]

ANS PHILA [perforated initials]

ANS 1994 label: *Lewisia rediviva* Pursh

APS printed label: Lewisia rediviva Pursh

88 *Lewisia triphylla* (S. Wats.) B. L. Robins., three-leaved lewisia; ANS-A; collected between Bald Mountain and Spring Hill, Lolo Trail, Idaho County, Idaho, on an affluent of the Clearwater (Kooskooskee) River, June 27, 1806

Deposited by American Philosophical Society [stamped]

BioSystems Analysis, Inc. *Lewisia triphylla* (Wats.) B. L. Robins. John M. Miller February 24, 1993 [printed label]

Lewisia triphylla. Rob. [Greenman] (Greenman) [Meehan?]

Claytonia linearis Dougl. (T. M) [Meehan]

On the waters of Kooskooskee within the Rocky mountains Jun: 27th 1806. [Pursh]

ANS PHILA [perforated initials]

APS printed label: Claytonia linearis Doug

89 *Leymus arenarius* (L.) Hochst., dune wildrye; ANS-A; collected at an unknown place and date

Deposited by American Philosophical Society [stamped]

This without a ticket appears to be Stipa robusta [Meehan?] Not Stipa. Probably Spartina gracilis (Scribner) [unknown]

ANS PHILA [perforated initials]

ANS 1994 label: *Elymus arenarius* L.

APS printed label: Spartina gracilis

90 *Liatris aspera* Michx., gay-feather; ANS-A; collected in Brule County, South Dakota, September 12, 1804

Deposited by American Philosophical Society [stamped]

Liatris Scariosa <Mx.> Willd. T. M [Meehan]

No. 58 12th September. growth of high & dry prarie— [Lewis] (Lewis) [Meehan?] As written above [unknown]

High dry prairies. Septb: 12, 1804. [Pursh]

Liatris spheroidea Michx. L H Shinners 1/9/1946

ANS PHILA [perforated initials]

ANS 1994 label: *Liatris spaeroidea* Michx.

APS printed label: Liatris scariosa Mich.

91 *Liatris pycnostachya* Michx., blazing star; ANS-A; collected above the mouth of the White River, Lyman or Brule County, South Dakota, September 18, 1804

Deposited by American Philosophical Society [stamped]

Liatris pycnostachya, Mx. [Greenman]

Liatris pycnostachya, Michx. (J. M. G.) 18 Sept; 1897. [Greenman]

Prairies, Septb: 15, 1804 [Pursh]

No 35 Sept. 18th growth of the praries [Lewis]

ANS PHILA [perforated initials]

ANS 1994 label: *Liatris pycnostachya* Michx.

APS printed label: Liatris pycnostachya Mx.

92a *Linum lewisii* Pursh var. *lewisii*, blue flax; ANS-A; Pursh, 210; collected on the Sun River, Lewis and Clark, Teton, or Cascade County, Montana, July 9, 1806

Deposited by American Philosophical Society [stamped]

Linum Lewisii Pursh T. M [Meehan]

Perennial Flax. Valleys of the Rocky mountains. July 9th 1806. 10 [Pursh]

Type collection [stamped]

ANS PHILA [perforated initials]

ANS 1994 label: *Linum lewisii* Pursh var. *Lewisii*

APS printed label: Linum Lewisii Pursh

92b *Linum lewisii* Pursh var. *lewisii*, blue flax; ANS-L; Pursh, 210; collected at an unknown place and date, perhaps on the Sun River, Lewis and Clark, Teton, or Cascade County, Montana, July 9, 1806

Ex. Herb. A. B. Lambert [stamped]

Pursh's spec [Meehan?]

Linum Lewisii, Fl: Amer: Pursh. [Lambert?]

Linum Lewisii Fl. Am: P. [Lambert?]

Upper Louisiana. Nuttall [unknown]

ANS PHILA [perforated initials]

ANS 1994 label: *Linum lewisii* Pursh var. *Lewisii*

ANS printed label: Linum perenne L.

93 *Lomatium cous* (S. Wats.) Coult. & Rose, cous; ANS-A; collected at the mouth of the Walla Walla River, Walla Walla County, Washington, April 29, 1806

Deposited by American Philosophical Society [stamped]

I think this must be Cymopterus campestris Nutt. T. M [Meehan]

Pursh's copy of Lewis ticket [Meehan?] An umbelliferous plant of the root of which the Wallowallows make a kind of bread. The natives calld it Shappalell. Aprl. 29th 1806. [Pursh]

Peucedanum cous = Lomatium cous [unknown]

Peucedanum probably P. Cous C. V. P. [Piper] ! M. E. M. [Mathias]

ANS PHILA [perforated initials]

ANS 1994 label: *Lomatium cous* (Wats.) Coult. & Rose

APS printed label: Cymopterus campestris Nutt.?

94 *Lomatium dissectum* (Nutt.) Mathias & Constance, fern-leaved lomatium; ANS-A; Pursh, 195; collected on the Clearwater (Kooskooskee) River, in the vicinity of Camp Chopunnish, Kamiah, Idaho County, Idaho, June 10, 1806

Deposited by American Philosophical Society [stamped]

Peucedanum utriculatum, Nutt.? (Phellandrium aquatium, Pursh not Linn.) [Greenman] (Greenman) [Meehan?]

Oenanthe Phellandrium Lam Phellandrium aquatium L. (T. M) [Meehan]

A great horse medicine among the natives. On the Kooskooskee Jun: 10th 1806. grows on rich upland. [Pursh] Pursh's copy of Lewis label [Meehan?]

Leptotaenia multifida? C. V. P. [Piper] !M. E. M. [Mathias]

ANS 1994 label: *Lomatium utriculatum* (Nutt. ex Torr. & Gray) Coult. & Rose

APS printed label: Peucedanum utriculatum Nutt.?

95 *Lomatium grayi* (Coult. & Rose) Coult. & Rose, Gray's lomatium; ANS-A; collected in the vicinity of Lower Memaloose Island (Sepulchre Rock), Klickitat County, Washington, or Wasco County, Oregon, April 14, 1806

Deposited by American Philosophical Society [stamped]

A large fusiform root, which the natives prepare by baking; Near the Sepulchre rock On the Columbia R. Aprl. 14th 1806. [Pursh]

This is apparently a mixture of material M. E. M. [Mathias]

P. grayi C. & R [unknown]

ANS PHILA [perforated initials]

ANS 1994 label: *Lomatium grayi* (Coult. & Rose) Coult. & Rose

APS printed label: Peucedanum?

96 *Lomatium nudicaule* (Pursh) Coult. & Rose, barestem lomatium; ANS-A; Pursh, 196; collected in the vicinity of The Dalles of the Columbia River, Klickitat County, Washington, or Wasco County, Oregon, April 15, 1806

Deposited by American Philosophical Society [stamped]

Peucedanum leiocarpum, Nutt. (Smyrnium nudicaule, Pursh) [Greenman] (Greenman) [Meehan?]

Type collection [stamped]

not [unknown] Peucedanum nudicaule Nutt. Smyrnium nudicaule Pursh (T. M) [Meehan]

Supposed to be a Smyrnium the natives eat the tops & boil it Sometimes with their Soup. On the Columbia Aprl. 15th 1806. [Pursh] Pursh's copy of Lewis ticket [Meehan?]

Cogswellia nudicaule M E M [Mathias]

ANS PHILA [perforated initials]

ANS 1994 label: *Lomatium nudicaule* (Pursh) Coult. & Rose

APS printed label: Peucedanum leiocarpum Nutt.

97 *Lomatium triternatum* (Pursh) Coult. & Rose, nine-leaf lomatium; ANS-A; Pursh, 197; collected on the Clearwater (Kooskooske) River, Nez Perce County, Idaho, May 6, 1806

Deposited by American Philosophical Society [stamped]

Peucedanum simplex Nutt. (T. M) [Meehan] or P. triternatum, Pursh [unknown] (Greenman) [Meehan?]

Pursh's copy of Lewis label [Meehan?] A root 5 or 6 inches long eaten raw or boiled by the natives. On the Kooskooske My. <17> 6th 1806. [Pursh]

Cogswellia platycarpa or triternata? M E M [Mathias]

ANS PHILA [perforated initials]

ANS 1994 label: *Lomatium triternatum* (Pursh) Coult. & Rose

APS printed label: Peucedanum simplex Nutt. or P. triternatum Pursh?

98 *Lomatium* sp.?, lomatium; ANS-A; collected in Skamania or Klickitat County, Washington, or Hood River or Wasco County, Oregon, April 14, 1806

Deposited by American Philosophical Society [stamped]

All eaten! [Meehan?]

To poor to determine now. [Meehan?]

The root not eaten by the natives. On the Columbia. Aprl. 14th 1806. [Pursh]

An umbelliferous plant of which the natives don't eat the root. On the Columbia Aprl. 14th 1806. [Pursh]

APS printed label: Peucedanum

99 *Lomatium* sp.?, lomatium; ANS-A; collected in the vicinity of The Dalles of the Columbia River, Klickitat County, Washington, or Wasco County, Oregon, April 15, 1806

Deposited by American Philosophical Society [stamped]

To poor to determine now. [Meehan?]

An umbelliferous plant with a large fusiform root, which the natives bake & eat On the Columbia. Aprl. 15th 1806. [Pursh]

ANS PHILA [perforated initials]

APS printed label: Peucedanum?

100a *Lonicera ciliosa* (Pursh) Poir. *ex* DC., trumpet honey-suckle; ANS-A; Pursh, 160; collected on the North Fork Salmon River, Lemhi County, Idaho, September 2, 1805, and near Hungery Creek, Lolo Trail, Idaho County, Idaho, June 16, 1806

Deposited by American Philosophical Society [stamped]

Lonicera ciliosa, Poir. [Greenman]

Rocky mountain June 16 1806. [Pursh] Pursh's copy [Meehan?]

No. [5?] found on the waters of the columbia Sept: 2nd 1805. the growth of a moist situation seldom rises higher than 6 or 8 feet—puts up a number of succulent sprouts forming a thick bush. [Lewis] Lewis [Meehan?]

Can't be L. ciliosa, perhaps ciliata was intended. The branch is not true L. ciliata C. V. P. or L. utahensis Wats. L. ebractulata Ryd. [Piper]

ANS PHILA [perforated initials]

ANS 1994 label: *Lonicera ciliosa* (Pursh) D.C.

APS printed label: Lonicera ciliosa Poir.

100b *Lonicera ciliosa* (Pursh) Poir. *ex* DC., trumpet honey-suckle; ANS-A; Pursh, 160; collected on the Clearwater (Kooskooskee) River, Camp Chopunnish, Kamiah, Idaho County, Idaho, June 5, 1806

Deposited by American Philosophical Society [stamped]

Lonicera ciliosa Poir Caprifolium ciliosum Pursh T. M. [Meehan]

Holotype Pursh, Fl. Am. Sept. 1 : 160. 1814. [typed label]

Revision of *Lonicera* subg. Caprifolium *Lonicera ciliosa* (Pursh) Poiret Charles H. Perino August 1975 North Carolina State University [printed label]

yellow; On the Kooskooskee Jun: 5th 1806. [Pursh] 8 Pursh's copy [Meehan?]

Type of Caprifolium ciliosum Pursh J. W. Braxton 1975

ANS PHILA [perforated initials]

ANS 1994 label: *Lonicera ciliosa* (Pursh) D.C.

APS printed label: Lonicera ciliosa Poir.

101 *Lonicera involucrata* Banks *ex* Spreng., bearberry honey-suckle; ANS-A; collected in the vicinity of Lewis and Clark Pass, Lewis and Clark County, Montana, July 7, 1806

Deposited by American Philosophical Society [stamped]

Lonicera involucrata Banks T. M. [Meehan]

A Shrub within the Rocky mountains found in moist grounds near branches of riverlets. Jul. 7th 1806. [Pursh]

ANS PHILA [perforated initials]

ANS 1994 label: *Lonicera involucrata* (Richards.) Banks ex Spreg.

APS printed label: Lonicera involucrata Banks

102a *Lupinus argenteus* Pursh, silvery lupine; ANS-A; Pursh, 468; collected on the Blackfoot (Cokahlaishkit) River, in the vicinity of Lewis and Clark Pass, Lewis and Clark County, Montana, July 7, 1806

Deposited by American Philosophical Society [stamped]

Lupinus argenteus Pursh T. M. [Meehan]

slide mount inside D. Dunn. [envelope]

On the Cokahlaishkit Jul. 7th 1806. Flowers yellowish white [Pursh]

ANS PHILA [perforated initials]

ANS 1994 label: *Lupinus argenteus* Pursh

APS printed label: Lupinus argenteus Pursh

102b *Lupinus argenteus* Pursh, silvery lupine; Kew; Pursh, 468; collected some distance east of the Clearwater (Kooskooskee) River, Idaho, July 1806

Lupinus argenteus* Kooskooskee. July, 1806 [Pursh]

Herbarium Hookerianum 1867 [stamped]

The original L. argenteus, Pursh. A. G. [Gray]

*F. Pursh scripsit **A. B. Lambert scripsit and on reverse of sheet. J. Ewan

Herb. Pursh propr. [Pamphlin] **Lupinus argenteus. Fl: Amer: Pursh. [Lambert]

America Sept. Fred: Pursh [Lambert] [reverse]

103 *Lupinus pusillus* Pursh, rusty lupine; Kew; Pursh, 468; collected at an unknown place and date, probably on the Missouri River

Lupin pusillus. dispermus pusillus. Fl. Amer* [Pursh]

Herbarium Hookerianum 1867 [stamped]

*F. Pursh scripsit; **A. B. Lambert scripsit. J. Ewan

Herb. Pursh propr. [Pamphlin] **Lupinus pusillus. Fl: Amer: Pursh [Lambert]

America Sept: Fred: Pursh [Lambert] [reverse]

104a *Lupinus sericeus* Pursh, silky lupine; ANS-A; Pursh, 468; collected on the Clearwater (Kooskooskee) River, Camp Chopunnish, Kamiah, Idaho County, Idaho, June 5, 1806

Deposited by American Philosophical Society [stamped]

Lupinus sericeus Pursh T. M [Meehan]

Slide mount inside D. Dunn [envelope]

New Species Flowers cream colored with a Small fringe of blue. On the Kooskooskee Jun: 5th 1806. [Pursh] Pursh's copy of Lewis [Meehan?]

Type collection [stamped]

ANS PHILA [perforated initials]

ANS 1994 label: *Lupinus sericeus* Pursh

APS printed label: Lupinus sericeus Pursh

104b *Lupinus sericeus* Pursh, silky lupine; Kew; Pursh, 468; collected on the Blackfoot (Cokahlaishkit) River, in the vicinity of Lewis and Clark Pass, Lewis and Clark County, Montana, July 7, 1806

Lupinus Sericeus.* Cokahlaishkit. Jul. 7, 1806? Flowers yellowish white [Pursh]

This leaf belongs clearly to the L. argenteus, Pursh; here by mistake A. G. 1868 [Gray]

Herbarium Hookerianum 1867 [stamped]

This was not collected at the place where the type was collected nor does it agree with description. "L. sericeus Pursh Fl. 2:468 perennis; caule foliisque sericeo-tomentosis, foliis digitatis; foliolis (7–8) lanceolatis acutis utrinque sericeis, calycibus subverticillatis inappendiculatis; labio superiore inciso; inferiore integro. On the banks of the Kooskoosky. M. Lewis. ♃ July v. s. in Herb. Lewis. Flowers pale purple or rose-colored." This is near the junction of Lewis & Clark river. Alice Eastwood, Oct. 1911.

This is a Lambert Herb. sheet: *Pursh scripsit; **Lambert scripsit; *** Wm. Pamphlin scripsit Cf. E. Coues' commentary on Lewis & Clark route for locality and date. Det. J. Ewan <Utrecht> 1955

***Herb. Pursh propr. [Pamphlin]

[*words illegible*] **Lupinus sericeus Flor: Amer: Pursh. [Lambert]

[Am]erica Sept: Fred: Pursh. [Lambert] [reverse]

105 *Machaeranthera canescens* (Pursh) Gray, hoary aster; ANS-A; collected on the Columbia River, October 1805

Deposited by American Philosophical Society [stamped]

Aplopappus sp? Certainly not A. spinulosus, DC. [Greenman] Greenman [Meehan?]

On the Columbia. Octbr. 1805. [Pursh] Lewis Pursh's copy [Meehan?]

Machaeranthera sp.—probably M. attenuata L H Shinners 1/9/1946

Apparently the common Columbia form of Aster canescens Pursh. Will send specimen to compare of Aster spinulosus Nutt. C. V. P. [Piper]

ANS 1994 label: *Machaeranthera canescens* (Pursh) Gray

APS printed label: Aplopappus

106 *Machaeranthera pinnatifida* (Hook.) Shinners ssp. *pinnatifida* var. *pinnatifida*, spiny goldenweed; ANS-A; Pursh, 564; collected above the mouth of the White River, Lyman or Brule County, South Dakota, September 15, 1804

Deposited by American Philosophical Society [stamped]

Aplopappus spinulosus, DC. [envelope] [Greenman?]

Lyman Co., S. Dakota, on the Missouri, passing mouth of White River. (v. Coues, Proc. Phila. Acad. 1898:304). [Shinners?]

Prairies, Septb: 15, 1804. [Pursh] Lewis Pursh's label [Meehan?]

Haplopappus spinulosus (Pursh) DC. subsp. *spinulosus* Det. R. C. Jackson 1971 [printed label]

Aplopappus spinulosus, DC. (Amellus spinulosus Pursh) Fl. 564 J. M. G. [Greenman]

Type. Amellus spinulosus Pursh, Fl. Am. Sept. 2:564. 1814. = Sideranthus (Aplopappus) spinulosus. L H Shinners 1/4/1946 !M. C. Johnston 4 I '58

ANS 1994 label: *Machaeranthera pinnatifidia* (Hook.) Shinners var. *pinnatifida*

APS printed label: Aplopappus spinulosus DC. Amellus spinulosus Pursh

107 *Maclura pomifera* (Raf.) Schneid., Osage orange; ANS-A; collected at an unknown place and date

Deposited by American Philosophical Society [stamped]

There is no label or memorandum with this in Herb Lewis. Maclura aurantiaca Nuttall T. M [Meehan]

ANS PHILA [perforated initials]

ANS 1994 label: *Maclura pomifera* (Raf.) Schneider

APS printed label: Maclura aurantiaca Nutt.

108 *Mahonia aquifolium* (Pursh) Nutt., Oregon grape; ANS-L; Pursh, 219; collected at the Cascades (Great Rapids) of the Columbia River, Skamania County, Washington, or Hood River County, Oregon, April 11, 1806

Lewisia ilicifolia. Great rapids of Columbia with Soil among rocks Aprl. 11, 1806. [Pursh]

Lewisia ilicifolia Nov: genus. Mountain Holly. The flowering stem Springs up from near the ground & is upright; the infertile Shoots trail along the ground. Rich Soil among rocks. Great rapids of Columbia. April 11th 1806. [Pursh] copy Lewis [Meehan?]

Pursh's specimen [Meehan?]

Torrey & Gray in Flora N. Amer 1:51 footnote say the separate leaflets are from a Menzies collection in the Banks herbarium. J. A. Mears 3/76

Ex. Herb. A. B. Lambert [stamped]

Type Collection [stamped]

N America Herb: Lewis & Clarck. Fred: Pursh. [Lambert] [reverse]

ANS PHILA [perforated initials]

ANS 1994 label: *Berberis aquifolium* (Pursh) Nutt.

ANS printed label: Berberis aquifolium Pursh.

109 *Mahonia nervosa* (Pursh) Nutt., dull Oregon grape; ANS-L; Pursh, 219; collected at the Cascades (Great Rapids) of the Columbia River, Skamania County, Washington, or Hood River County, Oregon, October [31?], 1805

Lewisia nervosa Great rapids of Columbia. Octbr: 1805. [Pursh]

Ex. Herb. A. B. Lambert [stamped]

Lewisia nervosa New genus. Mountain Holly fr[om] the great Rapids of t[he] Columbia R. Octbr: 1805. [Pursh]

Berberis aquifolium Pursh [unknown]

Berberis aquifolium Pursh [unknown]

Pursh's herb.! [Meehan?]

Type collection [stamped]

Written above [unknown]

America. Herb: Lewis & Clarck. Fred: Pursh [Lambert] [reverse]

ANS PHILA [perforated initials]

ANS 1994 label: *Berberis nervosa* (Pursh) Nutt.

ANS printed label: Berberis nervosa Pursh

110a *Matricaria discoidea* DC., pineapple weed; ANS-A; Pursh, 520; collected in the vinicity of Weippe Prairie, Clearwater County, Idaho, on an affluent of the Clearwater (Kooskooskee) River, June 12, 1806

Deposited by American Philosophical Society [stamped]

Matricaria discoidea D. C. <Authem> Santolina suaveolens Pursh T. M [Meehan]

Herbarium of the University of California *Matricaria matricarioides* (Less.) Porter Det. L. M. Moe Date March 1972 [typed and printed label]

"Camp Chopunnish." (v. Coues, Proc. Phila. Acad. 1898:306.) [Shinners]

An agreable Smell On the Kooskooskee Jun: [9th?] 12th 1806. [Pursh]

Type. Santolina suaveolens Pursh, Fl. Am. Sept. 2:520. 1814. (= Matricaria matricarioides (<Porter> Less.) Porter.) L H Shinners 1/9/1946

ANS PHILA [perforated initials]

APS printed label: Matricaria discoidea D. C. Santolina sauveolens Pursh

110b *Matricaria discoidea* DC., pineapple weed; ANS-L; Pursh, 520; collected in the vinicity of Weippe Prairie, Clearwater County, Idaho, on an affluent of the Clearwater (Kooskooskee) River, June 12, 1806

Santolina suaveolens. <Balsamila> <Kuscuskensis> Kooskooskee Jun. 12, 1806. [Pursh]

Ex. Herb. A. B. Lambert [stamped]

Pursh! [Meehan?]

Matricaria discoidea DC.! A Gr. [Gray]

Herb: Lewis & Clarcke. [Lambert]

Type of Santolina suaveolens Pursh Rickett 2 Mr 1949

Herbarium of the University of California *Matricaria matricarioides* (Less.) Porter Det. L. M. Moe Date March 1972 [typed and printed label]

From Matracaria metricaroides folder No. 9339 [unknown] [reverse]

ANS PHILA [perforated initials]

ANS printed label: Matricaria discoidea DC.

111 *Microseris lindleyi* (DC.) Gray, Lindley's microseris; ANS-A; collected at Rock Fort (Rock) Camp, The Dalles, Wasco County, Oregon, April 17, 1806

Deposited by American Philosophical Society [stamped]

Rock camp Aprl. 17th 1806. [Pursh]

Microseris macrochaeta, Gray (J. M. G.) [Greenman]

ANS PHILA [perforated initials]

ANS 1994 label: *Microseris laciniata* var. *lindleyi* (DC.) Gray

APS printed label: Microseris macrochaeta Gr.

112 *Mimulus guttatus* DC., yellow monkey-flower; ANS-A; Pursh, 426; collected on the Blackfoot River, above its

confluence with Clarks Fork (Clarks) River, Missoula County, Montana, July 4, 1806

Deposited by American Philosophical Society [stamped]

Mimulus luteus <Pursh> Linn. (T. M) [Meehan]

On the Waters of Clarks River. Jul. 4th 1806. [Pursh] Pursh's copy of Lewis ticket [Meehan?]

ANS PHILA [perforated initials]

ANS 1994 label: *Mimulus guttatus* Fisch. ex DC. ssp. *guttatus*

APS printed label: Mimulus luteus L.

113a *Mirabilis nyctaginea* (Michx.) MacM., wild four-o'clock; ANS-A; Pursh, 97; collected in Bon Homme County, South Dakota, or Knox County, Nebraska, September 1, 1804

Deposited by American Philosophical Society [stamped]

Open plains. Septbr: 1st 1804. [Pursh]

Oxybaphus nyctogineus, Sweet. [Greenman] Greenman [Meehan?]

Allionia ovata Pursh [Meehan?]

ANS PHILA [perforated initials]

ANS 1994 label: *Mirabilis nyctaginea* (Michx.) MacM.

APS printed label: Oxybaphus nyctagineus Sweet

113b *Mirabilis nyctaginea* (Michx.) MacM., wild four-o'clock; ANS-L; Pursh, 97; collected in Bon Homme County, South Dakota, or Knox County, Nebraska, September 1, 1804

Allionia albida? Walt. Open plains. Septbr: 1st 1804. [Pursh]

#1 Presumably Type of Allionia ovata Pursh. Rickett 1 Mr 1949

Type collection [stamped]

Ex. Herb. A. B. Lambert [stamped]

2 1 allionia nyctaginea [unknown]

1 America Sept: Herb: Lewis & Clark. 2 Lousiana Bradbery. [Lambert]

Allionia ovata [unknown]

ANS 1994 label: *Mirabilis nyctaginea* (Michx.) MacM.

ANS printed label: Oxytrophus nyctagineus Sweet var. oblongifolius Gr. (Allionia ovata Pursh)

114 *Nicotiana quadrivalvis* Pursh var. *quadrivalvis*, Indian tobacco; ANS-A; Pursh, 141; collected at the Arikara

(Ricare's) Indian villages, Campbell or Corson County, South Dakota, October 12, 1804

Deposited by American Philosophical Society [stamped]

12th of October at the Ricare's town. This is the to-bacco which they cultivate.—[Lewis] Lewis' ticket [Meehan?]

Nicotiana quadrivalvis Pursh (T. M) [Meehan]

No. 45. Specimen of the Ricara's tobacco—taken 12th of October 1804 [Lewis] (Lewis' [label?]) [Meehan?]

Type collection [stamped]

ANS PHILA [perforated initials]

ANS 1994 label: *Nicotiana bigelovii* (Torr.) Wats. var. *quadrivalus* (Pursh) Fast.

APS printed label: Nicotiana quadrivalvis Pursh

115a *Oenothera cespitosa* Nutt. ssp. *cespitosa*, gumbo evening primrose; ANS-A; Pursh, 263, 735; collected near the Great Falls of the Missouri River, Cascade County, Montana, July 17, 1806

Deposited by American Philosophical Society [stamped]

Oenothera caespitosa <Sims.> Nutt. T. M. [Meehan]

Oenothera caespitosa Nutt. subsp. *caespitosa* Isolectotype *Oenothera scapigera* Pursh, Fl. Amer. Sept. 1:263. 1814. Lectotype: PH Determined by Warren L. Wagner 1980 Missouri Botanical Garden Herbarium (MO) [typed and printed label]

Near the Falls of Missouri Jul. 17th 1806. [Pursh] Pursh's copy of Lewis [Meehan?]

PH [unknown]

ANS PHILA [perforated initials]

APS printed label: Oenothera caespitosa Nutt.

115b *Oenothera cespitosa* Nutt. ssp. *cespitosa*, gumbo evening primrose; ANS-L; Pursh, 263, 735; collected near the Great Falls of the Missouri River, Cascade County, Montana, July 17, 1806

Oenothera caespitosa [Pursh?]

Oenothera aborvitata Near the falls of Missouri Jul. 17 1806. [Pursh]

Lewis! [unknown]

Ex. Herb. A. B. Lambert [stamped]

Oenothera caespitosa Nutt. subsp. *caespitosa* Lectotype *Oenothera scapigera* Pursh, Fl. Amer. Sept. 1:263. 1814. 2 Determined by Warren L. Wagner 1980 [typed label]

This would be Type of O. caespitosa Pursh if it were not

for his notation of "very important specimen in Herb Lewis." Either this is not a Lewis specimen or it was added to by Pursh from plants from Herb. Fraser. It may be designated as Lectotype. Rickett 1 Mr 1949

PH [unknown]

1 Louisiana Bradbury 2 America Herb: Lewis & Clarke. Fred: Pursh. [Lambert] [reverse]

ANS PHILA [perforated initials]

ANS printed label: Oenothera caespitosa Nutt. (§ Euoenothera)

116 *Orthocarpus tenuifolius* (Pursh) Benth., thin-leaved owl-clover; ANS-A; Pursh, 429; collected in the valley of the Bitterroot (Clark's) River, Travelers' Rest, Missoula County, Montana, July 1, 1806

Deposited by American Philosophical Society [stamped]

Orthocarpus tenuifolius Benth Bartsia tenuifolius Pursh (T. M) [Meehan]

Valley of Clark's R. Jul. 1st 1806 [Pursh] Pursh's copy of Lewis label. [Meehan?]

Type collection [stamped]

Holotype Jepson Herbarium—University of California *Orthocarpus tenuifolius* (Pursh) Benth. T. I. Chuang & L. R. Heckard 1982 [typed, printed, and handwritten label]

ANS PHILA [perforated initials]

APS printed label: Orthocarpus tenuifolius Benth.

117 *Osmorhiza occidentalis* (Nutt. *ex* Torr. & Gray) Torr., western sweet-cicely; ANS-A; collected in Klickitat or Benton County, Washington, or Gilliam or Morrow County, Oregon, April 25, 1806

Deposited by American Philosophical Society [stamped]

all eaten! [unknown]

A Species of Fennel root eaten by the Indians of an Annis Seed taste. Flowers white. Columbia R. Aprl. 25th 1806. [Pursh]

ANS PHILA [perforated initials]

APS printed label: Ferula?

118a *Oxytropis nana* Nutt. var. *besseyi* (Rydb.) Isely, Bessey's crazyweed; ANS-A; Pursh, 473; collected on the Bitterroot (Clark's) River, Travelers' Rest, Missoula County, Montana, July [1?], 1806

Deposited by American Philosophical Society [stamped]

571. Oxytropis.... [*photocopy from Pursh, 473*]

As can be plainly seen from Pursh's words (above), this is not a type-specimen, Pursh merely misidentified Lewis's plant from near Missoula as the *Oxytropis argentata* (Pall.) DC., a morphologically similar but distinct species native to Siberia. The footnote from Barneby, Proc. Calif. Acad. Sci. IV, 27:232. 1952, is still relevant (see below). R. C. Barneby (NY) Jan. 1994 [printed and typed label]

5. This is the planted listed by Pursh, Fl. Amer. Sept. 471—1814 as *O. argentata* (not, however, of DC.), and according to Coues (Proc. Philad. Acad. 1898, p. 298—1899), who made a special study of Lewis and Clark's route, it must have been collected on July 1–2 in the Bitterroot valley at the mouth of its Lou-Lou branch, in the present Missoula County, Montana. This statement is difficult to reconcile with our knowledge of the range of *O. Besseyi* var. *Besseyi*, to which Lewis's plant unquestionably belongs. July, the month given also on the label, is late in the season for young flowering material of this species at an altitude not much exceeding 3,000 feet, and this may be some error in the original data. This specimen, which I studied at PH circa 1949, is somewhat ambiguous for lack of leaves or fruit, and *could* be a late-flowering example of *O. lagopus* Nutt. This is nothing, however, to exclude it from *O. besseyi*, which I myself have seen near Missoula, in flower in late June. R Barneby 1994 [printed, typed, and signed label]

Oxytropis argentea Pursh (T. M) [Meehan] Oxytropis argentata, Pursh [unknown] Greenman [Meehan?]

Near the head<th> of Clark's River Jul. 1806. [Pursh]

Type collection [stamped]

ANS PHILA [perforated initials]

ANS 1994 label: *Oxytropis besseyi* (Rydb.) Blank.

APS printed label: Oxytropis argentata Pursh

118b *Oxytropis nana* Nutt. var. *besseyi* (Rydb.) Isely, Bessey's crazyweed; ANS-L; Pursh, 473; collected on the Bitterroot (Clarck's) River, Travelers' Rest, Missoula County, Montana, July [1?] 1806

Oxytropis argentata Head of Clarcks river. July 1806. [Pursh] Pursh Flora II 473 [Meehan?] This label is for A, Oxytropis besseyi Rydb. [Schuyler]

Type Collection [stamped]

B is Bradbury collection (see Fl. Amer. Sept. p. 740) [Schuyler]

Type of Oxytropis Lambertii Pursh. Rickett 1 Mr 1949

= *O. Lagopus* Nutt (*O. Besseyi* Rydb.) C. L. Porter '47

A = Oxytropis Besseyi Rydb. (O. argentata Pursh, Flora; non (Pallas) Willd.) B. O. Lambertii Pursh, Flora 740 — Type R C Barneby 1946

[Lo]uisiana Bradbury. [Lambert] [reverse]

From Oxytropis Lambert folder (Idaho) No. 3767 [unknown] [reverse]

ANS PHILA [perforated initials]

ANS printed label: Oxytropis Lamberti Pursh Gray in his revisions—both 1863 & 1884—think Pursh's *O. argentata* may be *O. nana*, but Torrey & Gray in Flora I, 693 refer it to O. Lamberti & above specimens seem to say the same [unknown]

119a *Paxistima myrsinites* (Pursh) Raf., mountain-box; ANS-A; Pursh, 119; collected near the Pacific Ocean, Pacific County, Washington, November 16, 1805

Deposited by American Philosophical Society [stamped]

Pachystima myrsinites Raf Ilix? myrsinites Pursh T. M. [Meehan]

A Small Shrub about 4 feet high with a Small deep purple berry, evergreen! Near the Pacific Ocean Novbr: 16th 1805. [Pursh]

ANS PHILA [perforated initials]

ANS 1994 label: *Pachystima myrsinites* (Pursh) Raf.

APS printed label: [*blank*]

119b *Paxistima myrsinites* (Pursh) Raf., mountain-box; Kew; Pursh, 119; collected near the Pacific Ocean, Pacific County, Washington, November 16, 1805

Rhamnus berberidifolius Near the pacific ocean; Evergreen about 4 feet high; berry deep purple. Novr 16, 1805. [Pursh]

(Pursh scripsit) [Ewan]

Type Ilex myrsinites Pursh! ex Herb. Lambert—his writing at * and on back of sheet. Determinavit J. Ewan [printed and handwritten label]

Mygrinla mylifolia [unknown]

Herbarium Hookerianum 1867 [stamped]

Herb. Pursh propr [Pamphlin] *Ilex myrsinites, Fl: Amer: Pursh [Lambert] Ilex myrsinites Fl. amer. Ph. [unknown]

1 Menzies 2 America Herb: Lewis & Clarck. Fred: Pursh [Lambert] [reverse]

119c *Paxistima myrsinites* (Pursh) Raf., mountain-box; ANS-A; Pursh, 119; collected near Hungery Creek, Lolo Trail, Idaho County, Idaho, June 16, 1806

Deposited by American Philosophical Society [stamped]

Pachystima myrsinites Raf. Ilex? myrsinites Pursh [Meehan?]

Rocky mountain June 16th 1806. [Pursh] Pursh's copy of Lewis [Meehan?]

ANS PHILA [perforated initials]

ANS 1994 label: *Pachystima myrsinites* (Pursh) Raf.

APS printed label: [*blank*]

120 *Pedicularis cystopteridifolia* Rydb., fern-leaved lousewort; ANS-A; Pursh, 425; collected on the Blackfoot River, above its confluence with Clarks Fork (Clark's) River, Powell County, Montana, July 6, 1806

Deposited by American Philosophical Society [stamped]

Pedicularis scopulorum, Gray? (P. elata. Pursh not Willd.) [Greenman] (Greenman) [Meehan?]

P. cystopteridifolia [unknown]

Pedicularis Groenlandica Retz [*illegible word, crossed out*] (T. M) [Meehan]

Pursh's copy of Lewis ticket [Meehan?] On the low plains on the heath of Clarks R. Jul. 6th 1806 [Pursh] Pursh [Meehan?] P. unoinata Willd. ‖P. elata Willd [Pursh]

ANS PHILA [perforated initials]

ANS 1994 label: *Pedicularis cystopteridifolia* Rydb.

APS printed label: Pedicularis scopulorum, Gr.?

121 *Pedicularis groenlandica* Retz., pink elephants; ANS-A; Pursh, 426; collected on the Blackfoot River, above its confluence with Clarks Fork (Clark's) River, Powell County, Montana, July 6, 1806

Deposited by American Philosophical Society [stamped]

Pedicularis scopulorum, Gray? (P. elata. Pursh not Willd.) [Greenman] (Greenman) [Meehan?]

P. cystopteridifolia [unknown]

Pedicularis Groenlandica Retz [*illegible word, crossed out*] (T. M) [Meehan]

Pursh's copy of Lewis ticket [Meehan?] On the low plains on the heath of Clarks R. Jul. 6th 1806 [Pursh] Pursh [Meehan?] P. unoinata Willd. ‖P. elata Willd [Pursh]

ANS PHILA [perforated initials]

ANS 1994 label: *Pedicularis cystoperidifolia* Rydb.

APS printed label: Pedicularis scopulorum, Gr.?

122a *Pediomelum argophyllum* (Pursh) J. Grimes, silver-leaf scurf-pea; ANS-A; Pursh, 475; collected below the mouth of the Cannonball River, Sioux or Emmons County, North Dakota, October 17, 1804

Deposited by American Philosophical Society [stamped]

Psoralea argophylla Pursh T. M [Meehan]

No. 48. No. 103. October 17th 1804. a decoction of this plant used by the Indians to wash their wounds. [Lewis]

ANS PHILA [perforated initials]

ANS 1994 label: *Pediomelum argophylla* (Pursh) J. Grimes

APS printed label: Psoralea argophylla Pursh

122b *Pediomelum argophyllum* (Pursh) J. Grimes, silver-leaf scurf-pea; ANS-L; Pursh, 475; probably collected below the mouth of the Cannonball River, Sioux or Emmons County, North Dakota, October 17, 1804

Psoralea argophylla Missouri. [Pursh]

Ex. Herb. A. B. Lambert [stamped]

Pursh's specimen! [Meehan?]

Holotypus Psoralea argophyllus Pursh Fl. Amer. Sept. 475. 1814. =Pediomelum argophyullum (Pursh) J. Grimes Det. James Grimes, 1987 The University of Texas at Austin [printed and typed label]

Type of Psoralea argophylla Pursh Rickett 2 Mr 1949

N. America. Herb: Lewis & Clarck. [Lambert] [reverse]

From Psoralea argophyllum folder No. 3703 [unknown] [reverse]

ANS PHILA [perforated initials]

ANS printed label: Psoralea argophylla Pursh

123 *Pediomelum esculentum* (Pursh) Rydb., Indian breadroot; ANS-L; Pursh, 475; collected at an unknown place and date, probably on the Missouri River

Ex. Herb. A. B. Lambert

The University of Texas at Austin Pediomelum pentaphyllum (B. Juss.) J. Grimes var. scaposum (Gray) J. Grimes Det. James Grimes, 1987 [printed and typed label]

a new species P. esculenta Nutt. [Gray?]

P. hypogaea? N. L. B. [Britton?]

Type of Psoralea esculenta Pursh Rickett 2 Mr 1949

Holotypus Psoralea esculenta Pursh Fl. Amer. Sept. 2: 475. 1814. =Pediomelum esculentum (Pursh) Rydberg Det. James Grimes, 1987 The University of Texas at Austin [printed and typed label]

Lewis & Clark's herb [Meehan?]

Type collection [stamped]

Psoralea esculenta [unknown]

This plant produces the large root found in the [Canoes of Indians?] [*illegible, page torn*] [unknown]

N. America Herb: Lewis & Clarck. [Lambert] [reverse]

From Psoralea esculenta folder No. 3703 [unknown] [reverse]

ANS PHILA [perforated initials]

ANS printed label: Psoralea esculenta Pursh

124   *Penstemon fruticosus* (Pursh) Greene, shrubby penstemon; ANS-L; Pursh, 423; collected on the Lolo Trail, Clearwater or Idaho County, Idaho, June 15, 1806

Gerardia Suffruticosa. N. Sp. New Species A Small Shrub from the Rocky mountain, abundant in piny lands. Jun. 15th 1806. [Pursh]

(Pursh's copy of Lewis' label) [Pennell?]

Lewis & Clark Exped. [unknown]

Ex. Herb. A. B. Lambert [stamped]

Type collection [stamped]

Penstemon fruticosus (Pursh) Greene Type (Gerardia fruticosa Pursh) Specimen collected on Lewis and Clark Expedition, and studied by Pursh in England. How it came back to the Academy appears not to be known. [Pennell?]

an Penstemon [*words illegible*] [unknown]

Gerardia fruticosa Fl. Amer. Pursh [unknown]

written above [unknown]

N Ameria Lewis & Clarck. [Lambert] [reverse]

ANS PHILA [perforated initials]

ANS 1994 label: *Penstemon fruticosus* (Pursh) Greene

ANS printed label: Pentstemon Menziesii Hk.

125   *Penstemon wilcoxii* Rydb., Wilcox's penstemon; ANS-A; collected at Camp Chopunnish (Camp on the Kooskoosky), Kamiah, Idaho County, Idaho, May 20, 1806

Deposited by American Philosophical Society [stamped]

Pentstemon diffusus Dougl. (T. M) [Meehan]

Camp on the Kooskoosky May 20th 1806 [Pursh] Pursh's copy of Lewis label [Meehan?]

P. wilcoxii Rydb. F W P 1942 [Pennell]

ANS 1994 label: *Penstemon wilcoxii* Rydb.

APS printed label: Pentstemon diffusus Dougl.

126   *Pentaphylloides floribunda* (Pursh) A. L've, shrubby cinquefoil; ANS-A; Pursh, 355; collected at Nevada Val-

ley (Prairie of the Knobs), Blackfoot River, Powell County, Montana, July 6, 1806

Deposited by American Philosophical Society [stamped]

Potentilla fruticosa L T. M [Meehan]

Prairy of the Knobs. Jul. 6th 1806. [Pursh] Pursh's copy of Lewis' ticket [Meehan?]

ANS PHILA [perforated initials]

ANS 1994 label: *Potentilla fruticosa* L.

APS printed label: Potentilla fruticosa L.

127a   *Phacelia heterophylla* Pursh, varileaf phacelia; ANS-A; Pursh, 140; collected on the Clearwater (Kooskooskee) River, Camp Chopunnish, Kamiah, Idaho County, Idaho, June 9, 1806

Deposited by American Philosophical Society [stamped]

Phacelia circinata Jacq. P. heterophylla Pursh T. M [Meehan]

Root fibrous. plant from 3–4 high; dry Situation. On the Kooskooskee Jun. 9th 1806. [Pursh] Pursh copy of L. [Meehan?]

ANS PHILA [perforated initials]

ANS 1994 label: *Phacelia heterophylla* Pursh

APS printed label: Phacelia circinata Jacq.

127b   *Phacelia heterophylla* Pursh, varileaf phacelia; ANS-L; Pursh, 140; collected on the Clearwater (Kooskooskee) River, Camp Chopunnish, Kamiah, Idaho County, Idaho, June 9, 1806

Phacelia Scabiosaefolia Dry situations on the Kooskooske Jun. 9, 1806. [Pursh]

Ex. Herb. A. B. Lambert [stamped]

Type of Phacelia heterophylla Pursh Rickett 2 Mr 1949

Phacelia heterophylla. Fl. Am: Pursh [Lambert?]

[He]rb: Lewis & Clarck [Lambert]

Type collection [stamped]

From Phacelia heterophylla Pursh folder No. 7025 [unknown] [reverse]

ANS PHILA [perforated initials]

ANS 1994 label: *Phacelia heterophylla* Pursh

ANS printed label: Phacelia circinata Jacq. fil.

128   *Phacelia linearis* (Pursh) Holz., threadleaf phacelia; ANS-A; Pursh, 134; collected at Rock Fort (Rocky) Camp, The Dalles, Wasco County, Oregon, April 17, 1806

Deposited by American Philosophical Society [stamped]

Phacelia Menziesii, Torr. (Hydrophyllum lineare, Pursh) (J. M. G.) [Greenman]

Rocky Camp. Aprl. 17th 1806. [Pursh]

913784 [stamped]

ANS PHILA [perforated initials]

ANS 1994 label: *Phacelia lineare* (Pursh) Holz.

APS printed label: Phacelia menziesii Torr.

129   *Philadelphus lewisii* Pursh, Lewis's syringa; ANS-A; Pursh, 329; collected on the Clearwater (Kooskoosky) River, Nez Perce County, Idaho, May 6, 1806, and on the Blackfoot River, above its confluence with Clarks Fork (Clarks) River, Missoula County, Montana, July 4, 1806

Deposited by American Philosophical Society [stamped]

Philadelphus Lewisii Pursh (T. M) [Meehan]

Philadelphus Lewisii Pursh (T M) [Meehan]

Pursh's copy of Lewis ticket [Meehan?] A Shrub from the Kooskoosky. May 6th 1806. An Philadelphus? [Pursh] (Pursh) [Meehan?]

On the waters of Clarks R Jul. 4th 1806. [Pursh]

Type collection [stamped]

The two labels are interchanged P. A. R. [Rydberg?]

ANS PHILA [perforated initials]

ANS 1994 label: *Philadelphus lewisii* Pursh

APS printed label: Philadelphus Lewisii Pursh

130a   *Phlox speciosa* Pursh, showy phlox; ANS-A; Pursh, 149; collected in Nez Perce County, Idaho, May 7, 1806

Deposited by American Philosophical Society [stamped]

This is *Phlox speciosa*, but with narrower leaves than usual. A. A. Heller

Rather P. longifolia Nutt C. V. P. [Piper]

I am unable to locate this specimen. I have referred it temporarily to Philadelphus, from the appearance of wood and buds, the leaves protest against it! 1897 T. M [Meehan]

A Shrub about 4 feet high. On the plains of Columbia. May 7th 1806. [Pursh] Pursh's copy of Lewis [Meehan?]

Type collection [stamped]

Phlox speciosa *α* speciosa E. T. W. Genus Phlox: 14, 1955 [Wherry]

ANS PHILA [perforated initials]

ANS 1994 label: *Phlox speciosa* Pursh

APS printed label: Phlox speciosa Pursh

130b   *Phlox speciosa* Pursh, showy phlox; Kew; Pursh, 149; collected in Nez Perce County, Idaho, May 7, 1806

Phlox frutescens Plains of Columbia; about 4 feet high. May 7, 1806. [Pursh]

(F. Pursh scripsit! = copy as usual of Lewis's label. J. Ewan)

Herbarium Hookerianum 1867 [stamped]

Type Specimen. [printed label]

Phlox speciosa Pursh Typus. [unknown]

Herb. Pursh propr. [Pamphlin] Phlox speciosa Fl. Amer. Pursh [Lambert]

speciosa [unknown]

N. America Lewis & Clarck. Fred: Pursh [Lambert] [reverse]

131a   *Pinus ponderosa* P. & C. Lawson, ponderosa pine; ANS-A; collected in the vicinity of Canoe Camp, Clearwater (Kooskooskee) River, Clearwater County, Idaho, October 1, 1805

Deposited by American Philosophical Society [stamped]

Pinus ponderosa? T. M [Meehan]

as P. palustris in Pursh J A Mears 5/83

On the Kooskooskee On River bottoms in rich land, west of the mountains. Octbr: 1st 1805. [Pursh]

ANS PHILA [perforated initials]

ANS 1994 label: *Pinus ponderosa* Dougl.

APS printed label: Pinus ponderosa Doug.?

131b   *Pinus ponderosa* P. & C. Lawson, ponderosa pine; ANS-L; collected in the vicinity of Canoe Camp, Clearwater (Kooskooskee) River, Clearwater County, Idaho, October 1, 1805

Rocky Mountain Flora, Lat. 39°-41°. No. 528 Pinus ponderosa, Doug E. Hall & J. P. Harbour, Colls. 1862. [printed and handwritten label]

Pinus palustris? L. On the Kooskooskee, rich river bottoms. Oct: 1, 1805. [Pursh] Pursh Herb [Meehan?] Lewis & Clark [unknown]

ex Lamberth. deposit at PH [Mears?]

ANS PHILA [perforated initials]

ANS 1994 label: *Pinus ponderosa* Dougl.

ANS printed label: Pinus ponderosa Dgl. var. scopulorum Eng.

132 *Plagiobothrys tenellus* (Nutt. *ex* Hook.) Gray, slender plagiobothrys; ANS-A; collected at Rock Fort (Rocky) Camp, The Dalles, Wasco County, Oregon, April 17, 1806

Deposited by American Philosophical Society [stamped]

Plagiobothrys tenellus, Gray (J. M. G.) [Greenman]

Rocky Camp. Aprl. 17th 1806. [Pursh]

ANS PHILA [perforated initials]

ANS 1994 label: *Amsinkia intermedia* Fisch. & Mey.

APS printed label: Plagiobothrys tenellus Gr.

133 *Poa secunda* J. Presl, Sandberg's bluegrass; ANS-A; Pursh, 76; collected near the Clearwater (Kooskooskee) River, in the vicinity of Camp Chopunnish, Kamiah, Idaho County, Idaho, June 10, 1806

Deposited by American Philosophical Society [stamped]

Harvard University Herbaria Poa secunda Presl E. A. Kellogg 5 April 1983 [printed and handwritten label]

Poa sandbergii Vasey C. V. P. [Piper]

Aira brevifolia Pursh [Meehan?] Poa tenuifolia [Scribner?] Nutt [Meehan?] P. Buckleyana Nash [Scribner?]

= Poa Canbyi (Scribn) Piper Type Aira brevifolia Pursh, not Poa brevifolia DC Determined by A. S. Hitchcock [printed and handwritten label]

The most common grass through the plains of Columbia & near the Kooskooskee R. Jun: 10th 1806. [Pursh] Poa trivialis L. var. [Pursh?]

ANS PHILA [perforated initials]

ANS 1994 label: *Poa secunda* Presel

APS printed label: Poa tenuifolia Nutt.

134 *Polanisia dodecandra* (L.) DC. ssp. *trachysperma* (Torr. & Gray) Iltis, clammy-weed; ANS-A; collected at an unknown place and date

Deposited by American Philosophical Society [stamped]

Polanisia trachysperma, T. & G. [Greenman?]

Mixed with No. 43 [*Ed.: see 49a in this list*] August 25th growth of the open Praries. [Greenman] Greenman [Meehan?]

ANS PHILA [perforated initials]

ANS 1994 label: *Polanisia dodecandra* (L.) DC. ssp. *trachysperma* (Torr. & Gray) Iltis

APS printed label: Polanisia trachysperma T. & G.

135 *Polemonium caeruleum* L., western polemonium; ANS-A; collected between Bald Mountain and Spring Hill, Lolo Trail, Idaho County, Idaho, on an affluent of the Clearwater (Kooskoosky) River, June 27, 1806

Deposited by American Philosophical Society [stamped]

Polemonium caeruleum L. T. M. [Meehan]

Head waters of Kooskoosky June 27th 1806. [Pursh]

P. pulchellum C. V. P. [Piper]

ANS PHILA [perforated initials]

ANS 1994 label: *Polemonium* caeruleum L.

APS printed label: Polemonium caeruleum L.

136 *Polygala alba* Nutt., white milkwort; ANS-A; Pursh, 750; collected in Williams or McKenzie County, North Dakota, August 10, 1806

Deposited by American Philosophical Society [stamped]

Polygala alba Nutt. P. Sengea var. <angustifolia> tenuifolia, Pursh T. M. [Meehan]

Polygala A kind of Seneca Snake root. On the Missouri R. <Yellow Stone River> Augst: 10th 1806. [Pursh]

Leg. *M. Lewis Type* Polygala Senega var tenuifolia Pursh. Fl ed. 2, 2:750. 1816. = P. alba Nutt 1818. M. C. Johnston 1958

ANS PHILA [perforated initials]

ANS 1994 label: *Polygala alba* Nutt.

APS printed label: Polygala alba Nutt. var. tenuifolia Pursh

137 *Polygonum bistortoides* Pursh, American bistort; ANS-A; Pursh, 271; collected in the vinicity of Weippe Prairie (Quamash Flats), Clearwater County, Idaho, June 12, 1806

Deposited by American Philosophical Society [stamped]

Polygonum bistortoides, Pursh type [Greenman] (Greenman) [Meehan?]

Polygonum Bistortoides L. [Meehan?]

Polygonum Near to Bistorta [Pursh] Pursh [Meehan?] In moist grounds On the quamash flats. Jun: 12th 1806 [Pursh] Lewis [Meehan?] No. [1?] [Pursh]

Type collection [stamped]

Pursh, Fl. Am. Sept. i:271 [Pennell?]

ANS PHILA [perforated initials]

ANS 1994 label: *Polygonum bistortoides* Pursh

APS printed label: Polygonum bistortoides Pursh

138   *Populus balsamifera* L. ssp. *trichocarpa* (Torr. & Gray *ex* Hook.) Brayshaw, black cottonwood; ANS-A; collected at an unknown place, June 1806

Deposited by American Philosophical Society [stamped]

Populus trichocarpa, Torr. & Gray [Greenman] (Greenman) [Meehan?]

Cotton tree of the Columbia River. Jun: 1806. [Pursh] Pursh's copy of Lewis' ticket [Meehan?]

ANS PHILA [perforated initials]

ANS 1994 label: *Populus balsamifera* L. ssp. *tricocarpa* (Torr. & Gray) Brayshaw

APS printed label: Populus trichocarpa T & G.

139   *Populus deltoides* Bartr. *ex* Marsh. ssp. *monilifera* (Ait.) Eckenwalder, cottonwood; ANS-A; collected at an unknown place, August 1806

Deposited by American Philosophical Society [stamped]

Populus monolifera Ait. (P. angulata Ait.) (T. M) [Meehan]

Cotton tree of the Misisippi & Missouri. Augst. 1806. [Pursh] Pursh's copy of Lewis ticket [Meehan?]

ANS PHILA [perforated initials]

ANS 1994 label: *Populus deltoides* Bartr. ex Marsh. ssp. *monilifera* (Ait.) Eckenwalder

APS printed label: Populus monilifera Ait.

140   *Prunus emarginata* (Dougl. *ex* Hook.) Walp. var. *emarginata*, bitter cherry; ANS-A; collected on the Clearwater (Kooskooske) River, Camp Chopunnish, Kamiah, Idaho County, Idaho, May 29, 1806

Deposited by American Philosophical Society [stamped]

Cerasus pumila Nutt.? T. M [Meehan]

Prunus A Smaller Shrub than the Choak cherry, the natives count it a good fruit. On the Kooskooskee May 29th 1806. [Pursh] Pursh's copy of Lewis label [Meehan?]

Very probably Prunus emarginata Dougl. C. V. P. [Piper]

ANS PHILA [perforated initials]

ANS 1994 label: *Prunus emarginata* var. *emarginata* (Dougl.) Walp.

APS printed label: Cerasus pumila Nutt?

141a   *Prunus virginiana* L., choke cherry; ANS-A; collected on the Clearwater (Kooskoosky) River, Camp Chopunnish, Kamiah, Idaho County, Idaho, May 29, 1806

Deposited by American Philosophical Society [stamped]

Prunus virginiana L. T. M [Meehan]

Prunus Choak or Pidgeon Cherry On the waters of Kooskoosky May 29th 1806. [Pursh] Pursh's copy of Lewis ticket [Meehan?]

ANS PHILA [perforated initials]

ANS 1994 label: *Prunus virginiana* var. *demissa* (Nutt.) Torr.

APS printed label: Prunus Virginiana L.

141b   *Prunus virginiana* L., choke cherry; ANS-A; collected in Williams or McKenzie County, North Dakota, August 10, 1806

Deposited by American Philosophical Society [stamped]

Prunus demissa Nutt. T. M [Meehan]

Prunus A Cherry found near the beaver bents on the Missouri—Augst: 10th 1806. [Pursh] Pursh's copy of Lewis ticket [Meehan?]

ANS PHILA [perforated initials]

ANS 1994 label: *Prunus virginiana* L.

APS printed label: Prunus demissia Nutt.

142   *Pseudoroegneria spicata* (Pursh) A. Löve, bluebunch wheatgrass; ANS-A; Pursh, 83; collected in the vicinity of Camp Chopunnish, Kamiah, Idaho County, Idaho, June 10, 1806

Deposited by American Philosophical Society [stamped]

Festuca spicata Pursh [Meehan?] Agropyron divergens [Scribner?]

= Agropyron spicatum (Pursh) S & S Type Festuca spicata Pursh Determined by A. S. Hitchcock [printed and handwritten label]

On the plains of Columbia Jun: 10th 1806. [Pursh]

ANS PHILA [perforated initials]

ANS 1994 label: *Agropyron spicatum* (Pursh) Scribn. & Smith

APS printed label: Agropyron divergens

143   *Psoralidium lanceolatum* (Pursh) Rydb., lemon scurf-pea; ANS-L; Pursh, 475; collected at an unknown place and date, probably on the Missouri River

Ex. Herb. A. B. Lambert [stamped]

Psoralea lanceolata Missouri. [Pursh]

Lewis & Clark's herb. [Meehan?]

Holotypus Psoralea lanceolata Pursh Fl. Amer. Sept. 2: 475. 1814. = Psoralidum lanceolatum (Pursh) Rydberg Det. James Grimes, 1987 The University of Texas at Austin [printed and typed label]

Type of Psoralea lanceolata Pursh Rickett 2 Mr 1949

[N.] America. Herb: Lewis & Clarck. [Lambert] [reverse]

ANS PHILA [perforated initials]

ANS printed label: Psoralea lanceolata Pursh

144a *Psoralidium tenuiflorum* (Pursh) Rydb., wild alfalfa; ANS-A; Pursh, 475; collected at the Big Bend of the Missouri River, Lyman County, South Dakota, September 21, 1804

Deposited by American Philosophical Society [stamped]

Psoralea tenuiflora, Pursh (J. M. G.) [Greenman]

Big bend of the Missouri Septbr: 21, 1804 [Pursh] Lewis Pursh's label [Meehan?]

Type collection [stamped]

ANS PHILA [perforated initials]

ANS 1994 label: *Psoralidium tenuiflorum* (Pursh) Rydb.

APS printed label: Psoralea tenuiflora Pursh

144b *Psoralidium tenuiflorum* (Pursh) Rydb., wild alfalfa; ANS-L; Pursh, 475; collected at the Big Bend of the Missouri River, Lyman County, South Dakota, September 21, 1804

Ex. Herb. A. B. Lambert

Psoralea tenuiflora Big bend of Missouri Septbr: 21, 1804 [Pursh]

Lewis & Clark's herb. [Meehan?]

Holotypus Psoralea tenuiflora Pursh Fl. Amer. Sept. 2: 475. 1814. = Psoralidum tenuiflorum (Pursh) Rydberg Det. James Grimes, 1987 The University of Texas at Austin [printed and typed label]

Type collection [stamped]

Type of Psoralea tenuiflora Pursh. Rickett 2 Mr 1949

[N.] America. Herb: Lewis & Clarck. [Lambert] [reverse]

ANS PHILA [perforated initials]

ANS printed label: Psoralea tenuiflora Pursh

145 *Purshia tridentata* (Pursh) DC., antelope-brush; ANS-A; Pursh, 333; collected at Nevada Valley (Prairie of the Knobs), Blackfoot River, Powell County, Montana, July 6, 1806

Deposited by American Philosophical Society [stamped]

Purshia tridentata DC T. M [Meehan]

The University of Texas Herbarium (LL, TEX) Purshia tridentata (Pursh) DC. ex Poir. in Lam. Encycl. Meth. Bot. suppl. 4 (2): 623 (14 Dec) 1816. Holotype of: Tigarea tridentata Pursh Fl. Am. sept. 333, T. 15. 1814. J. Henrickson, June 1995 [printed label]

A Shrub common to the open prairie of the Knobs. Jul. 6th 1806. [Pursh] Pursh's copy of Lewis ticket [Meehan?]

Herbarium Acad. Nat. Sci. Phila. Type Collection No. Type of: Coll. Loc. [printed label]

Tigarea Pursh [unknown]

Type collection [stamped]

ANS PHILA [perforated initials]

APS printed label: Purshia tridentata DC.

146a *Quercus garryana* Dougl. *ex* Hook., Garry oak; ANS-A; collected in Cowlitz County, Washington, or Columbia County, Oregon, March 26, 1806

Deposited by American Philosophical Society [stamped]

Quercus Garryana Dougl. <a sort of white oak Columbia R> T. M [Meehan]

A Sort of white Oak Columbia. March 26th 1806. [Pursh] Pursh's copy of Lewis [Meehan?]

ANS PHILA [perforated initials]

ANS 1994 label: *Quercus garryana* Dougl. ex Hook

APS printed label: Quercus Garryana Dougl.

146b *Quercus garryana* Dougl. *ex* Hook., Garry oak; ANS-L; collected in Cowlitz County, Washington, or Columbia County, Oregon, March 26, 1806

Quercus bicolor West Chester, Pa. 1829. Wm Darlington

Quercus garryana Hook. A E Schuyler 1996

Quercus alba var. Columbia March 26, 1806. [Pursh] Pursh [Meehan?]

Barton Herb? [unknown]

Lambert Herb? [unknown]

Conrad herb [Mears?]

Monoecia Polyandria Quercus bicolor [unknown]

Q bicolor [unknown]

Recorded U. of Pa. Catalog Pa. Plants [stamped]

Chester Co. [unknown]

ANS PHILA [perforated initials]

ANS printed label: Quercus bicolor Willd.

147a *Quercus macrocarpa* Michx., bur oak; ANS-A; collected above the Niobrara River, Knox County, Nebraska, or Charles Mix County, South Dakota, September 5, 1804

Deposited by American Philosophical Society [stamped]

Quercus macrocarpa Mx. var. depressa Engel. T. M [Meehan]

No. 34 The leaf of oak which is common to the Praries 5th September 1804. [Lewis]

circinata Common to the prairies Septb: 5, 1804 [Pursh]

ANS PHILA [perforated initials]

ANS 1994 label: *Quercus macrocarpa* Michx.

APS printed label: Quercus macrocarpa var. depressa Engl.

147b *Quercus macrocarpa* Michx., bur oak; ANS-L; collected above the Niobrara River, Knox County, Nebraska, or Charles Mix County, South Dakota, September 5, 1804

Quercus macrocarpa Mississippi [Pursh] Pursh! [Meehan?]

Quercus macrocarpa circinata Common to the prairie Septb. 5, 1804. [Pursh] Pursh! [Meehan?]

ANS PHILA [perforated initials]

ANS 1994 label: *Quercus macrocarpa* Michx.

ANS printed label: Quercus macrocarpa Mx.

148 *Rhus trilobata* Nutt. var. *trilobata*, fragrant sumac; ANS-A; collected near the mouth of the Cheyenne River, Dewey, Sully, or Stanley County, South Dakota, October 1, 1804

Deposited by American Philosophical Society [stamped]

Rhus Canadensis, Marsh var. trilobata, Gray [Greenman?]

No. 57. October 1st 1804 first discovered in the neighborhood of the Kancez River—now very common, the growth of the little cops which appear on the steep declivities of the hills where they are sheltered from the ravages of the fire—[Lewis] Lewis [Meehan?]

Common on the declivity of hills Octb: 1, 1804 [Pursh] (Pursh) [Meehan?]

ANS PHILA [perforated initials]

ANS 1994 label: *Rhus trilobata* var. *trilobata* (Nutt.) Gray

APS printed label: Rhus canadensis Marsh var. trilobata Gray

149a *Ribes aureum* Pursh, golden currant; ANS-A; Pursh, 164; collected in the vicinity of the Three Forks of the Missouri River, Gallatin County, Montana, July 29, 1805, and near The Dalles (Narrows) of the Columbia River, Klickitat County, Washington, or Wasco County, Oregon, April 16, 1806

Deposited by American Philosophical Society [stamped]

Ribes aureum Pursh T. M [Meehan]

Yellow Currant of the Missouri. Jul. 29th 1805. [Pursh]

Type collection [stamped]

Yellow Flowering Currant. Near the narrows of Columbia R. Aprl. 16th 1806. [Pursh]

ANS PHILA [perforated initials]

ANS 1994 label: *Ribes aureum* Pursh

APS printed label: Ribes aureum Pursh

149b *Ribes aureum* Pursh, golden currant; Kew; Pursh, 164; collected near The Dalles (Narrows) of the Columbia River, Klickitat County, Washington, or Wasco County, Oregon, April 16, 1806

Ribes flavum Narrows of Columbia Aprl. 16th 1806.** [Pursh]

Kew Negative No. 1676 Date Intls. [printed label]

Lewis & Clarke Exped. [unknown]

= Lewis and Clark coll. Orig. label copied by Pursh *Pursh scripsit ** Lambert scripsit J. Ewan

Herbarium Hookerianum 1867 [stamped]

Herb. Pursh propr. [Pamphlin]

**Ribes aureum Fl: Amer: Pursh [Lambert]

America Herb Lewis & Clarke. Fred: Pursh [Lambert] [reverse]

150 *Ribes divaricatum* Pursh, straggly gooseberry; ANS-A; collected above the mouth of the Sandy River, Multnomah County, Oregon, or Skamania County, Washington, April 8, 1806

Deposited by American Philosophical Society [stamped]

Ribes Menziesii Pursh (T. M) [Meehan]

Deep purple Gooseberry Columbia R. Aprl. 8th 1806. [Pursh] Pursh's copy of Lewis label [Meehan?]

Probably R. divaricatum Dougl. C. V. P. [Piper]

ANS PHILA [perforated initials]

ANS 1994 label: *Ribes divaricatum* Dougl.

APS printed label: Ribes Menziesii Pursh

151 *Ribes sanguineum* Pursh, red currant; ANS-A; Pursh, 164; collected near the mouth of the Cowlitz River, Cowlitz County, Washington, or Columbia County, Oregon, March 27, 1806

Deposited by American Philosophical Society [stamped]

Ribes Sanguineum Pursh (T. M) [Meehan]

Columbia. March 27th 1806. [Pursh] Pursh's copy of Lewis label [Meehan?]

ANS PHILA [perforated initials]

ANS 1994 label: *Ribes sanguineum* Pursh

APS printed label: Ribes Sanguineum Pursh

152a *Ribes viscosissimum* Pursh, sticky currant; ANS-A; Pursh, 163; collected near Hungery Creek, Lolo Trail, Idaho County, Idaho, June 16, 1806

Deposited by American Philosophical Society [stamped]

Ribes viscosissimum Pursh (T. M) [Meehan]

Fruit indifferent & gummy The hights of the Rocky mountain. Jun: 16th 1806. [Pursh] Pursh's copy of Lewis label [Meehan?]

R. viscosissimum [unknown]

Type collection [stamped]

ANS PHILA [perforated initials]

ANS 1994 label: *Ribes viscossissimum* Pursh

APS printed label: Ribes viscosum Pursh

152b *Ribes viscosissimum* Pursh, sticky currant; Kew; Pursh, 163; collected near Hungery Creek, Lolo Trail, Idaho County, Idaho, June 16, 1806

Isotype Ribes viscosissimum Pursh *Pursh scripsit **Lambert scripsit J. Ewan, 1955

Herbarium Hookerianum 1867 [stamped]

*Ribes viscosum glandulosum, Flor. per. Hights of the Rocky mountain. Jun. 16, 1806. [Pursh]

Herb. Pursh propr. [Pamphlin]

**Ribes viscosissimum. Fl: Amer: Pursh [Lambert]

New York Botanical Garden Exploration of Montana and Yellowstone Park No. 4256 Ribes viscosissimum Pursh. Bridger Mountains, Mont., June 14, 1897 P. A.

Rydberg, Ernst A. Bessey, collectors Altitude, 6500 feet [printed label]

Royal Gardens Kew 10 March 00 [stamped]

153 *Rosa arkansana* Porter, prairie wild rose; ANS-A; collected above the Niobrara River, Knox County, Nebraska, or Charles Mix County, South Dakota, September 5, 1804, and near the mouth of the Cannonball River, Morton, Sioux, or Emmons County, North Dakota, October 18, 1804

Deposited by American Philosophical Society [stamped]

Rosa Open prairies Septb: 5, 1804 [Pursh] Pursh's copy of Lewis ticket [Meehan?]

No. 50 Octobr 18th The small Rose of the praries it rises from 12 to 14 Inches high does not vine [Lewis] (Lewis) [Meehan?]

Rosa woodsii Lindl. T. M [Meehan]

ANS PHILA [perforated initials]

ANS 1994 label: *Rosa arkansana* Porter

APS printed label: Rosa Woodsii Lindl.

154 *Rubus parviflorus* Nutt., thimbleberry; ANS-A; collected in the vicinty of The Dalles of the Columbia River, Klickitat County, Washington, or Wasco County, Oregon, April 15, 1806

Deposited by American Philosophical Society [stamped]

Rubus nutkaensis <Moç.> Moç. T. M [Meehan]

Rubus Nutkanus Moç. var. velutina Brewer [Greenman] Greenman [Meehan?]

A Shrub of which the natives eat the young Sprout without kooking. On the Columbia Aprl. 15th 1806. [Pursh] Pursh's copy of Lewis ticket [Meehan?]

ANS PHILA [perforated initials]

ANS 1994 label: *Rubus spectabilis* Pursh var. *spectabilis*

APS printed label: Rubus Nutkanus Moç var. velutinus Brewer

155 *Rubus spectabilis* Pursh, salmonberry; ANS-A; Pursh, 348; collected near the mouth of the Cowlitz River, Cowlitz County, Washington, or Columbia County, Oregon, March 27, 1806

Deposited by American Philosophical Society [stamped]

Rubus spectabilis Pursh T. M [Meehan]

Fruit like a Rasberry Columbia. March 27th 1806. [Pursh] Pursh's copy of Lewis ticket [Meehan?]

ANS PHILA [perforated initials]

ANS 1994 label: *Rubus spectabilis* Pursh

APS printed label: Rubus spectabilis Pursh

156a *Salvia reflexa* Hornem., lance-leaved sage; ANS-A; Pursh, 19; collected at the Big Bend of the Missouri River, Lyman County, South Dakota, September 21, 1804

Deposited by American Philosophical Society [stamped]

Big bend of Missouri Septbr. 21, 1804. [Pursh]

Salvia lanceolata Willd. <Broun? Brouss?> Salvia trichostemmoides Pursh T M [Meehan]

ANS PHILA [perforated initials]

ANS 1994 label: *Salvia reflexa* Hornem.

APS printed label: Salvia lanceolata Willd.

156b *Salvia reflexa* Hornem., lance-leaved sage; ANS-L; Pursh, 19; collected at the Big Bend of the Missouri River, Lyman County, South Dakota, September 21, 1804

Salvia trichostemmoides. Big bend of Missouri Septbr: 21, 1804 [Pursh]

Trichostemme sp. [unknown]

Type of Salvia trichostemmoides Pursh Rickett 2 Mr 1949

America Sept: Herb: Lewis & Clark. [Lambert]

X Salvia lanceolata [unknown]

Pursh's Herb [Meehan?]

Salvia trichostemmoides Pursh Fl: Amer: [Lambert?]

Type collection [stamped]

ANS PHILA [perforated initials]

ANS 1994 label: *Salvia reflexa* Hornem.

ANS printed label: Salvia lanceolata Willd. 491

157 *Sarcobatus vermiculatus* (Hook.) Torr., greasewood; ANS-A; collected on the Marias River, Toole County, Montana, July 20, 1806

Deposited by American Philosophical Society [stamped]

Sarcobatus vermiculatus Torr. T. M. [Meehan]

A Small branchy Shrub from the plains of Missouri— July 20th 1806. [Pursh] Pursh's copy of Lewis [Meehan?]

ANS PHILA [perforated initials]

ANS 1994 label: *Sarcobatus vermiculatus* (Hook.) Torr. var. *vermiculatus*

APS printed label: Sarcobatus vermiculatus Torr.

158 *Scutellaria angustifolia* Pursh ssp. *angustifolia*, narrow-leaved skullcap; ANS-A; Pursh, 412; collected on the Clearwater (Kooskooskee) River, Camp Chopunnish, Kamiah, Idaho County, Idaho, June 5, 1806

Deposited by American Philosophical Society [stamped]

Scutellaria angustifolia Pursh T. M [Meehan]

Type collection [stamped]

On the Kooskooskee Jun: 5th 1806. [Pursh]

Holotype! *Scutellaria angustifolia* Pursh subsp. *angustifolia* Det. by Richard Olmstead 1987 University of Washington [typed and handwritten label]

ANS PHILA [perforated initials]

APS printed label: Scutellaria angustifolia Pursh

159 *Sedum stenopetalum* Pursh, wormleaf stonecrop; ANS-A; Pursh, 324; collected on the Clearwater (Kooskooskee) River, Camp Chopunnish, Kamiah, Idaho County, Idaho, June 5, 1806, and in the valley of the Bitterroot (Clarks) River, Travelers' Rest, Missoula County, Montana, July 1, 1806

Deposited by American Philosophical Society [stamped]

Type of Sedum stenopetalum (inflorescences) and loose leaves of S.? coerulescens. Haw. R. T. Clausen 1946, Nov. 30

Type collection [stamped]

Sedum? coerulescens Haw. R. T. Clausen 1946, Nov. 30

Sedum stenopetalum, Pursh type (J. M. G.) [Greenman]

Valley of Clarks R. Jul. 1st 1806. [Pursh]

On the naked rocks on the Kooskooskee. Jun: 5th 1806. [Pursh]

ANS PHILA [perforated initials]

ANS 1994 label: *Sedum stenopetalum* Pursh

APS printed label: Sedum stenopetalum Pursh

160a *Shepherdia argentea* (Pursh) Nutt., buffaloberry; ANS-A; Pursh, 115; collected at the mouth of the Niobrara (Quiccourre) River, Knox County, Nebraska, or Bon Homme County, South Dakota, about September 4, 1804

Deposited by American Philosophical Society [stamped]

B No. 39. [Lewis?]

Shepherdia argentea Nutt. Hippophaea argentea
Pursh T. M. [Meehan]

A No. 39. [H?] obtained at the mouth of the River
Quiccourre from which place upwards it is abundant
in the Missouri bottoms it is a pleasent burry to eat—
it has much the flavor of the cranbury, and continues
on the brush through the winter—this is an evergreen
shrub—some plants are sent down by the barge to the
care of Capt. Stoddard at St. Louis [Lewis]

From the mouth of the river Quiccourre & from there
upwards in all the Missouri bottoms; The berry pleasant, acid like Cranberry & hang on all winter Evergreen. [Pursh]

ANS PHILA [perforated initials]

ANS 1994 label: *Shepherdia argentea* (Pursh) Nutt.

APS printed label: Shepherdia argentea Nutt. Hippophaea argentea Pursh

160b *Shepherdia argentea* (Pursh) Nutt., buffaloberry; ANS-L;
Pursh, 115; collected at the mouth of the Niobrara
(Quiccourre) River, Knox County, Nebraska, or Bon
Homme County, South Dakota, about September 4,
1804

Ex. Herb. A. B. Lambert [stamped]

Hippophäe argentea From the mouth of the River
Quiccourre & from there upwards in all the Missouri
bottoms; The berry pleasant, acid like Cranberry hang
on all winter; Evergreen. [Pursh]

America Herb: Lewis & Clarcke [Lambert]

Ex. Herb Pursh—per Lambert [unknown]

Type collection [stamped]

Type of Hippophae argentea Pursh Rickett 1 Mr 1949

ANS PHILA [perforated initials]

ANS 1994 label: *Shepherdia argentea* (Pursh) Nutt.

ANS printed label: Shepherdia argentea (Nutt.) Greene
(Hippophae Pursh)

161 *Solidago rigida* L., rigid goldenrod; ANS-A; collected in
Brule County, South Dakota, if September 12, 1804,
but more likely in Doniphan or Atchison County, Kansas, or Buchanan County, Missouri, September 12,
1806

Deposited by American Philosophical Society
[stamped]

Solidago rigida L T. M [Meehan]

High dry prairies Septb: 12 [13?], 1804. [1806?]
[Pursh] [Lewis?] Pursh label [Meehan?]

ANS PHILA [perforated initials]

ANS 1994 label: *Solidago rigida* L.

APS printed label: Solidago rigida L.

162 *Sorbus scopulina* Greene, mountain ash; ANS-A; collected
on the North Fork Salmon River, Lemhi County, Idaho,
September 2, 1805, and between Bald Mountain and
Spring Hill, Lolo Trail, Idaho County, Idaho, June 27,
1806

Deposited by American Philosophical Society
[stamped]

Spcm. Sorbus Sambucifolia Ch. & Schlt T. M [Meehan]
Pyrus sambucifolia Ch. & Sch. [Greenman] Greenman
[Meehan?]

No. 24. found the [2th?] day of Sepbr. 1805. a small
growth only rising to the hight of 15 feet moist situations it seems to prefer. it is a handsome growth.—
[Lewis] Lewis' ticket [Meehan?]

On the top of the highest peaks & mountains. Jun. 27th
1806 In the Rocky mountains. [Pursh] Pursh's copy of
Lewis [Meehan?]

Sorbus scopulina Greene det. G. N. Jones 1944

P. sitchensis (Roem.) Piper [unknown]

ANS PHILA [perforated initials]

ANS 1994 label: *Sorbus scopulina* Greene

APS printed label: Pyrus sambucifolia Ch. & Sch

163a *Sphaeralcea coccinea* (Nutt.) Rydb., red false mallow;
ANS-A; Pursh, 453; collected on the Marias River, Toole
County, Montana, July 20, 1806

Deposited by American Philosophical Society
[stamped]

Malvastrum coccineum Gray Cristaria coccinea Pursh
[Meehan?]

A malvaceous Small plant probably a Species of
Malope. Plains of Missouri. Jul. 20th 1806. [Pursh]

ANS PHILA [perforated initials]

ANS 1994 label: *Sphaeralcea coccinea* (Nutt.) Rydb.

APS printed label: Malvastrum coccineum Gray

163b *Sphaeralcea coccinea* (Nutt.) Rydb., red false mallow;
ANS-L; Pursh, 453; collected on the Marias River, Toole
County, Montana, July 20, 1806

Cristaria stellata. <Lagunaea multifida> Plains of Missouri Jul. 20, 1806. [Pursh] Lewis & Clark [unknown]

Type collection [stamped]

Type of Cristaria coccinea Pursh Rickett 1 Mr 1949

Ex. Herb. A. B. Lambert [stamped]

Ex. Pursh Herbarium [Meehan?]

America. Lewis & Clarcke. <Herb> [Lambert] [reverse]

ANS PHILA [perforated initials]

ANS 1994 label: *Sphaeralcea coccinea* (Nutt.) Rydb.

ANS printed label: Malvastrum coccineum Gr. (Malva Nutt.) (Cristaria Pursh)

164   *Stipa comata* Trin. & Rupr., needle-and-thread; ANS-A; Pursh, 72; collected in Lewis and Clark or Teton County, Montana, July 8, 1806

50 [unknown]

Stipa spartea Trin. S. juncea Pursh, but not of Linn. [Meehan?] *Stipa comata* Trin F L S [Scribner]

Valeys of the Missouri on the Rocky mountain. Jul. 8th 1806. [Pursh]

Revisionary Studies in the Stipeae *Stipa comata* Trinius & Ruprecht var. *comata* M. Barkworth 1983 Intermountain Herbarium—Utah State University [printed and typed label]

= Stipa comata Trn & Rupr Basis of S. juncea misapplied by Pursh Determined by A. S. Hitchcock [printed and handwritten label]

ANS PHILA [perforated initials]

APS printed label: Stipa comata Trin.

165   *Symphoricarpos albus* (L.) Blake, snowberry; CM; Pursh, 162; collected at an unknown place and date, probably on the Missouri River

Symphoricarpos missouri—N. S. Lewis [Collins?]

folius inferioribu[s] [unknown]

Symphoria racemosa, Mx-Pursh secund [Collins?]

Mr. Collins [Elliott]

166a   *Synthyris missurica* (Raf.) Pennell, mountain kittentails; ANS-A; Pursh, 10; collected on Hungery Creek, Lolo Trail, Idaho County, Idaho, June 26, 1806

Deposited by American Philosophical Society [stamped]

Synthyris reniformis, Benth var. major, Hook. [Greenman] (Greenman) [Meehan?]

Synthyris reniformis Benth Veronica reniformis Pursh ?? (T. M) [Meehan]

Veronica reniformis Pursh [Mears?]

On hungry creek Jun: 26th 1806. [Pursh] Pursh's copy of Lewis' label [Meehan?]

S. missurica (Raf.) F W P 1932 [Pennell]

ANS 1994 label: *Synthyris missurica* (Raf.) Pennell

APS printed label: Synthyris reniformis Benth

166b   *Synthyris missurica* (Raf.) Pennell, mountain kittentails; ANS-L; Pursh, 10; collected on Hungery Creek, Lolo Trail, Idaho County, Idaho, June 26, 1806

Holotype University of Montana Herbarium Veronica reniformis Pursh Determined by Clak Schaack 4-21-75 [printed and handwritten label]

University of Montana Herbarium = Synthyria missurica (Raf.) Pennell Det. C. G. Schaack 1975 [printed, typed, and handwritten label]

Synthyria missurica (Raf.) F W P 1932 Type [Pennell]

Ex. Herb. A. B. Lambert [stamped]

Pursh's specimen [Meehan?]

Veronica reniformis Hungry creek Jun. 26 1806. [Pursh]

Type [Pennell?]

N. America Herb: Lewis & Clarke. [Lambert]

Wulfenia reniformis D Don [unknown]

Others removed from this sheet were *Synthyris rotundifolia* Gray of the Pacific coast region F W P [Pennell]

A. Gray [unknown]

775778 [stamped]

Flora of Northwestern U.S.A. Collected by J. William Thompson Idaho 13 862 15 July 1937 Synthyria missurica (Raf.) Pennell Valley Co: Alpine slopes near summit of high ridge west of Cascade, Payette National Forest, 8000 ft. Det. by Dr. S. F. [F. W.?] Pennell [printed and typed label]

University of Montana Herbarium Synthyria missurica (Raf.) Pennell Det. C. G. Schaack 1975 [printed, typed, and handwritten label]

ANS PHILA [perforated initials]

167a   *Trifolium macrocephalum* (Pursh) Poir., big-head clover; ANS-A; Pursh, 479; collected at Rock Fort (Rockford) Camp, The Dalles, Wasco County, Oregon, April 17, 1806

Deposited by American Philosophical Society [stamped]

Dept. of Agriculture Ottawa Canada (DAO) 1299 [printed and handwritten ruler label]

Holotype of *Lupinaster macrocephalus* Pursh Fl. Am. Sept. 2:479. 1814. Pursh gave the locality as "Headwaters of the Missouri, *Lewis.*" Nuttall merely changed the name of Pursh's species because he cited Pursh's name in synonymy. It is therefore based on the same type. The correct name then is *Trifolium macrocephalum* (Pursh) Poir. Encycl. Suppl. 5:336. 1817. This combination is a year earlier than Nuttall's change anyhow. J. M. Gillett, 1963 Department of Agriculture, Ottawa, Canada [typed and printed label]

Holotype *Lupinaster macrocephalus* Pursh = *Trifolim macrocephalum* (Pursh) Poir. Michael A. Vincent (MU) 1995 [printed label]

Type Collection [stamped]

Trifolium megacephalum, Nutt. (J. M. G.) [Greenman]

(Greenman's label of identification, 1897) [Pennell?]

A Species of Clover near Rockford Camp on high hills Aprl. 17th 1806. [Pursh]

(Pursh's copy of Lewis' label) [Pennell?]

("April 17, 1806. Rock Fort [not 'Rockford'] Camp at The Dalles of the Columbia.["] Ex. E. Coues) [Pennell?]

ANS PHILA [perforated initials]

APS printed label: Trifolium megacephalum Nutt.

167b   *Trifolium macrocephalum* (Pursh) Poir., big-head clover; ANS-L; Pursh, 479; collected at Rock Fort (Rockford) Camp, The Dalles, Wasco County, Oregon, April 17, 1806

Ex. Herb. A. B. Lambert [stamped]

Isotype Lupinaster macrocephalus Pursh = *Trifolium macrocephalum* (Pursh) Poir. Michael A. Vincent (MU) 1995 [printed label]

Lewis & Clark's herb. Pursh's specimen [Meehan?]

Trifolium microcephalum Rockford camp, high hills. Aprl. 17, 1806. [Pursh]

N. America Lewis & Clarck. [Lambert]

ANS PHILA [perforated initials]

168a   *Trifolium microcephalum* Pursh, small-head clover; ANS-A; Pursh, 478; collected in the valley of the Bitterroot (Clark's) River, Travelers' Rest, Missoula County, Montana, July 1, 1806

Deposited by American Philosophical Society [stamped]

Annotation Label Trifolium microcephalum Pursh James S. Martin 1942 [typed and printed label]

Type collection [stamped]

Trifolium microcephalum Pursh—T. M [Meehan]

Valley of Clarks R. Jul. 1st 1806. [Pursh]

For locality see Proc. Acad. Nat. Sci. Phila. :299. 1898. [Pennell?]

ANS PHILA [perforated initials]

ANS 1994 label: *Trifolium microcephalum* Pursh

APS printed label: Trifolium microcephalum Pursh

168b   *Trifolium microcephalum* Pursh, small-head clover; ANS-L; Pursh, 478; collected in the valley of the Bitterroot (Clarks) River, Travelers' Rest, Missoula County, Montana, July 1, 1806

Ex. Herb. A. B. Lambert [stamped]

Trifolium <ariculatum> parviflorum. Valley of Clarks River. Jul. 1st 1806. [Pursh]

[Lewis] & Clark's herb. [Meehan?]

Herb Lewis & Clarck. [Lambert]

"Nuttall" [unknown] *Thicaphyllum microcephalum. Trifolium microcephalum Ph Columbia wood [Nuttall?]

Lieut A. W. Whipple Exploration of a Railway Route, from the Mississippi River to the Pacific Ocean, near the 35th parallel of Latitude, in 1853–4. Collected by Dr. J. M. Bigelow, Surgeon and Botanist to the expedition Trifolium microcephalum California Tamulpais Torrey [printed and handwritten label]

From Trifolium microcephalum Pursh folder No. 3690 [unknown] [reverse]

ANS PHILA [perforated initials]

ANS 1994 label: *Trifolium microcephalum* Pursh

ANS printed label: Trifolium microcephalum Pursh

169   *Trillium ovatum* Pursh, white trillium; ANS-A; Pursh, 245; collected near the Cascades (Rapids) of the Columbia River, Skamania County, Washington, or Hood River County, Oregon, April 10, 1806

Deposited by American Philosophical Society [stamped]

Columbia R. near the rapids. Aprl. 10th 1806. [Pursh]

Holotype The University of Tennessee Knoxville, Tennessee, U.S.A. Lewis and Clark exped. *Trillium ovatum* Pursh 1814. Flora Americae Septentrionalis. 1:245. Thomas S. Patrick 1980 [typed and printed label]

Trillium ovatum Pursh T. M [Meehan]

0943823 [stamped]

Type collection [stamped]

Pursh Fl. Am. Sept. 1:245 [Pennell?]

ANS PHILA [perforated initials]

APS printed label: Trillium ovatum Pursh PH-932

170   *Trillium petiolatum* Pursh, purple trillium; ANS-A; Pursh, 244; collected on an affluent of the Clearwater (Koos-

kooskee) River, Lolo Trail, Clearwater or Idaho County, Idaho, June 15, 1806

Deposited by American Philosophical Society [stamped]

Trillium petiolatum Pursh T. M. [Meehan]

Holotype *Trillium petiolatum* Pursh. Fl. Am. Sept. I, p. 244, 1814. Examined in a revisionary study of sessile-flowered *Trillium* L. (Lilliaceae) John D. Freeman 1967 [printed and typed label]

Type collection [stamped]

Pursh, Fl. Am. Sept. i:244 [Pennell?]

folium—The flowers brown with a fruit of brick red;—On the waters of the Kooskooskee Jun. 15th 1806. [Pursh]

ANS PHILA [perforated initials]

ANS 1994 label: *Trillium petiolatum* Pursh

APS printed label: Trillium petiolatum Pursh PH-931

171a *Triteleia grandiflora* Lindl., Douglas' brodiaea; ANS-A; Pursh, 223; collected in vicinity of The Dalles of the Columbia River, Klickitat County, Washington, or Wasco County, Oregon, April 20, 1806

Deposited by American Philosophical Society [stamped]

Brodiaea Douglasii, Wats. [Greenman] Greenman [Meehan?]

Hyacinth of Columbia plains.—Aprl. 20th 1806. [Pursh]

900263 [stamped]

Herbarium of the University of California, Berkeley Triteleia grandiflora Lindl. Theodore Niehaus May 1975 <1968> [printed, typed, and handwritten label]

ANS PHILA [perforated initials]

APS printed label: Brodiaea Douglasii Wats.

171b *Triteleia grandiflora* Lindl., Douglas' brodiaea; ANS-L; Pursh, 223; collected in vicinity of The Dalles of the Columbia River, Klickitat County, Washington, or Wasco County, Oregon, April 20, 1806

Millea umbellata Hookera coronaria. Par. lond. Hyacinth of the plains of Columbia. Aprl. 20, 1806. [Pursh]

Ex. Herb. A. B. Lambert [stamped]

N. America. Lewis & Clarke. [Lambert]

900262 [stamped]

Tritelleria grandiflora, D[ouglassi] Millea umbellata, Pursh Oregon, Lewis & Clark from Lambert's her-

barium c[ollection] probably the specimen on which Pur[sh] established the diagnosis of Brodiea grandiflora [unknown]

Herbarium of the University of California, Berkeley Triteleia grandiflora var. Howellii Hoover Theodore Niehaus May 1975 <1968> [printed, typed, and handwritten label]

ANS PHILA [perforated initials]

ANS printed label: Brodiaea grandiflora Sm.

172 *Vaccinium myrtillus* L., dwarf bilberry; ANS-A; collected at Fort Clatsop, Clatsop County, Oregon, January 20, 1806

Deposited by American Philosophical Society [stamped]

Vaccinium Myrtillus, L. (J. M. G.) [Greenman]

New Species. With a purple Small berry eatable, an evergreen Fort Clatsop Jan. 20th 1806. [Pursh] Pursh's copy of Lewis label [Meehan?]

ANS PHILA [perforated initials]

ANS 1994 label: *Vaccinium myrtillus* L.

APS printed label: Vaccinium Myrtillus L.

173 *Vaccinium ovatum* Pursh, evergreen huckleberry; ANS-A; Pursh, 290; collected in the vicinity of Fort Clatsop, Clatsop County, Oregon, January 27, 1806

Deposited by American Philosophical Society [stamped]

Vaccinium ovatum Pursh (T. M) [Meehan]

A Shrub of 7 or 8 feet high, Supposed to be a Species of Vaccinium; the berries are eaten by the natives. On the Pacific Ocean Fort Clatsop. Jan: 27th 1806. [Pursh] Pursh's copy of Lewis ticket [Meehan?]

ANS PHILA [perforated initials]

ANS 1994 label: *Vaccinium ovatum* Pursh

APS printed label: Vaccinium ovatum Pursh

174 *Veratrum californicum* Dur., California false hellebore; ANS-A; collected on Hungery Creek, Lolo Trail, Idaho County, Idaho, June 25, 1806

Deposited by American Philosophical Society [stamped]

Veratrum californicum Durand? [Meehan?]

A plant growing in wet places with a Single Stem, & leaves clasping around one another; no flowers observed. On the Kooskooskee Jun: 25th 1806 [Pursh]

ANS PHILA [perforated initials]

ANS 1994 label: *Veratrum californicum* Durand.

APS printed label: Veratrum Californicum Durand?

175a *Xerophyllum tenax* (Pursh) Nutt., Indian basket-grass; ANS-A; Pursh, 243; collected in the Rocky Mountains, Lolo Trail, Clearwater or Idaho County, Idaho, June 15, 1806

Deposited by American Philosophical Society [stamped]

Xerophyllum asphodeloides Nutt. Helonias tenax Pursh T. M [Meehan]

Xerophyllum tenax, Nutt. [Greenman] (Greenman) [Meehan?]

The leaves are made use of by the natives, to make baskets & other ornaments. On high land, Rocky mountains Jun. 15th 1806. [Pursh]

Type collection [stamped]

Pursh, Fl. Am. Sept. i:243. [Pennell?]

Helonias tenax Pursh [unknown]

ANS PHILA [perforated initials]

ANS 1994 label: *Xerophyllum tenax* (Pursh) Nutt.

APS printed label: Xerophyllum tenax Nutt.

175b *Xerophyllum tenax* (Pursh) Nutt., Indian basket-grass; Kew; Pursh, 243; collected in the Rocky Mountains, Lolo Trail, Clearwater or Idaho County, Idaho, June 15, 1806

Helonias tenax. Rocky mountain; high lands Jun. 15, 1806. *Leaves used to make baskets. [Pursh]

Herbarium Hookerianum 1867 [stamped]

*F. Pursh scripsit! **A. B. Lambert scripsit! J. Ewan

Melanthececae [unknown]

Herb Pursh propr. [Pamphlin]

**Helonias tenax. Pursh: Fl: Amer: [Lambert]

America Herb: Lewis & Clarck. F. Pursh. [Lambert] [reverse]

176 *Zigadenus elegans* Pursh, white camass; ANS-A; Pursh, 241; collected on the Blackfoot (Cokahlaishkit) River, in the vicinity of Lewis and Clark Pass, Lewis and Clark County, Montana, July 7, 1806

Deposited by American Philosophical Society [stamped]

Zygadenus elegans Pursh T. M. [Meehan]

On the Cokahlaishkit R Jul. 7th 1806. [Pursh]

Type collection [stamped]

Annotation Label Zigadenus elegans Pursh Det. O. S. Walsh Type May 1940 [printed and handwritten label]

Type [unknown]

ANS PHILA [perforated initials]

ANS 1994 label: *Zigadenus elegans* Pursh

APS printed label: Zygadenus elegans Pursh

177 *Zizania palustris* L. var. *interior* (Fassett) Dore, wild rice; ANS-A; collected in Charles Mix or Gregory County, South Dakota, or Boyd County, Nebraska, September 8, 1804

Deposited by American Philosophical Society [stamped]

Ziz. palustris L. var. *interior* (Fassett) Dore (Can. Dept. Agric. Bull 1393:1969) Annotated 30 Sept., 1975. By William G. Dore [handwritten and printed label]

Zizania aquatica L. [Meehan?]

No. 59. 8th Sept. the growth of moist and very wet prairies [Lewis] (Lewis) [Meehan?]

Very wet prairies Septb: 8, 1804 [Pursh]

ANS PHILA [perforated initials]

APS printed label: Zizania aquatica L.

Herbarium of the Lewis & Clark Expedition

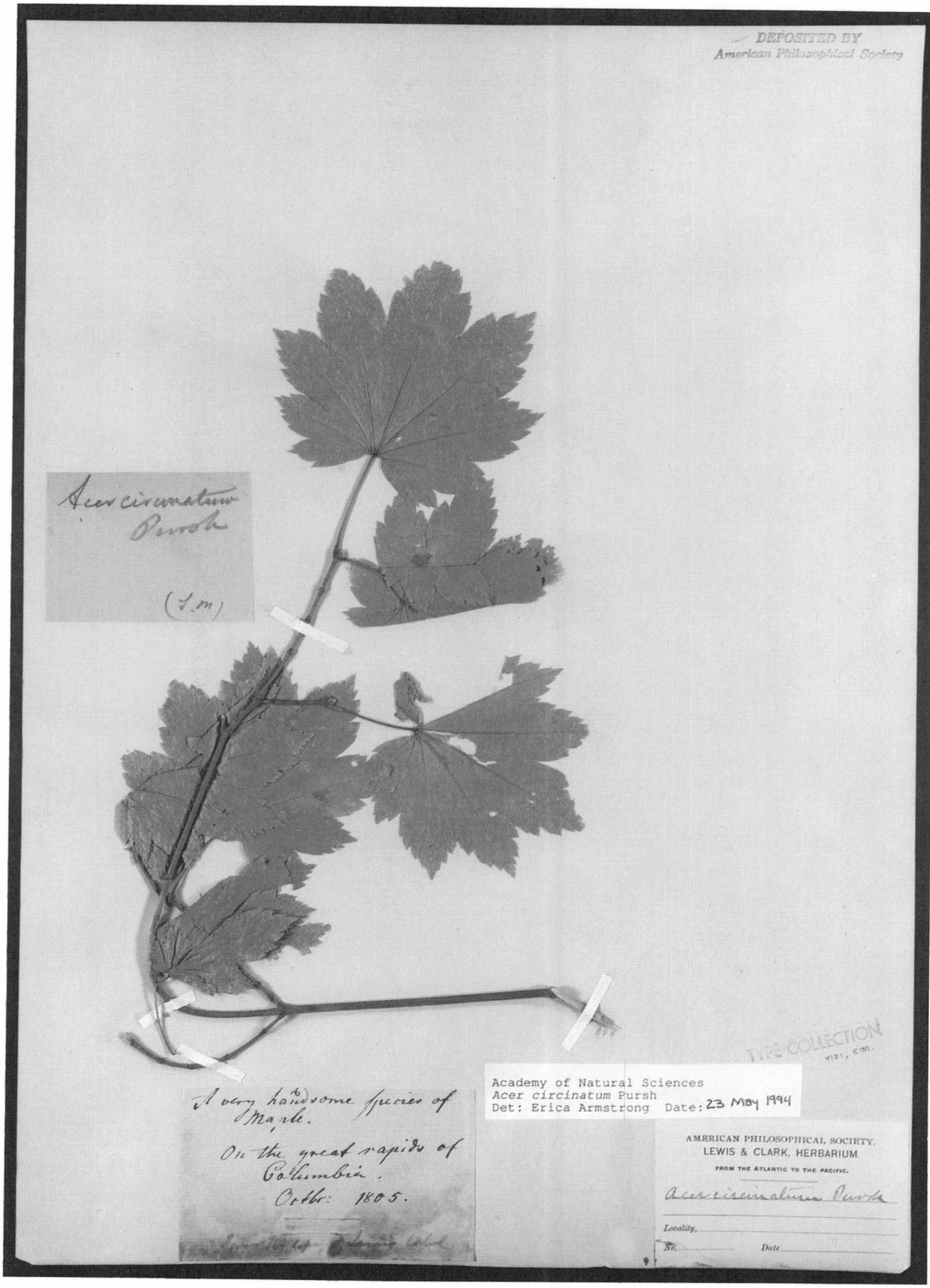
DEPOSITED BY
American Philosophical Society
Acer circinatum
Pursh
(F.m)
TYPE COLLECTION
Academy of Natural Sciences
Acer circinatum Pursh
Det: Erica Armstrong Date: 23 May 1994
A very handsome species of
Maple.
On the great rapids of
Columbia.
Octbr: 1805.
AMERICAN PHILOSOPHICAL SOCIETY.
LEWIS & CLARK, HERBARIUM.
FROM THE ATLANTIC TO THE PACIFIC.
Acer circinatum Pursh
Locality,
No.
Date

1a. *Acer circinatum* Pursh, vine maple

Acer circinatum
Great rapids of Columbia
Colbia 1805.

Pursh's specimen!

nenea Xte Columbia Herb: Lewis & Clarke. J.

AS WRITTEN ABOVE

HERBARIUM OF
ACADEMY OF NATURAL SCIENCES, PHILADELPHIA.

Acer circinatum Pursh

Academy of Natural Sciences
Acer circinatum Pursh
Det: Erica Armstrong Date: 17 May 1994

1b. *Acer circinatum* Pursh, vine maple

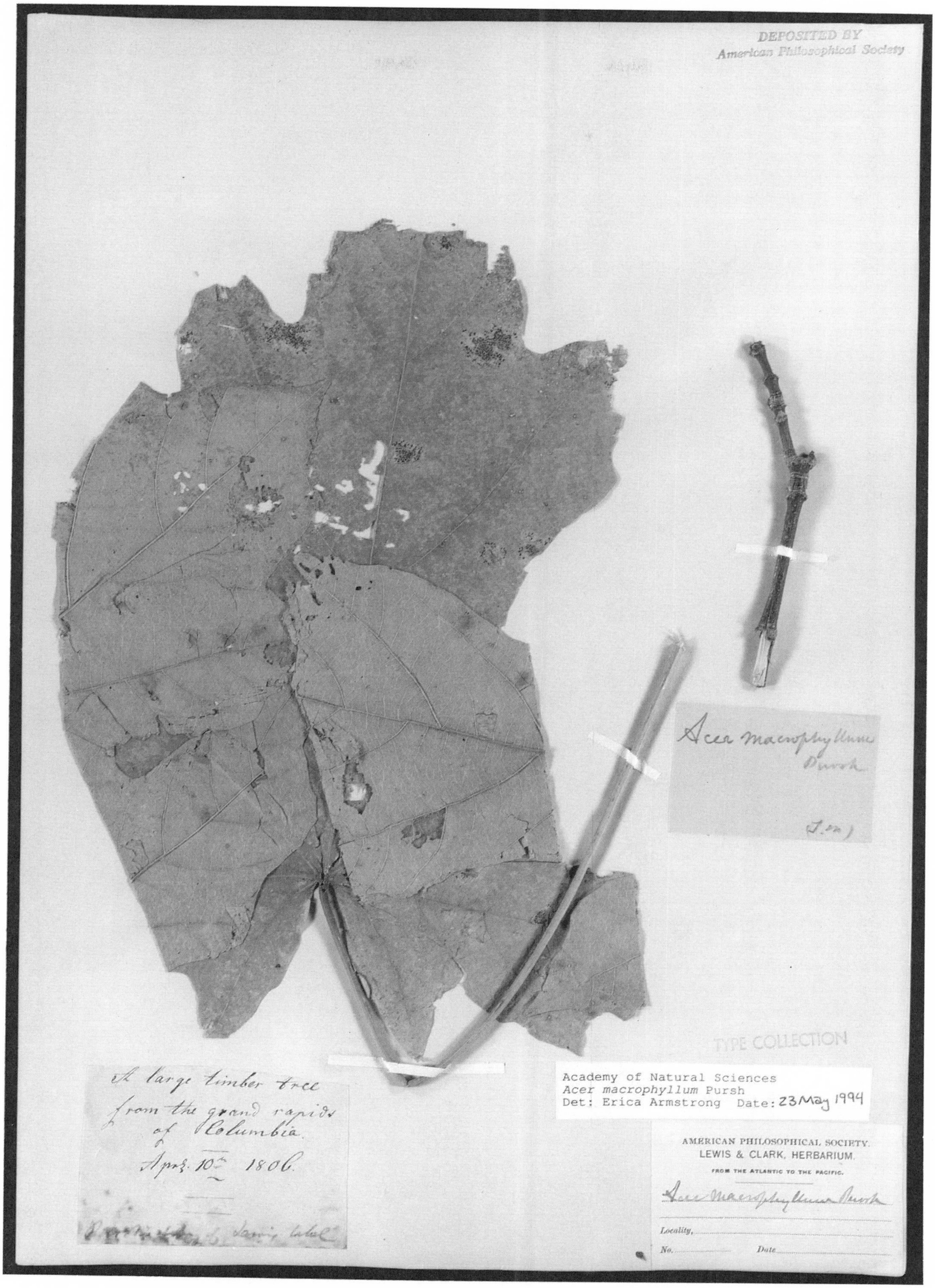

Acer macrophyllum
Pursh

(L.m)

A large timber tree
from the grand rapids
of Columbia.
Apr. 10ᵗʰ 1806.

Academy of Natural Sciences
Acer macrophyllum Pursh
Det: Erica Armstrong   Date: 23 May 1994

AMERICAN PHILOSOPHICAL SOCIETY.
LEWIS & CLARK, HERBARIUM.
FROM THE ATLANTIC TO THE PACIFIC.

Acer macrophyllum Pursh

Locality,
No.   Date

2a. *Acer macrophyllum* Pursh, big-leaf maple

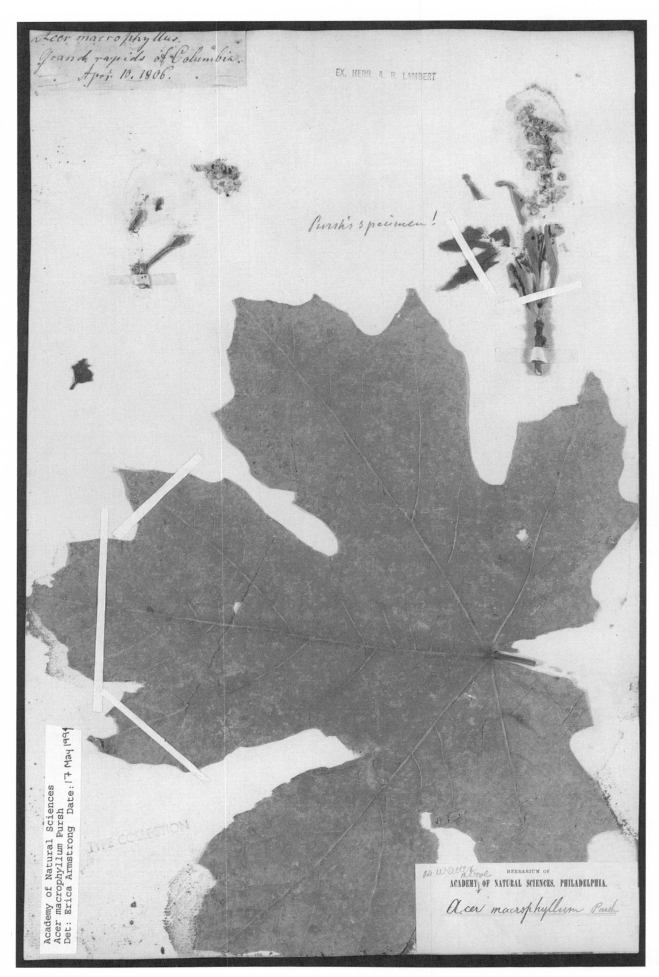

2b. *Acer macrophyllum* Pursh, big-leaf maple

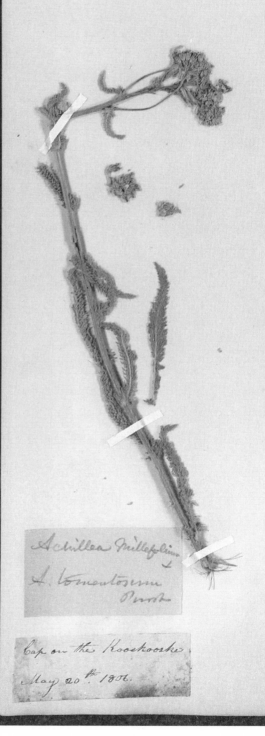

Achillea Millefolium
L.
A. tomentosum
Pursh

Cap on the Kooskooske.
May 20th 1806.

Academy of Natural Sciences
Achillea millefolium L.
Det: Erica Armstrong   Date: 17 May 1994

AMERICAN PHILOSOPHICAL SOCIETY.
LEWIS & CLARK, HERBARIUM.
FROM THE ATLANTIC TO THE PACIFIC.

Achillea millefolium L.
A. tomentosum Pursh

Locality,
No.   Date.

3a. *Achillea millefolium* L., yarrow

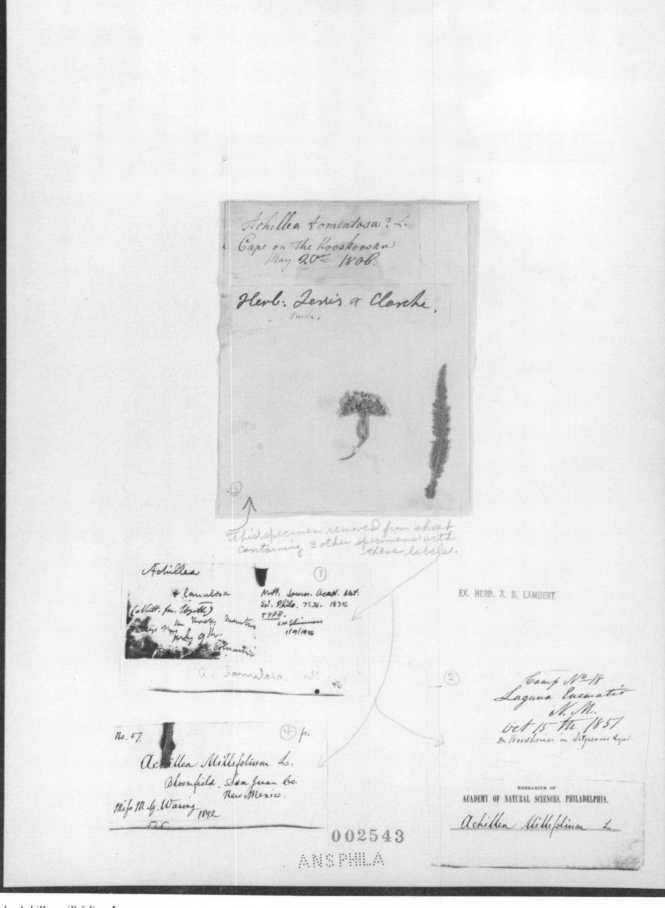

3b. *Achillea millefolium* L., yarrow

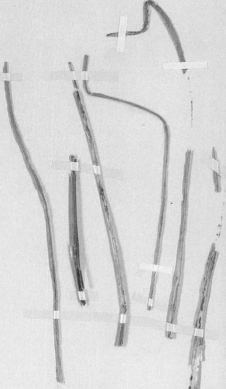

Allium Pursh
Kuskuskiense.

Lewis Purshicspy form.

On the waters of Kooskooskee
April 30th 1806.

Academy of Natural Sciences
Allium textile A. Nels. & J.F. Macbr.
Det: Erica Armstrong   Date: 17 May 1994

A. reticulatum does not
occur in the Kooskooskie.
R.V.R.

AMERICAN PHILOSOPHICAL SOCIETY.
LEWIS & CLARK, HERBARIUM.
FROM THE ATLANTIC TO THE PACIFIC.

Allium reticulatum Fraser

Locality,
No.   Date

4. *Allium textile* A. Nels. & J. F. Macbr., textile onion

Academy of Natural Sciences
Alnus rubra Bong.
Det: Erica Armstrong   Date: 17 May 1994

Black Alder of the Pacific
Ocean, grows to a large
size.
March 26ᵗʰ 1806.

AMERICAN PHILOSOPHICAL SOCIETY.
LEWIS & CLARK, HERBARIUM.
FROM THE ATLANTIC TO THE PACIFIC.

Alnus rubra Bong.?

Locality.

No.   Date.

5. *Alnus rubra* Bong., red alder

*Amelanchier
alnifolia* Nutt.

S.n

Service berry
A small bush
the Narrows of Columbia R.
April 15th 1806.

Pursh's copy of Lewis's label

AMERICAN PHILOSOPHICAL SOCIETY.
LEWIS & CLARK, HERBARIUM.
FROM THE ATLANTIC TO THE PACIFIC.

Amelanchier alnifolia
Nutt.

Locality,

No.   Date

Academy of Natural Sciences
Amelanchier alnifolia (Nutt.)Nutt.
Det: Erica Armstrong   Date: 17 May 1994

6. *Amelanchier alnifolia* (Nutt.) Nutt. *ex* M. Roemer, western serviceberry

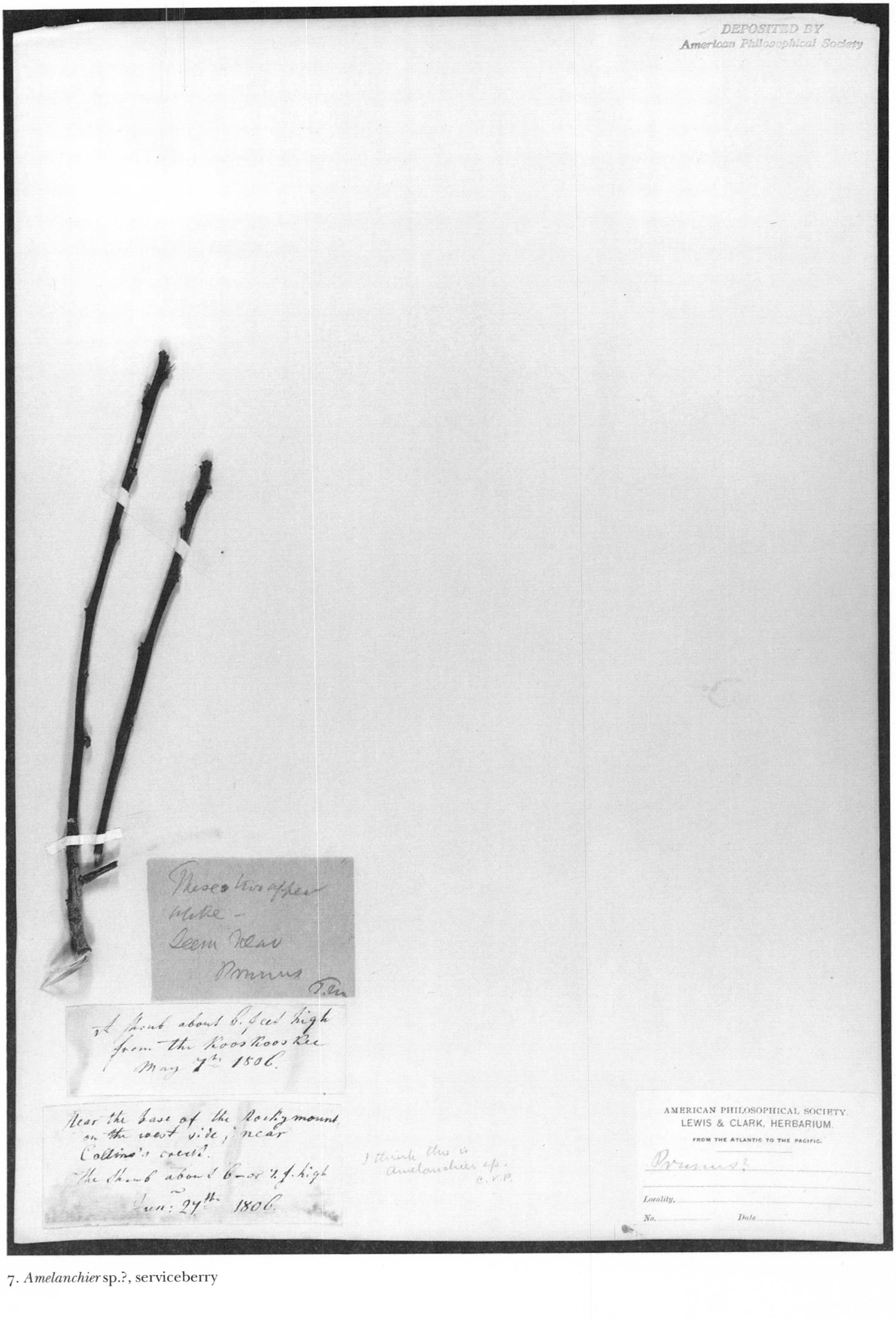

These two appear
to be —
Seem near
Prunus

A shrub about 6 feet high
from the Kooskooskee
May 7th 1806.

Near the base of the Rocky mount.
on the west side; near
Collins's creek.
The shrub about 6 or 7 f. high
Jun: 27th 1806.

I think this is
Amelanchier sp.
C. v. P.

7. *Amelanchier* sp.?, serviceberry

Amorpha fruticosa L.
V angustifolia Pursh

fruticosa.
On the great bend of
the Missouri.
August 27th 1806.

Academy of Natural Sciences
Amorpha fruticosa L.
Det: Erica Armstrong   Date: 17 May 1994

8a. *Amorpha fruticosa* L., false indigo

8b. *Amorpha fruticosa* L., false indigo

Academy of Natural Sciences
Ampelopsis cordata Michx.
Det: Erica Armstrong   Date: 17 May 1994

near Council Bluffs
Missouri.
Sept. 14th 1806.

ANS PHILA

9. *Ampelopsis cordata* Michx., raccoon grape

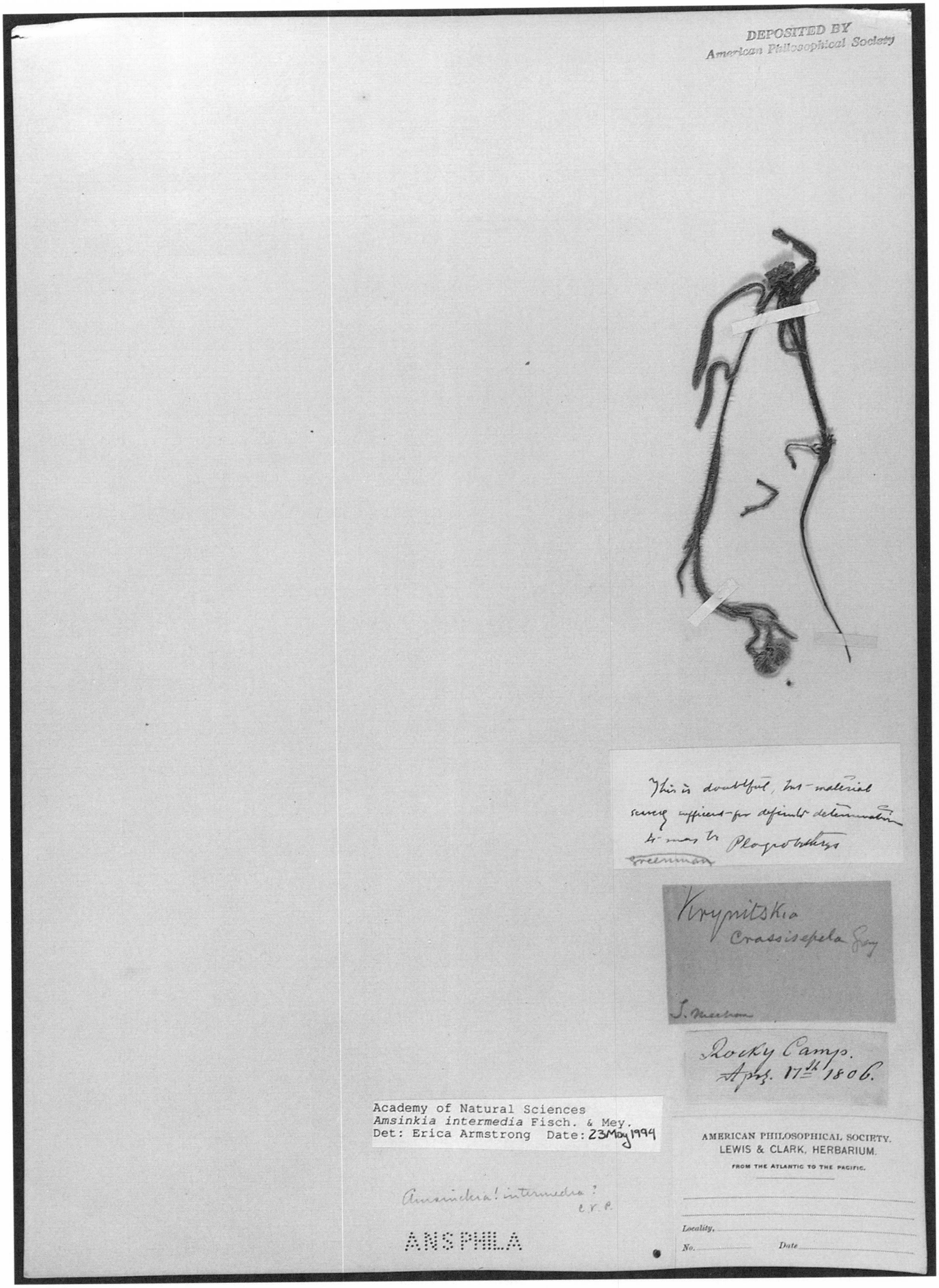

This is doubtful, but material scarcely sufficient for definite determination & was to Plagiobothrys
Greenman

Krynitzkia
crassisepela Gray

S. Meehan

Rocky Camp.
Aprl. 17th 1806.

Academy of Natural Sciences
Amsinkia intermedia Fisch. & Mey.
Det: Erica Armstrong   Date: 23 May 1994

Amsinckia! intermedia?
C. V. P.

ANS PHILA

10. *Amsinckia intermedia* Fisch. & C. A. Mey., ranchers fiddleneck

Anemone
dichotoma L.
A. Pennsylvania L.

T.M

Anemone Canadensis. L.

Greenman

Prairies, in the camp near the
old Maha village Augt. 17. 1804

[Lewis]

Academy of Natural Sciences
Anemone canadensis L.
Det: Erica Armstrong   Date: 17 May 1994

11. *Anemone canadensis* L., meadow anemone

Anemone nemorosa

J. M.

Anemone quinquefolia, L.
(A. nemorosa of Amer. authors)
(Greenman)

On the waters of Koos Koosnee
Jun: 15th 1866.

Parotis edge of Lewis' Label

Academy of Natural Sciences
Anemone quinquifolia L.
Det: Erica Armstrong   Date: 17 May 1994

12. *Anemone quinquefolia* L., wood anemone

all cne!

Angelica within the
Rocky mountains
in moist places.
Jan. 25th 1806.

The flowering one taken in
Septh. 3d 1805.

13. *Angelica* sp.?, angelica

Arbutus menziesii
Pursh

(Tm)

A middle sizes tree with a
remarkable smooth bark
which scales off in the manner
of the birch; & red berries
in clusters.
Columbia R.
Novbr: 1st 1805.

(Pursh's own)

Academy of Natural Sciences
Arbutus menzisii Pursh
Det: Erica Armstrong   Date: 17 May 1994

AMERICAN PHILOSOPHICAL SOCIETY.
LEWIS & CLARK, HERBARIUM.

FROM THE ATLANTIC TO THE PACIFIC.

Arbutus menziesii Pursh

Locality,
No.   Date

14. *Arbutus menziesii* Pursh, Pacific madrone

Fort Mandan, open plains,
Evergreen, calld Sacacommis;
natives smoke its leaves.

Nº 13 B.

an evergreen plant which grows in the open plains usually...
the natives smoke its leaves, and mixed with tobacco
called by the French engages Sacacommis.
obtained at Fort Mandan *(Lewis)*

AMERICAN PHILOSOPHICAL SOCIETY,
LEWIS & CLARK, HERBARIUM
FROM THE ATLANTIC TO THE PACIFIC.

Arctostaphylos Uva ursi 8/06.

Locality,
No.   Date

Arctostaphylos Uva-ursi; Spreng.
(Jus. G.)

Academy of Natural Sciences
Arctostaphylos uva-ursi Spreng.
Det: Erica Armstrong   Date: 17 May 1994

15. *Arctostaphylos uva-ursi* (L.) Spreng., bearberry

*Potentilla
anserina, L.*

I. m

*The roots are eat by the
natives, & taste like Sweet
Patatoes, grows in marshy ground
Fort Clatsop
March 13= 1806.*

Academy of Natural Sciences
Potentilla anserina L.
Det: Erica Armstrong   Date: 17 may 1994

ANS PHILA

16. *Argentina anserina* (L.) Rydb., silverweed

Academy of Natural Sciences
Artemisia cana Pursh
Det: Erica Armstrong   Date: 23 May 1994

TYPE OF:

Artemisia cana Pursh, Fl. Am. Sept. 521. 1814.
(Holotype originally in Herb. Lewis)
det. L. Shultz 1982

Intermountain Herbarium (UTC) — Rancho Santa Ana Botanic Garden (RSA)

Artemisia cana Pursh (JMS)

"In Lookout Bend of the Missouri ...
now called Little Bend, passing mouth
of Big Cheyenne River." (Coues, Proc.
Phila. Acad. 1899: 304.)

TYPE Artemisia cana Pursh
Fl. Am. Sept. 2: 521. 1814.
(Lectotype)   LH Shinners 11/9/1946

N° 60.

On the bluffs. Octr. 1. 1804.

Pursh

1804 October 1st another variety of ...

ANSP HLA

17a. *Artemisia cana* Pursh, dwarf sagebrush

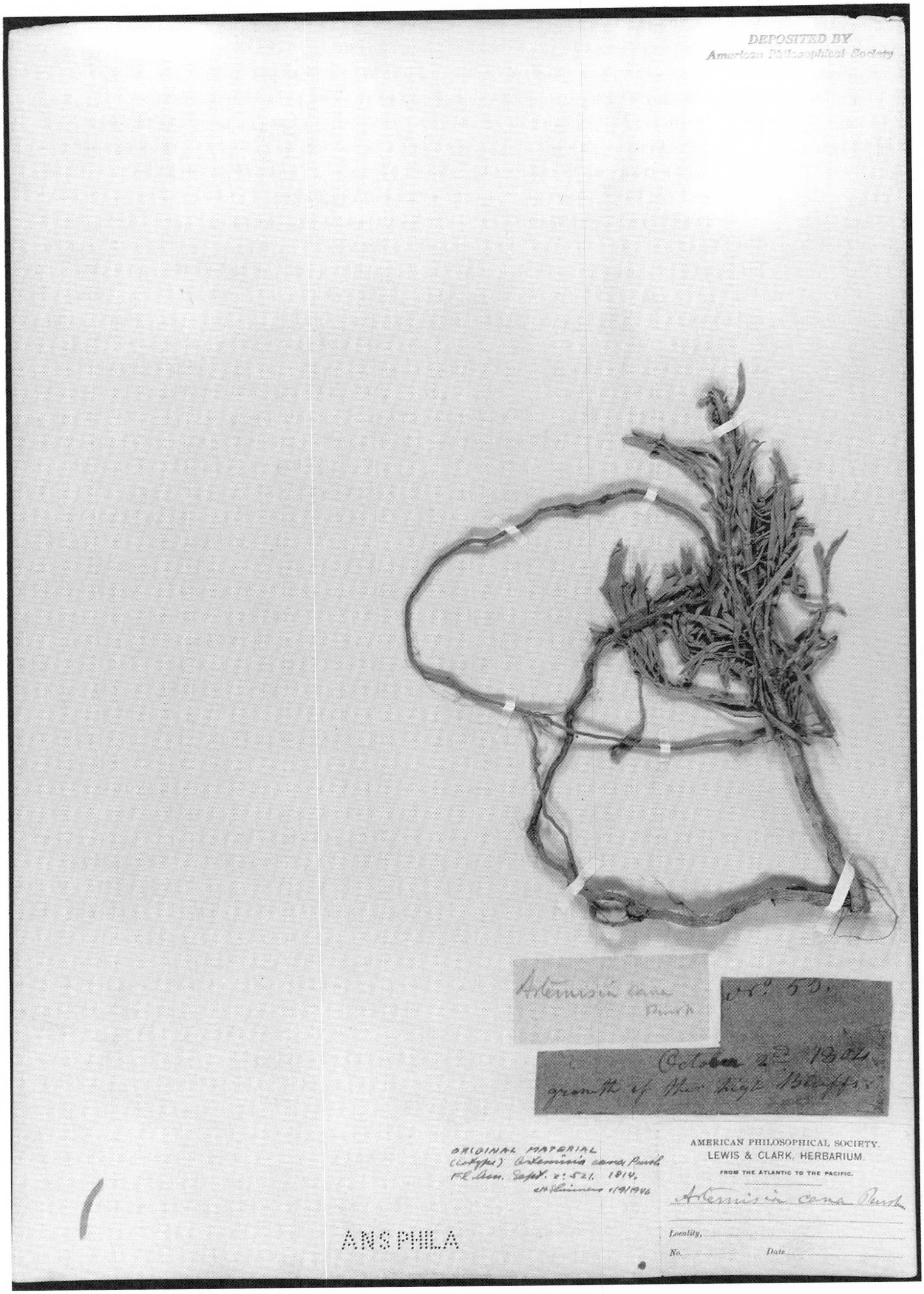

Artemisia cana
Pursh

Nº 55

October 2nd 1804
growth of the high Bluffs

ORIGINAL MATERIAL
(cotype) Artemisia cana Pursh
Fl. Am. Sept. 2: 521. 1814,
H. Rinnen 1/91/1946

AMERICAN PHILOSOPHICAL SOCIETY.
LEWIS & CLARK, HERBARIUM.
FROM THE ATLANTIC TO THE PACIFIC.

Artemisia cana Pursh

Locality,
No. Date

17b. *Artemisia cana* Pursh, dwarf sagebrush

On the Bluffs, Oct: 2. 1804.

Pursh GM

Artemisia cana, Pursh

(Greenman)

Academy of Natural Sciences
Artemisia cana Pursh
Det: Erica Armstrong   Date: 23 May 1994

ORIGINAL MATERIAL (salype).
Artemisia cana Pursh
Fl. Am. Sept. 2: 521. 1814.
C H Shinners 119/1946

AMERICAN PHILOSOPHICAL SOCIETY.
LEWIS & CLARK, HERBARIUM.
FROM THE ATLANTIC TO THE PACIFIC.

Artemisia cana Pursh

Locality,
No.   Date

17c. *Artemisia cana* Pursh, dwarf sagebrush

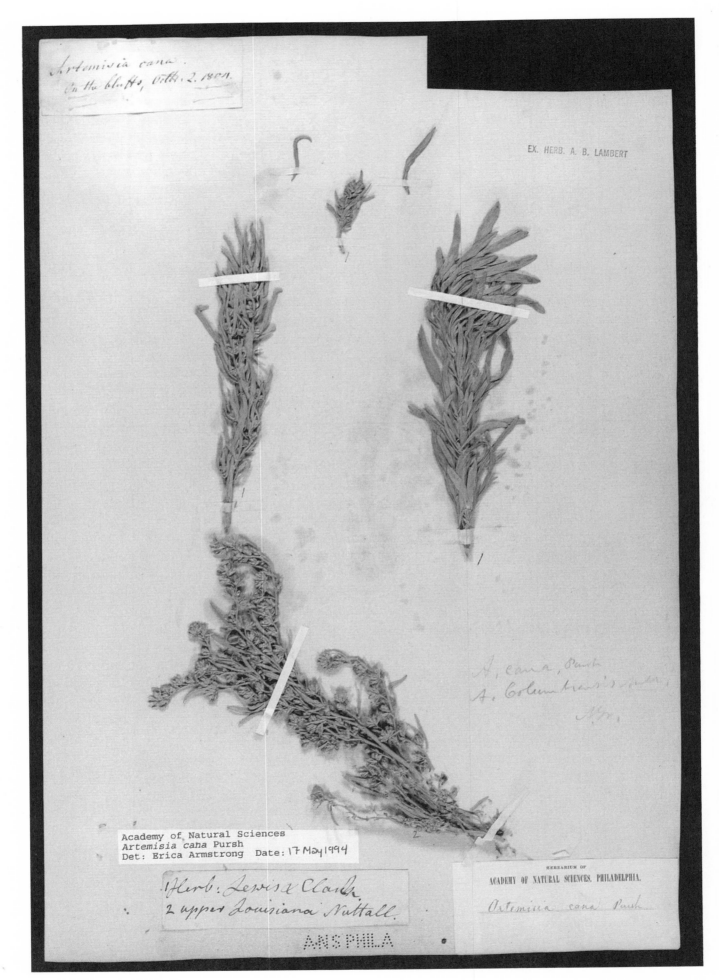

17d. *Artemisia cana* Pursh, dwarf sagebrush

Academy of Natural Sciences
Artemisia dracunculus L.
Det: Erica Armstrong   Date: 17 May 1994

AMERICAN PHILOSOPHICAL SOCIETY.
LEWIS & CLARK, HERBARIUM.
FROM THE ATLANTIC TO THE PACIFIC.

Locality,
No.   Date

18. *Artemisia dracunculus* L., silky wormwood

Academy of Natural Sciences
Artemisia frigida Willd.
Det: Erica Armstrong Date: 17 May 1994

Artemisia frigida L.
Willd.

J.M

On the bluffs. Sept. 2. 1804.

Rush lake

N° 41.   Lewis & Clark

found on the old Bluffs the 2d of Septr 1804.
is the growth of other high situations

AMERICAN PHILOSOPHICAL SOCIETY.
LEWIS & CLARK, HERBARIUM.
FROM THE ATLANTIC TO THE PACIFIC.

Artemisia frigida Willd

Locality,
No.   Date

19a. *Artemisia frigida* Willd., pasture sagewort

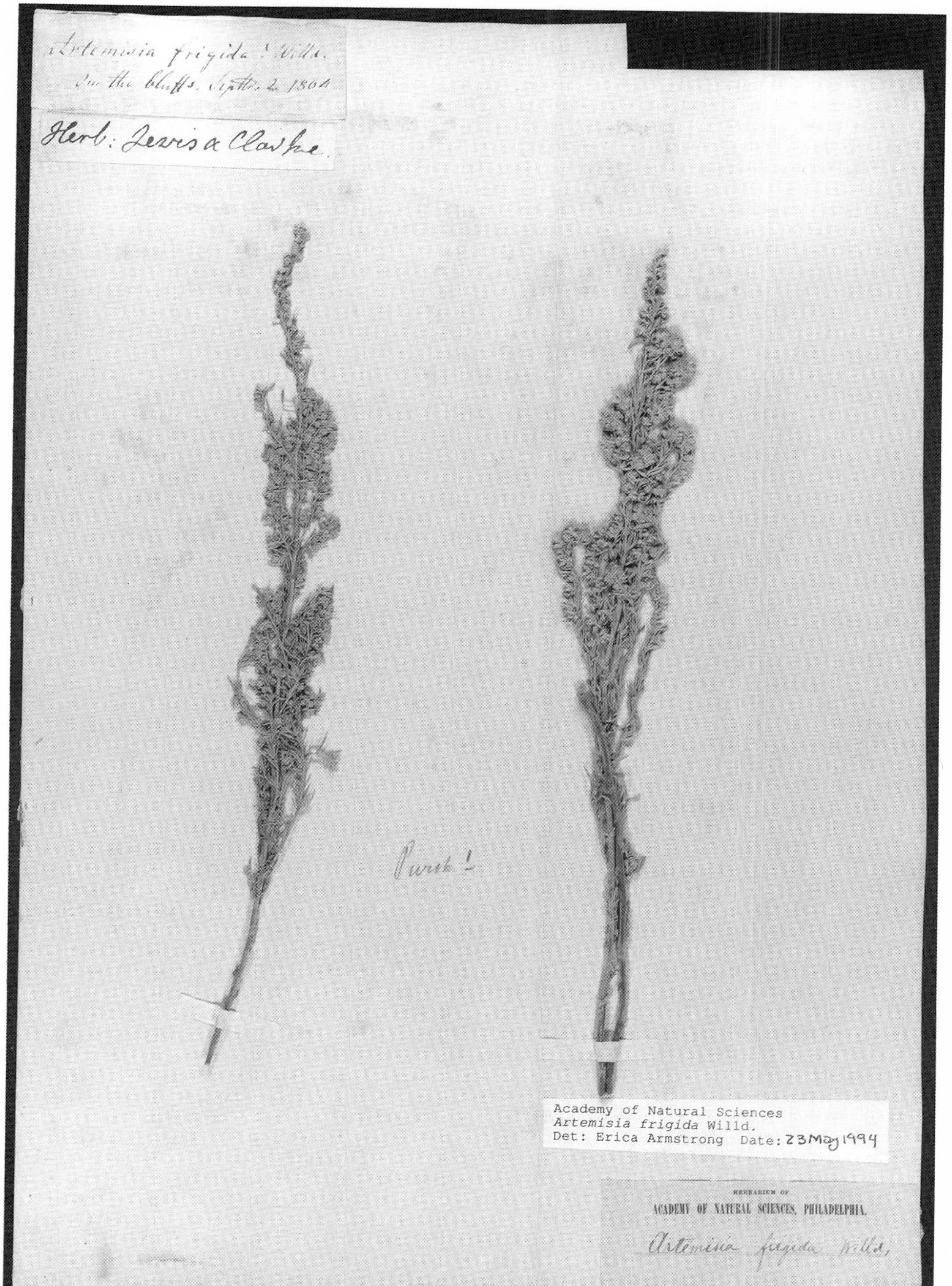

Artemisia frigida ? Willd.
On the bluffs. Septr. 2 1804
Herb: Lewis a Clarke.
Pursh !
Academy of Natural Sciences
Artemisia frigida Willd.
Det: Erica Armstrong Date: 23 May 1994
HERBARIUM OF
ACADEMY OF NATURAL SCIENCES, PHILADELPHIA.
Artemisia frigida Willd.

19b. *Artemisia frigida* Willd., pasture sagewort

Artemisia frigida Willd.

Academy of Natural Sciences
Artemisia frigida Willd.
Det: Erica Armstrong Date: 23 May 1994

AMERICAN PHILOSOPHICAL SOCIETY.
LEWIS & CLARK, HERBARIUM.
FROM THE ATLANTIC TO THE PACIFIC.

Artemisia frigida Willd

Locality,
No.   Date

19c. *Artemisia frigida* Willd., pasture sagewort

Artemisia longifolia, Nutt.
(A. integrifolia, Pursh)

Artemisia
integrifolia Pursh

Nº 53

October 3ᵈ flavor like the
camomile radix perennial
growth of the high Bluffs. Lewis

Wild Sage, on the bluffs.
Octbr. 1. 1804.
Pursh etc.

Academy of Natural Sciences
Artemisia longifolia Nutt.
Det: Erica Armstrong   Date: 17 May 1994

AMERICAN PHILOSOPHICAL SOCIETY.
LEWIS & CLARK, HERBARIUM.
FROM THE ATLANTIC TO THE PACIFIC.

Artemisia longifolia Nutt.
A. integrifolia Pursh

Locality,
No.   Date

20. *Artemisia longifolia* Nutt., long-leaved sage

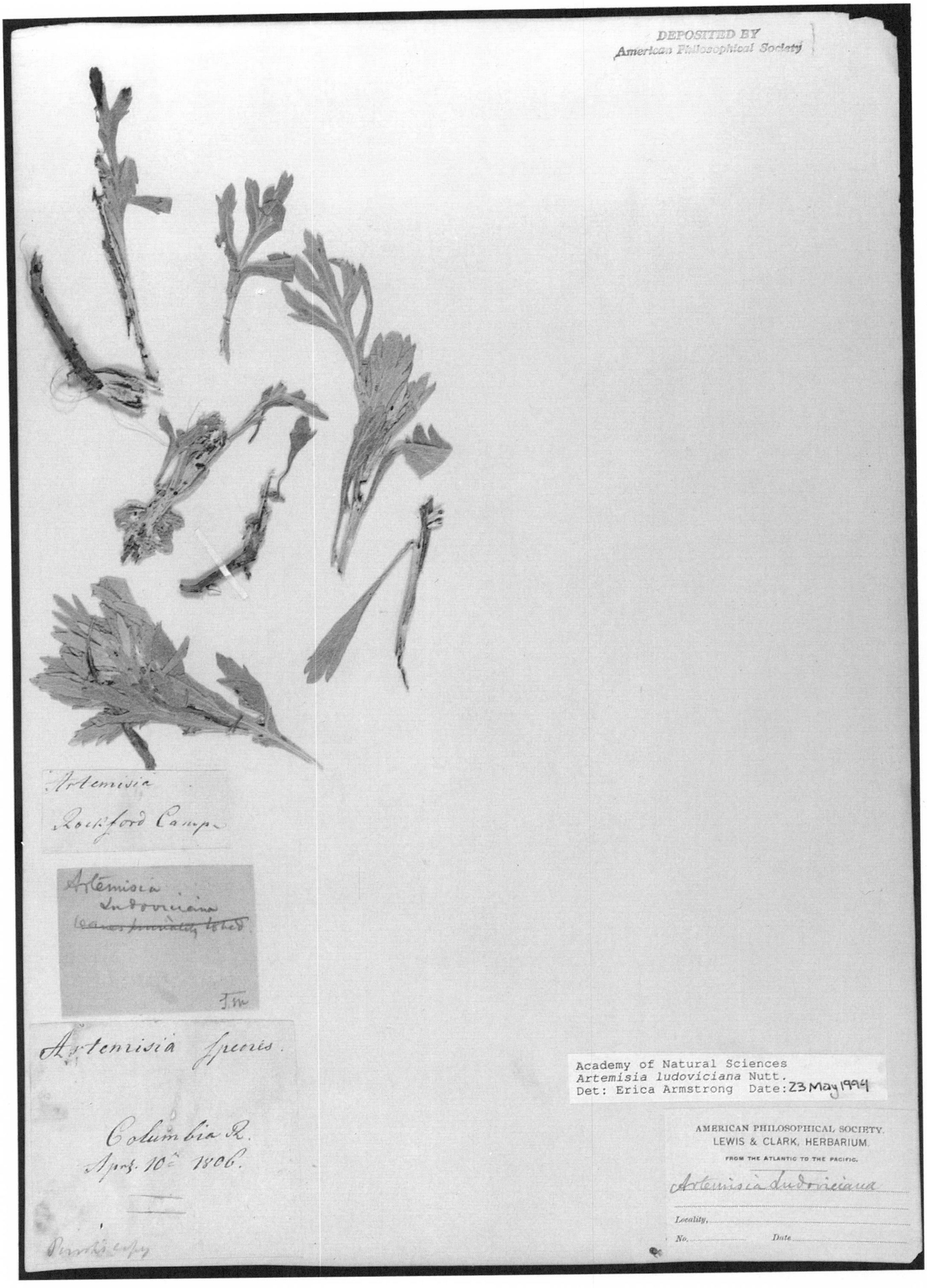

Artemisia
Rockford Camp

Artemisia
Ludoviciana
(canoflanninating) 46465

J.M.

Artemisia Species.

Columbia R.
Aprs. 10ᵗ 1806.

Academy of Natural Sciences
Artemisia ludoviciana Nutt.
Det: Erica Armstrong   Date: 23 May 1994

21a. *Artemisia ludoviciana* Nutt., white sage

Artemisia integrifolia &
Wild Sage on the bluffs.
Octob. 1804.

Academy of Natural Sciences
Artemisia ludoviciana Nutt.
Det: Erica Armstrong   Date: 17 May 1994

¹Herb: Lewis & Clark.
2 upper Louisiana. Nuttall.

37

Artemisia Ludoviciana Nutt

21b. *Artemisia ludoviciana* Nutt., white sage

Lasallea oblongifolia (Nutt.) Semple &
                                    Brouillet

DETERMINAVIT   John C. Semple
        1980
Herbarium WAT   University of Waterloo

Big bend of the Missouri
Septbr. 21. 1804.
Lewis & Pursh = label

Aster oblongifolius. Nutt.

Greenman

AMERICAN PHILOSOPHICAL SOCIETY.
LEWIS & CLARK, HERBARIUM.
FROM THE ATLANTIC TO THE PACIFIC.

Aster oblongifolius Nutt.

Locality,
No.   Date

ANS PHILA

22. *Aster oblongifolius* Nutt., aromatic aster

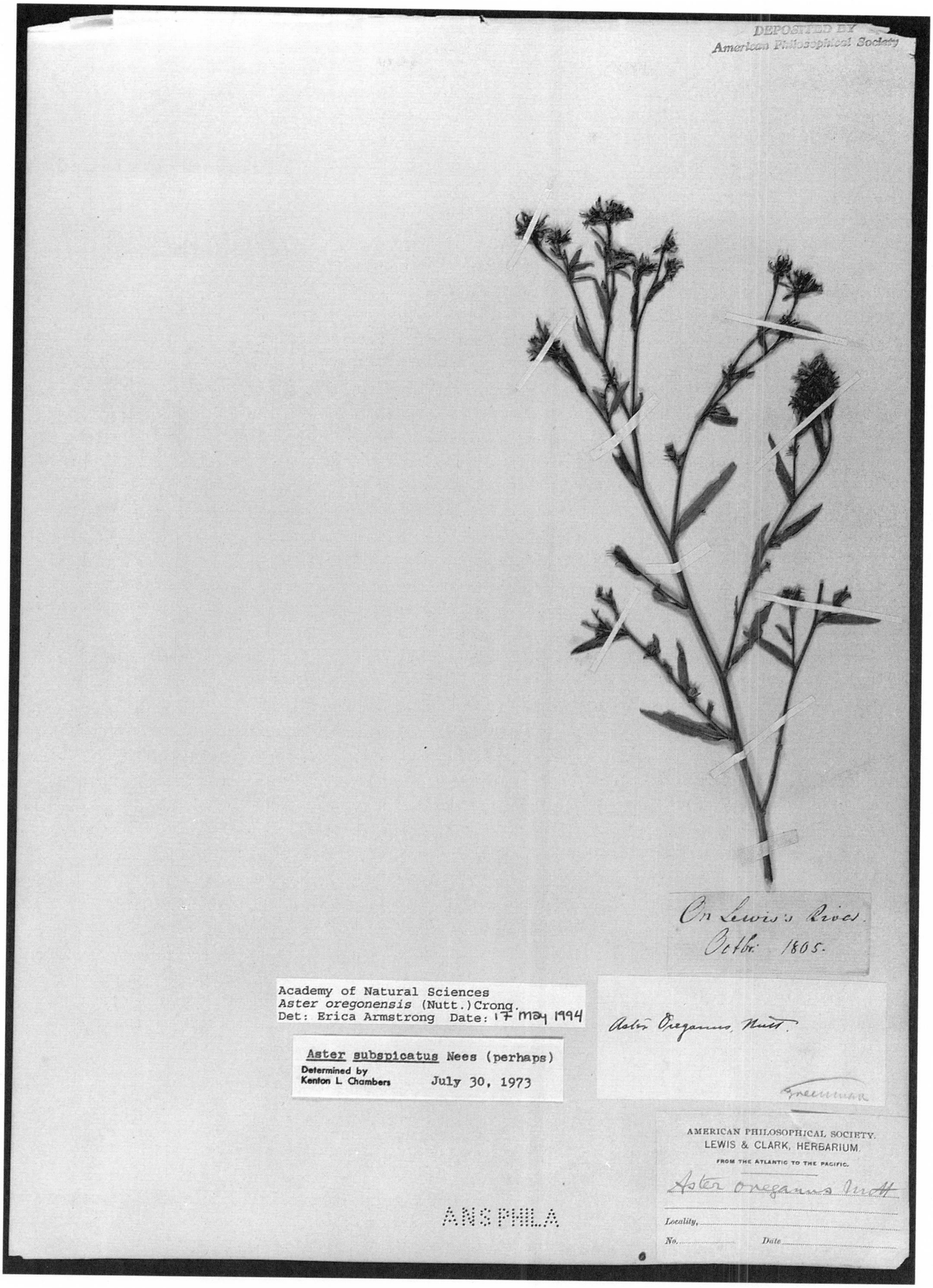

On Lewis's River.
Octbr. 1805.

Academy of Natural Sciences
Aster oregonensis (Nutt.) Cronq.
Det: Erica Armstrong Date: 17 May 1994

Aster Oreganus, Nutt.

Aster subspicatus Nees (perhaps)
Determined by
Kenton L. Chambers   July 30, 1973

Greenman

AMERICAN PHILOSOPHICAL SOCIETY.
LEWIS & CLARK, HERBARIUM.
FROM THE ATLANTIC TO THE PACIFIC.

Aster oreganus Nott

Locality,
No.   Date

ANS PHILA

23. *Aster oregonensis* (Nutt.) Cronq., Oregon white-topped aster

Astragalus mortoni Nutt

Astragalus   Noo:spec:
Open prairies Septh: 5. 1804.
   May be A. utalensis? L.

No. 46.   (Lewis)
The growth of the open prairies
     taken 15th of Sept. 1804.

Academy of Natural Sciences
Astragalus canadensis var. *mortonii* (Nutt.) Wats.
Det: Erica Armstrong   Date: 17 May 1994

24. *Astragalus canadensis* L., Canada milk-vetch

Astragalus missouriensis
Nutt.

S. 1 vis

N.° 36

18th. of Sept. the grown of the high

Prarie

Lewis

Academy of Natural Sciences
Astragalus missouriensis Nutt.
Det: Erica Armstrong   Date: 17 may 1994

AMERICAN PHILOSOPHICAL SOCIETY.
LEWIS & CLARK, HERBARIUM.
FROM THE ATLANTIC TO THE PACIFIC.

Astragalus missouriensis
nutt.

Locality,
No.   Date

25. *Astragalus missouriensis* Nutt., Missouri milk-vetch

26. *Atriplex canescens* (Pursh) Nutt., four-wing saltbush

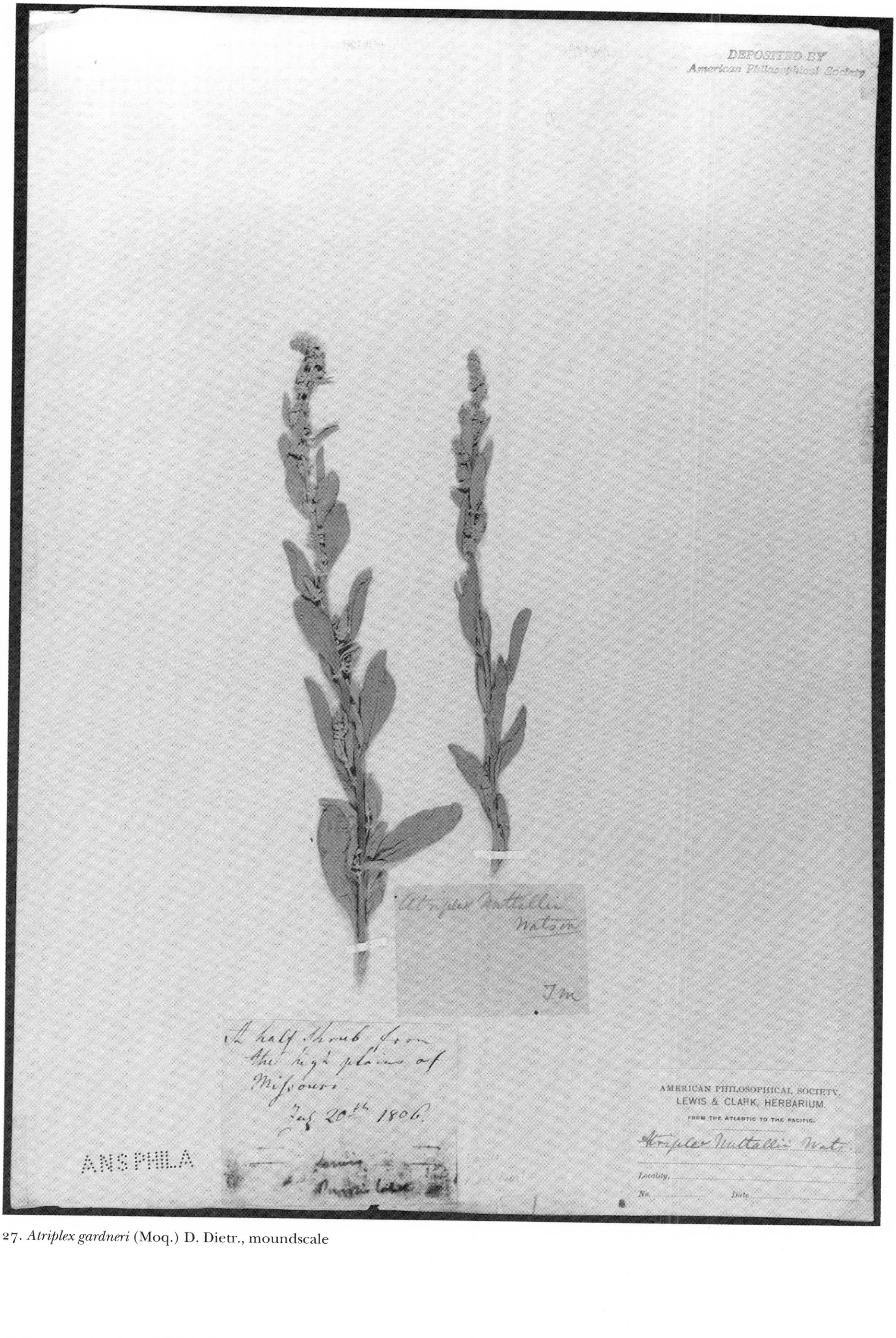
DEPOSITED BY
American Philosophical Society
Atriplex Nuttallii
Watson
T.M
A half shrub from
the high plains of
Missouri.
Jul. 20th 1806.
AMERICAN PHILOSOPHICAL SOCIETY.
LEWIS & CLARK, HERBARIUM.
FROM THE ATLANTIC TO THE PACIFIC.
Atriplex Nuttallii Wats.
Locality,
No.
Date
ANSPHILA

27. *Atriplex gardneri* (Moq.) D. Dietr., moundscale

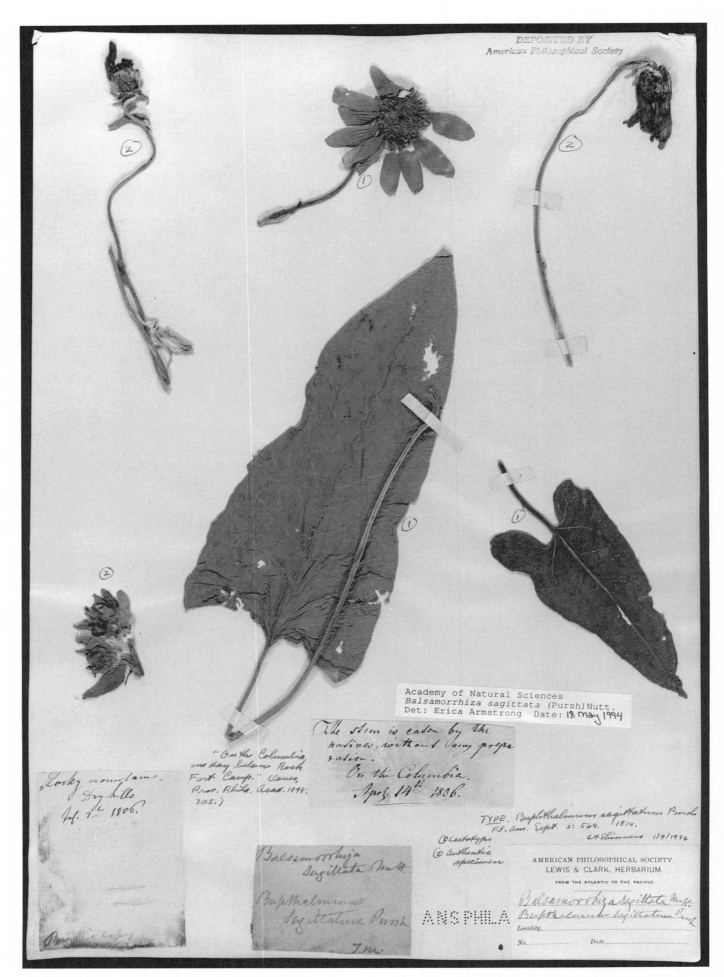

Academy of Natural Sciences
Balsamorrhiza sagittata (Pursh) Nutt.
Det: Erica Armstrong   Date: 18 May 1994

The stem is eaten by the natives, without any preparation.
On the Columbia.
April 14th 1806.

"On the Columbia one day below Rock Fort Camp." (Cones, Proc. Phila. Acad. 1898: 305.)

Rocky mountains. Dry hills July 7th 1806.

TYPE. *Buphthalmum sagittatum Pursh*
Fl. Am. Sept. 2: 564. 1814.
(a) Lectotype
(b) authentic specimen
CA Sinners 119/1946

Balsamorrhiza sagittata Nutt.

Buphthalmum sagittatum Pursh
J.M.

AMERICAN PHILOSOPHICAL SOCIETY.
LEWIS & CLARK, HERBARIUM.
FROM THE ATLANTIC TO THE PACIFIC.
Balsamorrhiza sagittata Nutt.
Buphthalmum sagittatum Pursh
Locality,
No.   Date

ANS PHILA

28. *Balsamorhiza sagittata* (Pursh) Nutt., arrowleaf balsamroot

A moss used by the natives
as a yellow dye.

Grows on the Pines of
the Rocky mountain.
July 1st 1806

ANS PHILA

29. *Bazzania trilobata* (L.) S. F. Gray, liverwort

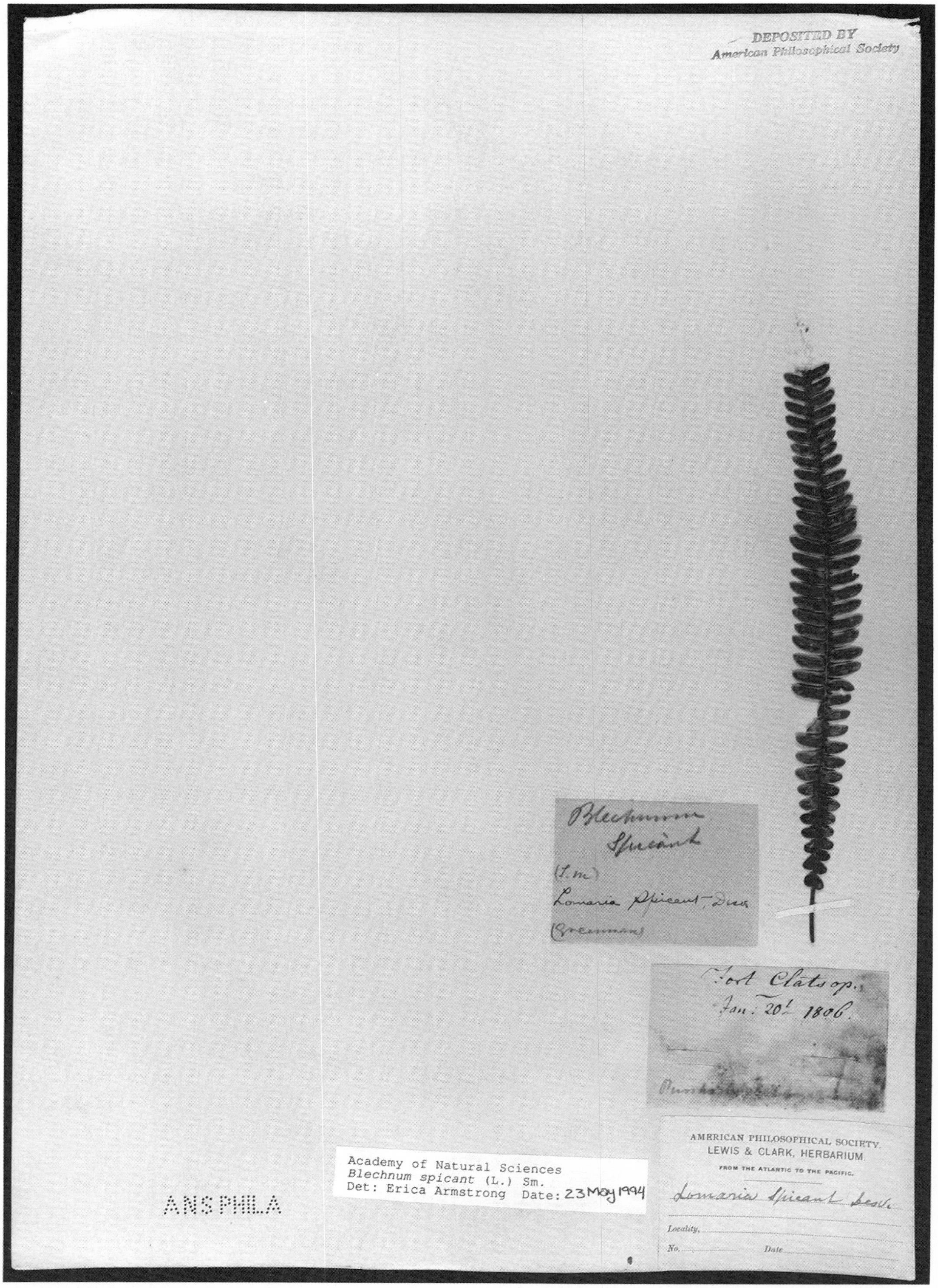
DEPOSITED BY
American Philosophical Society
Blechnum
Spicant
(S.m)
Lomaria Spicant, Desv.
(Greenman)
Fort Clatsop.
Jan: 20th 1806.
AMERICAN PHILOSOPHICAL SOCIETY.
LEWIS & CLARK, HERBARIUM.
FROM THE ATLANTIC TO THE PACIFIC.
Lomaria Spicant Desv.
Locality,
No.
Date
Academy of Natural Sciences
Blechnum spicant (L.) Sm.
Det: Erica Armstrong Date: 23 May 1994
ANSPHILA

30a. *Blechnum spicant* (L.) Roth, deer-fern

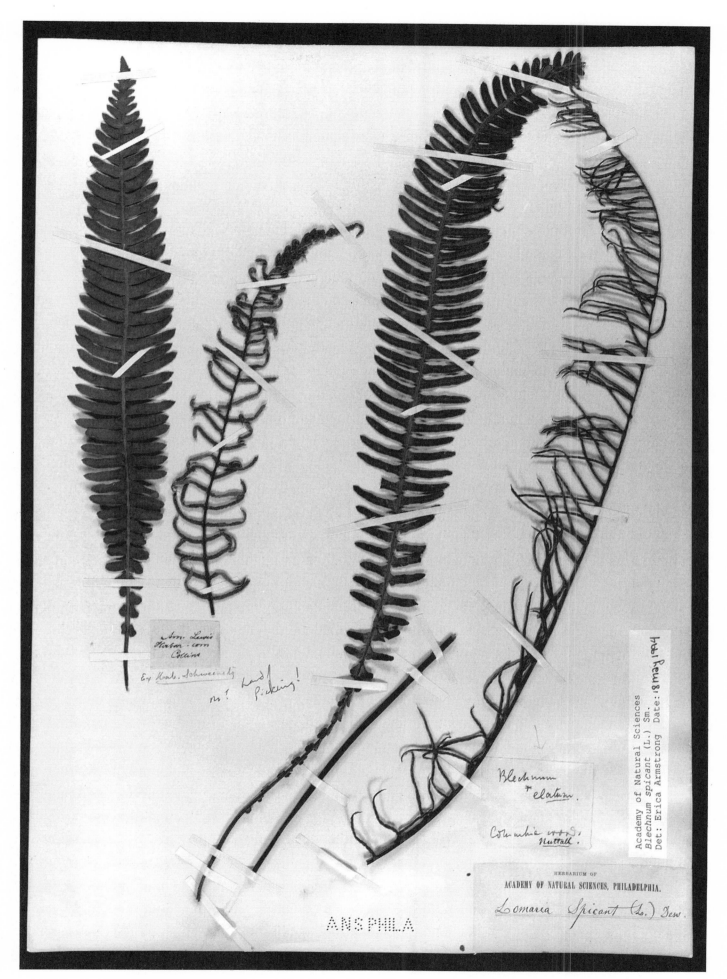

Academy of Natural Sciences
Blechnum spicant (L.) Sm.
Det: Erica Armstrong Date: 18 may 1994

Blechnum
+ elatum.

Columbia woods,
Nuttall.

HERBARIUM OF
ACADEMY OF NATURAL SCIENCES, PHILADELPHIA.

Lomaria Spicant (L.) Dew.

ANS PHILA

30b. *Blechnum spicant* (L.) Roth, deer-fern

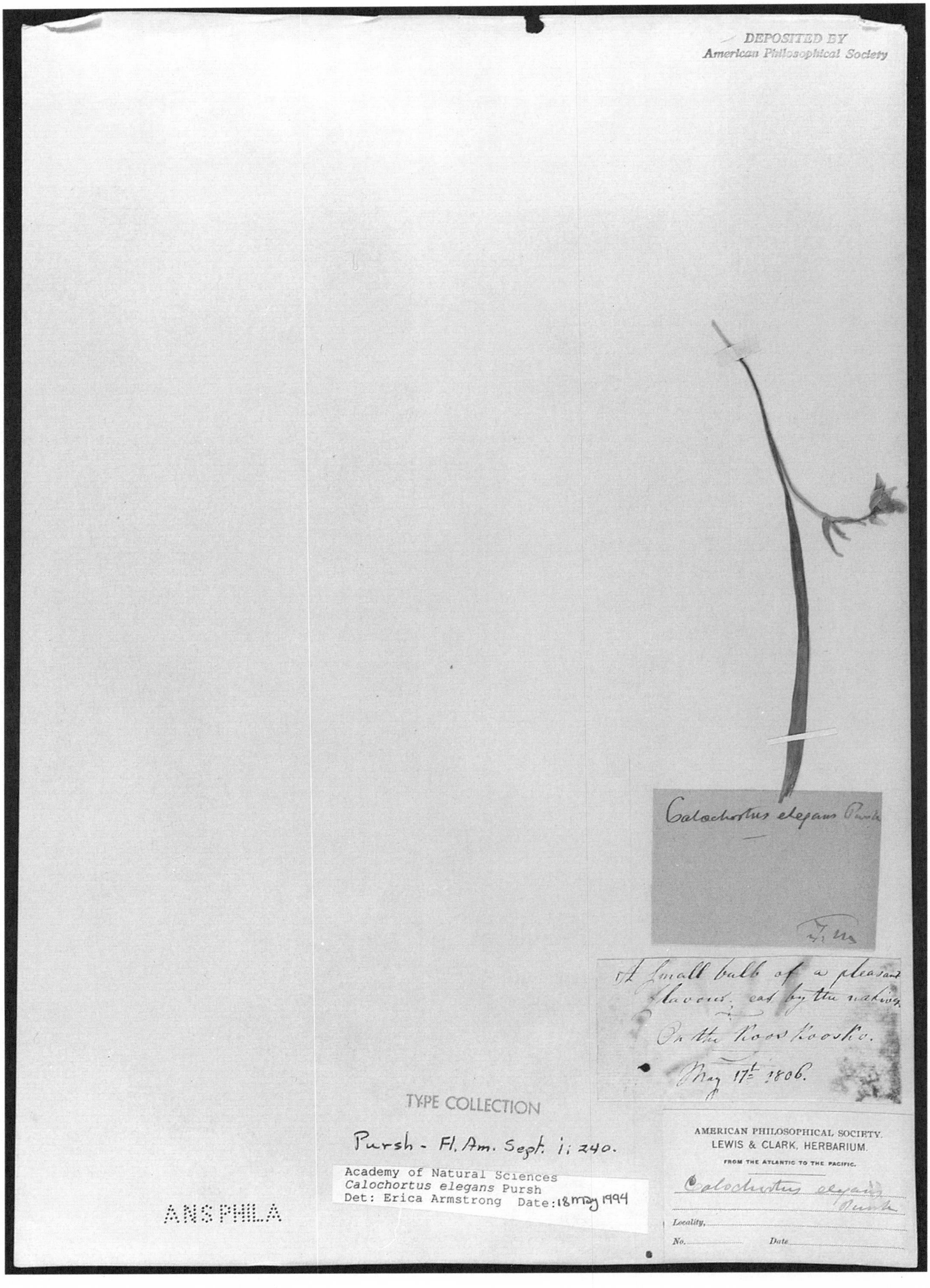
DEPOSITED BY
American Philosophical Society
Calochortus elegans Pursh
A small bulb of a pleasant flavour. eat by the natives.
On the Koos koosko.
May 17th 1806.
TYPE COLLECTION
Pursh - Fl. Am. Sept. 1: 240.
Academy of Natural Sciences
Calochortus elegans Pursh
Det: Erica Armstrong Date: 18 May 1994
ANSPHILA
AMERICAN PHILOSOPHICAL SOCIETY.
LEWIS & CLARK, HERBARIUM.
FROM THE ATLANTIC TO THE PACIFIC.
Calochortus elegans Pursh
Locality,
No.
Date

31. *Calochortus elegans* Pursh, northwest mariposa

Calypso borealis, Salisb.

(Greenman)

waters of hungry creeks.
Rocky mountain.
June 16th 1806.

(Nuttis copy of Lewis)

Academy of Natural Sciences
Calypso bulbosa (L.)Oakes.
Det: Erica Armstrong   Date: 18 may 1994

ANS PHILA

32. *Calypso bulbosa* (L.) Oakes, fairy-slipper

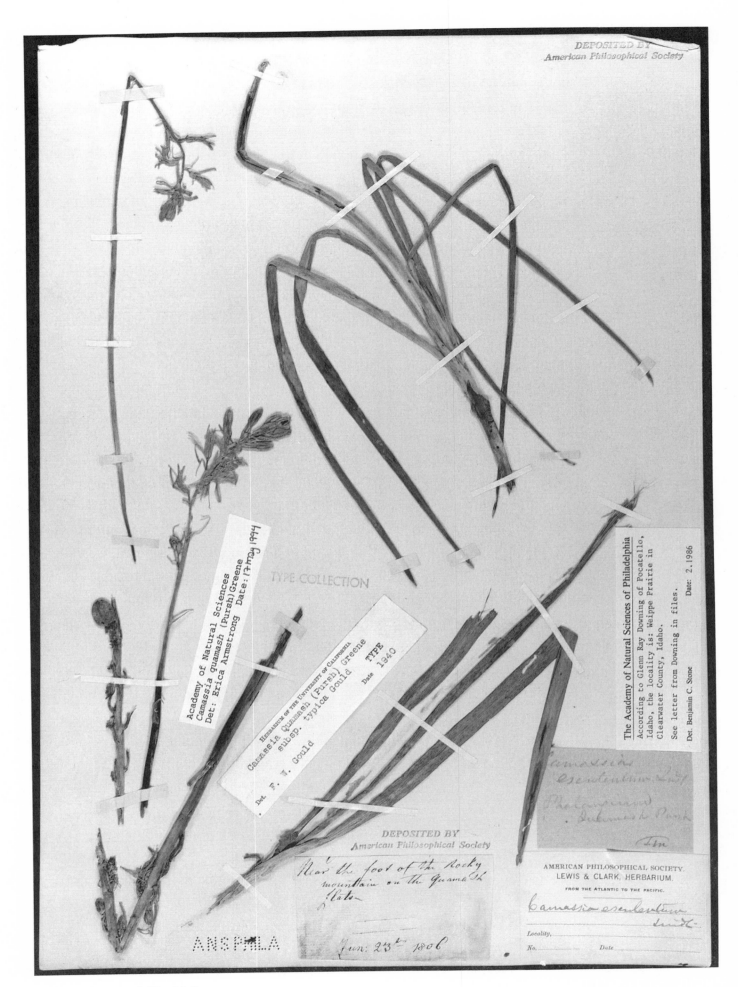

Academy of Natural Sciences
Camassia quamash (Pursh)Greene
Det: Erica Armstrong Date:17 May 1994

TYPE COLLECTION

HERBARIUM OF THE UNIVERSITY OF CALIFORNIA

Camassia Quamash (Pursh) Greene   TYPE

subsp. typica Gould   Date 1940

Det. F. W. Gould

The Academy of Natural Sciences of Philadelphia
According to Glenn Ray Downing of Pocatello,
Idaho, the locality is: Weippe Prairie in
Clearwater County, Idaho.

See letter from Downing in files.

Det. Benjamin C. Stone   Date: 2, 1986

Near the foot of the Rocky
mountain on the Quama sh
plate—

Jun: 23ᵈ 1806

ANSPHLA

AMERICAN PHILOSOPHICAL SOCIETY.
LEWIS & CLARK, HERBARIUM.
FROM THE ATLANTIC TO THE PACIFIC.

Camassia esculentum
Lindl—

Locality,
No.   Date

33. *Camassia quamash* (Pursh) Greene, camas

Jussieua subacaulis Pursh
9APM 3/83

pub na

Oenothera heterantha, Nutt.

(Greenman)

In moist ground on the Squamash flats.
Jun: 14th 1806

Pursh copy of Lewis

Part of type of
Camissonia
subacaulis
(Pursh) Raven

Academy of Natural Sciences
Camissonia subacaulis (Pursh) Raven
Det: Erica Armstrong   Date: 17 May 1994

ANS PHILA

AMERICAN PHILOSOPHICAL SOCIETY
LEWIS & CLARK, HERBARIUM.
FROM THE ATLANTIC TO THE PACIFIC.

Oenothera heterantha Nutt

Locality,
No.   Date

34. *Camissonia subacaulis* (Pursh) Raven, long-leaf evening primrose

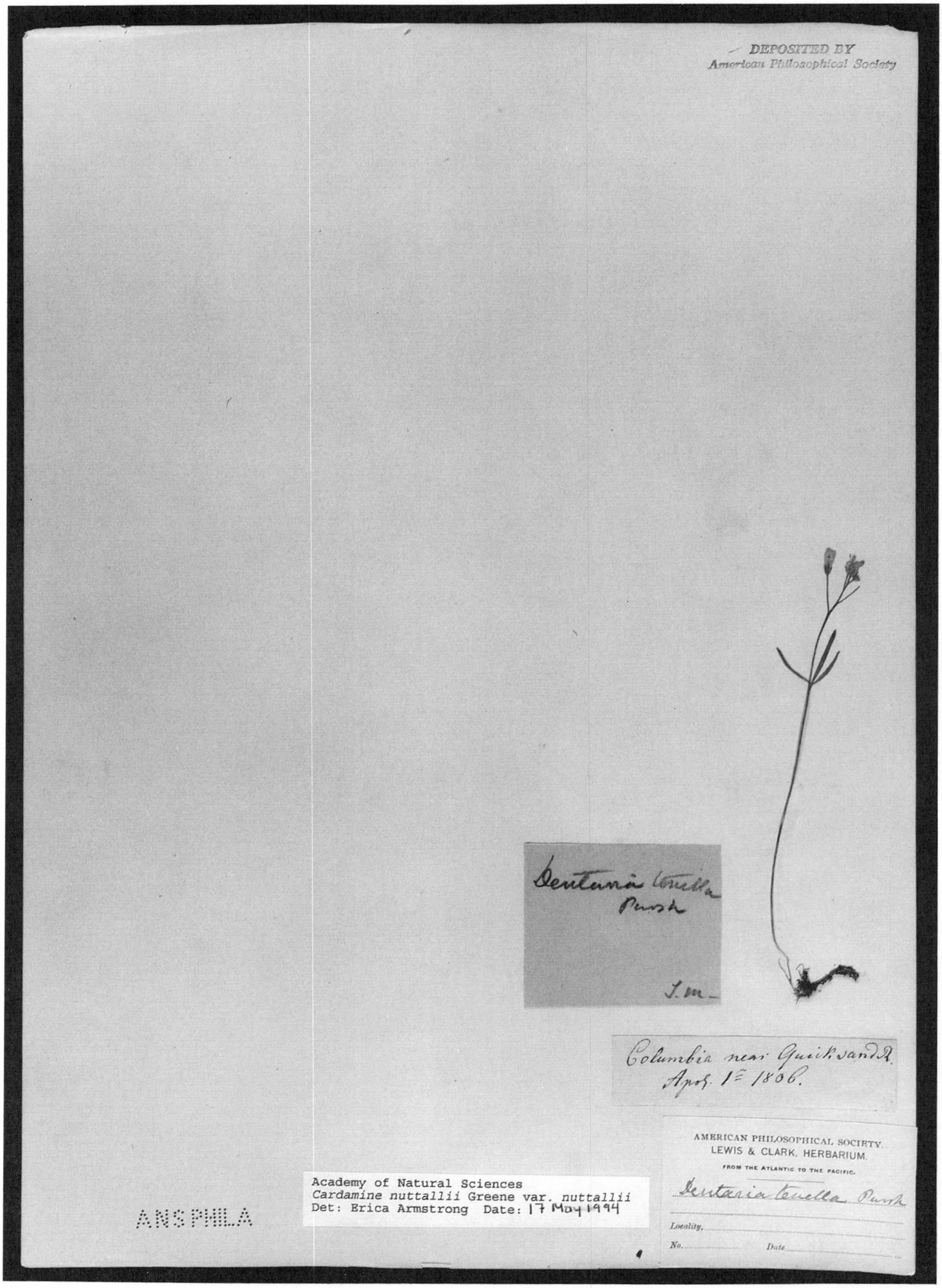

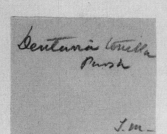

Dentaria tenella
Pursh

I.m.

Columbia near Quicksand R.
Apof 1<u>e</u> 1806.

Academy of Natural Sciences
Cardamine nuttallii Greene var. nuttallii
Det: Erica Armstrong   Date: 17 May 1994

ANSPHILA

35a. *Cardamine nuttallii* Greene, slender toothwort

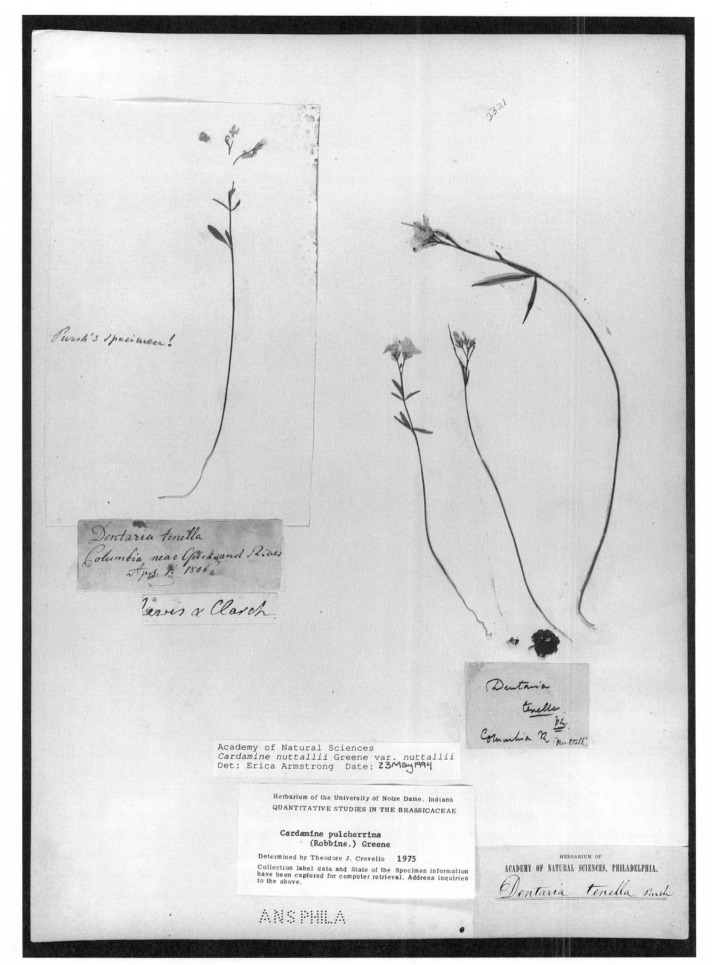

Pursh's specimen!

Dentaria tenella
Columbia near Quicksand River
Aps 1: 1806.

Lewis & Clark.

Dentaria
tenella
ph.
Columbia R nuttall:

Academy of Natural Sciences
Cardamine nuttallii Greene var. *nuttallii*
Det: Erica Armstrong   Date: 23May1994

Herbarium of the University of Notre Dame, Indiana
QUANTITATIVE STUDIES IN THE BRASSICACEAE

**Cardamine pulcherrima
(Robbins.) Greene**

Determined by Theodore J. Crovello   1975
Collection label data and State of the Specimen information
have been captured for computer retrieval. Address inquiries
to the above.

HERBARIUM OF
ACADEMY OF NATURAL SCIENCES, PHILADELPHIA.

Dentaria tenella Pursh

ANS PHLA

35b. *Cardamine nuttallii* Greene, slender toothwort

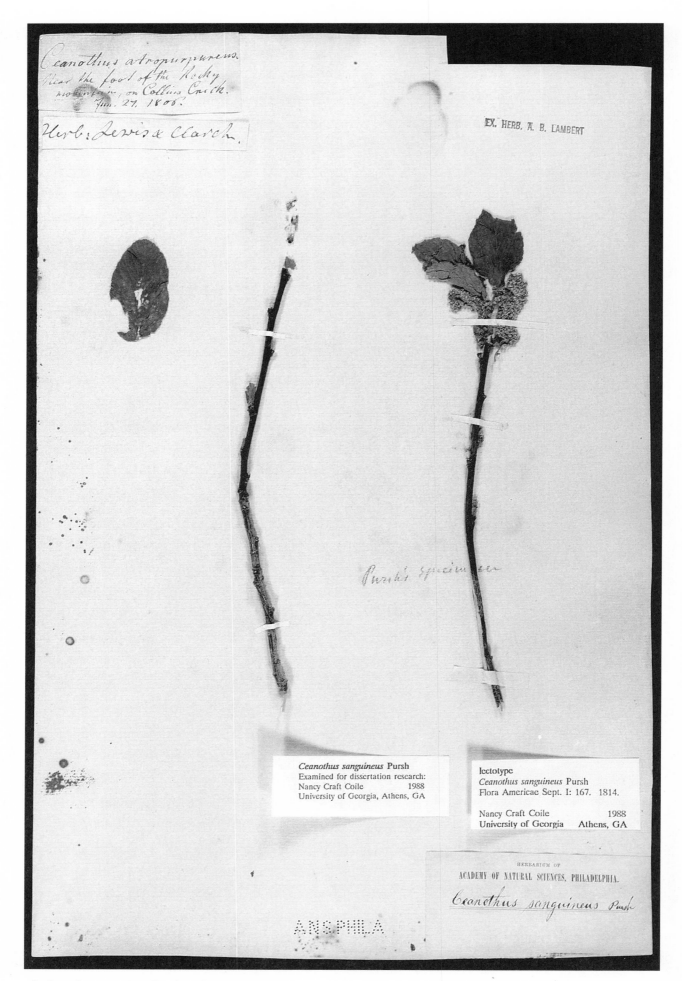

Ceanothus atropurpureus.
Near the foot of the Rocky
mountain, on Collins Crick.
Jun. 27, 1806.

Herb. Lewis & Clark.

EX. HERB. A. B. LAMBERT

Pursh's specimen

| Ceanothus sanguineus Pursh |
| Examined for dissertation research: |
| Nancy Craft Coile   1988 |
| University of Georgia, Athens, GA |

lectotype
Ceanothus sanguineus Pursh
Flora Americae Sept. I: 167. 1814.

Nancy Craft Coile   1988
University of Georgia   Athens, GA

HERBARIUM OF
ACADEMY OF NATURAL SCIENCES, PHILADELPHIA.

Ceanothus sanguineus Pursh

ANSPHILA

36. *Ceanothus sanguineus* Pursh, redstem ceanothus

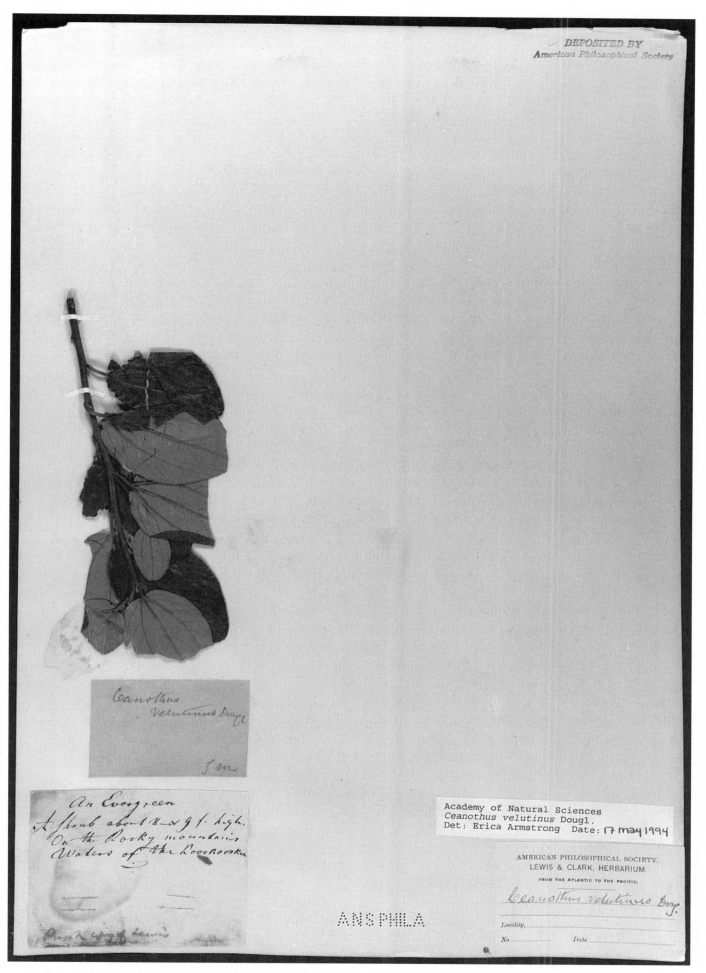

Ceanothus
velutinus Doug

S. m.

An Evergreen
A shrub about 8 – 9 f. high.
On the Rocky mountains
Waters of the Kooskooske

Academy of Natural Sciences
Ceanothus velutinus Dougl.
Det: Erica Armstrong   Date: 17 may 1994

ANS PHILA

37. *Ceanothus velutinus* Dougl. *ex* Hook., mountain balm

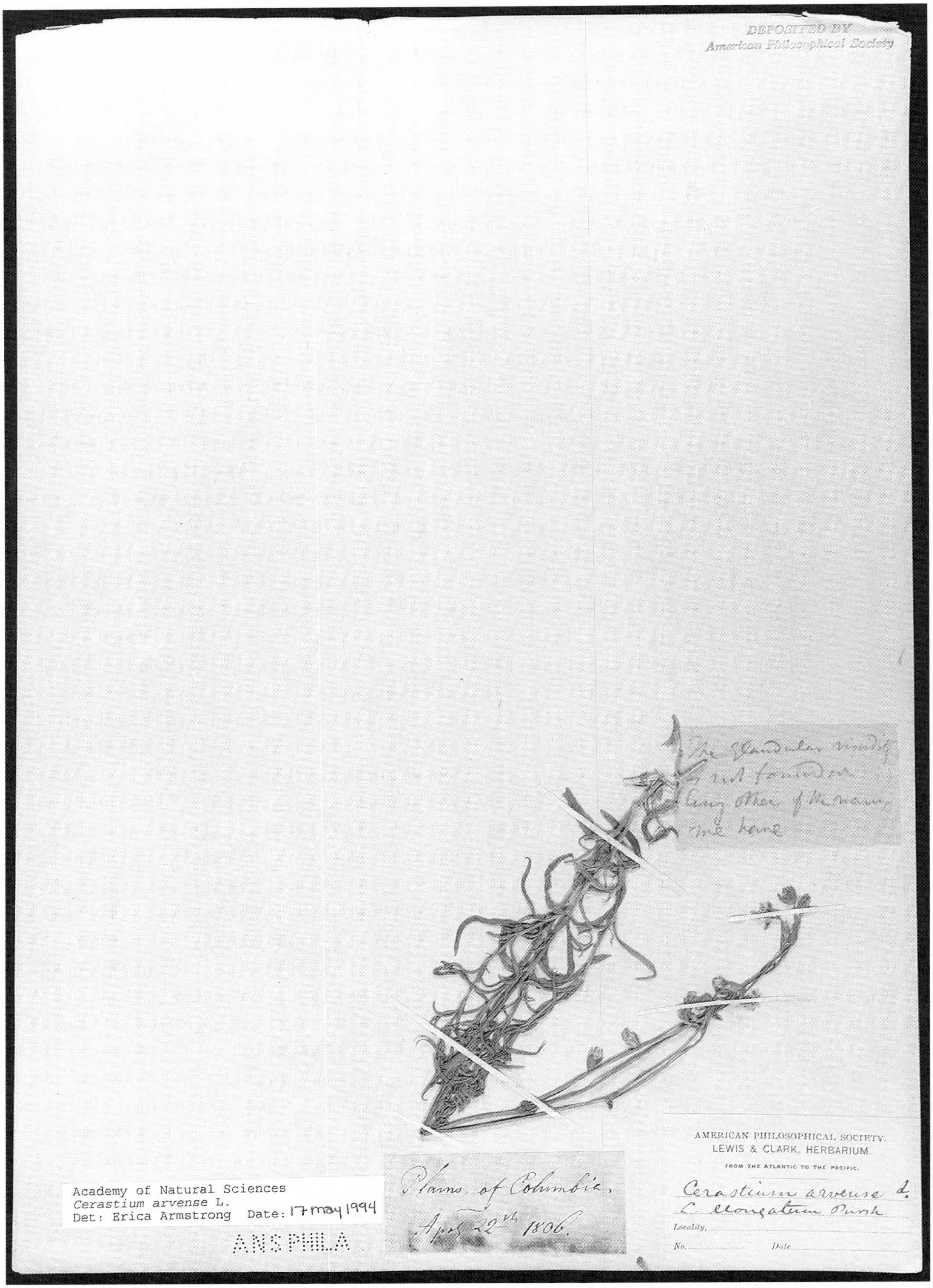

The glandular viscidity
is not found on
any other of the mann
we have

Academy of Natural Sciences
Cerastium arvense L.
Det: Erica Armstrong   Date: 17 May 1994

ANS PHILA.

Plains of Columbia.
Apl 22th 1806.

AMERICAN PHILOSOPHICAL SOCIETY.
LEWIS & CLARK, HERBARIUM.

FROM THE ATLANTIC TO THE PACIFIC.

Cerastium arvense L.
C. elongatum Pursh

Locality,

No.   Date

38. *Cerastium arvense* L., field chickweed

The Academy of Natural Sciences of Philadelphia

Chrysothamnus nauseosus
ssp. graveolens

Det. Harvey M. Hall   Date: 1924.

The Academy of Natural Sciences of Philadelphia

H. M. Hall det should be
taken as authoritative   L+C Journal Proj.
Det. A. T. Harrison   9-5-84
                              Univ of Neb   Date:

yes! probably C. nauseosus graveolens
(tomentose twigs, keep it out of Gutierrezia)
H M Hall. 1924

Chrysothamnus

Gutierrezia Euthamiae, Torr. & Gray.
(Solidago Sarothrae, Pursh.)
Greenman

Gutierrezia
Euthamia T.&G.

No. 32.   Upper part of the big bend of
the Missouri. Septbr. 21. 1804.

ANS PHILA

Specimen of aromatic plants on which the
Atelope feeds — these were obtained 21st of Sept.
1805. at the upper part of the bigg bend of the
Missouri.

AMERICAN PHILOSOPHICAL SOCIETY.
LEWIS & CLARK, HERBARIUM.
FROM THE ATLANTIC TO THE PACIFIC.

Gutierrezia Euthamia T.&G.
Solidago Sarothra Pursh

Locality,

No.   Date.

39a. *Chrysothamnus nauseosus* (Pallas *ex* Pursh) Britt. ssp. *graveolens* (Nutt.) Piper, rabbit brush

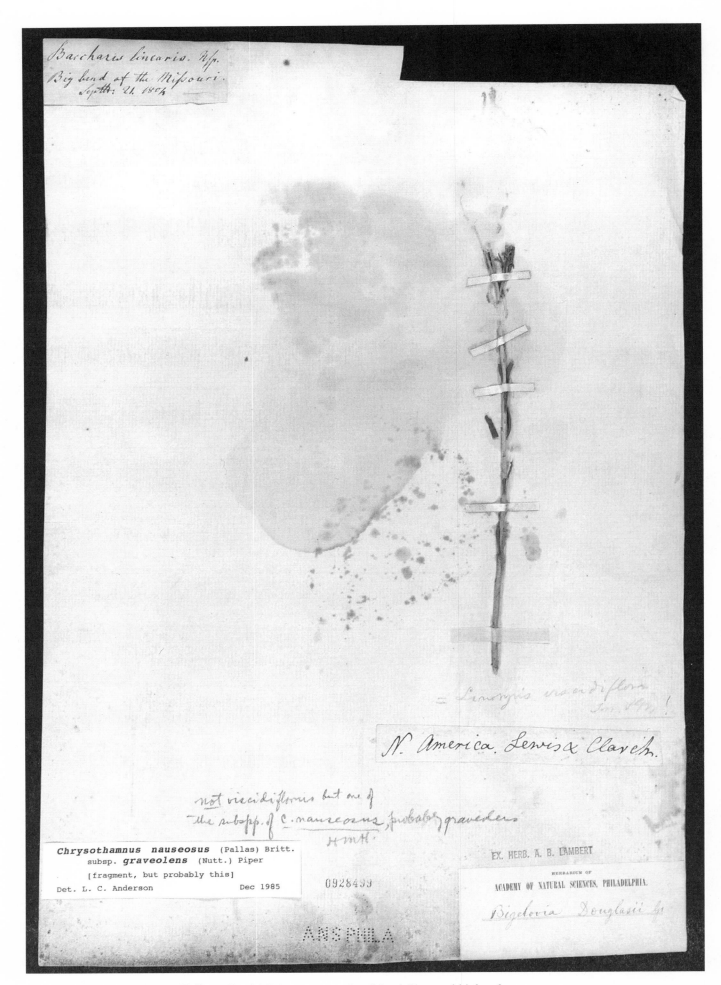

Baccharis linearis. Ph.
Big bend of the Missouri.
Septbr: 21. 1804

= *Linosyris viscidiflora*
Torr & Gr. !

N. America. Lewis & Clark.

not viscidiflorus but one of
the subspp. of C. nauseosus, probably graveolens
HMH.

Chrysothamnus nauseosus (Pallas) Britt.
subsp. *graveolens* (Nutt.) Piper
[fragment, but probably this]
Det. L. C. Anderson   Dec 1985

0928499

39b. *Chrysothamnus nauseosus* (Pallas *ex* Pursh) Britt. ssp. *graveolens* (Nutt.) Piper, rabbit brush

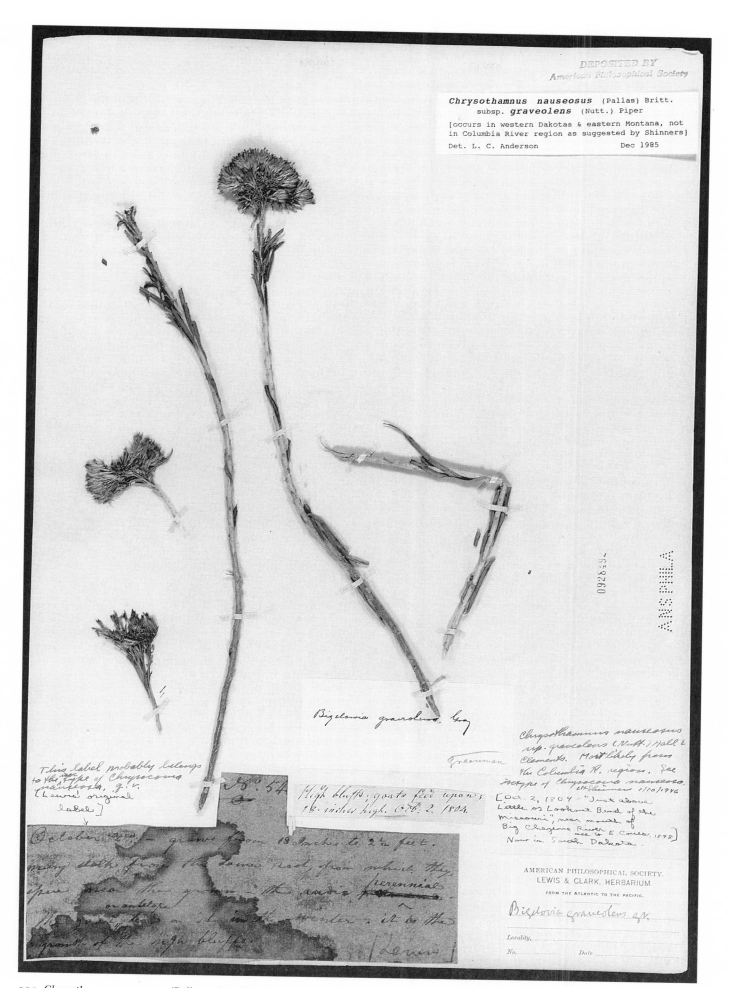

Chrysothamnus nauseosus (Pallas) Britt.
subsp. **graveolens** (Nutt.) Piper
[occurs in western Dakotas & eastern Montana, not
in Columbia River region as suggested by Shinners]
Det. L. C. Anderson   Dec 1985

Bigelowia graveolens, Gray

Greenman

This label probably belongs
to the type of Chrysocoma
nauseosa, q. v.
[Lewis' original
label]

Nº 54

High bluffs, goats feed upon;
18 inches high. Oct. 2. 1804.

Chrysothamnus nauseosus
ssp. graveolens (Nutt.) Hall &
Clements. Most likely from
the Columbia R. regions. See
isotype of Chrysocoma nauseosa.
LCAnderson 1/10/1986
[Oa. 2, 1804 - "Just above
Little or Lookout Bend of the
Missouri", near mouth of
Big Cheyenne River acc to E.Coues, 1878]
Now in South Dakota.

October 1804 — grows from 18 inches to 2½ feet.
many stalks from the same root, from which they
spring ... perennial
... antelope
... the winter ; it is the
growth of the high bluffs.   [Lewis]

AMERICAN PHILOSOPHICAL SOCIETY,
LEWIS & CLARK, HERBARIUM.
FROM THE ATLANTIC TO THE PACIFIC.

Bigelowia graveolens gr.

Locality.
No.   Date

092849

AMS PHILA

39c. *Chrysothamnus nauseosus* (Pallas *ex* Pursh) Britt. ssp. *graveolens* (Nutt.) Piper, rabbit brush

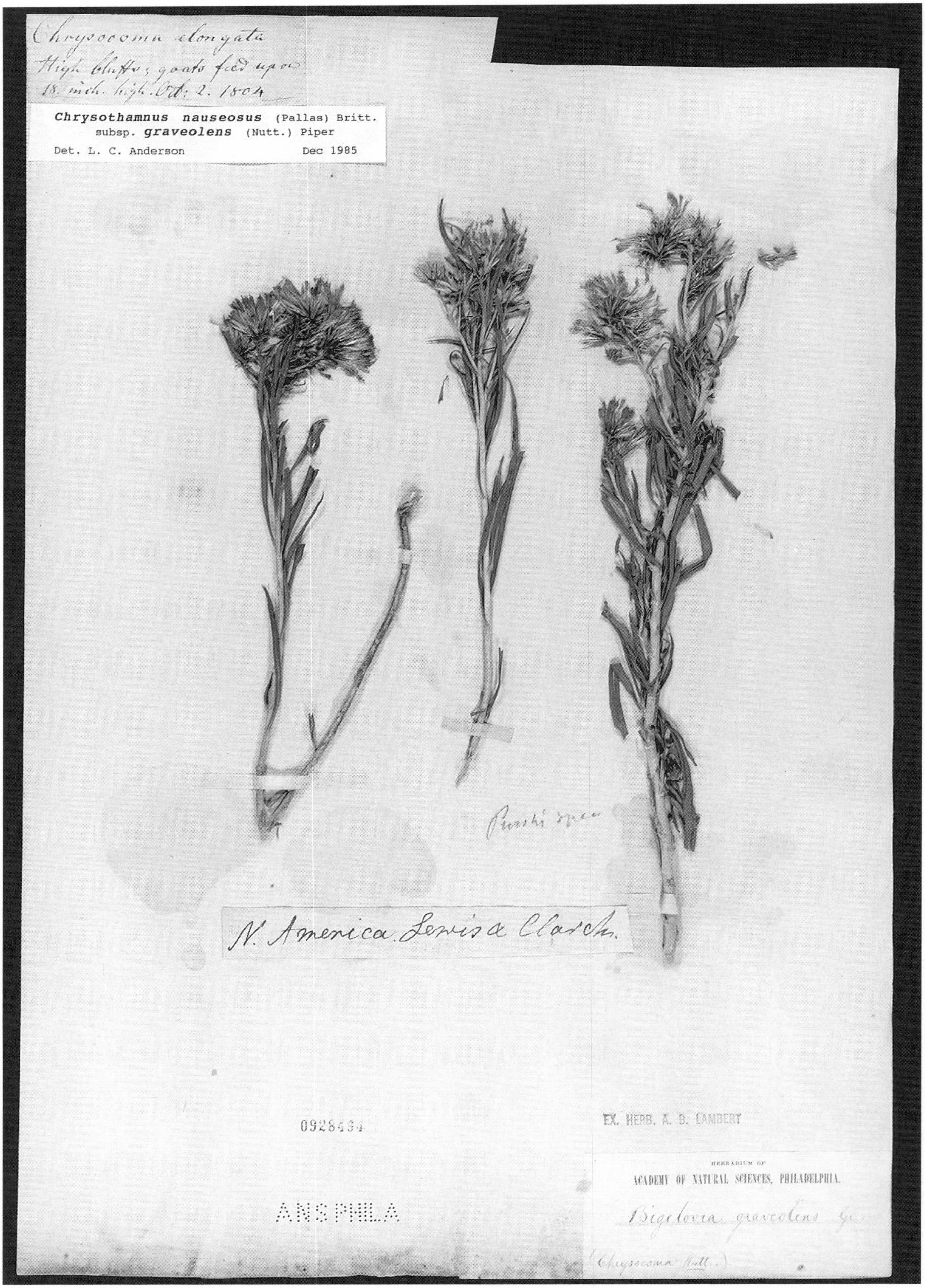

Chrysocoma elongata
High bluffs; goats feed upon
18. inch. high. Oct. 2. 1804

Chrysothamnus nauseosus (Pallas) Britt.
subsp. graveolens (Nutt.) Piper
Det. L. C. Anderson   Dec 1985

Pursh spec.

N. America. Lewis & Clark.

0928434

EX. HERB. A. B. LAMBERT

Bigelovia graveolens Gr.
(Chrysocoma Nutt.)

ANS PHILA

39d. *Chrysothamnus nauseosus* (Pallas *ex* Pursh) Britt. ssp. *graveolens* (Nutt.) Piper, rabbit brush

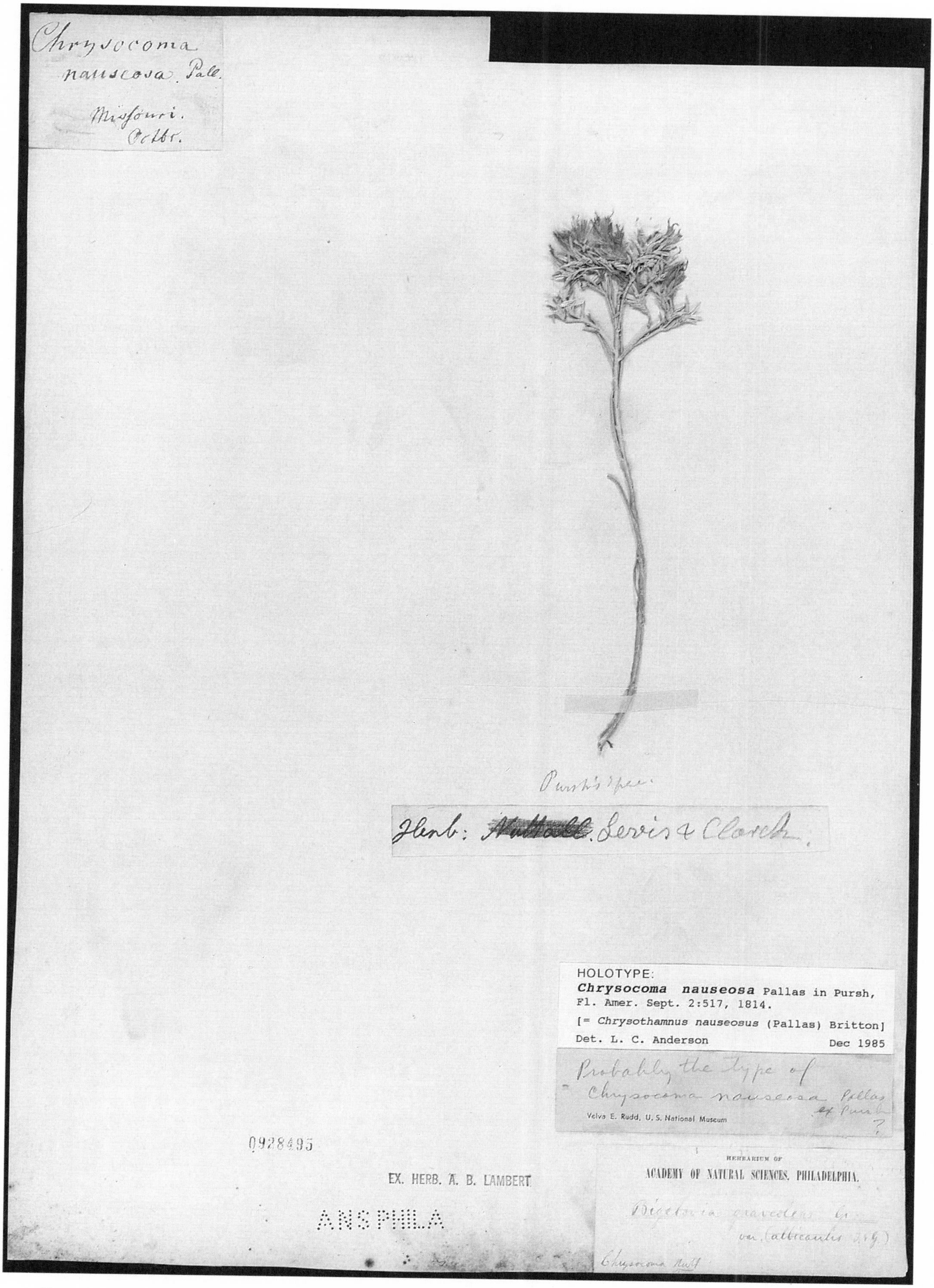

Chrysocoma
nauseosa. Pal.

Missouri.
Octbr.

Pursh's spec.

Herb: ~~Nuttall~~ Lewis & Clark.

HOLOTYPE:
Chrysocoma nauseosa Pallas in Pursh,
Fl. Amer. Sept. 2:517, 1814.

[= *Chrysothamnus nauseosus* (Pallas) Britton]

Det. L. C. Anderson   Dec 1985

Probably the Type of
Chrysocoma nauseosa Pallas
ex Pursh
Velva E. Rudd, U. S. National Museum   *?*

0928495

EX. HERB. A. B. LAMBERT.

ANSPHILA

HERBARIUM OF
ACADEMY OF NATURAL SCIENCES, PHILADELPHIA.

Bigelovia graveolens Gr
var. albicaulis (A.G.)

Chrysocoma Nutt

40a. *Chrysothamnus nauseosus* (Pallas *ex* Pursh) Britt. ssp. *nauseosus*, rabbit brush

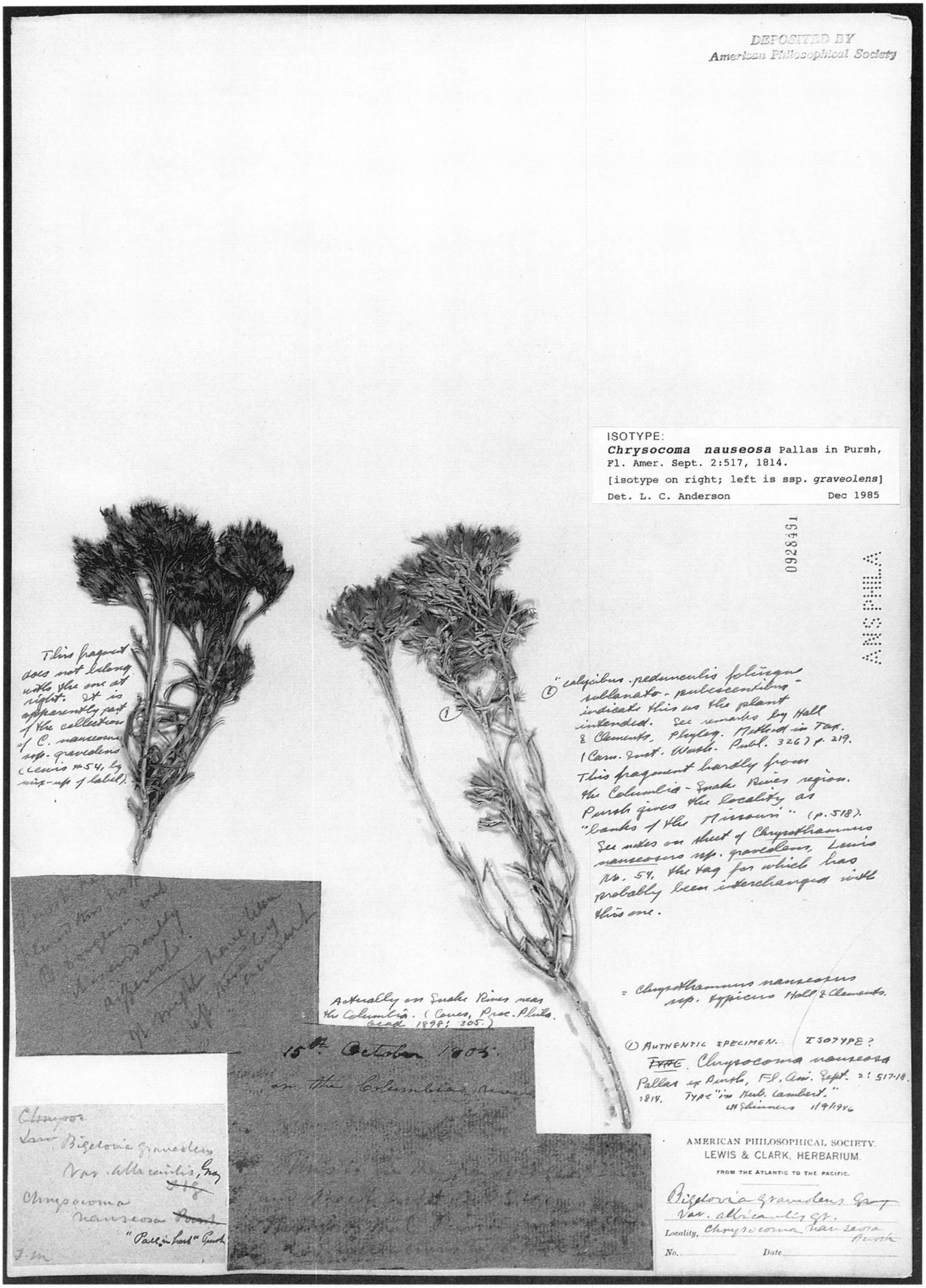

DEPOSITED BY
American Philosophical Society
ISOTYPE:
Chrysocoma nauseosa Pallas in Pursh,
Fl. Amer. Sept. 2:517, 1814.
[isotype on right; left is ssp. graveolens]
Det. L. C. Anderson Dec 1985
00928491
ANS PHILA
15th October 1805
AMERICAN PHILOSOPHICAL SOCIETY.
LEWIS & CLARK, HERBARIUM.
FROM THE ATLANTIC TO THE PACIFIC.
Locality,
No.
Date

40b. *Chrysothamnus nauseosus* (Pallas *ex* Pursh) Britt. ssp. *nauseosus,* rabbit brush

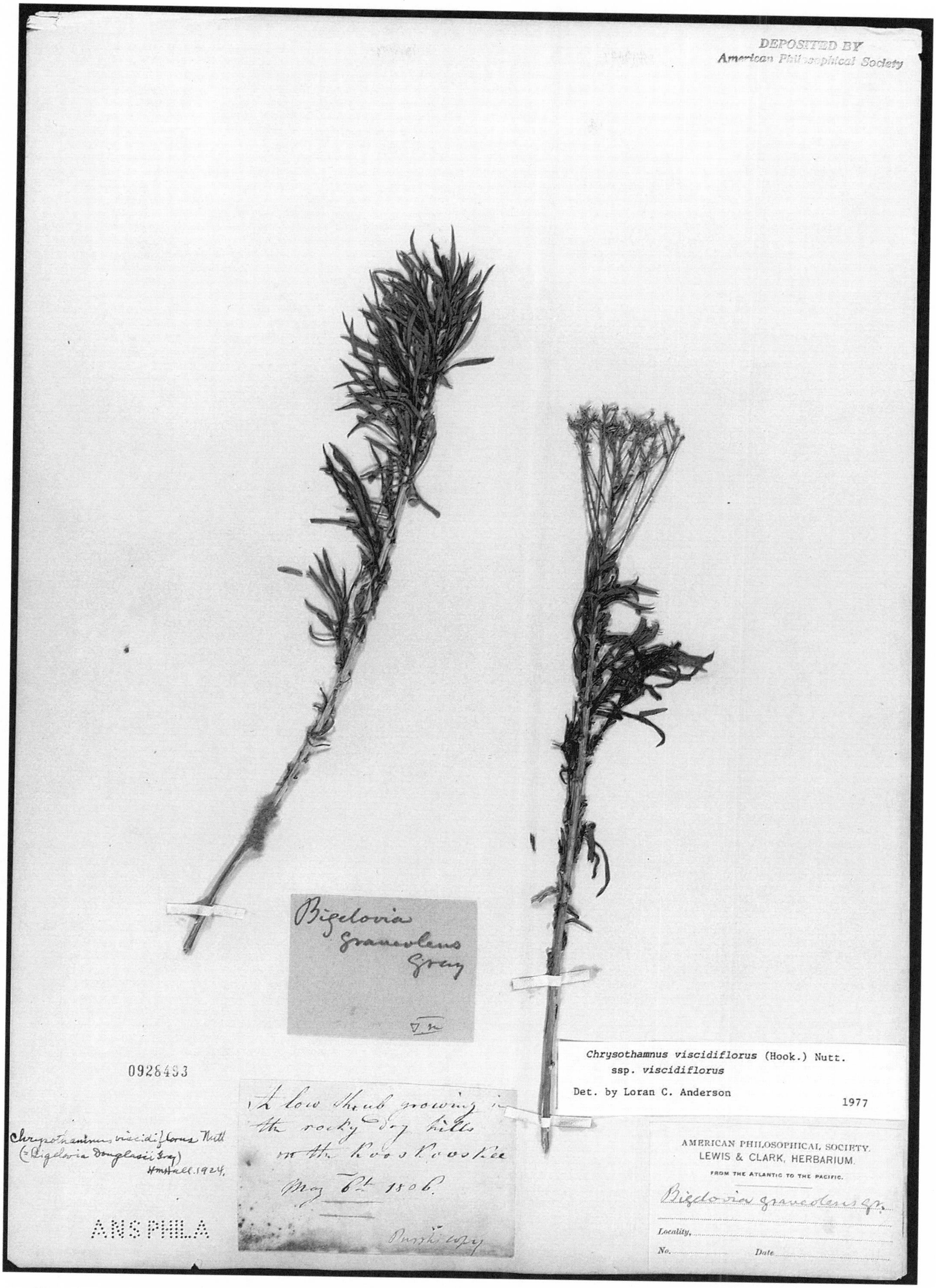

*Bigelovia
graveolens
Gray*

0928493

Chrysothamnus viscidiflorus (Hook.) Nutt.
ssp. *viscidiflorus*

Det. by Loran C. Anderson   1977

*Chrysothamnus viscidiflorus Nutt.
(=Bigelovia Douglasii Gray)
HMHall 1924.*

*A low shrub growing in
the rocky dry hills
on the Kooskooskee
May 6th 1806.*

Pursh copy

ANS PHILA

AMERICAN PHILOSOPHICAL SOCIETY.
LEWIS & CLARK, HERBARIUM.
FROM THE ATLANTIC TO THE PACIFIC.

Bigelovia graveolens sp.

Locality,
No.   Date

41. *Chrysothamnus viscidiflorus* (Hook.) Nutt., green rabbit brush

Cnicus edulis Gray

I. m

Carduus

~~Leaf of the Shappellel~~
or Thistel
Roots eatable
Fort Clatsop.
March 13 1806.

Private copy of Lewis

Academy of Natural Sciences
Cirsium edule Nutt.
Det: Erica Armstrong   Date: 17 May 1994

ANS PHILA

42. *Cirsium edule* Nutt., edible thistle

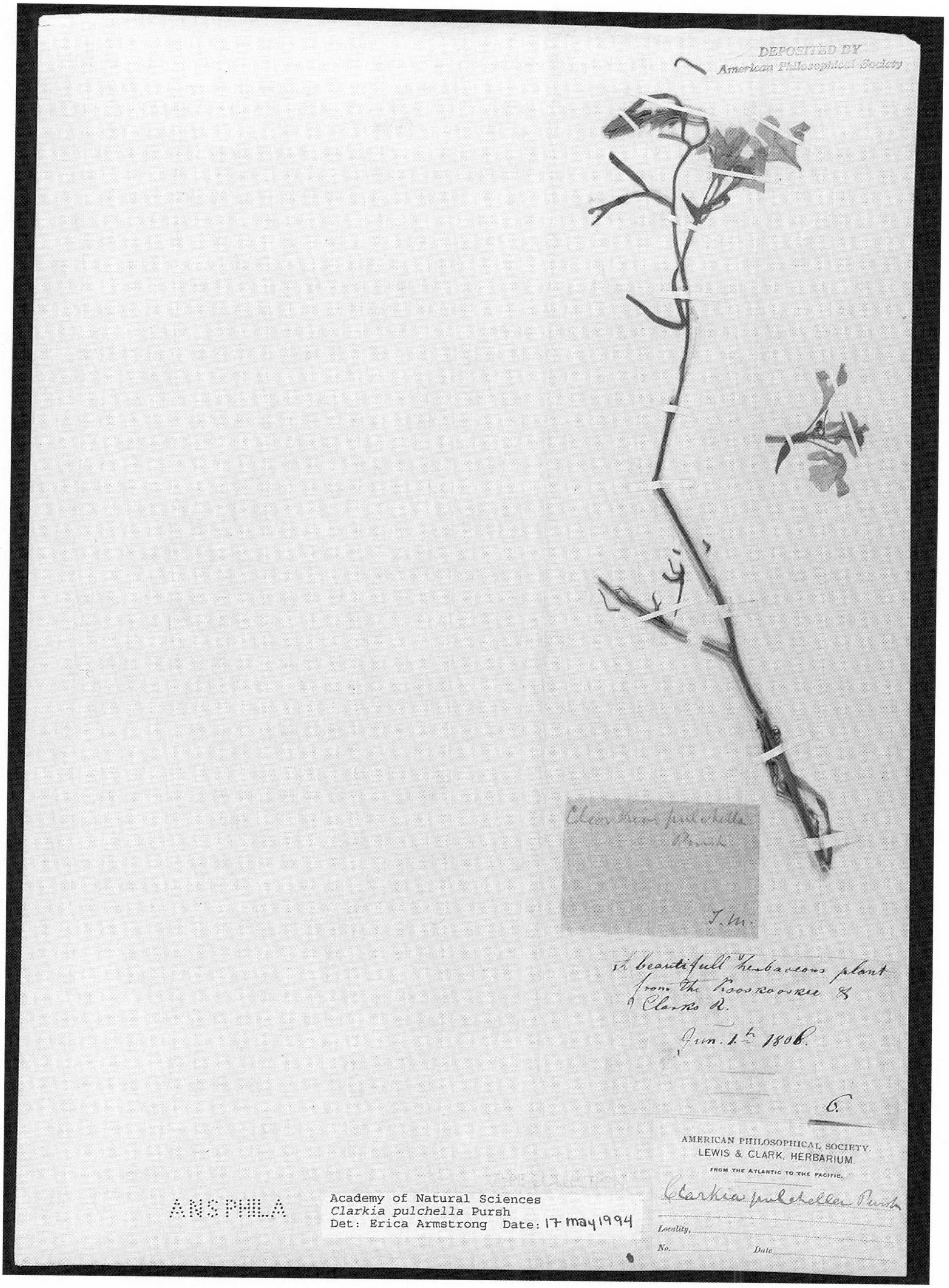

Clarkia pulchella
Pursh

T. M.

A beautifull herbaceous plant
from the Kooskooskee &
Clarks R.

Jun. 1st 1806.

6.

ANS PHILA

Academy of Natural Sciences
Clarkia pulchella Pursh
Det: Erica Armstrong   Date: 17 May 1994

TYPE COLLECTION

43. *Clarkia pulchella* Pursh, ragged robin

Claytonia
lanceolata Pursh

J.M.

Head waters of Koos Kooski
June 27th 1806.

Pursh's copy of Lewis

Monographic Studies of *Claytonia*
BioSystems Analysis, Inc. & Oregon
State University

HOLOTYPE

Claytonia lanceolata Pursh

Fl. Am. Sept. 1: 175. 1814.

John M. Miller & Kenton L. Chambers
September 3, 1993

TYPE COLLECTION
Pursh, Fl. Am. Sept. 1, 175 t 3

ANSPHILA

44. *Claytonia lanceolata* Pursh, western springbeauty

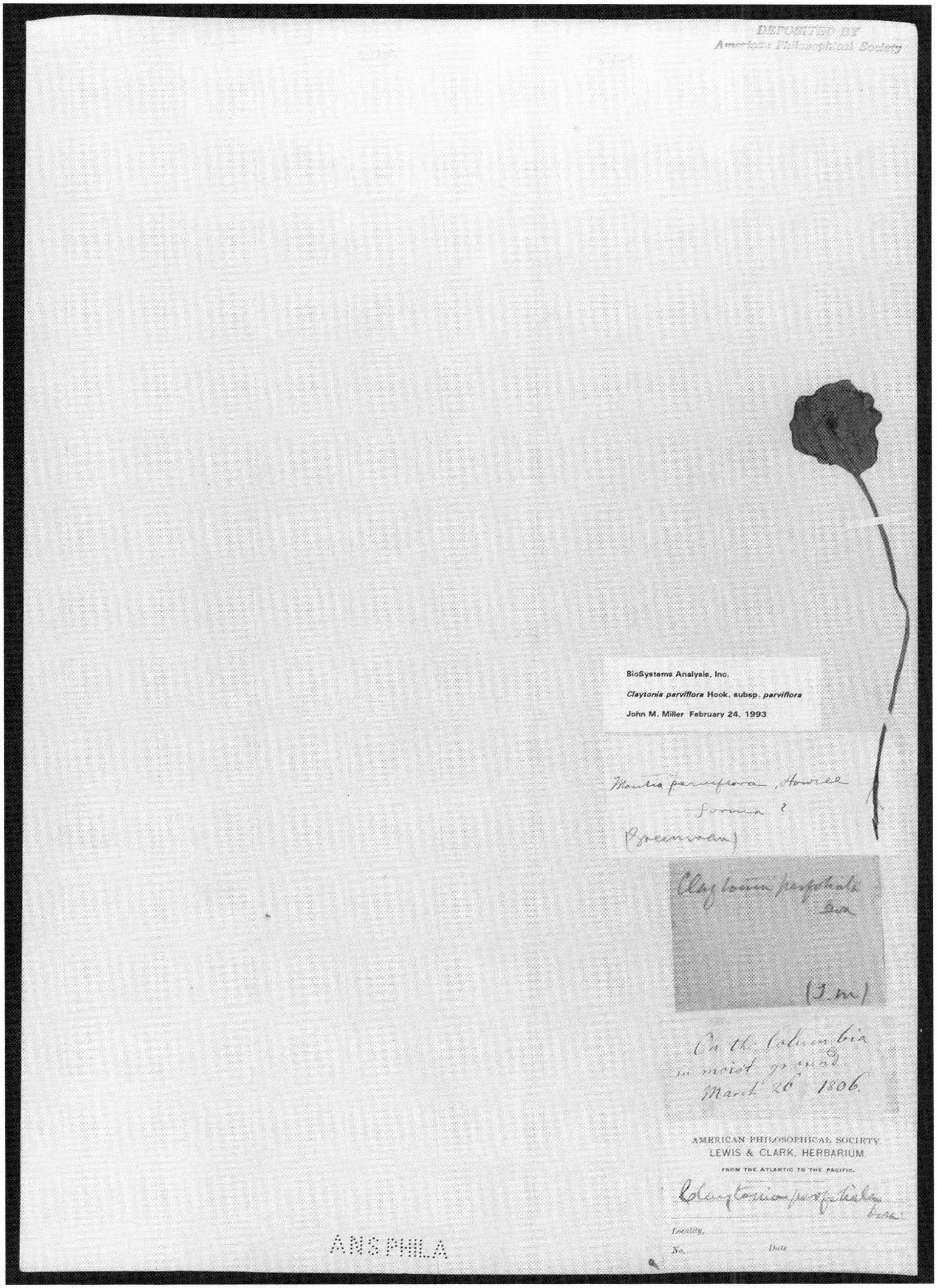

BioSystems Analysis, Inc.

Claytonia parviflora Hook. subsp. *parviflora*

John M. Miller   February 24, 1993

Montia parviflora, Howell
forma ?
(Greenman)

Claytonia perfoliata
Don

(J. m.)

On the Columbia
in moist ground
March 26, 1806.

AMERICAN PHILOSOPHICAL SOCIETY,
LEWIS & CLARK, HERBARIUM.
FROM THE ATLANTIC TO THE PACIFIC.

Claytonia perfoliata
Don

Locality,

No.   Date

ANS PHILA

45. *Claytonia parviflora* Dougl. *ex* Hook., littleleaf montia

Claytonia perfoliata Don

(J. M)

Rocky camp.
Apl. 17th 1806

Montia parviflora, Howell
Claytonia perfoliata, Pursh. Fl. i. 176 non Don
(Greenman)

Oregon State University Herbarium

Claytonia perfoliata ssp. *perfoliata* Donn
ex Willdenow

John M. Miller   May-July 1991

ANS PHILA

46. *Claytonia perfoliata* Donn *ex* Willd. ssp. *perfoliata,* miner's lettuce

Columbia R.
Apl. 8th 1806.

Montia sibirica Howell
(Claytonia sibirica, L.)
((Claytonia alsinoides, Pursh.)

AMERICAN PHILOSOPHICAL SOCIETY.
LEWIS & CLARK, HERBARIUM.
FROM THE ATLANTIC TO THE PACIFIC.

Claytonia sibirica L.

Locality,
No.   Date

ANS PHILA

47. *Claytonia sibirica* L., Siberian montia

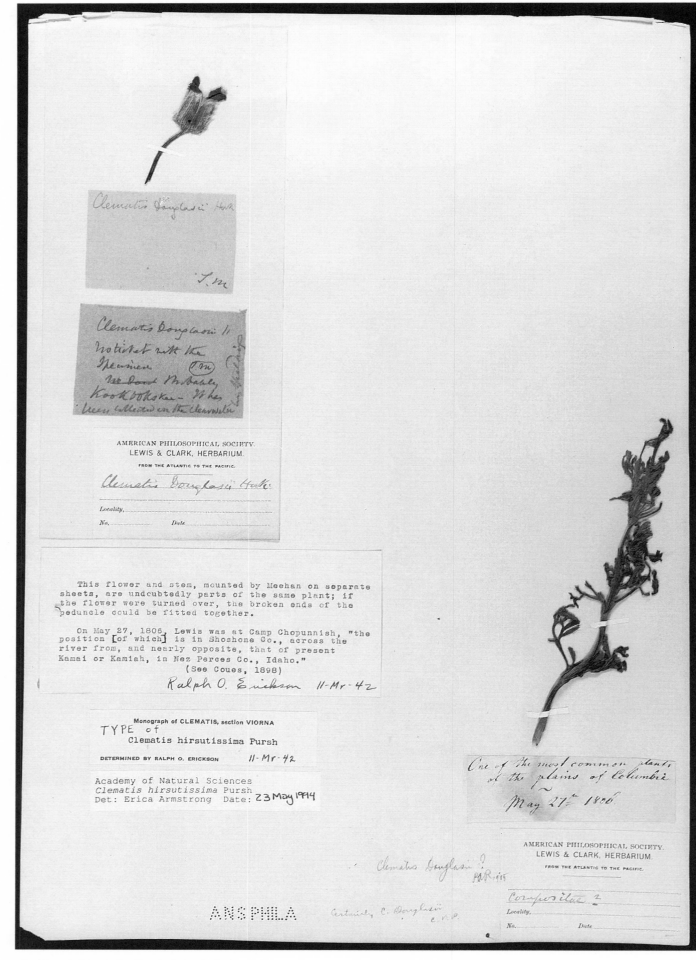

48. *Clematis hirsutissima* Pursh, Douglas's clematis

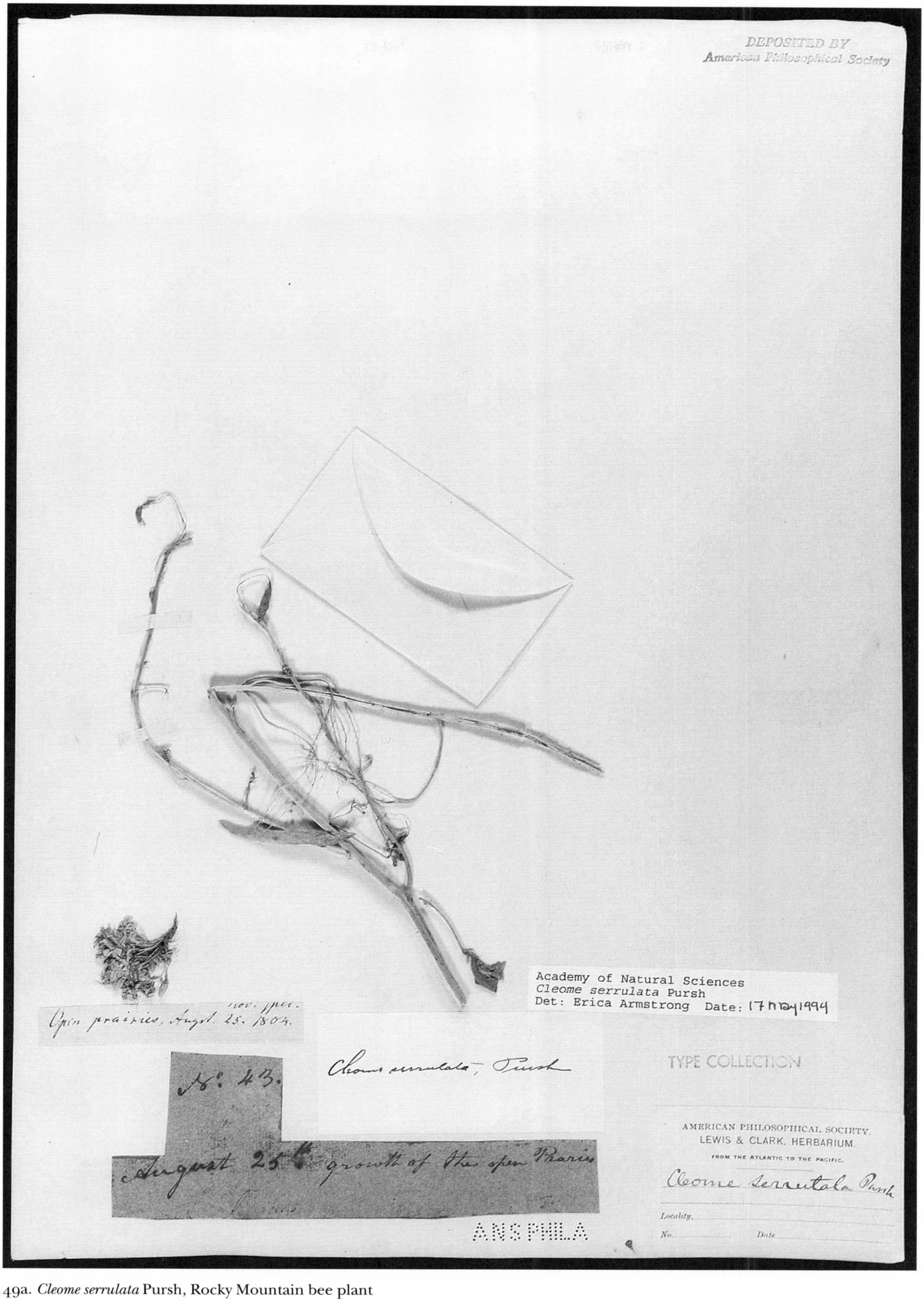
DEPOSITED BY
American Philosophical Society
Academy of Natural Sciences
Cleome serrulata Pursh
Det: Erica Armstrong Date: 17 May 1994
nov. spec.
Open prairies, Augst. 25. 1804.
No. 43.
Cleome serrulata, Pursh
TYPE COLLECTION
AMERICAN PHILOSOPHICAL SOCIETY.
LEWIS & CLARK, HERBARIUM.
FROM THE ATLANTIC TO THE PACIFIC.
Cleome serrutala Pursh
Locality,
No.
Date
August 25th growth of the open Praries
ANSPHILA

49a. *Cleome serrulata* Pursh, Rocky Mountain bee plant

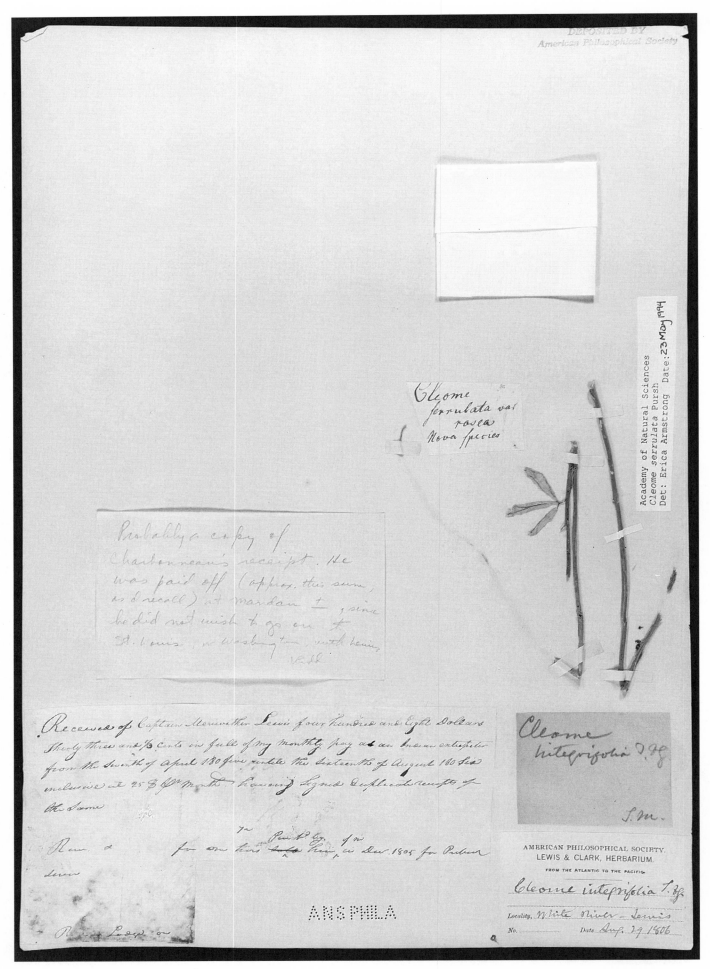

Academy of Natural Sciences
Cleome serrulata Pursh
Det: Erica Armstrong Date: 23 May 1994

*Cleome
serrulata var
rosea
Nova species*

Probably a copy of
Charbonneau's receipt. He
was paid off (approx. this sum,
as I recall) at mandan ± , since
he did not wish to go on to
St. Louis, or Washington, with Lewis.
v.dd

Received of Captain Meriwether Lewis four hundred and Eight Dollars
thirty three and ⅓ cents in full of my monthly pay as an Indian enterpeter
from the fourth of April 180 five until the sixteenth of August 180 Six
inclusive at 25 $ ⅌ month having Signed Duplicate receipts of
the Same

*Cleome
integrifolia* T.fg

S. M.

AMERICAN PHILOSOPHICAL SOCIETY.
LEWIS & CLARK, HERBARIUM.
FROM THE ATLANTIC TO THE PACIFIC

Cleome integrifolia T. fg

Locality, White River - Lewis
No.   Date Aug. 29 1806

A N S PHILA

49b. *Cleome serrulata* Pursh, Rocky Mountain bee plant

Cleome serrulata alba
Open prairies, Augt. 25. 1804

EX. HERB. A. B. LAMBERT.

Pursh's specimen!

rica. Herb: Lewis Clark. Jrd: Pursh.

Academy of Natural Sciences
Cleome serrulata Pursh
Det: Erica Armstrong   Date: 23 May 1994

HERBARIUM OF
ACADEMY OF NATURAL SCIENCES, PHILADELPHIA.
Cleome integrifolia Torr. & G.

49c. *Cleome serrulata* Pursh, Rocky Mountain bee plant

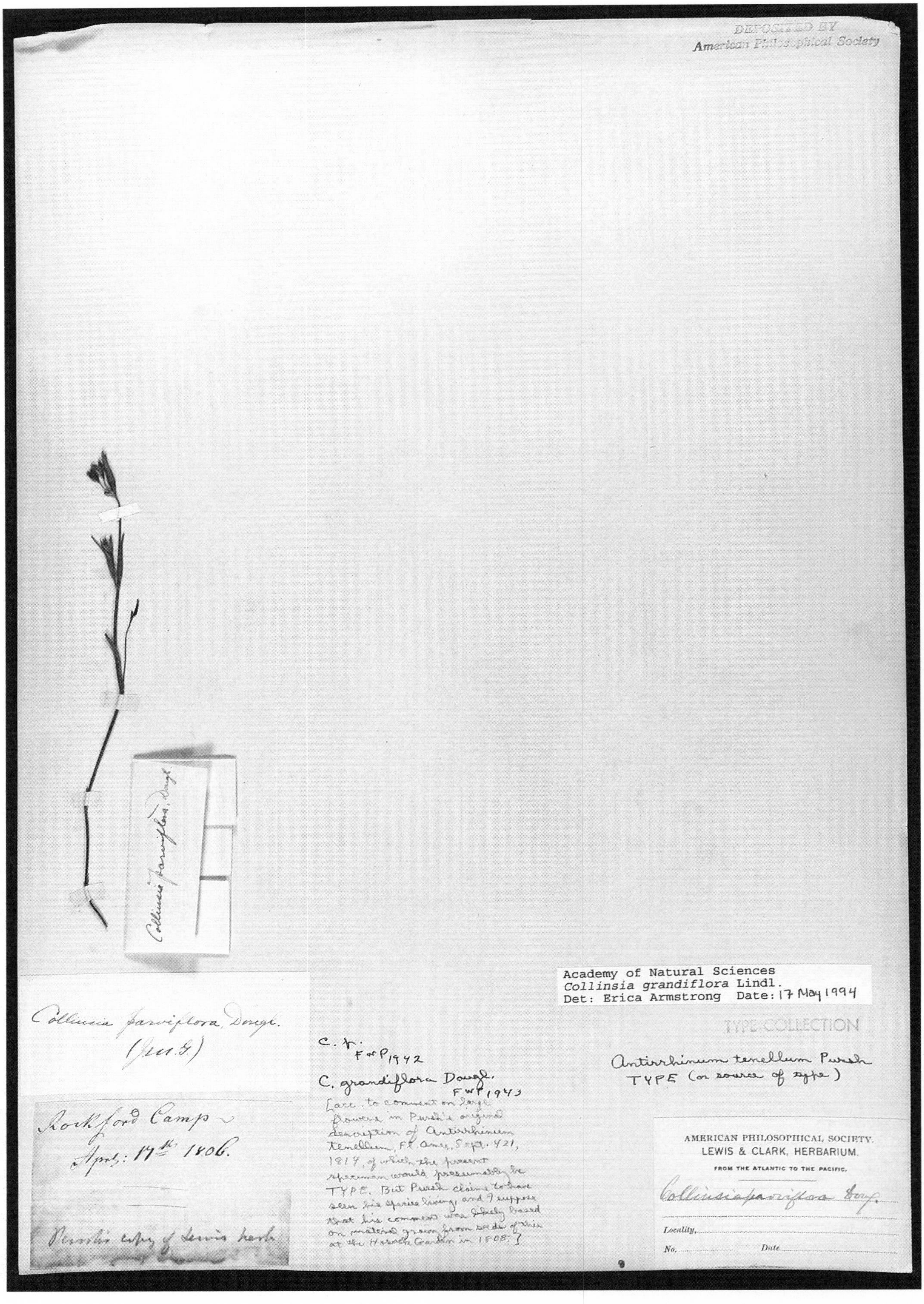

Collinsia parviflora, Dougl.

Academy of Natural Sciences
Collinsia grandiflora Lindl.
Det: Erica Armstrong   Date: 17 May 1994

Collinsia parviflora, Dougl.
(Jun. 9)

C. r.
F & P 1942

C. grandiflora Dougl.
F & P 1943

Lace. to comment on large
flowers in Pursh's original
description of Antirrhinum
tenellum, Ft. Ames, Sept. 421,
1814, of which the present
specimen would presumably be
TYPE. But Pursh claims to have
seen his species living, and I suppose
that his comment was likely based
on material grown from seeds of this
at the Harold Garden in 1808.

Antirrhinum tenellum Pursh
TYPE (or source of type)

Rockford Camp
April: 17th 1806.

Pursh's copy of Lewis herb.

AMERICAN PHILOSOPHICAL SOCIETY.
LEWIS & CLARK, HERBARIUM.
FROM THE ATLANTIC TO THE PACIFIC.

Collinsia parviflora Doug.

Locality,
No.   Date

50. *Collinsia parviflora* Lindl. var. *grandiflora* (Lindl.) Ganders & Krause, small-flowered blue-eyed Mary

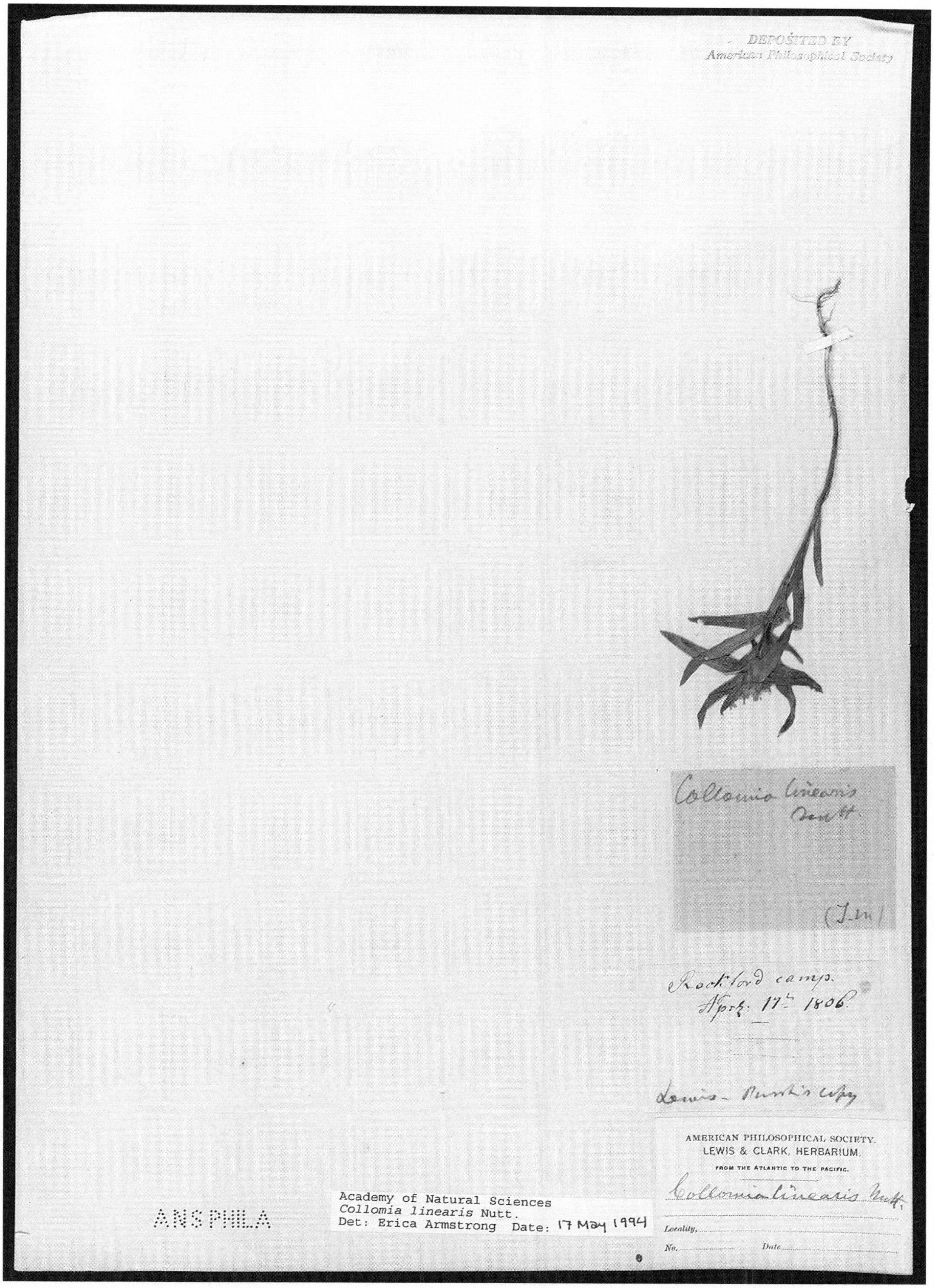

Collomia linearis
Nutt.

(T.N)

Rockford camp.
Apl: 17th 1806.

Lewis — Nutt's copy

Academy of Natural Sciences
Collomia linearis Nutt.
Det: Erica Armstrong   Date: 17 May 1994

ANS PHILA

51. *Collomia linearis* Nutt., narrow-leaf collomia

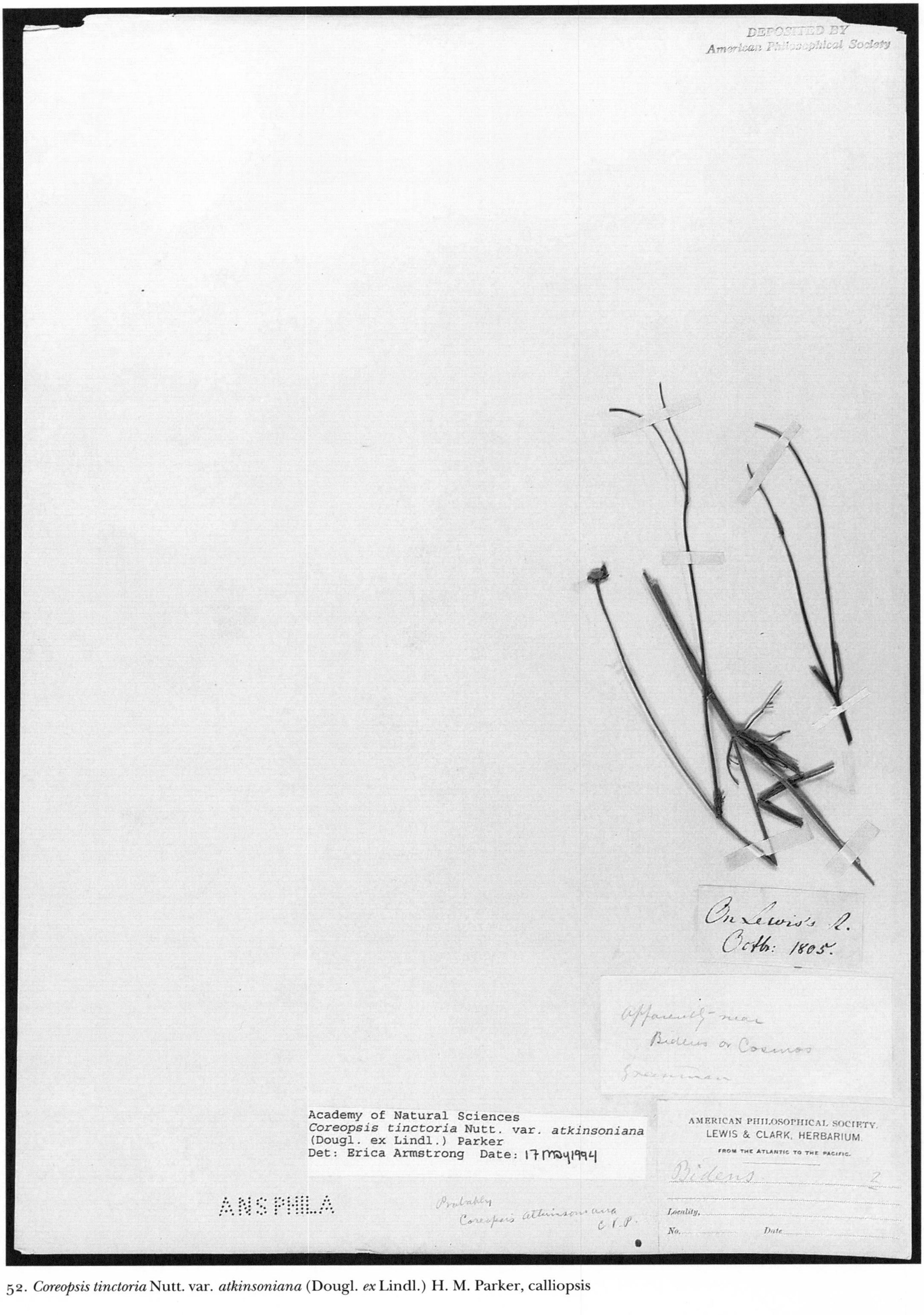

On Lewis's R.
Octb: 1805.

apparently near
Bidens or Cosmos
Greenman

Academy of Natural Sciences
Coreopsis tinctoria Nutt. var. *atkinsoniana*
(Dougl. *ex* Lindl.) Parker
Det: Erica Armstrong   Date: 17 May 1994

ANS PHILA

Probably
Coreopsis atkinsoniana
C. V. P.

52. *Coreopsis tinctoria* Nutt. var. *atkinsoniana* (Dougl. *ex* Lindl.) H. M. Parker, calliopsis

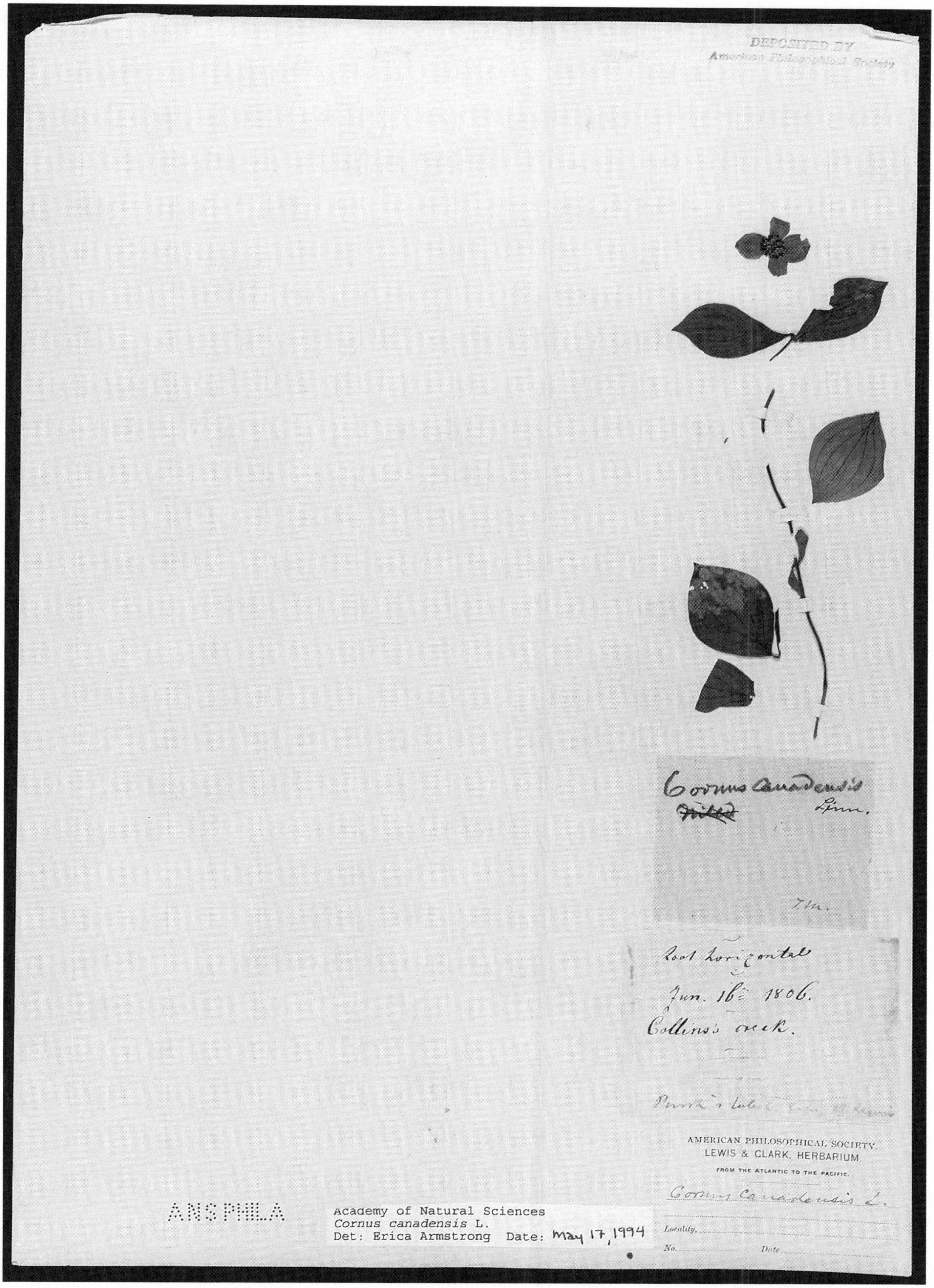

Cornus canadensis Linn.

~~killed~~

7m.

Root horizontal
Jun. 16th 1806.
Collins's creek.

Academy of Natural Sciences
Cornus canadensis L.
Det: Erica Armstrong   Date: May 17, 1994

53. *Cornus canadensis* L., bunchberry

Crataegus Douglasii
Lindl.

S. en

Deep purple Haw.

Columbia R.
April 29th 1806.

Crataegus
C. oxperi
c.v.s.

ANS PHILA

Academy of Natural Sciences
Crataegus douglasii Lindl.
Det: Erica Armstrong   Date: 17 May 1994

AMERICAN PHILOSOPHICAL SOCIETY.
LEWIS & CLARK, HERBARIUM.
FROM THE ATLANTIC TO THE PACIFIC.

Crataegus douglasii Lindl.

Locality,

No.   Date

54. *Crataegus douglasii* Lindl., black hawthorn

Petalostemum
violaceus Mx.

1 m

On the Missouri
Sep. 2nd 1806.

Petalosteman
violaceus, Michx.?
(J.M.G.)

Academy of Natural Sciences
Dalea purpureum Vent.
Det: Erica Armstrong   Date: 17 may 1994

ANS PHILA

found September 2nd the Indians use it
as an application to fresh wounds. they
bruise they leaves adding a little water and
apply it.

55. *Dalea purpurea* Vent., purple prairie clover

Delphinium Menziesii, DC.

(Greenman)

A sort of Larkspur with 3
styles,
On the Columbia
Apr. 14th 1806.

Perrolis copy of Lewis's ticket

Academy of Natural Sciences
Delphinium menziesii DC.
Det: Erica Armstrong   Date: 17 Nov 1994

ANS PHILA

56. *Delphinium menziesii* DC., Menzies' larkspur

Collected by Meriwether Lewis on Lewis
and Clark Expedition, the original label
having been copied by Pursh. Deposited
by the American Philosophical Society.

*Dodecatheon
meadea L*

*Near the narrows of
Columbia R.
Aprl 16. 1806.*

Academy of Natural Sciences
Dodecatheon meadia L.
Det: Erica Armstrong   Date: 17 May 1994

ANSPHILA

AMERICAN PHILOSOPHICAL SOCIETY.
LEWIS & CLARK, HERBARIUM.
FROM THE ATLANTIC TO THE PACIFIC.

Dodecatheon meadea L.

Locality,
No.   Date

57. *Dodecatheon jeffreyi* Van Houtte, Jeffrey's shooting star

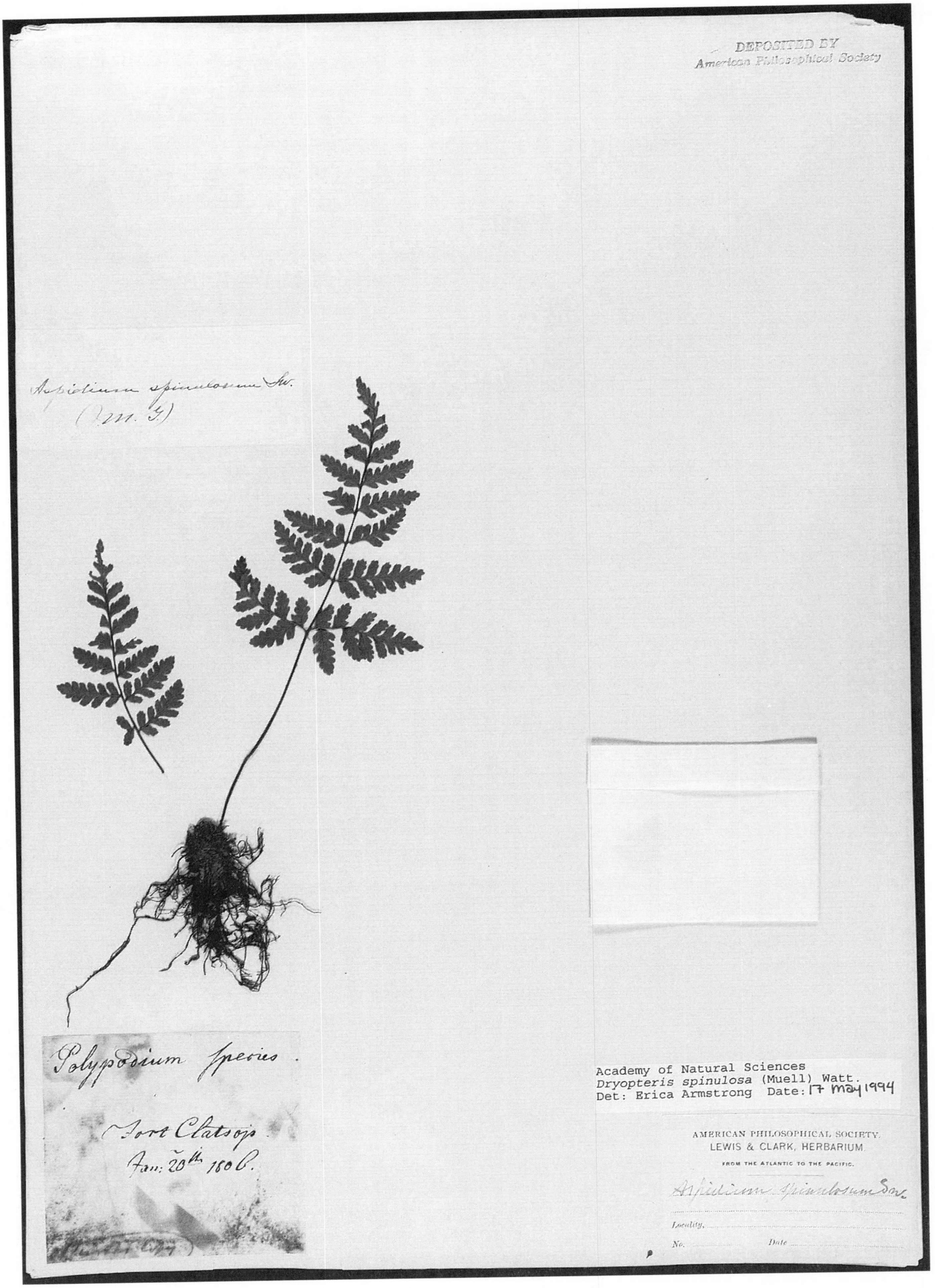

Aspidium spinulosum Sw.
(M. Y)

Polypodium species.

Fort Clatsop
Jan: 20th 1806.

Academy of Natural Sciences
Dryopteris spinulosa (Muell) Watt.
Det: Erica Armstrong   Date: 17 May 1994

58. *Dryopteris expansa* (K. Presl) Fraser-Jenkins & Jermy, mountain wood-fern

DEPOSITED BY
American Philosophical Society
Egregia Menziesii (Turn.) Aresch.
(Phyllospora Menziesii.)
(determined at Cambridge)
Fucus
From the mouth of the Columbia River on the Pacific Ocean.
Novr. 17th 1805.
AMERICAN PHILOSOPHICAL SOCIETY.
LEWIS & CLARK, HERBARIUM.
FROM THE ATLANTIC TO THE PACIFIC.
Egregia Menziesii Aresch.
Locality,
No.
Date
ANSPHILA
Academy of Natural Sciences
Egrigia menziesii (Turn.)Aresch.
Det: Erica Armstrong Date: 17 May 1994

59. *Egregia menziesii* (Turn.) Aresch., Menzies' rockweed

Elaeagnus argentea, Pursh
(& m G) type

Silver tree of the Missouri

From the prairi of
the Knobs.
Feb. 6ᵗʰ 1806.

Academy of Natural Sciences
Elaeagnus commutata Bernh. ex Rydb.
Det: Erica Armstrong   Date: 17 May 1994

ANS PHILA

60a. *Elaeagnus commutata* Bernh. *ex* Rydb., silverberry

6ob. *Elaeagnus commutata* Bernh. *ex* Rydb., silverberry

Sandbanks on the Missouri
Augt. 18. 1804

No. 31.

Academy of Natural Sciences
Equisetum arvense L.
Det: Erica Armstrong   Date: 17 May 1994

ANS PHILA

Equisetum arvense 2

(7mm)

AMERICAN PHILOSOPHICAL SOCIETY,
LEWIS & CLARK, HERBARIUM
FROM THE ATLANTIC TO THE PACIFIC.

Equisetum arvense L.

Locality,
No.   Date

61a. *Equisetum arvense* L., field horsetail

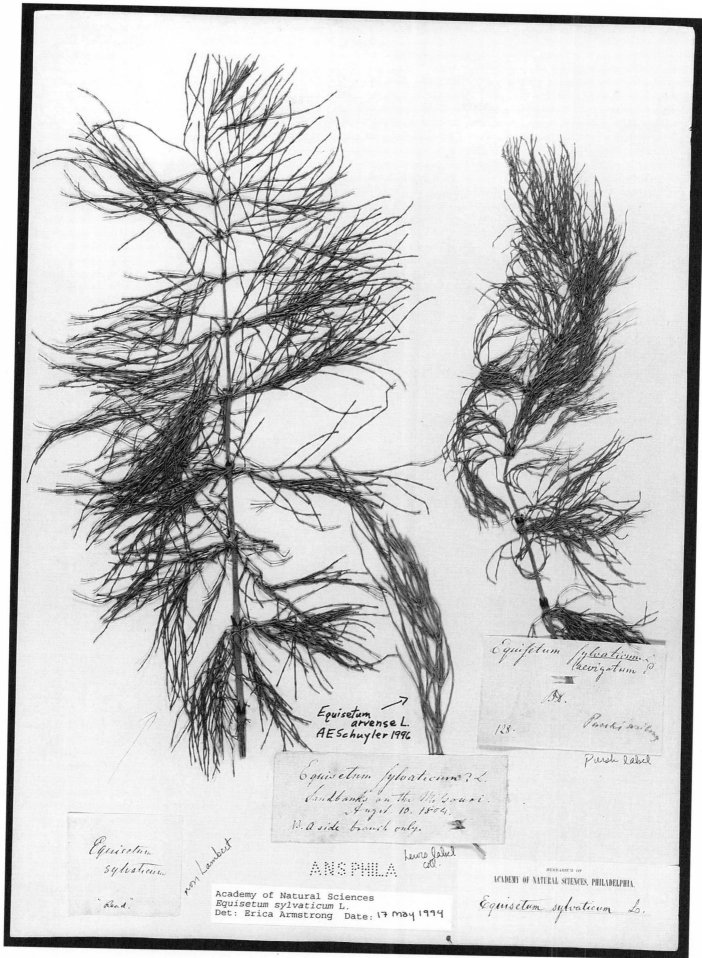

Equisetum arvense L.
AE Schuyler 1996

Equisetum sylvaticum? L.
Sandbanks on the Missouri.
August 10. 1804.
N. a side branch only.

Equisetum
sylvaticum

"Read."

non Lambert

Lewis label
coll.

ANSPHILA

Academy of Natural Sciences
Equisetum sylvaticum L.
Det: Erica Armstrong Date: 17 May 1994

Equisetum Sylvaticum
laevigatum δ

B.

128.

Pursh's writing

Pursh label

Equisetum sylvaticum L.

61b. *Equisetum arvense* L., field horsetail

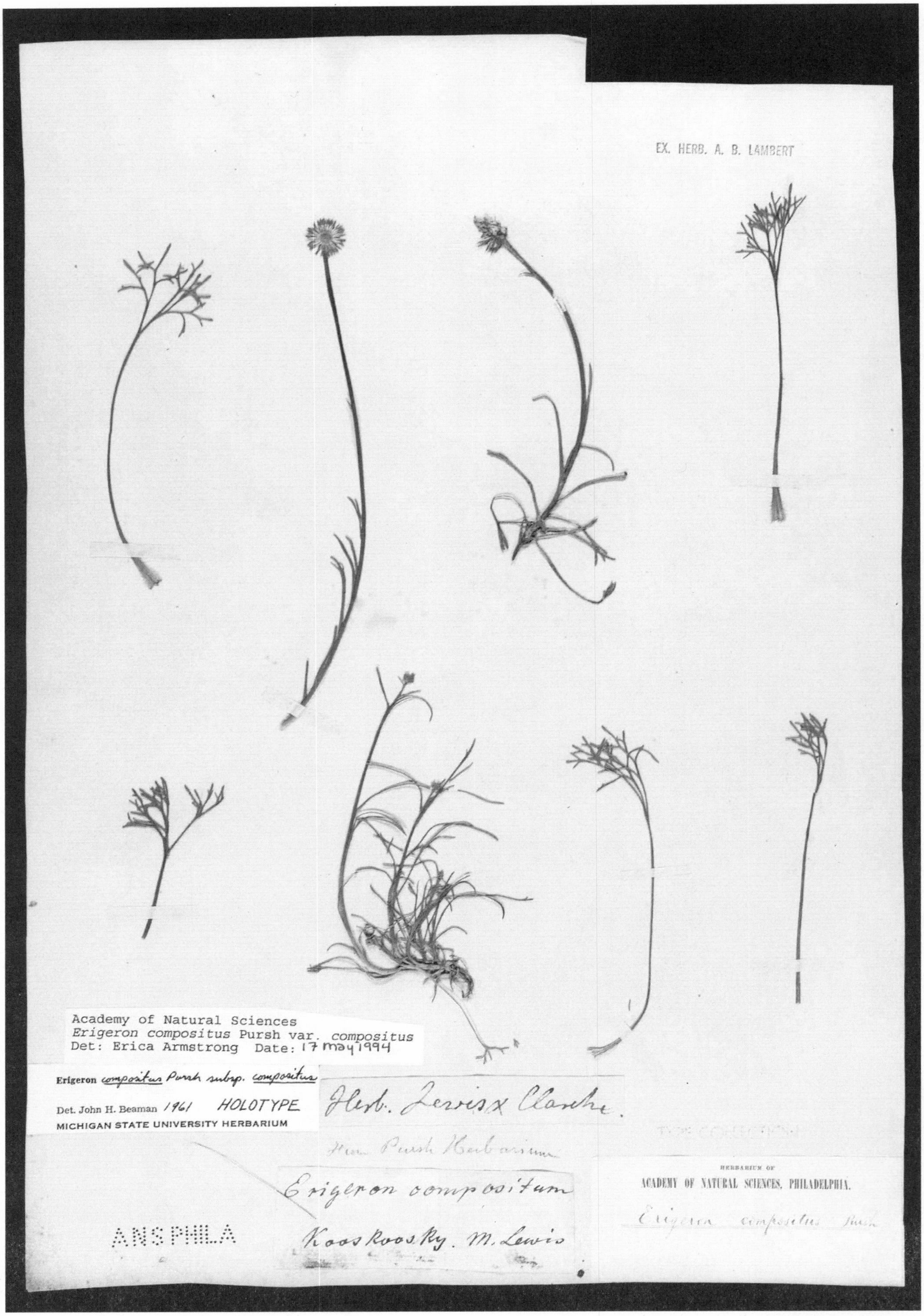

Academy of Natural Sciences
Erigeron compositus Pursh var. *compositus*
Det: Erica Armstrong   Date: 17 may 1994

Erigeron *compositus* Pursh subsp. *compositus*

Det. John H. Beaman *1961*   HOLOTYPE
MICHIGAN STATE UNIVERSITY HERBARIUM

Herb. Lewis & Clarke.

Non Pursh Herbarium

Erigeron compositum

ANS PHILA

Roos Roos Ky. M. Lewis

HERBARIUM OF
ACADEMY OF NATURAL SCIENCES, PHILADELPHIA.

Erigeron compositus Pursh

62. *Erigeron compositus* Pursh, cut-leaved daisy

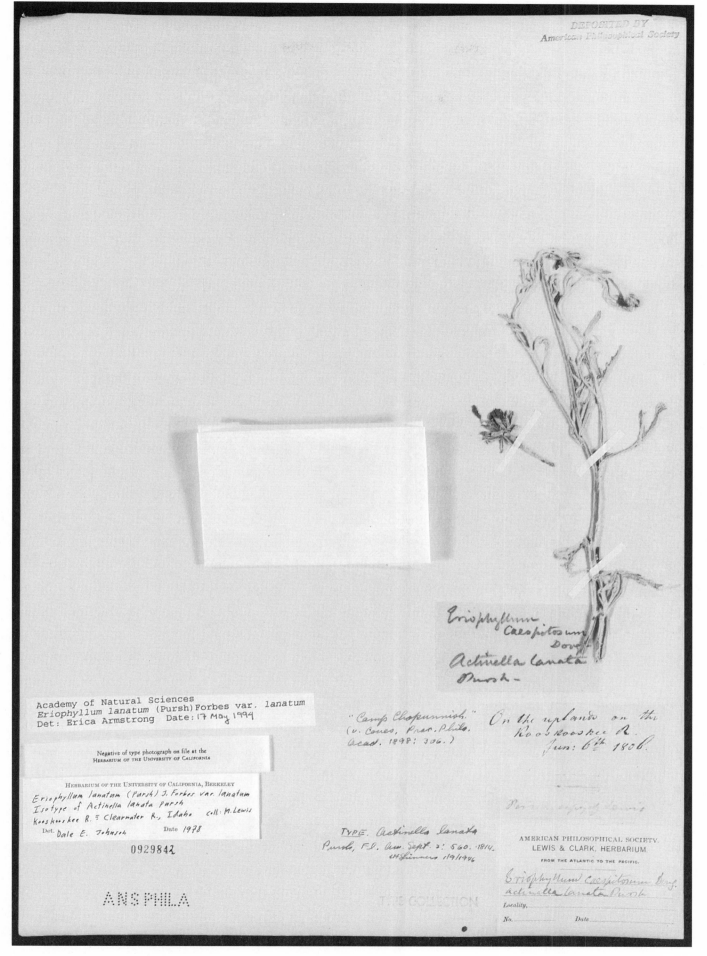

Eriophyllum
Caespitosum
Dou
Actinella lanata
Pursh

Academy of Natural Sciences
Eriophyllum lanatum (Pursh) Forbes var. lanatum
Det: Erica Armstrong   Date: 17 May 1994

Negative of type photograph on file at the
HERBARIUM OF THE UNIVERSITY OF CALIFORNIA

HERBARIUM OF THE UNIVERSITY OF CALIFORNIA, BERKELEY
Eriophyllum lanatum (Pursh) J. Forbes var. lanatum
Isotype of Actinella lanata Pursh
Kooskoorskee R. = Clearwater R., Idaho.   coll: M. Lewis
Det. Dale E. Johnson   Date 1978
0929842

ANS PHILA

"Camp Chopunnish."
(v. Cones, Proc. Phila.
Acad. 1898: 306.)

On the uplands on the
Kooskooskee R.
Jun: 6th 1806.

TYPE. Actinella lanata
Pursh, Fl. Am. Sept. 2: 560. 1814.
M. Linnerz 119/1946

AMERICAN PHILOSOPHICAL SOCIETY.
LEWIS & CLARK, HERBARIUM.
FROM THE ATLANTIC TO THE PACIFIC.

Eriophyllum caespitosum Doug
actinella lanata Pursh

Locality,
No.   Date

63a. *Eriophyllum lanatum* (Pursh) Forbes var. *lanatum,* common eriophyllum

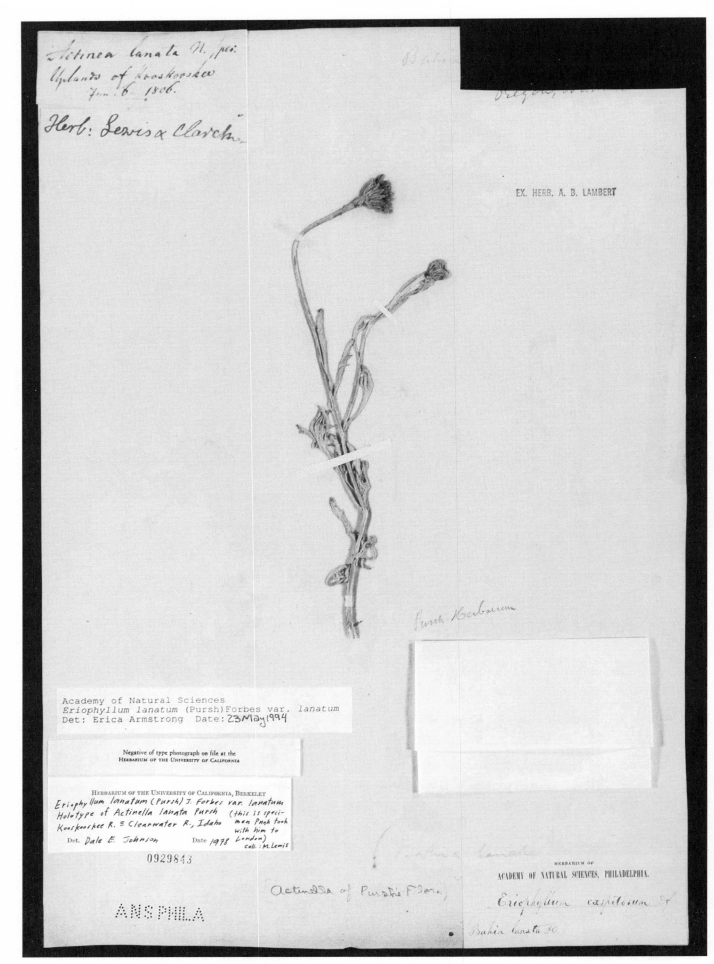

Actinea lanata N. spei:
Uplands of Kooskooskee
Jun. 6. 1806.

Herb: Lewis & Clark.

EX. HERB. A. B. LAMBERT

Pursh Herbarium

Academy of Natural Sciences
Eriophyllum lanatum (Pursh)Forbes var. lanatum
Det: Erica Armstrong Date: 23May1994

Negative of type photograph on file at the
HERBARIUM OF THE UNIVERSITY OF CALIFORNIA

HERBARIUM OF THE UNIVERSITY OF CALIFORNIA, BERKELEY
Eriophyllum lanatum (Pursh) J. Forbes var. lanatum
Holotype of Actinella lanata Pursh (this is speci-
Kooskooskee R. = Clearwater R., Idaho men Pursh took
Det. Dale E. Johnson   Date 1978 with him to
                                        London)
                                        coll.: M. Lewis

0929843

ANS PHILA

(Actinella of Pursh's Flora)

HERBARIUM OF
ACADEMY OF NATURAL SCIENCES, PHILADELPHIA.

Eriophyllum caespitosum

Bahia lanata

63b. *Eriophyllum lanatum* (Pursh) Forbes var. *lanatum,* common eriophyllum

Erysimum
asperum, DC.

(*E. lanceolatum,*
Pursh
not R.Br.)
Greenman

On the Koos Kooskee
Jun: 1st 1806.

Pursh's copy

Academy of Natural Sciences
Erysimum asperum (Nutt.)DC.
Det: Erica Armstrong   Date:17 may 1994

ANS PHILA

64. *Erysimum asperum* (Nutt.) DC., rough wallflower

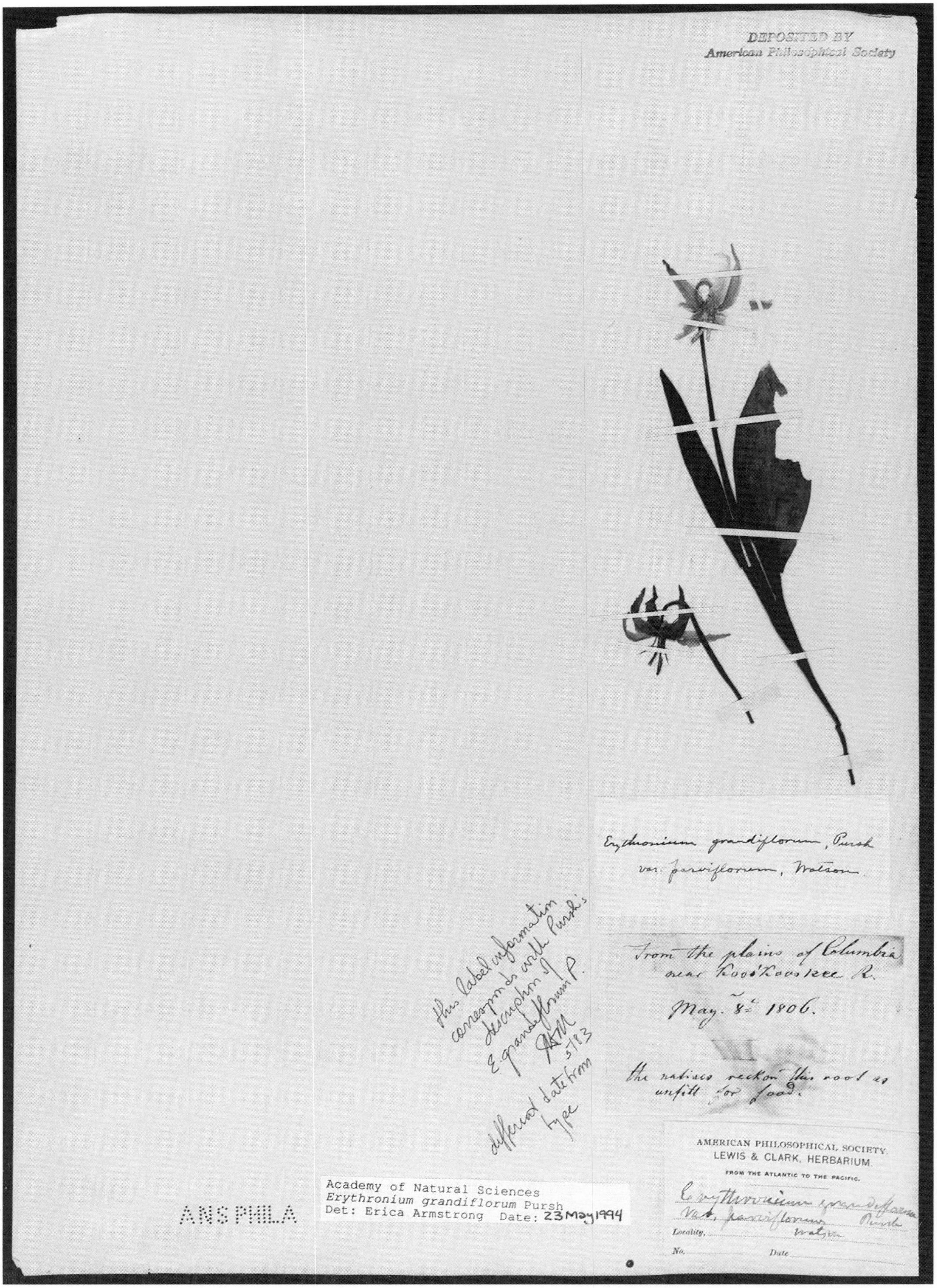

Erythronium grandiflorum, Pursh
var. parviflorum, Watson.

From the plains of Columbia
near Koos'Koos'kee R.

May. 8ᵗ 1806.

the natives reckon this root as
unfitt for food.

This label information
corresponds with Pursh's
description of
E. grandiflorum P.
different date from
type
AMM
3183

AMERICAN PHILOSOPHICAL SOCIETY.
LEWIS & CLARK, HERBARIUM.
FROM THE ATLANTIC TO THE PACIFIC.

Erythronium grandiflorum
var. parviflorum Pursh
Locality, Watson
No.   Date.

Academy of Natural Sciences
Erythronium grandiflorum Pursh
Det: Erica Armstrong   Date: 23May1994

ANS PHILA

65a. *Erythronium grandiflorum* Pursh, pale fawn-lily

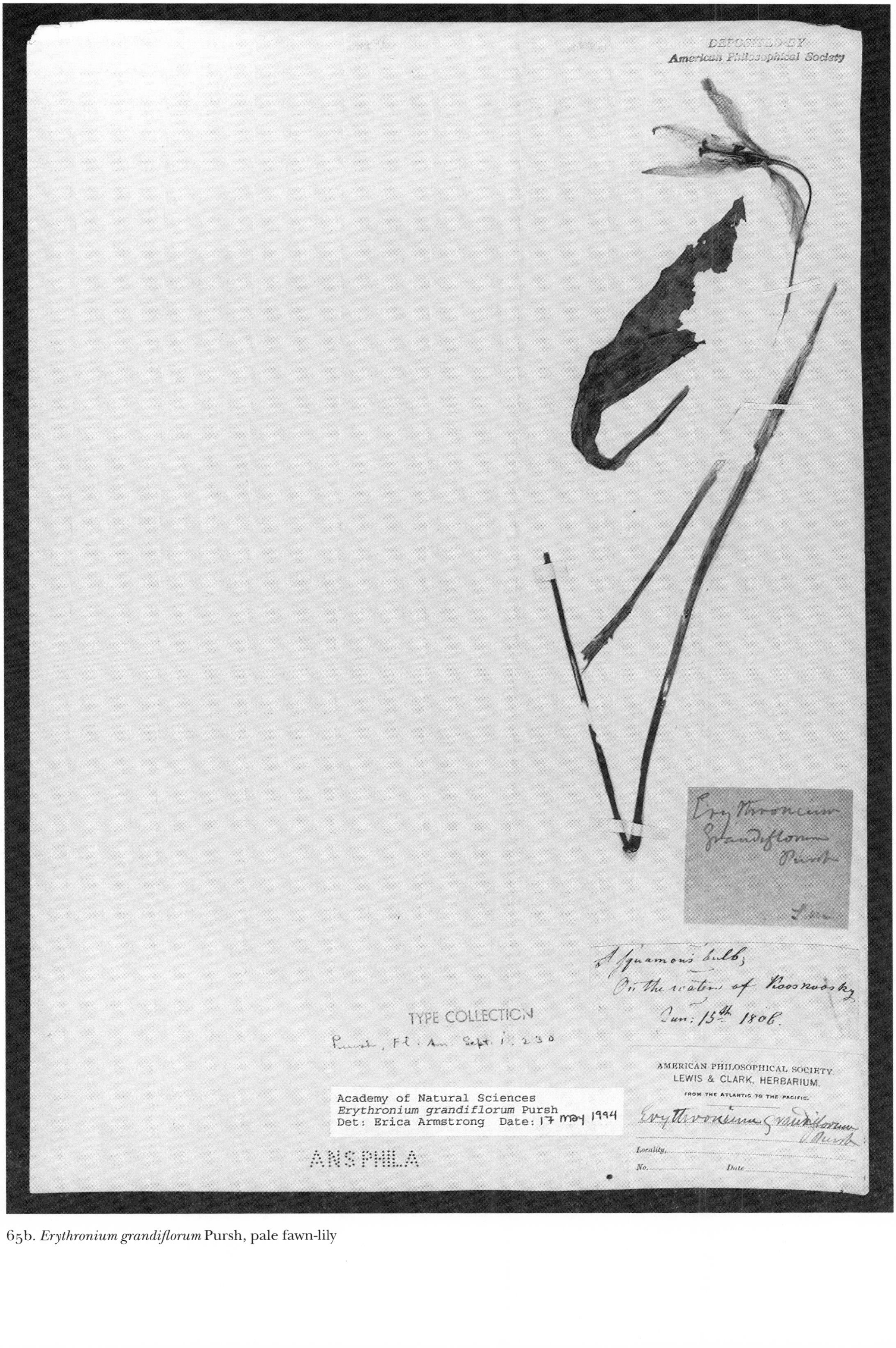

Erythronium Grandiflorum Pursh

A /guamons bulb;
On the waters of Roosnoosky
Jun: 15th 1806.

TYPE COLLECTION

Pursh, Fl. Am. Sept. i: 230

Academy of Natural Sciences
Erythronium grandiflorum Pursh
Det: Erica Armstrong   Date: 17 May 1994

Erythronium Grandiflorum
V. Pursh

Locality,
No.   Date

65b. *Erythronium grandiflorum* Pursh, pale fawn-lily

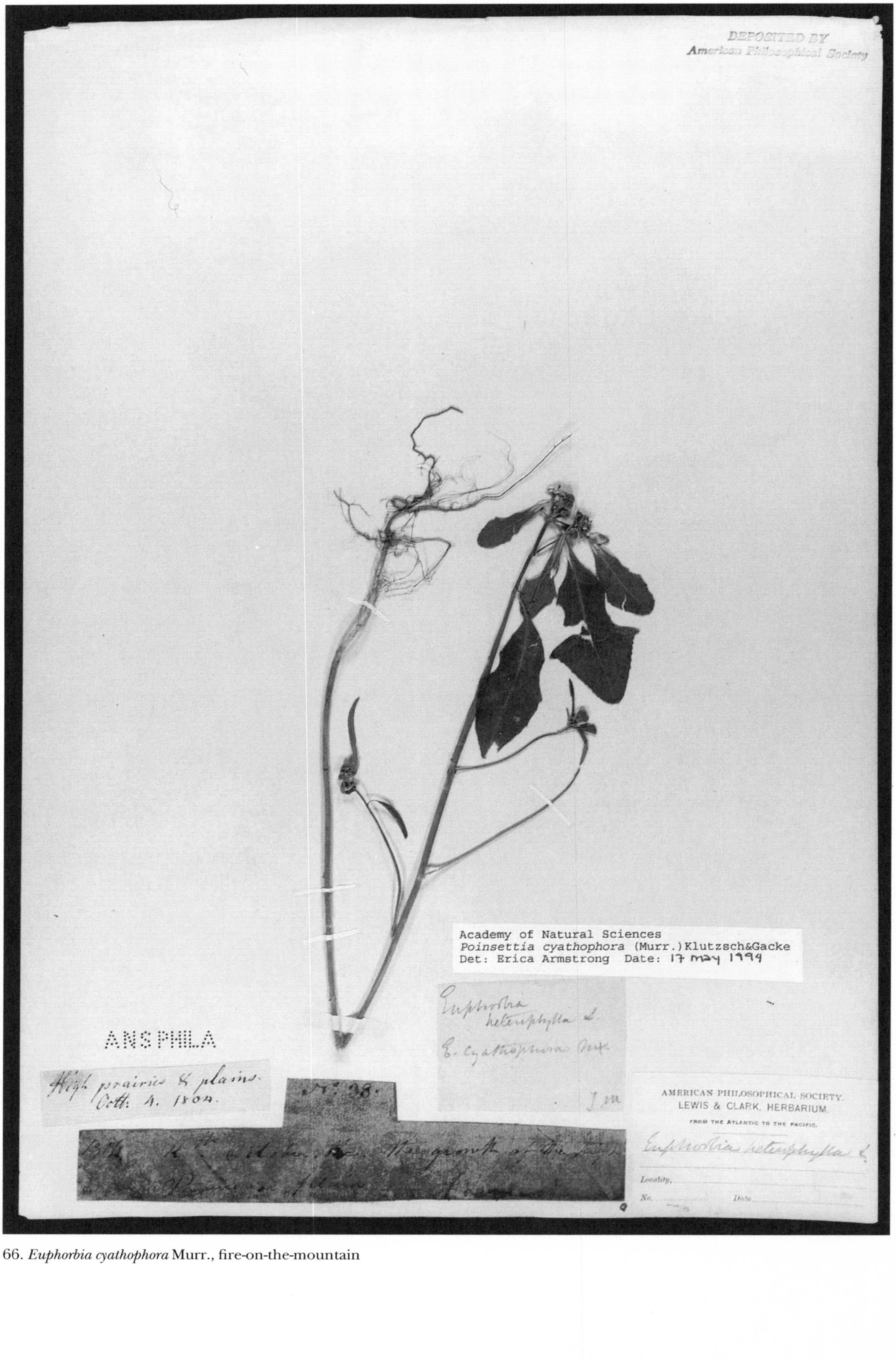

Academy of Natural Sciences
Poinsettia cyathophora (Murr.) Klutzsch & Gacke
Det: Erica Armstrong   Date: 17 may 1994

ANS PHILA

High prairies & plains.
Octb. 4. 1804.

No. 28.

Euphorbia
heterophylla L.
E. cyathophora Mx.

Euphorbia heterophylla L.

Locality,
No.   Date

66. *Euphorbia cyathophora* Murr., fire-on-the-mountain

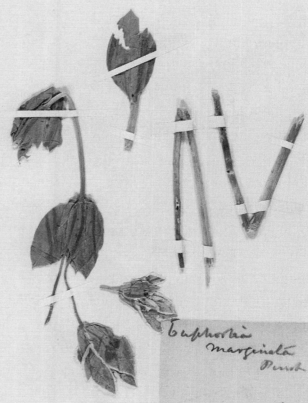

Academy of Natural Sciences
Euphorbia marginata Pursh
Det: Erica Armstrong   Date: 17 May 1994

TYPE

Euphorbia marginata Pursh, Fl. Amer.

Sept. 2: 607. 1814.

Louis C. Wheeler 1938

*Euphorbia
marginata
Pursh*

J. M.

*In the Yellowstone River.
Jul. 28th 1806.*

(Pursh's copy)

*Euphorbia marginata
Pursh*

Locality,

No.   Date

ANS PHILA

ANNOTATION LABEL
Revision of New World Euphorbieae

Euphorbia marginata Pursh

Det.: Louis C. Wheeler 1938
GRAY HERBARIUM

67. *Euphorbia marginata* Pursh, snow-on-the-mountain

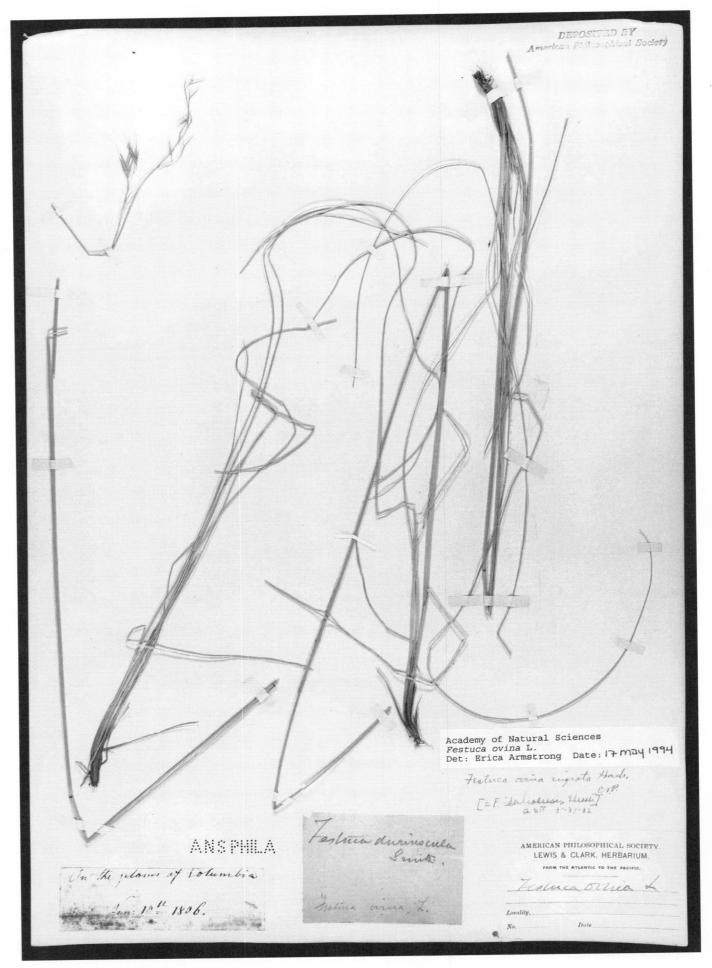

Academy of Natural Sciences
Festuca ovina L.
Det: Erica Armstrong   Date: 17 May 1994

Festuca ovina migrato Hack.
[= F. idahoensis Elmer]
a btt 5-31-82

ANS PHILA

On the plains of Columbia
Jun: 10th 1806.

Festuca duriuscula
Smith.

Festuca ovina, L.

AMERICAN PHILOSOPHICAL SOCIETY.
LEWIS & CLARK. HERBARIUM.
FROM THE ATLANTIC TO THE PACIFIC.

Festuca ovina L

Locality.
No.   Date

68. *Festuca idahoensis* Elmer, Idaho fescue

Rhamnus Purshiana, DC.
Prodr. ii. 25.
(fen 1)

A Shrub apparently a species
of Rhamnus. (Pursh!
About 12 feet high, in Clumps.
fruit a 3-valved purple berry
which the natives eat & esteem
highly; the berry depressed
globous.
On the waters of the Kooskooskee
May. 29th 1806.
Lewis trithat

Academy of Natural Sciences
Rhamnus purshiana DC.
Det: Erica Armstrong   Date: 23 May 1994

ANSPHILA

69a. *Frangula purshiana* (DC.) Cooper, cascara

Rhamnus ovalifolius.

Academy of Natural Sciences
Rhamnus purshiana DC.
Det: Erica Armstrong   Date: 17 May 1994

ANSPHILA

HERBARIUM OF
ACADEMY OF NATURAL SCIENCES, PHILADELPHIA.

Rhamnus Purshiana DC.

69b. *Frangula purshiana* (DC.) Cooper, cascara

In moist & wet places
On the Squamash flats.
Jun: 14th 1806.

Frasera thyrsiflora, Hook.
(Swertia fastigiata, Pursh)

TYPE COLLECTION

AMERICAN PHILOSOPHICAL SOCIETY.
LEWIS & CLARK, HERBARIUM.
FROM THE ATLANTIC TO THE PACIFIC.

Academy of Natural Sciences
Frasera fastigata (Pursh) Heller
Det: Erica Armstrong   Date: 18 May 1994

Frasera thyrsiflora Hook.
Swertia fastigiata Pursh

Locality,

ANS PHILA

No.   Date

70. *Frasera fastigiata* (Pursh) Heller, clustered frasera

Academy of Natural Sciences
Fritillaria lanceolata Pursh
Det: Erica Armstrong   Date: 17 May 1994

Pursh states "On the headwaters of the Missouri
and Columbia. M.Lewis   July (Fl.Am.Sept.1:230
1814)Brant Is not at headwaters. Not type."
Examined in a revisionary study of *Fritillaria* L. (Liliaceae) at the University
of California, Davis.

Donald O. Santana   Dec. 1977

TYPE COLLECTION

*Fritillaria
lanceolata* Pursh

0927824

ANS PHILA

Brant island Apl. 10. 1806.
Bulb squamous, eaten by the natives,
who call it tel-lak-thil-pah.

AMERICAN PHILOSOPHICAL SOCIETY
LEWIS & CLARK, HERBARIUM.
FROM THE ATLANTIC TO THE PACIFIC.

Fritillaria lanceolata
Pursh

Locality,

No.   Date

71a. *Fritillaria lanceolata* Pursh, checker lily

Fritillaria occidentalis.
Brand islans. *April. 10. 1806.*
Bulb squamous, eaten by the natives,
who call it tel-lak-thlt-pah.
Lewis & Clark.

Purshs specimen!

TYPE COLLECTION

Pursh Fl. Am. Sept. i.; 220

ANS PHILA

Academy of Natural Sciences
Fritillaria lanceolata Pursh
Det: Erica Armstrong Date: 23 May 1994

HERBARIUM OF
ACADEMY OF NATURAL SCIENCES, PHILADELPHIA.

Fritillaria lanceolata
Pursh.

71b. *Fritillaria lanceolata* Pursh, checker lily

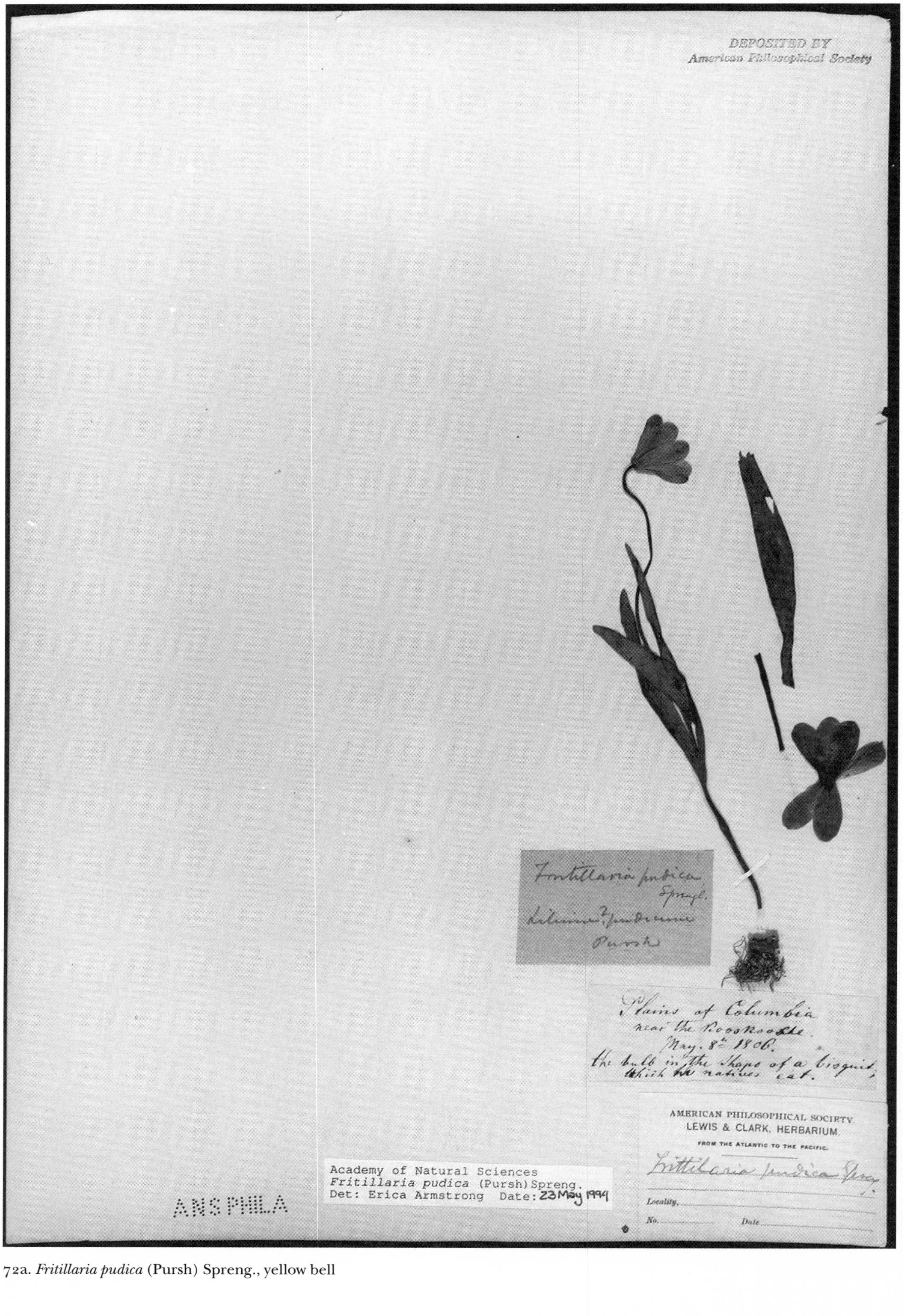

Frittillaria pudica
Sprengl.
Lilium? pudicum
Pursh

Plains of Columbia
near the Rooshooshe.
May. 8th 1806.
the bulb in the shape of a bisquit,
which the natives eat.

Academy of Natural Sciences
Fritillaria pudica (Pursh)Spreng.
Det: Erica Armstrong   Date: 23 May 1994

ANSPHILA

72a. *Fritillaria pudica* (Pursh) Spreng., yellow bell

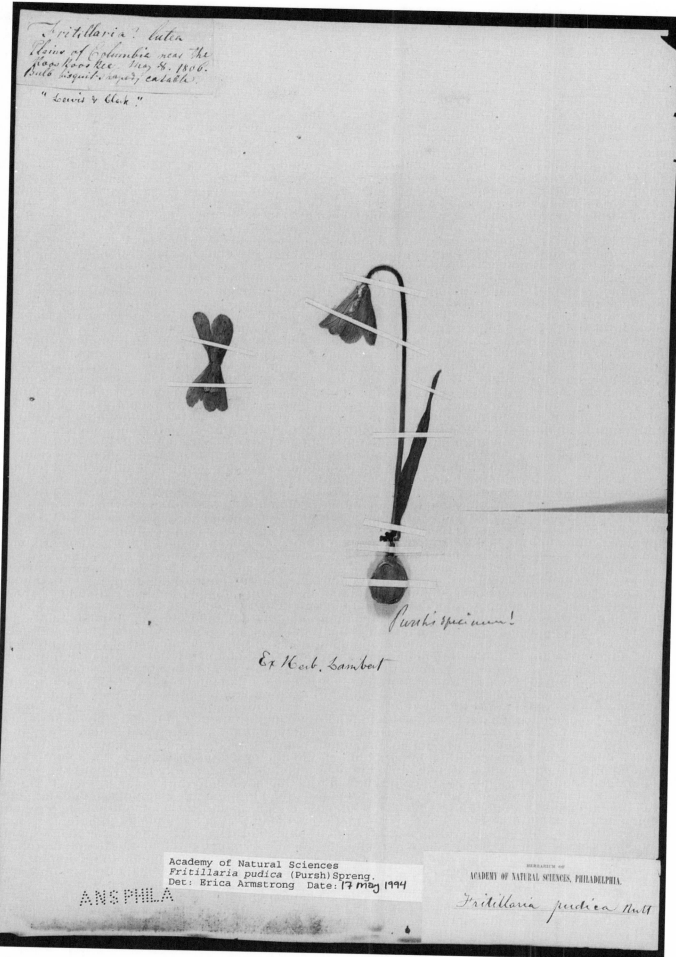

Academy of Natural Sciences
Fritillaria pudica (Pursh) Spreng.
Det: Erica Armstrong   Date: 17 May 1994

HERBARIUM OF
ACADEMY OF NATURAL SCIENCES, PHILADELPHIA.

72b. *Fritillaria pudica* (Pursh) Spreng., yellow bell

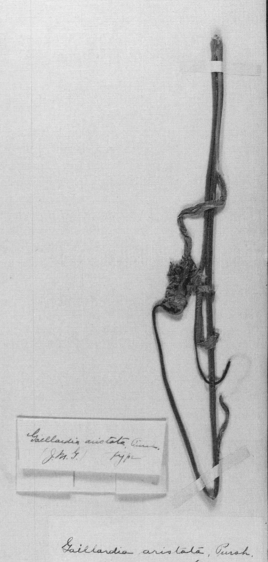

Gaillardia aristata, Pursh.
(J.M.G.)   Type

Academy of Natural Sciences
Gaillardia aristata Pursh
Det: Erica Armstrong   Date: 18 may 1994

Gaillardia aristata, Pursh.
(J.M.G.)   Type

"Lewis & Clark's Pass of the
Continental Divide, near head
of Big Blackfoot River, in
Deer Lodge Co., Montana." (Coues,
Proc. Phila. Acad. 1898: 305-306.)

Rocky mountains
Dry hills.
July 7th 1806.

Copy of Lewis.

TYPE. Gaillardia ("Galardia")
aristata Pursh, Fl. Am. Sept. 2:
573. 1814.   LHShinners 1/4/1946

AMERICAN PHILOSOPHICAL SOCIETY.
LEWIS & CLARK, HERBARIUM.
FROM THE ATLANTIC TO THE PACIFIC.

Gaillardia aristata Pursh

Locality,
No.   Date

ANS PHILA

73. *Gaillardia aristata* Pursh, blanket flower

Gaultheria
Shallon
Pursh

I.M.

The Shallon; Supposed To
be a Species of Vaccinium.
Pursh
On the Coast of the
Pacific Ocean.
Jan: 20th 1806
Lewis

Academy of Natural Sciences
Gaultheria shallon Pursh
Det: Erica Armstrong   Date: 18 May 1994

ANS PHILA

74. *Gaultheria shallon* Pursh, salal

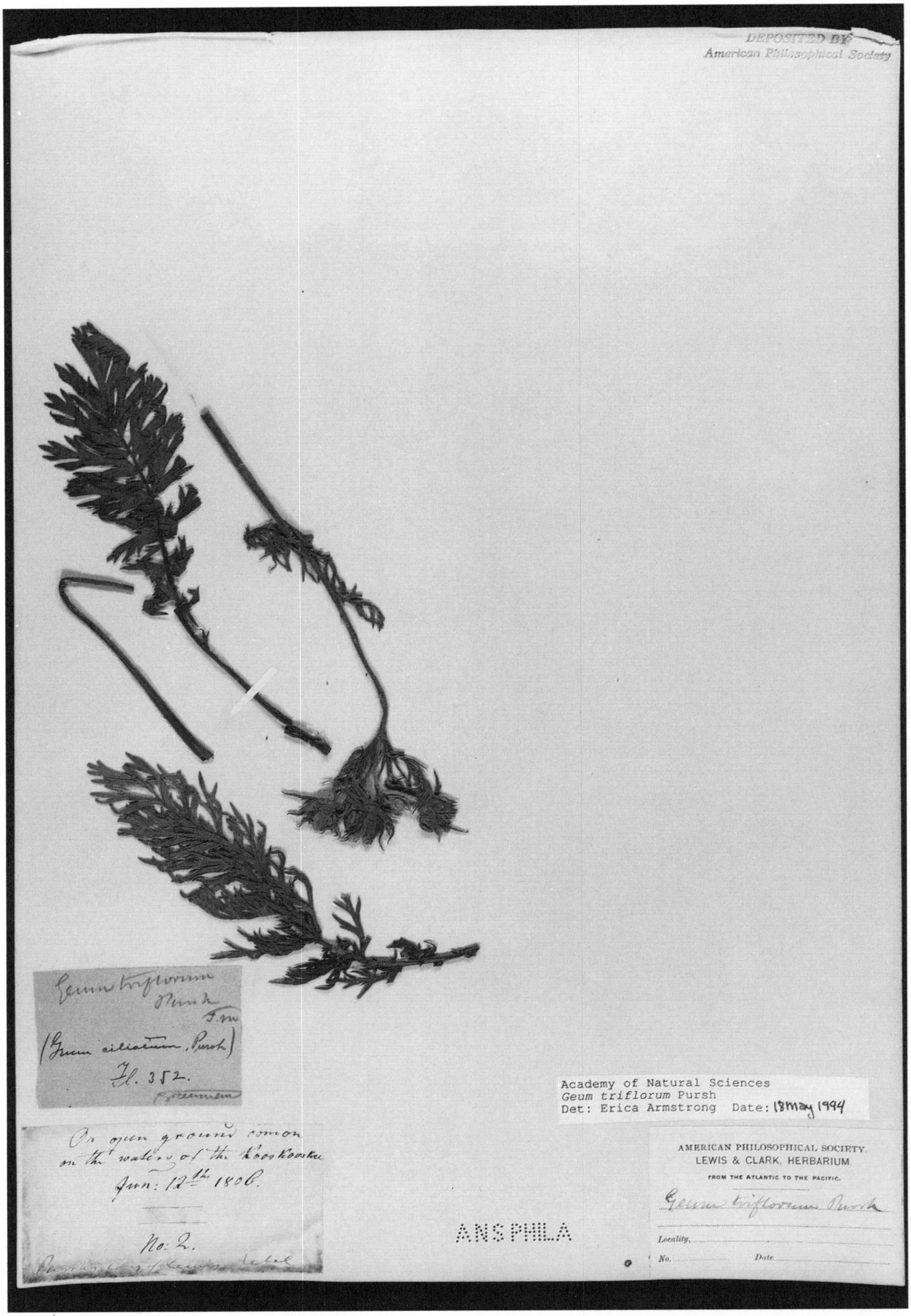

Geun triflorum
Pursh
S.m
(Geum ciliatum, Pursh)
Fl. 352.
Frremem

On open ground common
on the waters of the Kooskooskee
Jun: 12th 1806.

No: 2.

Academy of Natural Sciences
Geum triflorum Pursh
Det: Erica Armstrong   Date: 18 May 1994

ANS PHILA

AMERICAN PHILOSOPHICAL SOCIETY.
LEWIS & CLARK, HERBARIUM.
FROM THE ATLANTIC TO THE PACIFIC.

Geum triflorum Pursh

Locality,
No.   Date

75. *Geum triflorum* Pursh, old man's whiskers

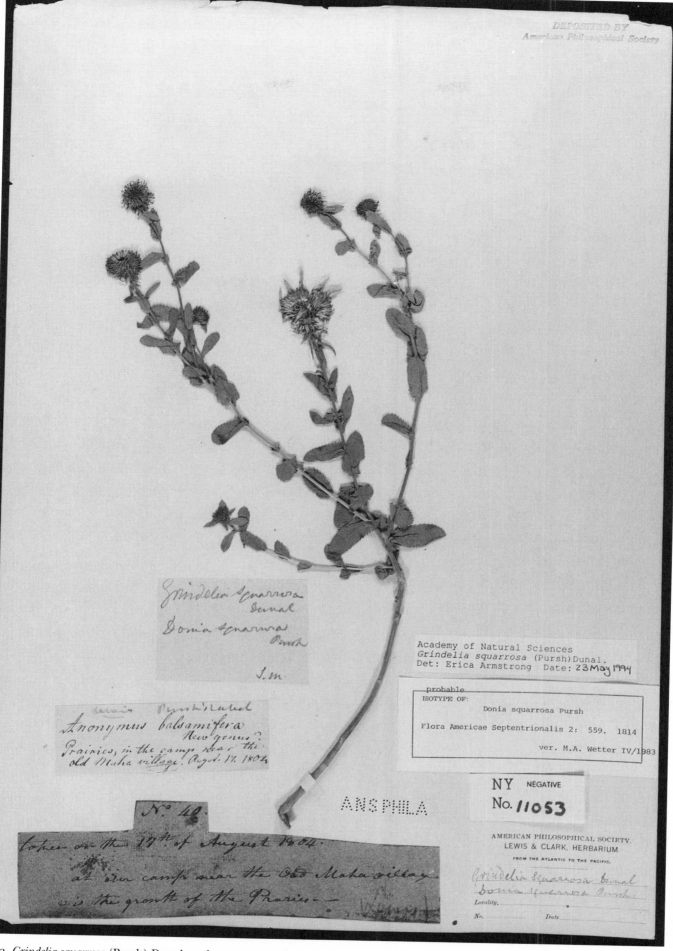

Grindelia squarrosa
Dunal
Donia squarrosa
Pursh

S. m.

Anonymus balsamifera
New genus?
Prairies, in the camp near the
old Maha village. August 17. 1804

Academy of Natural Sciences
Grindelia squarrosa (Pursh)Dunal.
Det: Erica Armstrong   Date: 23May 1994

probable
ISOTYPE OF:
Donia squarrosa Pursh

Flora Americae Septentrionalis 2: 559. 1814

ver. M.A. Wetter IV/1983

No. 40

taken on the 27th of August 1804.

at our camp near the Old Maha village
is the growth of the Prairies —

ANS PHILA

NY   NEGATIVE
No. 11053

AMERICAN PHILOSOPHICAL SOCIETY.
LEWIS & CLARK, HERBARIUM.
FROM THE ATLANTIC TO THE PACIFIC.

Grindelia squarrosa Dunal
Donia squarrosa Pursh

Locality.

No.   Date

76a. *Grindelia squarrosa* (Pursh) Dunal, curly-top gumweed

Anonymus balsamifera
Prairies; in the camp near the
old Maha village Augt. 17. 1804

Academy of Natural Sciences
Grindelia squarrosa (Pursh) Dunal.
Det: Erica Armstrong Date: 17 May 1994

written
below

NO.

Grindelia squarrosa (Pursh) Dunal

DETERMINATION BY *J. A. Steyermark* 3/19/33

probable
ISOTYPE OF: Donia squarrosa Pursh
Flora Americae Septentrionalis 2: 559. 1814.
ver. M. A. Wetter IV/1983

N America Lewis & Clark.

HERBARIUM OF
ACADEMY OF NATURAL SCIENCES. PHILADELPHIA.

Grindelia squarrosa Dunal.

(Donia Pursh.)

Pursh.

ANSPHILA

76b. *Grindelia squarrosa* (Pursh) Dunal, curly-top gumweed

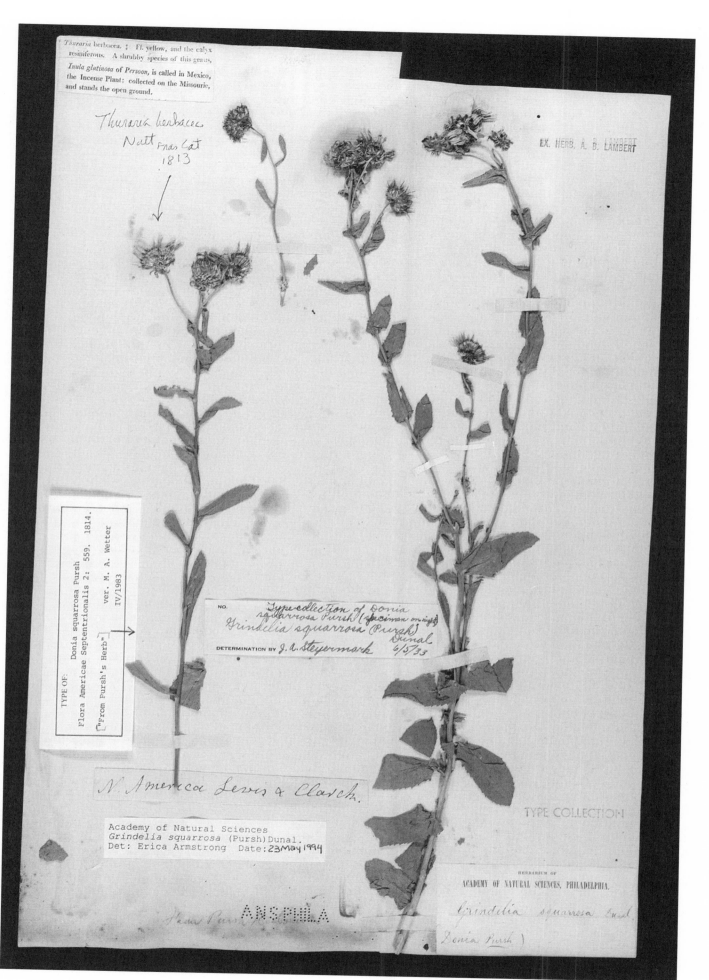

76c. *Grindelia squarrosa* (Pursh) Dunal, curly-top gumweed

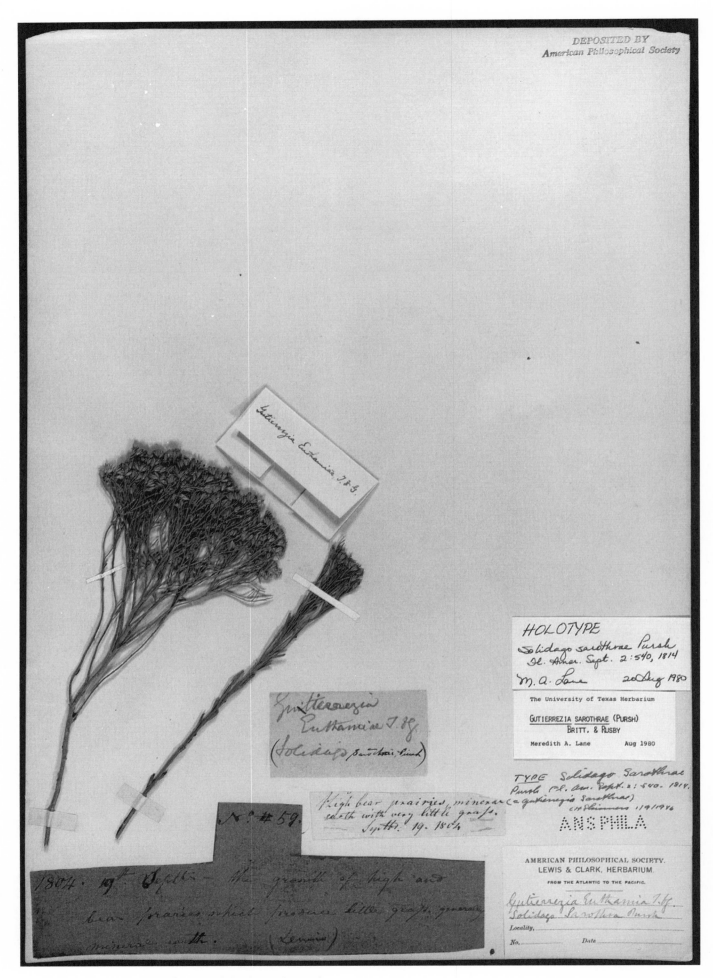

Gutierrezia Euthamiae T.&G.

*Gutierrezia
Euthamiae T.&G.
(Solidago sarothrae Pursh)*

HOLOTYPE
Solidago sarothrae Pursh
Fl. Amer. Sept. 2:540, 1814
M. A. Lane   20 Aug 1980

The University of Texas Herbarium

GUTIERREZIA SAROTHRAE (PURSH)
BRITT. & RUSBY

Meredith A. Lane   Aug 1980

*High bear prairies, mineral
earth with very little grass.
Sept. 19. 1804.*

TYPE Solidago Sarothrae
Pursh Fl. Am. Sept. 2: 540. 1814.
(= gutierrezia Sarothrae)
C.H. Shinners 11/4/1946

ANSPHILA

AMERICAN PHILOSOPHICAL SOCIETY.
LEWIS & CLARK, HERBARIUM.
FROM THE ATLANTIC TO THE PACIFIC.

*Gutierrezia Euthamia T.&g.
Solidago Sarothra Pursh*

Locality,
No.   Date

No. #59.

*1804. 19th Septr — the growth of high and
bear prairies which produce little grass, generally
mineral earth. (Lewis)*

77a. *Gutierrezia sarothrae* (Pursh) Britt. & Rusby, snakeweed

Sarothrae:

Solidago tenuifolia.

High bear prairies with little grass Sept: 19. 1804

F. Pursh scripsit!

J. Swan

Herb. Pursh propr.

Solidago sarothrae (Pursh) Britton Rusby

+ A. B. Lambert scripsit and also verso.

77b. *Gutierrezia sarothrae* (Pursh) Britt. & Rusby, snakeweed

Spiraea discolor
Pursh

Holodiscus discolor (Pursh) Maxim.
AE Schuyler 1996

A shrub growing much in the
manner of Nine bark
On the waters of RoosRooskee
May 29th 1806.

ANS PHILA

78a. *Holodiscus discolor* (Pursh) Maxim., creambush ocean-spray

Holodiscus dumosus (Hook.) Heller
AE Schuyler 1996

Spiraea betulifolia discolor
Kooskooskee. May 29, 1806.

L. Lambert

Holodiscus discolor (Pursh) Maxim.
AE Schuyler 1996

ANS PHILA

78b. *Holodiscus discolor* (Pursh) Maxim., creambush ocean-spray

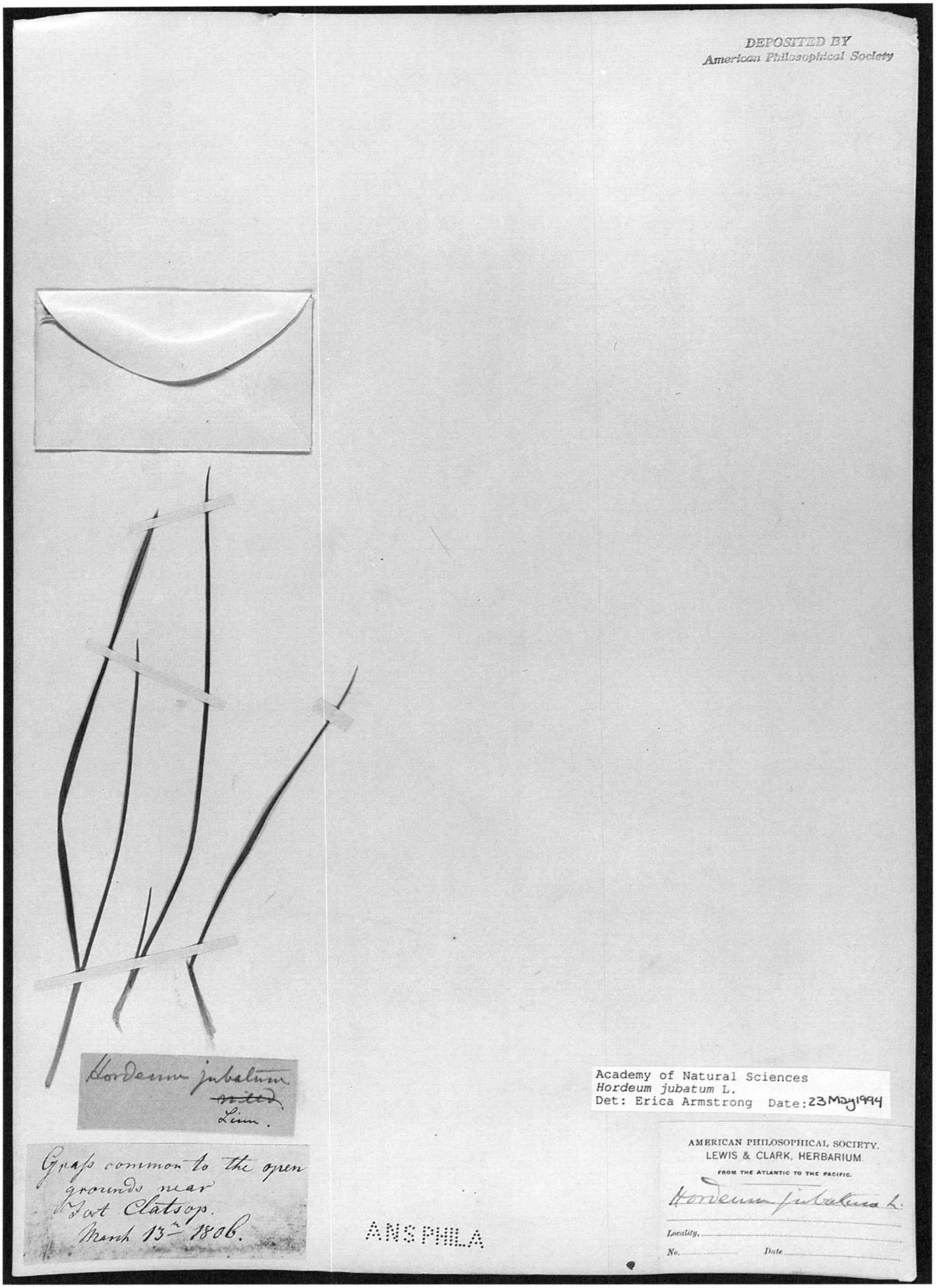

DEPOSITED BY
American Philosophical Society
Hordeum jubatum
~~mited~~
Linn.
Grass common to the open
grounds near
Fort Clatsop.
March 13th 1806.
ANS PHILA
Academy of Natural Sciences
Hordeum jubatum L.
Det: Erica Armstrong Date: 23 May 1994
AMERICAN PHILOSOPHICAL SOCIETY.
LEWIS & CLARK, HERBARIUM.
FROM THE ATLANTIC TO THE PACIFIC.
Hordeum jubatum L.
Locality,
No.
Date

79a. *Hordeum jubatum* L., foxtail barley

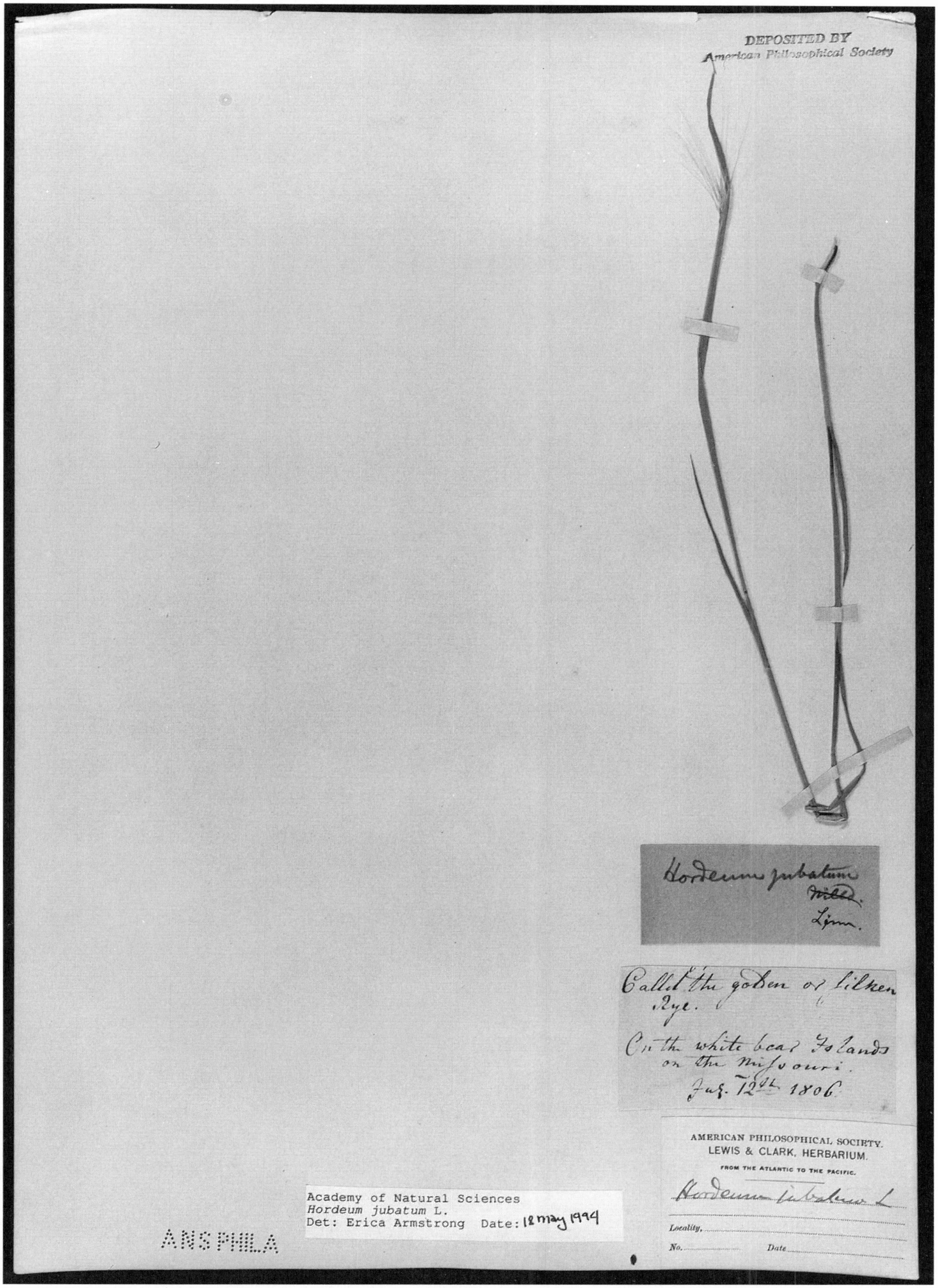

Hordeum jubatum
Willd.
Linn.

Called the golden or silken Rye.

On the white bear Islands on the Missouri.
Aug. 12th 1806.

Academy of Natural Sciences
Hordeum jubatum L.
Det: Erica Armstrong   Date: 18 May 1994

ANS PHILA

79b. *Hordeum jubatum* L., foxtail barley

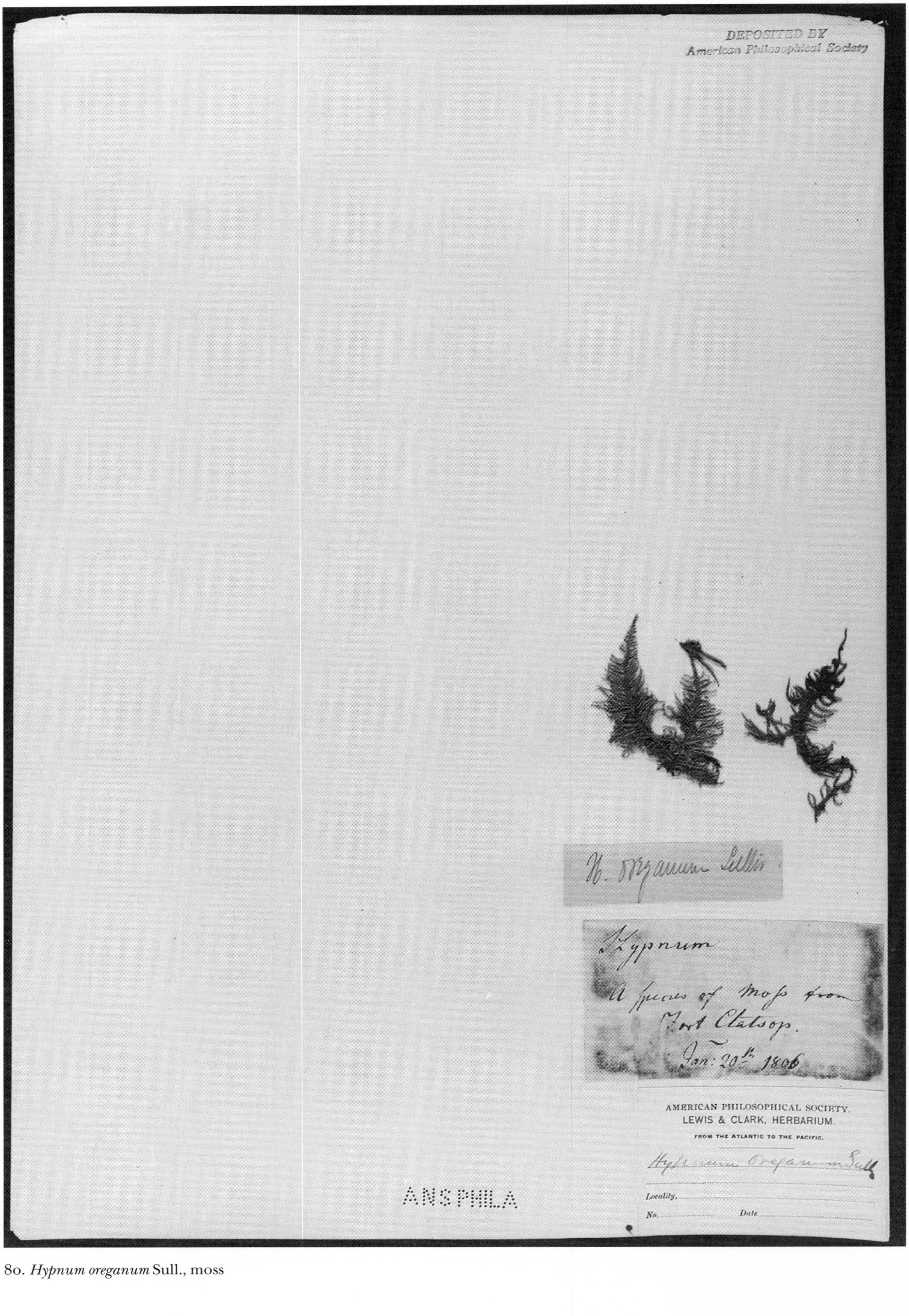

H. *oreganum* Sulliv.

Hypnum

A species of Moss from
Fort Clatsop.
Jan: 20th 1806

AMERICAN PHILOSOPHICAL SOCIETY,
LEWIS & CLARK, HERBARIUM.
FROM THE ATLANTIC TO THE PACIFIC.

Hypnum oreganum Sull.

Locality,
No.   Date

ANS PHILA

80. *Hypnum oreganum* Sull., moss

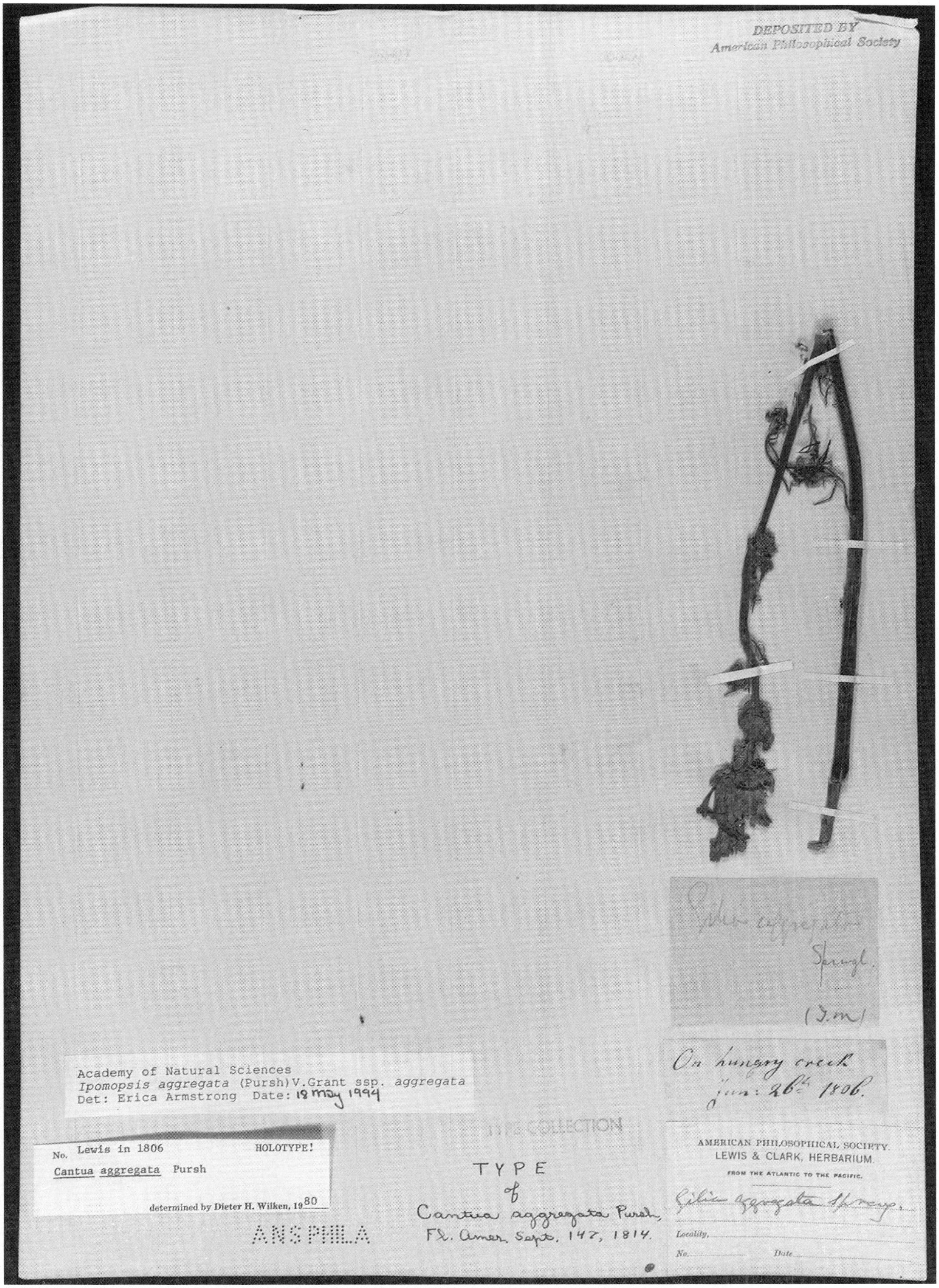

Academy of Natural Sciences
Ipomopsis aggregata (Pursh)V.Grant ssp. *aggregata*
Det: Erica Armstrong   Date: 18 May 1994

No. Lewis in 1806   HOLOTYPE!

Cantua aggregata Pursh

determined by Dieter H. Wilken, 1980

ANS PHILA

TYPE COLLECTION

TYPE
of
Cantua aggregata Pursh,
Fl. Amer. Sept. 147, 1814.

Gilia aggregata
Sprngl.
(J.m)

On hungry creek
Jun: 26th 1806.

AMERICAN PHILOSOPHICAL SOCIETY.
LEWIS & CLARK, HERBARIUM.
FROM THE ATLANTIC TO THE PACIFIC.

Gilia aggregata Sprnys.

Locality,

No.   Date

· 81. *Ipomopsis aggregata* (Pursh) V. Grant ssp. *aggregata*, scarlet gilia

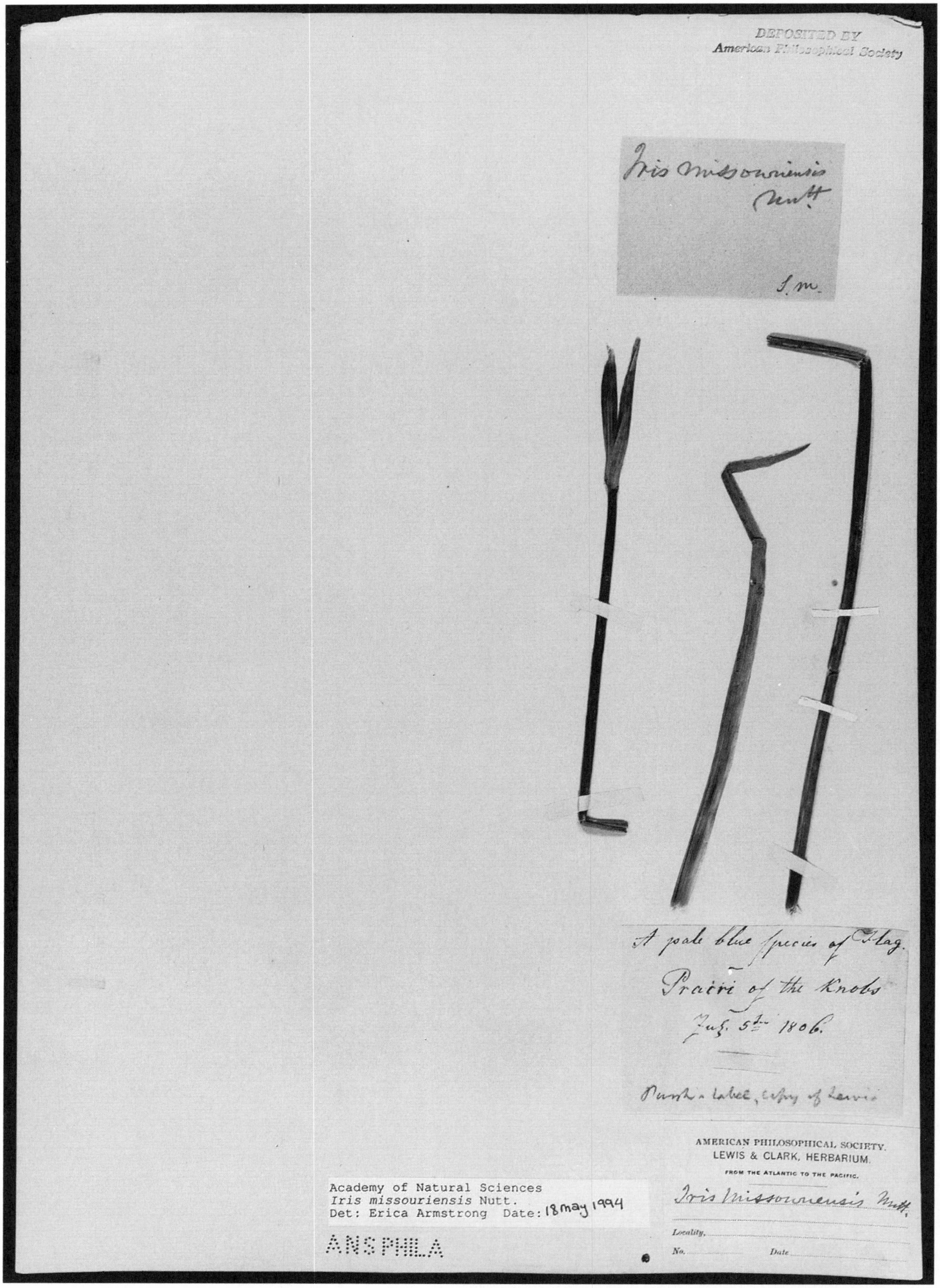

Iris missouriensis
Nutt.

S. m.

A pale blue species of Flag.
Prairi of the Knobs
Aug. 5th 1806.

Pursh's label, copy of Lewis

Academy of Natural Sciences
Iris missouriensis Nutt.
Det: Erica Armstrong   Date: 18 May 1994

ANSPHILA

82. *Iris missouriensis* Nutt., western blue flag

Common to the bluffs.
Octbr: 17. 1804.

Pursh's copy

a species of Juniper common to the

bluffs   October

Juniperus Communis

AMERICAN PHILOSOPHICAL SOCIETY.
LEWIS & CLARK, HERBARIUM.
FROM THE ATLANTIC TO THE PACIFIC.

Juniperus Communis L.

Locality,
No.   Date

Academy of Natural Sciences
Juniperus communis L.
Det: Erica Armstrong   Date: 23 May 1994

83a. *Juniperus communis* L. var. *depressa* Pursh, common juniper

ANS PHILA

83b. *Juniperus communis* L. var. *depressa* Pursh, common juniper

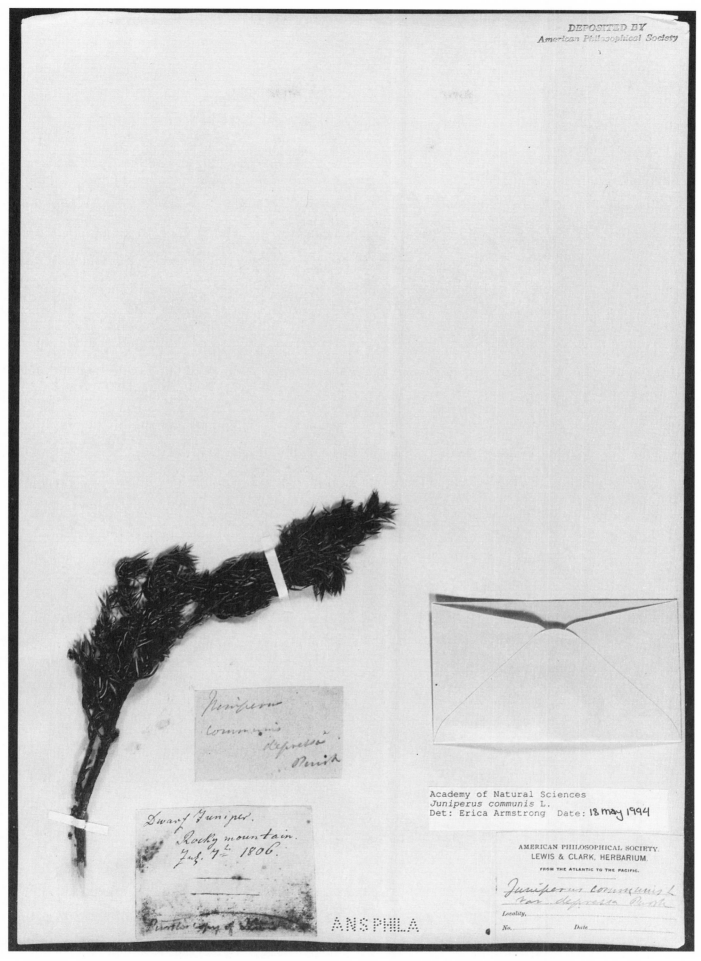

*Juniperus
communis
depressa
Pursh*

Academy of Natural Sciences
Juniperus communis L.
Det: Erica Armstrong Date: 18 May 1994

Dwarf Juniper.
Rocky mountain.
Jul. 7th 1806.

AMERICAN PHILOSOPHICAL SOCIETY.
LEWIS & CLARK, HERBARIUM.
FROM THE ATLANTIC TO THE PACIFIC.

*Juniperus communis L.
var. depressa Pursh*

Locality,

No.   Date

ANSPHILA

83c. *Juniperus communis* L. var. *depressa* Pursh, common juniper

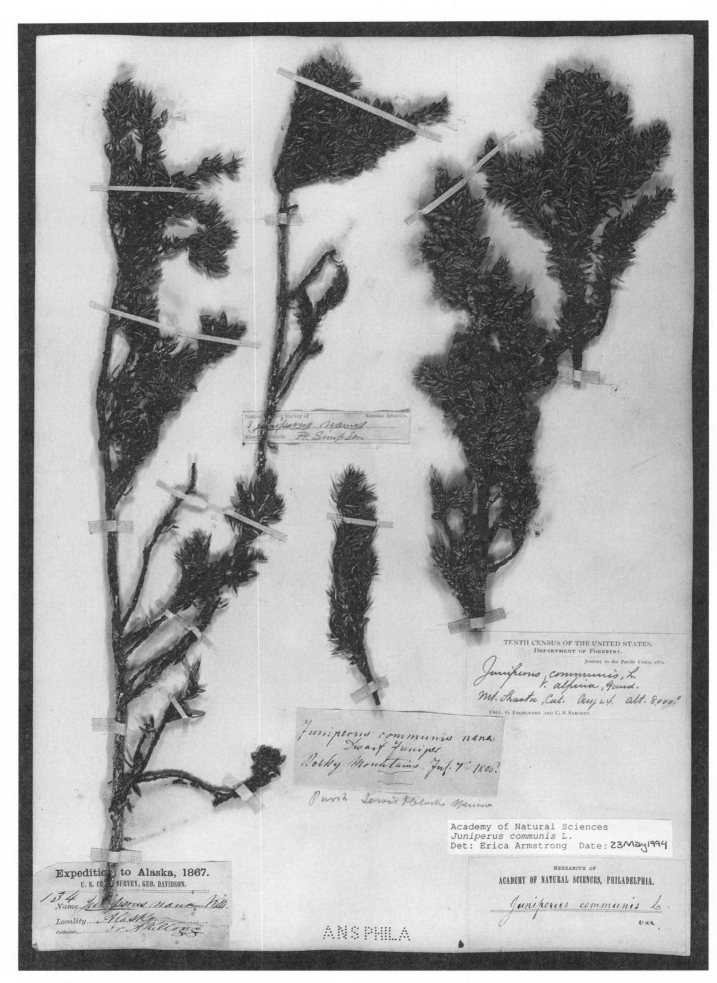

83d. *Juniperus communis* L. var. *depressa* Pursh, common juniper

Juniperus Sabina,
Procumbens Pursh

Dwarf Cedar, never more than
6 inches high, open prairies.
Oct: 16. 1804.

Academy of Natural Sciences
Juniperus horizontalis Moench.
Det: Erica Armstrong   Date: 17 May 1994

ANS PHILA

84a. *Juniperus horizontalis* Moench, creeping juniper

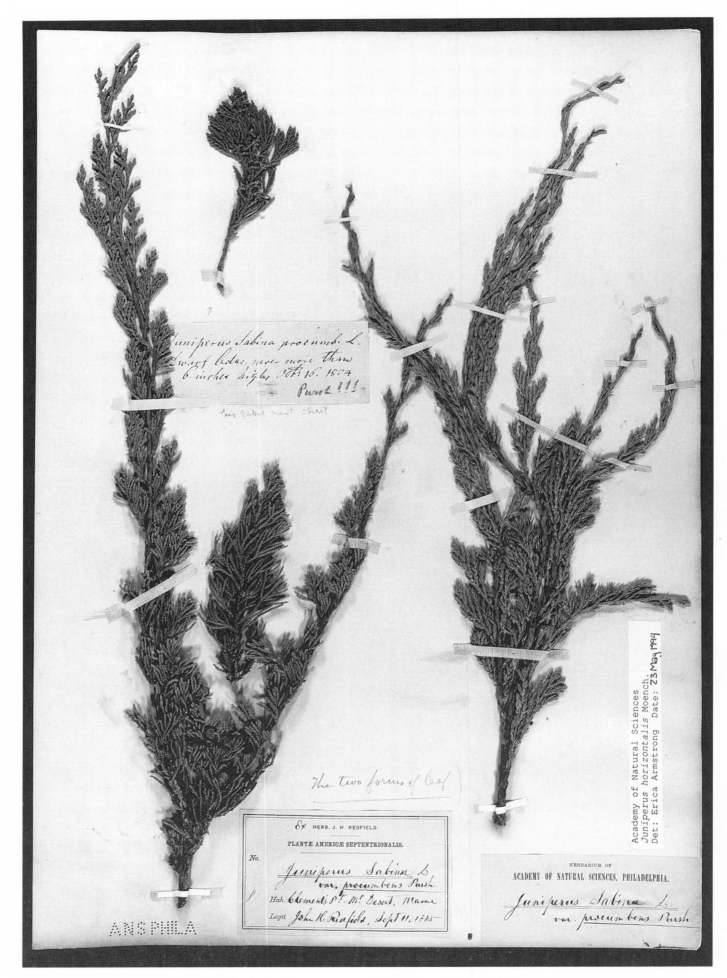

Juniperus Sabina procumb. L.
Dwarf Cedar; never more than
6 inches high; Octr 16. 1804.
Pursh !!!

The two forms of leaf

84b. *Juniperus horizontalis* Moench, creeping juniper

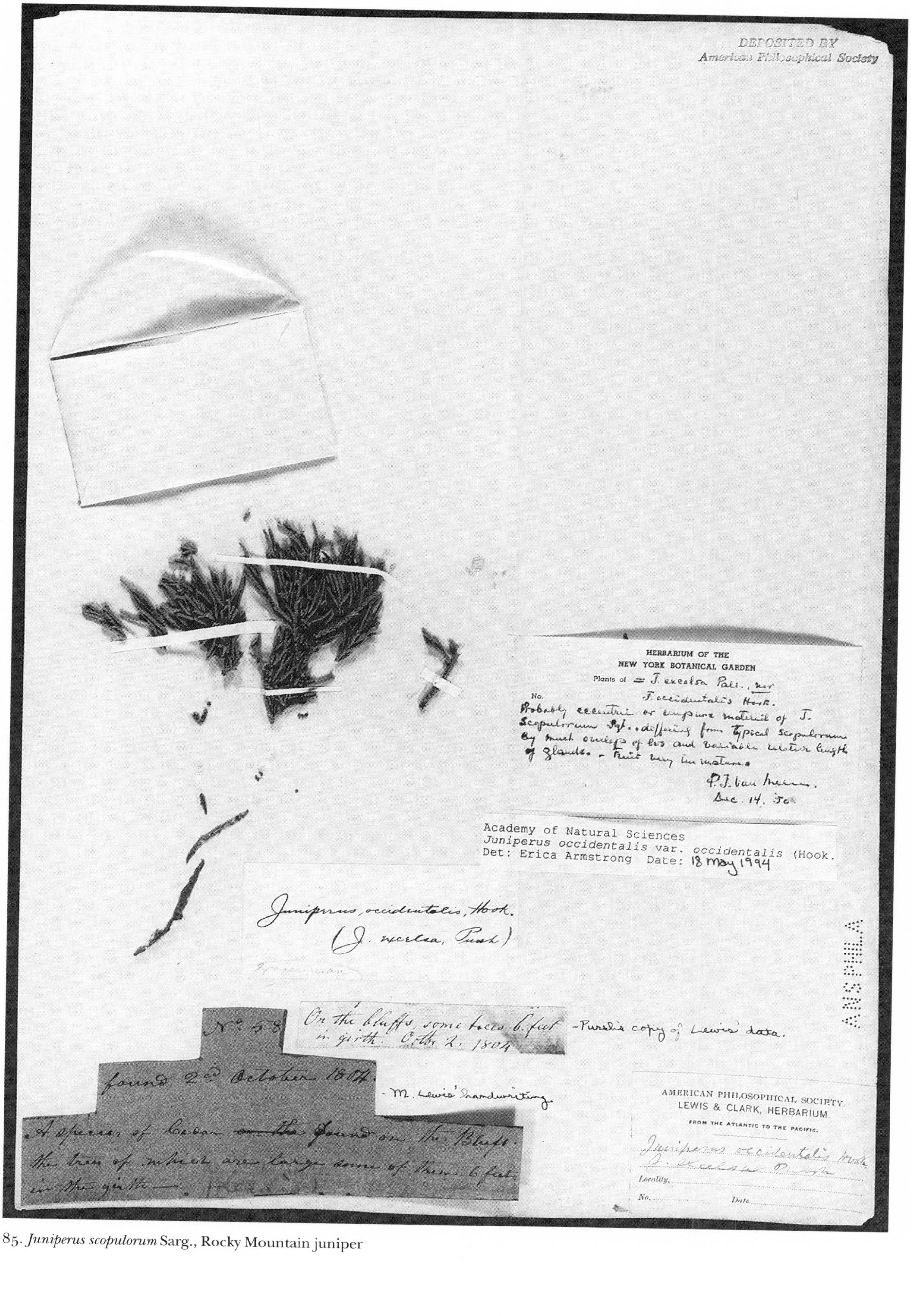

DEPOSITED BY
American Philosophical Society
HERBARIUM OF THE
NEW YORK BOTANICAL GARDEN
Plants of = J. excelsa Pall., nor
No.
J. occidentalis Hook.
Probably eccentric or impure material of J. scopulorum Sarg. differing from typical scopulorum by much overlap of lvs and variable relative length of glands. – Fruit very immature.
P. J. van Melle.
Dec. 14. 50
Academy of Natural Sciences
Juniperus occidentalis var. occidentalis (Hook.
Det: Erica Armstrong Date: 18 May 1994
Juniperus, occidentalis, Hook.
(J. excelsa, Pursh)
No. 58
On the bluffs, some trees 6. feet in girth. Octbr 2. 1804
– Pursh's copy of Lewis' data.
found 2nd October 1804
– M. Lewis' handwriting
A species of Cedar on the found on the Bluffs. the trees of which are large some of them 6 feet in the girth —
AMERICAN PHILOSOPHICAL SOCIETY.
LEWIS & CLARK, HERBARIUM.
FROM THE ATLANTIC TO THE PACIFIC.
Juniperus occidentalis Hook
J. excelsa Pursh
Locality,
No.
Date
ANSPHILA

85. *Juniperus scopulorum* Sarg., Rocky Mountain juniper

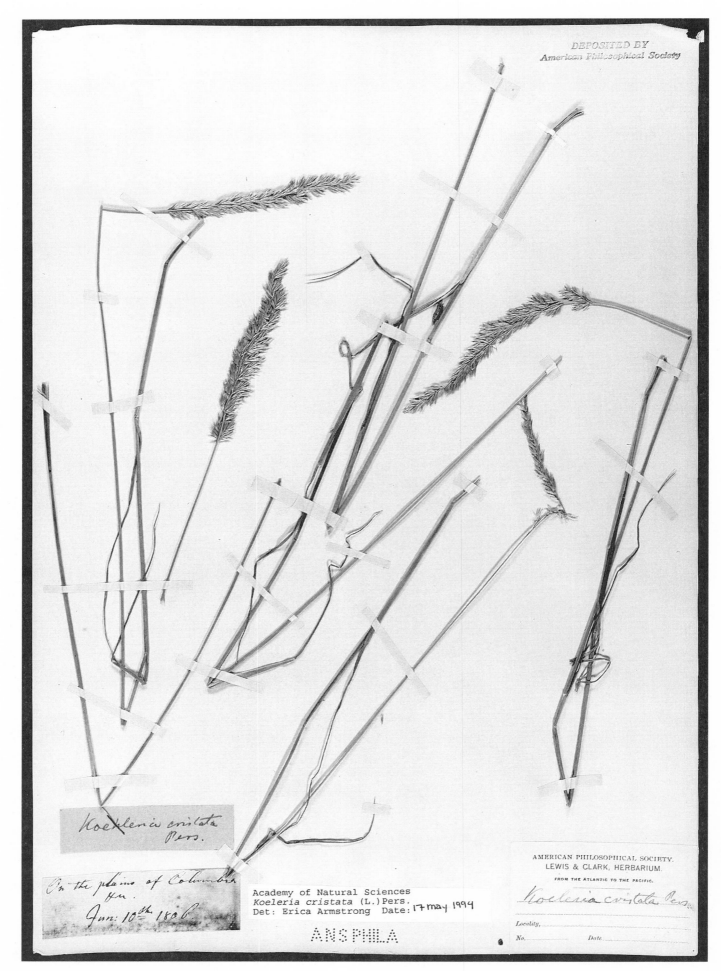

Koeleria cristata
Pers.

On the plains of Columbia
&c.
Jun: 10th 1806

Academy of Natural Sciences
Koeleria cristata (L.) Pers.
Det: Erica Armstrong   Date: 17 may 1994

ANSPHILA

AMERICAN PHILOSOPHICAL SOCIETY.
LEWIS & CLARK, HERBARIUM.
FROM THE ATLANTIC TO THE PACIFIC.

Koeleria cristata Pers.

Locality,
No.   Date.

86. *Koeleria macrantha* (Ledeb.) J. A. Schultes, prairie Junegrass

Lewisia rediviva
Pursh

(F.m)

The Indians eat the root of this
Near Clarks R.
Aug. 1st 1806 Lewis
The Calyx consist of 6 or 7. leaves
the Corolla many petals and stami-
na many. Fig. 9. Capsula.
Pursh

Academy of Natural Sciences
Lewisia rediviva Pursh
Det: Erica Armstrong   Date: 17 May 1994

ANS PHILA

87. *Lewisia rediviva* Pursh, bitterroot

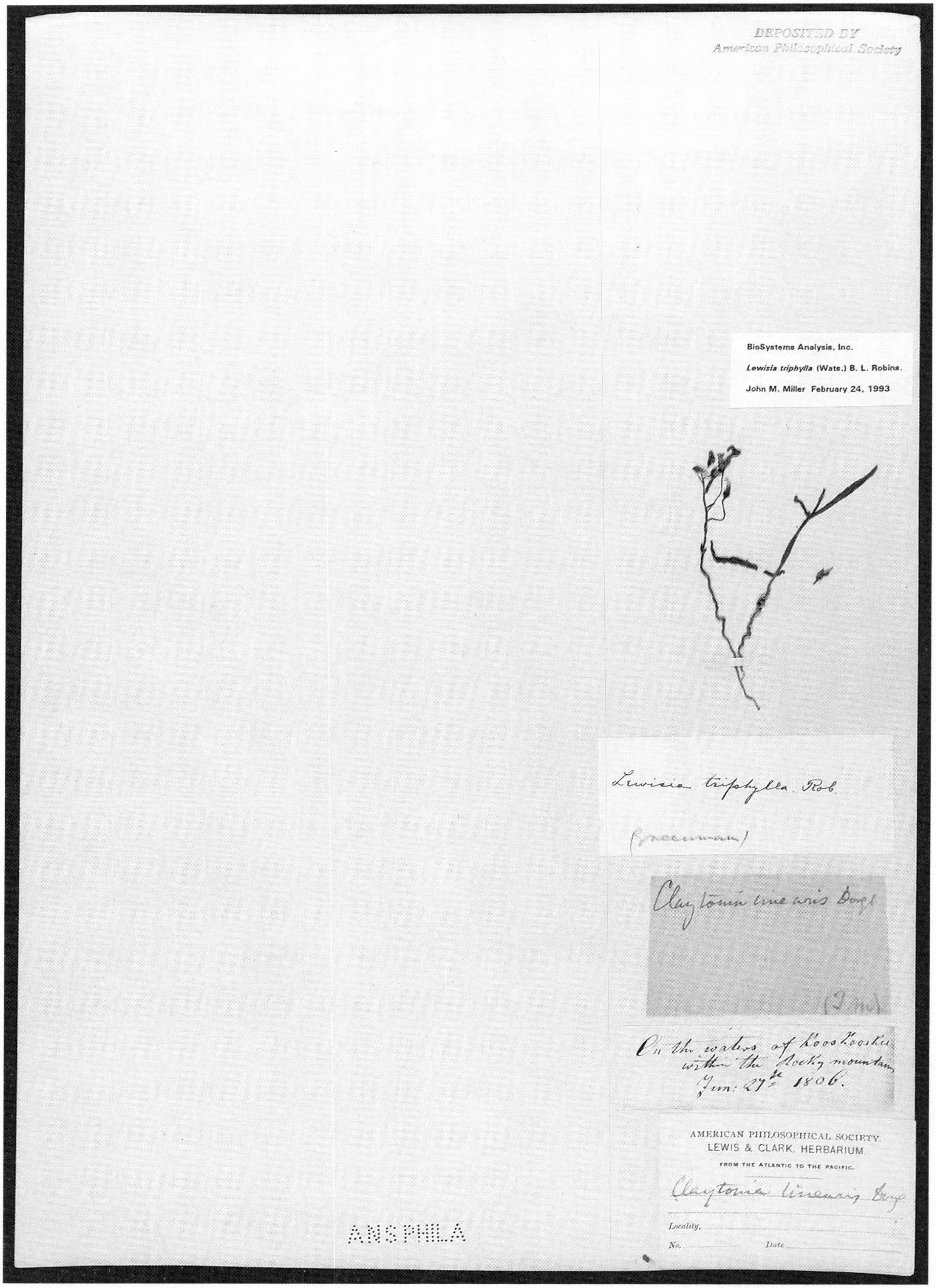

BioSystems Analysis, Inc.

Lewisia triphylla (Wats.) B. L. Robins.

John M. Miller February 24, 1993

Lewisia triphylla. Rob.

(Greenman)

Claytonia linearis Dougl.

(J.M.)

On the waters of KoosKooskie
within the Rocky mountains
Jun: 27th 1806.

Claytonia linearis Dougl.

Locality,
No.   Date

88. *Lewisia triphylla* (S. Wats.) B. L. Robins., threeleaved lewisia

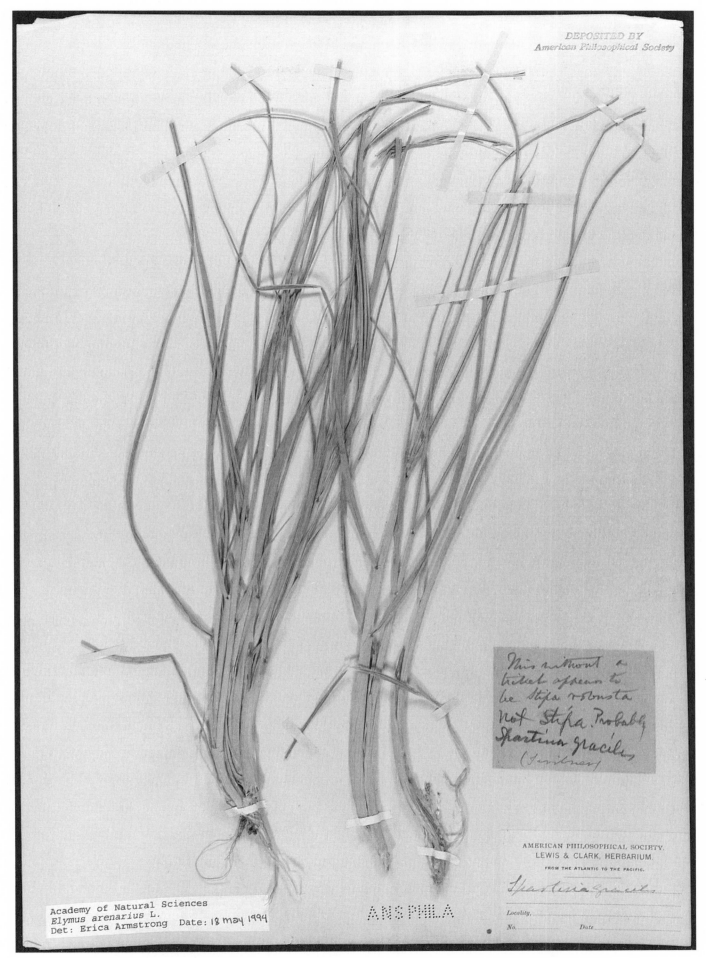

This without a
tiebel appears to
be Stipa robusta
Not Stipa. Probably
Spartina gracilis
(Scribner)

Academy of Natural Sciences
Elymus arenarius L.
Det: Erica Armstrong   Date: 18 May 1994

ANSPHILA

89. *Leymus arenarius* (L.) Hochst., dune wildrye

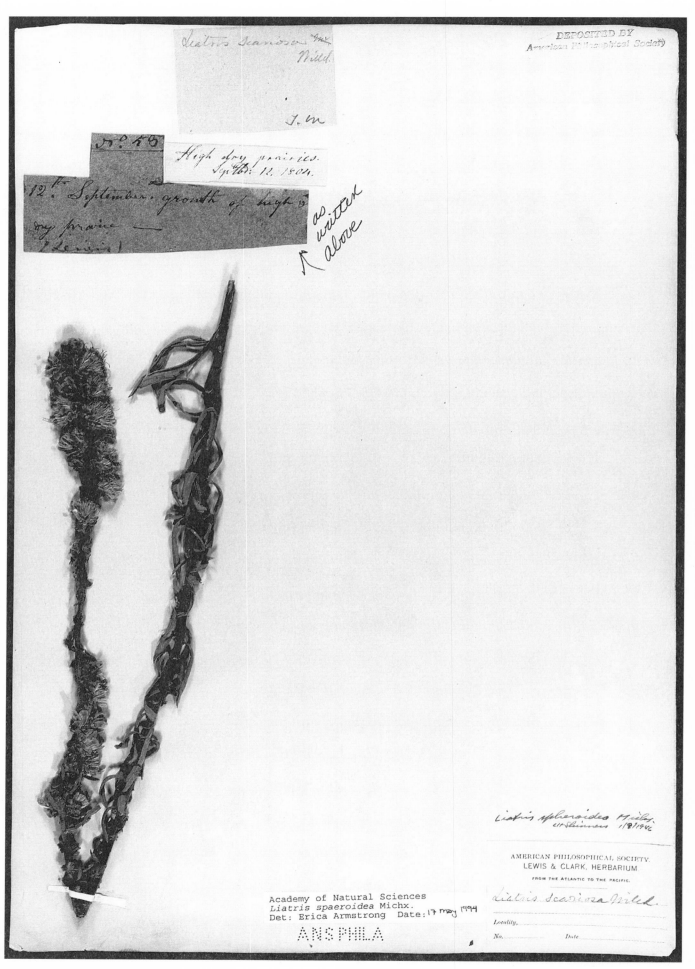

Liatris scariosa Willd.

J. M.

No. 58

High dry prairies.
Septbr. 12. 1804.

12th September. growth of high &
dry prairie —
? Lewis) —

as
written
above

Liatris sphaeroidea Michx.
Lit Shinners 1/8/1946

Liatris scariosa Willd.

Locality,

No.   Date

Academy of Natural Sciences
Liatris spaeroidea Michx.
Det: Erica Armstrong   Date: 17 may 1994

ANS PHILA

90. *Liatris aspera* Michx., gay-feather

Liatris pycnostachya. Mx.

Liatris pycnostachya Michx.

(Mx S.)

18 Nov., 1897.

Prairies, Septb. 15. 1804

N° 35

Sept. 13.th growth of the Prairies

Academy of Natural Sciences
Liatris pycnostachya Michx.
Det: Erica Armstrong   Date: 17 May 1994

ANS PHILA

91. *Liatris pycnostachya* Michx., blazing star

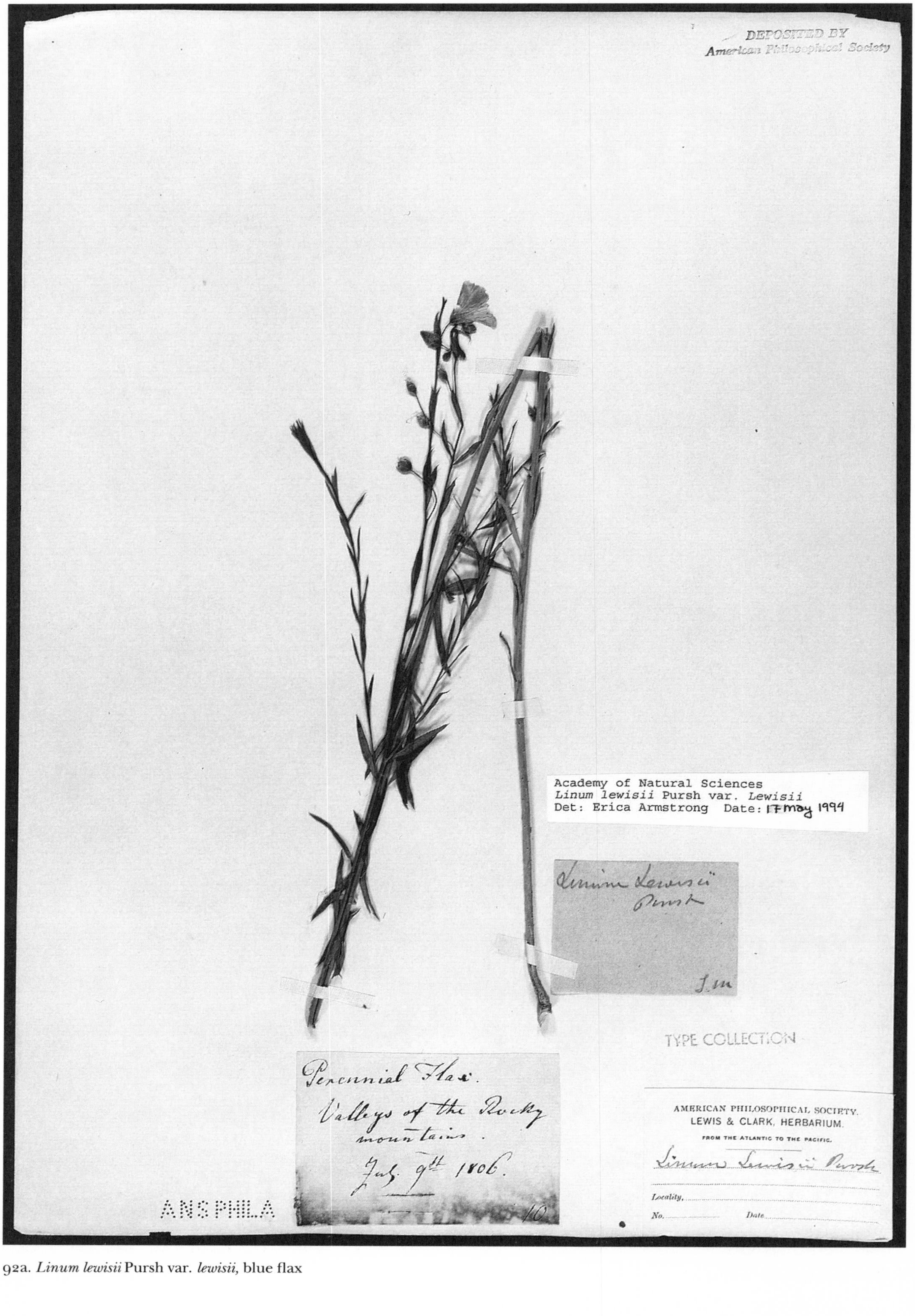

Academy of Natural Sciences
Linum lewisii Pursh var. *Lewisii*
Det: Erica Armstrong   Date: 17 May 1994

Linum Lewisii
Pursh

J. m

Perennial Flax.
Valleys of the Rocky
mountains.
July 9th 1806.

ANS PHILA

TYPE COLLECTION

AMERICAN PHILOSOPHICAL SOCIETY.
LEWIS & CLARK, HERBARIUM.
FROM THE ATLANTIC TO THE PACIFIC.

Linum Lewisii Pursh

Locality,
No.   Date

92a. *Linum lewisii* Pursh var. *lewisii*, blue flax

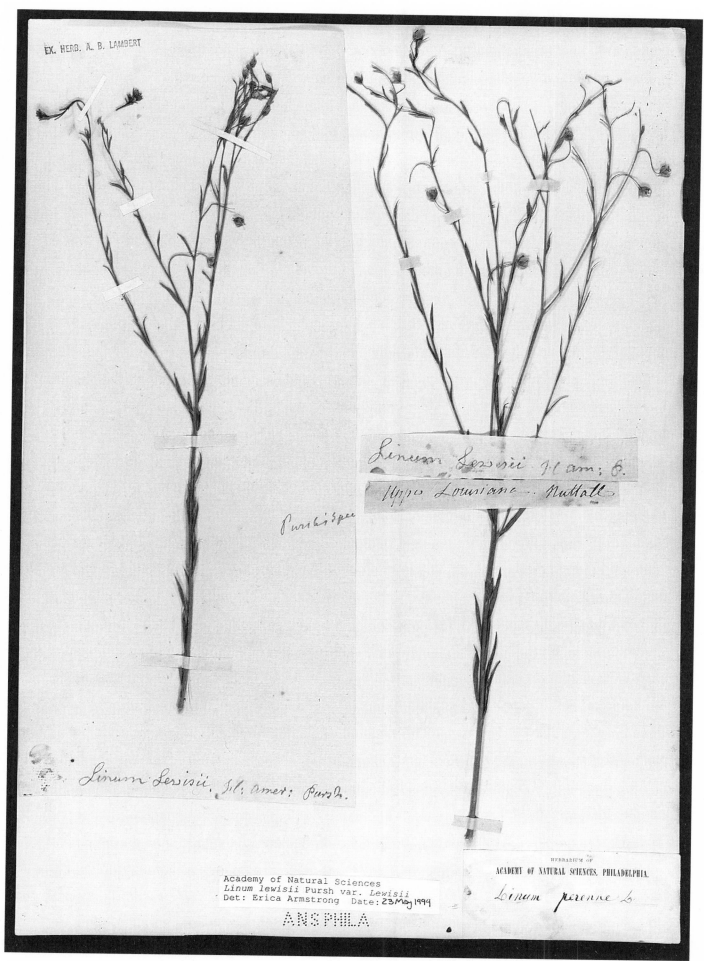

Linum Lewisii. Fl: am: ß.

Uppo Louisiana. Nuttall

Pursh: Spec

Linum Lewisii. Fl: amer: Pursh.

Academy of Natural Sciences
Linum lewisii Pursh var. *Lewisii*
Det: Erica Armstrong   Date: 23 May 1994

ANSPHILA

Linum perenne L.

92b. *Linum lewisii* Pursh var. *lewisii*, blue flax

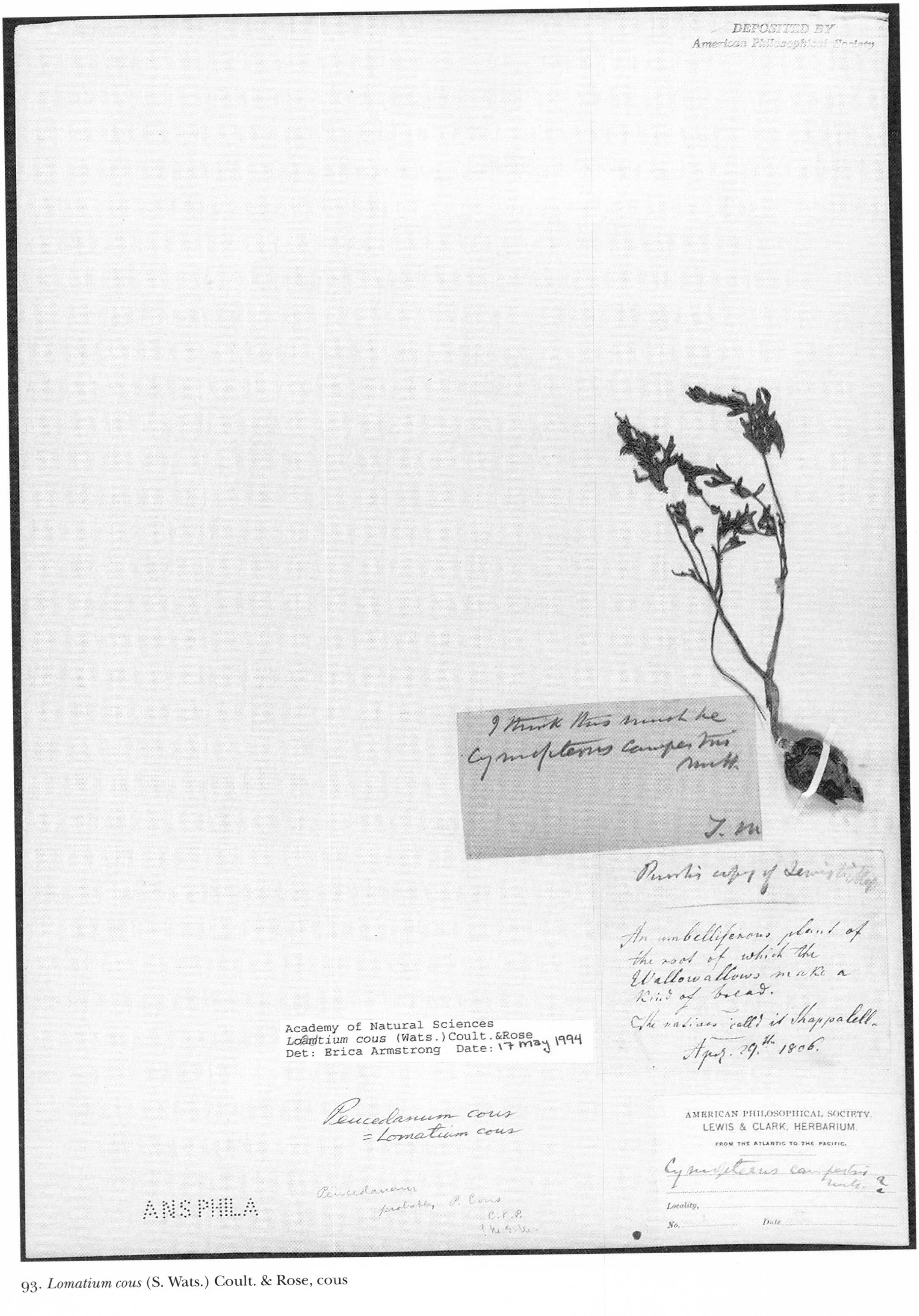

I think this much be
Cymopterus campestris
Nutt.

J. M.

Prints copy of Lewis's ?

An umbelliferous plant of
the root of which the
Wallowallows make a
kind of bread.
The natives call'd it Shappalell.
Aug. 29th 1806.

Academy of Natural Sciences
Lomatium cous (Wats.)Coult.&Rose
Det: Erica Armstrong   Date: 17 May 1994

Peucedanum cous
= Lomatium cous

AMERICAN PHILOSOPHICAL SOCIETY,
LEWIS & CLARK, HERBARIUM.
FROM THE ATLANTIC TO THE PACIFIC.

Cymopterus campestris
Nutt. ?

Locality,
No.   Date

Peucedanum
probably, P. Cous
C.V.P.

ANS PHILA

93. *Lomatium cous* (S. Wats.) Coult. & Rose, cous

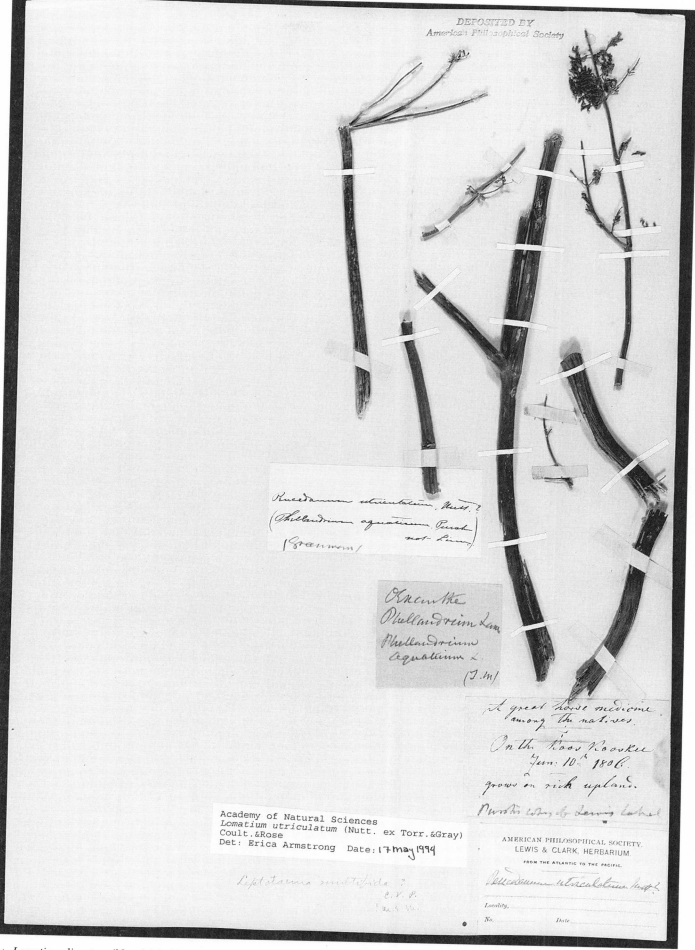

Peucedanum utriculatum, Nutt.?
(Phellandrium aquaticum. Pursh)
not Linn.)
(Granum)

Oenanthe
Phellandrium Linn
Phellandrium
aquaticum L.
(J.M)

A great horse medicine
among the natives.

On the Koos Kooskee
Jun. 10th 1806.
grows on rich upland.

Nuttis copy of Lewis label

Academy of Natural Sciences
Lomatium utriculatum (Nutt. ex Torr. &Gray)
Coult.&Rose
Det: Erica Armstrong   Date: 17 May 1994

AMERICAN PHILOSOPHICAL SOCIETY.
LEWIS & CLARK, HERBARIUM.
FROM THE ATLANTIC TO THE PACIFIC.

Peucedanum utriculatum Nutt?

Locality.
No.   Date.

Leptotaenia multifida ?
C.V.P.

94. *Lomatium dissectum* (Nutt.) Mathias & Constance, fern-leaved lomatium

Academy of Natural Sciences
Lomatium grayi (Coult.&Rose) Coult.&Rose
Det: Erica Armstrong   Date: 17 may 1994

A large fusiform root, which the
natives prepare by baking;
Near the Sepulchre rock
On the Columbia R.
Apr.ᵉ 14.ᵗʰ 1806.

This is apparently a
mixture of material
U. S. no.

ANSPHILA

O. grayi C. + R

AMERICAN PHILOSOPHICAL SOCIETY,
LEWIS & CLARK, HERBARIUM.
FROM THE ATLANTIC TO THE PACIFIC.

Umbellum   2

Locality,
No.   Date

95. *Lomatium grayi* (Coult. & Rose) Coult. & Rose, Gray's lomatium

Peucedanum leiocarpum. Nutt.
(Smyrnium nudicaule, Pursh)
(Erennon)

not Peucedanum
Nudicaule Nutt

Smyrnium
Nudicaule Pursh

(T. m)

Supposed to be a Smyrnium
the natives eat the tops &
boil it sometimes with their
soup.
On the Columbia
Apr. 15th 1806.

coquellia nudicaule
nom

Academy of Natural Sciences
Lomatium nudicaule (Pursh) Coult. & Rose
Det: Erica Armstrong   Date: 18 May 1994

ANS PHILA

96. *Lomatium nudicaule* (Pursh) Coult. & Rose, barestem lomatium

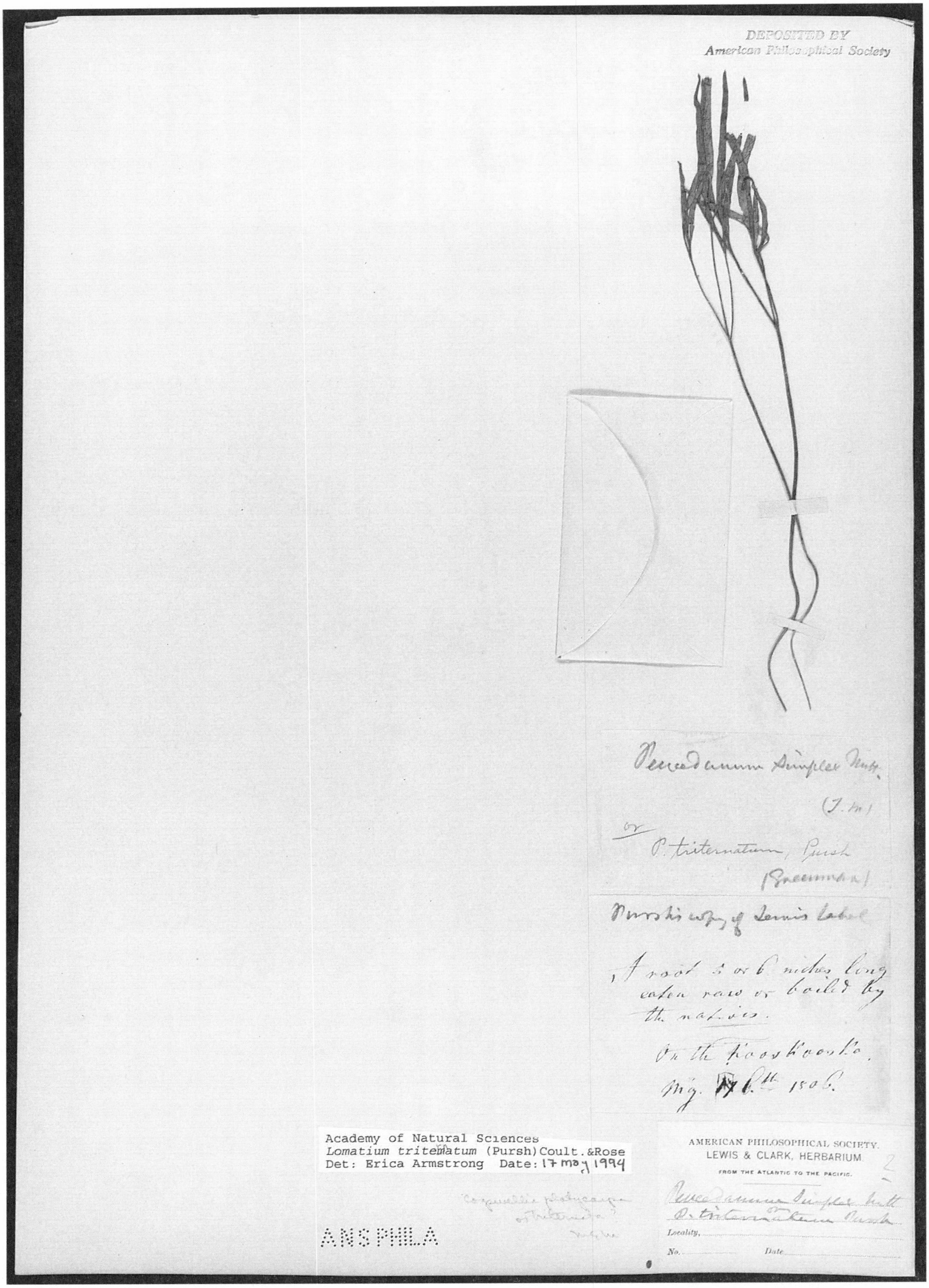

Peucedanum Simplex Nutt.

(T.M.)

or

P. triternatum, Pursh
(Greenman)

Nuttall's copy of Lewis label

A root 5 or 6 inches long
eaten raw or boiled by
the natives.

On the Kooskooske.
May 6th 1806.

Academy of Natural Sciences
Lomatium triternatum (Pursh) Coult. & Rose
Det: Erica Armstrong Date: 17 may 1994

Carpuelia podocarpa
of triternata?

ANS PHILA

97. *Lomatium triternatum* (Pursh) Coult. & Rose, nine-leaf lomatium

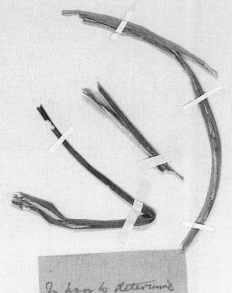

DEPOSITED BY
American Philosophical Society
All Eaten!
The root not eaten by
the natives.
On the Columbia.
Apr. 14th 1806.
To poor to determine
now.
An umbelliferos plant of
which the natives don't
eat the root.
On the Columbia
Apr. 14th 1806.
AMERICAN PHILOSOPHICAL SOCIETY.
LEWIS & CLARK, HERBARIUM.
FROM THE ATLANTIC TO THE PACIFIC.
Locality,
No.
Date

98. *Lomatium* sp.?, lomatium

To poor to determine now.

An umbelliferous plant with a large fusiform root, which the natives bake & eat on the Columbia. Aprl 15th 1806.

ANS PHILA

99. *Lomatium* sp.?, lomatium

Lonicera ciliosa. Poir.

Rocky mountain

June 16ᵗʰ 1806.

Pursh's copy

Nᵒ found on the waters of the columbia Sept. 2ⁿᵈ 1805. the growth of a moist situation seldom rises higher than 6 or 8 feet puts up a number of succulent sprouts forming a thick bush.

Lewis

Can't be L. ciliosa; perhaps ciliata was intended.

the branch is not true L. ciliata

ANSPHILA

L. ciliata ?

Academy of Natural Sciences
Lonicera ciliosa (Pursh) D.C.
Det: Erica Armstrong   Date: 17 May 1994

100a. *Lonicera ciliosa* (Pursh) Poir. *ex* DC., trumpet honeysuckle

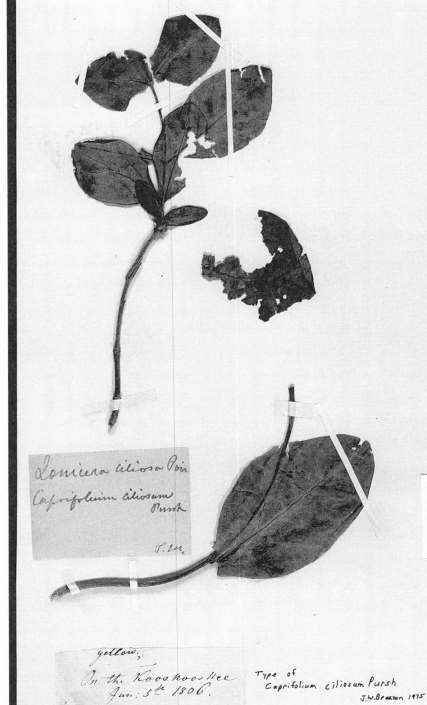

Academy of Natural Sciences
Lonicera ciliosa (Pursh)D.C.
Det: Erica Armstrong Date:23 May 1994

HOLOTYPE

Pursh, Fl. Am. Sept. 1:160.1814.

Revision of *Lonicera* subg. Caprifolium

Lonicera ciliosa (Pursh) Poiret

Charles H. Perino   August 1975
North Carolina State University

Lonicera ciliosa Poir

Caprifolium ciliosum Pursh

S. Lu.

yellow,
On the Kooskooskee
Jun: 5th 1806.

Type of
Caprifolium ciliosum Pursh
J.W.Braxton 1975

AMERICAN PHILOSOPHICAL SOCIETY.
LEWIS & CLARK, HERBARIUM.
FROM THE ATLANTIC TO THE PACIFIC.

Lonicera ciliosa Poir.

Locality,
No.   Date

8.

ANS PHILA

100b. *Lonicera ciliosa* (Pursh) Poir. *ex* DC., trumpet honeysuckle

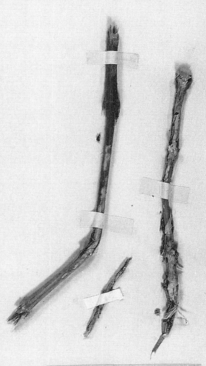

*Lonicera
involucrata* Banks

J. M.

A Shrub within the Rocky
mountains. found in moist
grounds near branches of
rivulets.
20. July 7th 1806.

Academy of Natural Sciences
Lonicera involucrata (Richards.) Banks ex Spreg.
Det: Erica Armstrong   Date: 17 May 1994

ANS PHILA

101. *Lonicera involucrata* Banks *ex* Spreng., bearberry honeysuckle

Academy of Natural Sciences
Lupinus argenteus Pursh
Det: Erica Armstrong   Date: 17 May 1994

Lupinus
argenteus
Pursh

1 m

slide mount
inside
D. Dunn.

On the Cokahlaishkit.
July 7th 1806.

flowers yellowish white

102a. *Lupinus argenteus* Pursh, silvery lupine

Lupinus argenteus. *
Kooskooskee.
July 1806

P

* F. Pursh scripsit
** A. B. Lambert scripsit on **
reverse of sheet.

The original *L. argenteus, Pursh.*

Herb. Pursh propr.

Lupinus argenteus, Fl. Amer. Pursh.

102b. *Lupinus argenteus* Pursh, silvery lupine

103. *Lupinus pusillus* Pursh, rusty lupine

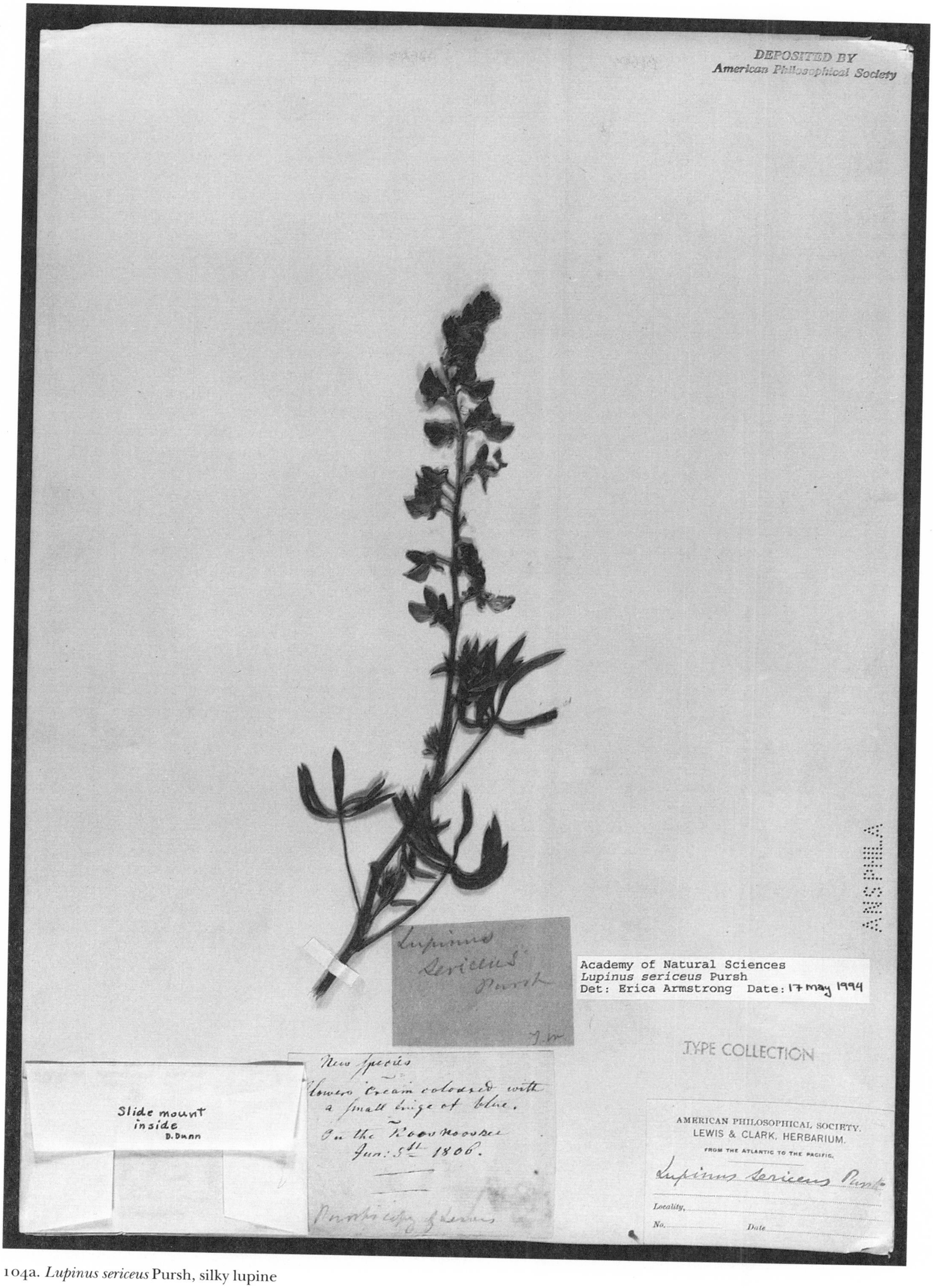
DEPOSITED BY
American Philosophical Society
ANS PHILA
Lupinus sericeus Pursh
Academy of Natural Sciences
Lupinus sericeus Pursh
Det: Erica Armstrong Date: 17 May 1994
TYPE COLLECTION
Slide mount inside
D. Dunn
New Species
Flowers Cream coloured with a small tinge of blue.
On the Kooskooskee
Jun: 5th 1806.
AMERICAN PHILOSOPHICAL SOCIETY.
LEWIS & CLARK. HERBARIUM.
FROM THE ATLANTIC TO THE PACIFIC.
Lupinus sericeus Pursh
Locality,
No.
Date

104a. *Lupinus sericeus* Pursh, silky lupine

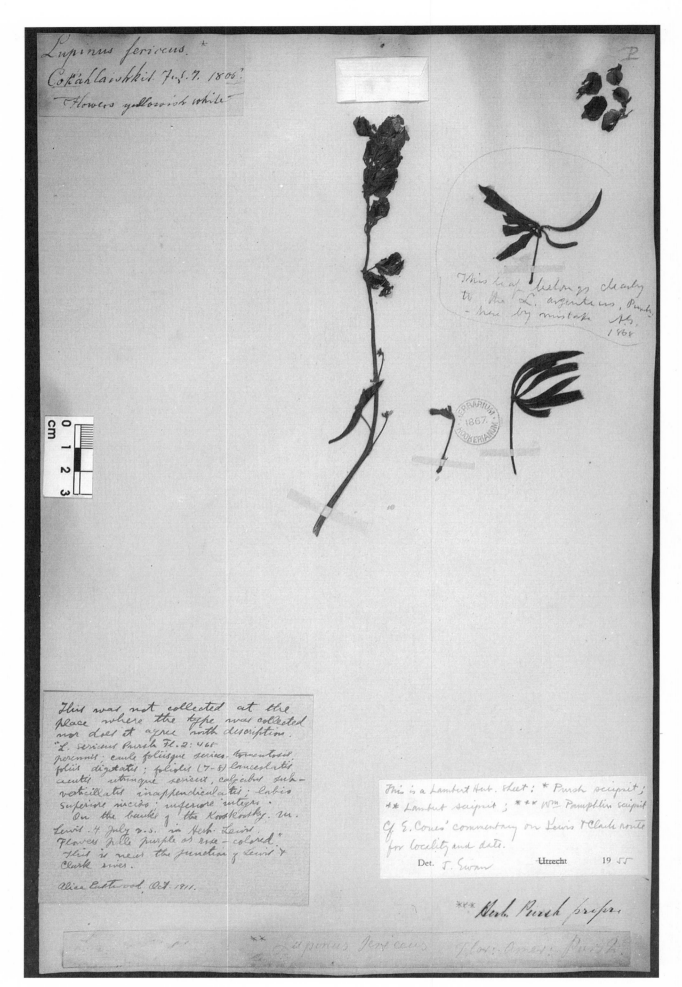

104b. *Lupinus sericeus* Pursh, silky lupine

Aplopappus sp ?

Certainly not

A. spinulosus, DC.

Greene

On the Columbia.
Octbr: 1805.

Lewis

Newlis Coby

Academy of Natural Sciences
Machaeranthera canescens (Pursh) Gray
Det: Erica Armstrong   Date: 17 May 1994

Machaeranthera sp. – possibly M. attenuata.
M. Shinners 1/9/1946

Apparently the common Columbia
form: of Aster canescens Pursh.
Will send specimen to compare.
of Aster spinulosus Nutt.   C.V.P.

105. *Machaeranthera canescens* (Pursh) Gray, hoary aster

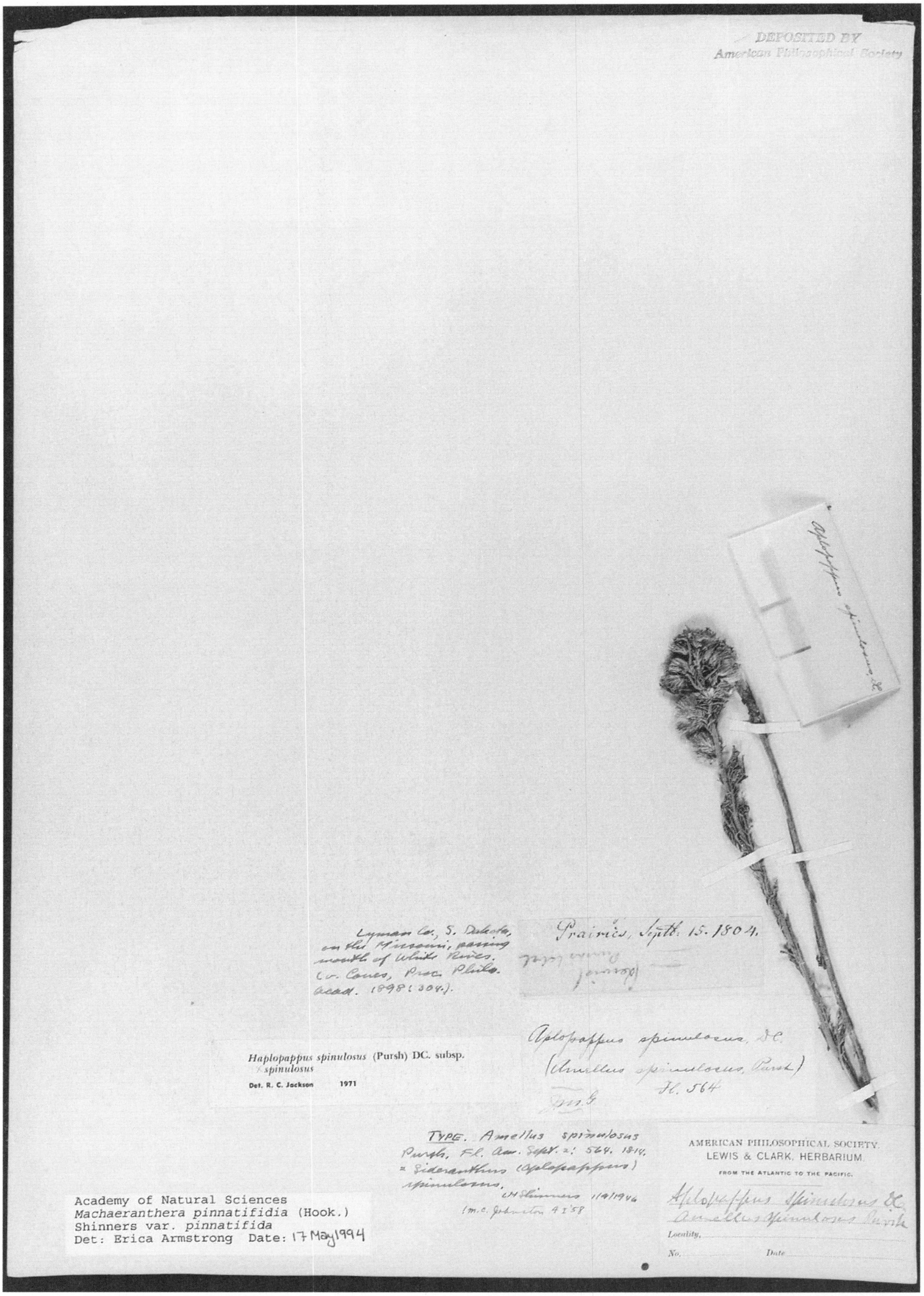

Lyman Co., S. Dakota,
on the Missouri, passing
mouth of White River.
(v. Coues, Proc. Phila.
Acad. (1898: 304.).

Prairies, Sept. 15. 1804.

Haplopappus spinulosus (Pursh) DC. subsp.
× spinulosus

Det. R. C. Jackson   1971

Aplopappus spinulosus, DC.
(Amellus spinulosus, Pursh)
Fl. 564

TYPE. Amellus spinulosus
Pursh, Fl. Am. Sept. 2: 564, 1814,
× Sideranthus (Aplopappus)
spinulosus.
                    H. Shinners 11/1/1946
                    (m.c. Johnston 4 1 58

Academy of Natural Sciences
Machaeranthera pinnatifidia (Hook.)
Shinners var. pinnatifida
Det: Erica Armstrong   Date: 17 May 1994

106. *Machaeranthera pinnatifida* (Hook.) Shinners ssp. *pinnatifida* var. *pinnatifida*, spiny goldenweed

There is no label or memorandum with this in Herb. Lewis.

Maclura aurantiaca Nuttall

J.M.

Academy of Natural Sciences
Maclura pomifera (Raf.)Schneider
Det: Erica Armstrong   Date: 17 May 1994

ANSPHILA

107. *Maclura pomifera* (Raf.) Schneid., Osage orange

108. *Mahonia aquifolium* (Pursh) Nutt., Oregon grape

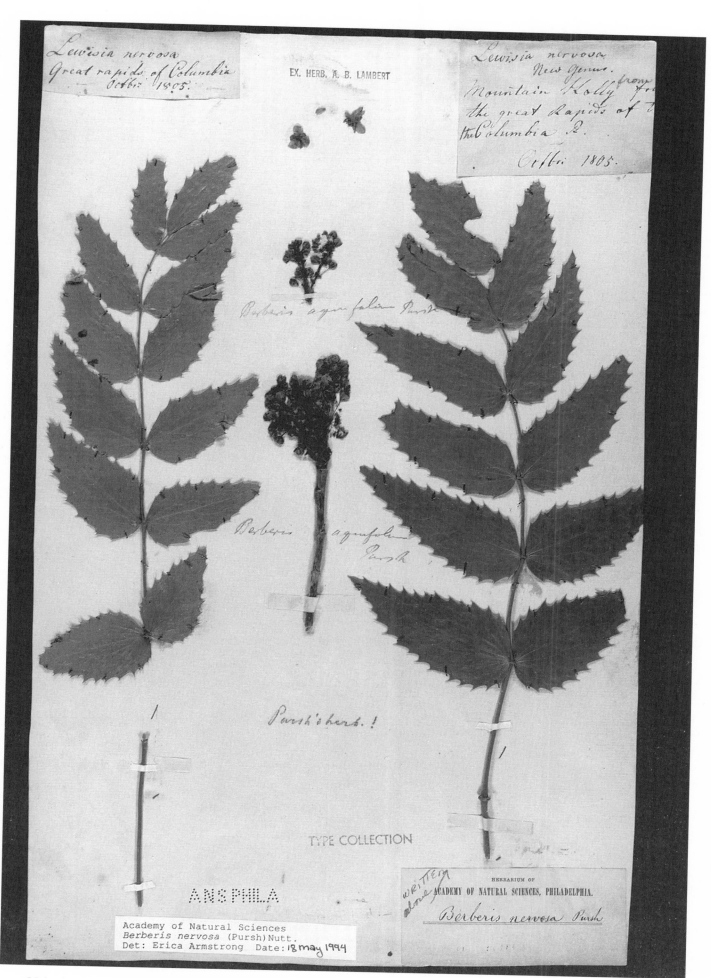

Lewisia nervosa
Great rapids of Columbia
Octbr: 1805.

Lewisia nervosa
New Genus.
Mountain Holly from
the great Rapids of
the Columbia R.
Octbr 1805.

Berberis aquifolia Pursh

Berberis aquifolia
Pursh.

Pursh's herb.!

1

1

TYPE COLLECTION

ANSPHILA

WRITTEN above

Berberis nervosa Pursh

Academy of Natural Sciences
Berberis nervosa (Pursh)Nutt.
Det: Erica Armstrong   Date:18 May 1994

109. *Mahonia nervosa* (Pursh) Nutt., dull Oregon grape

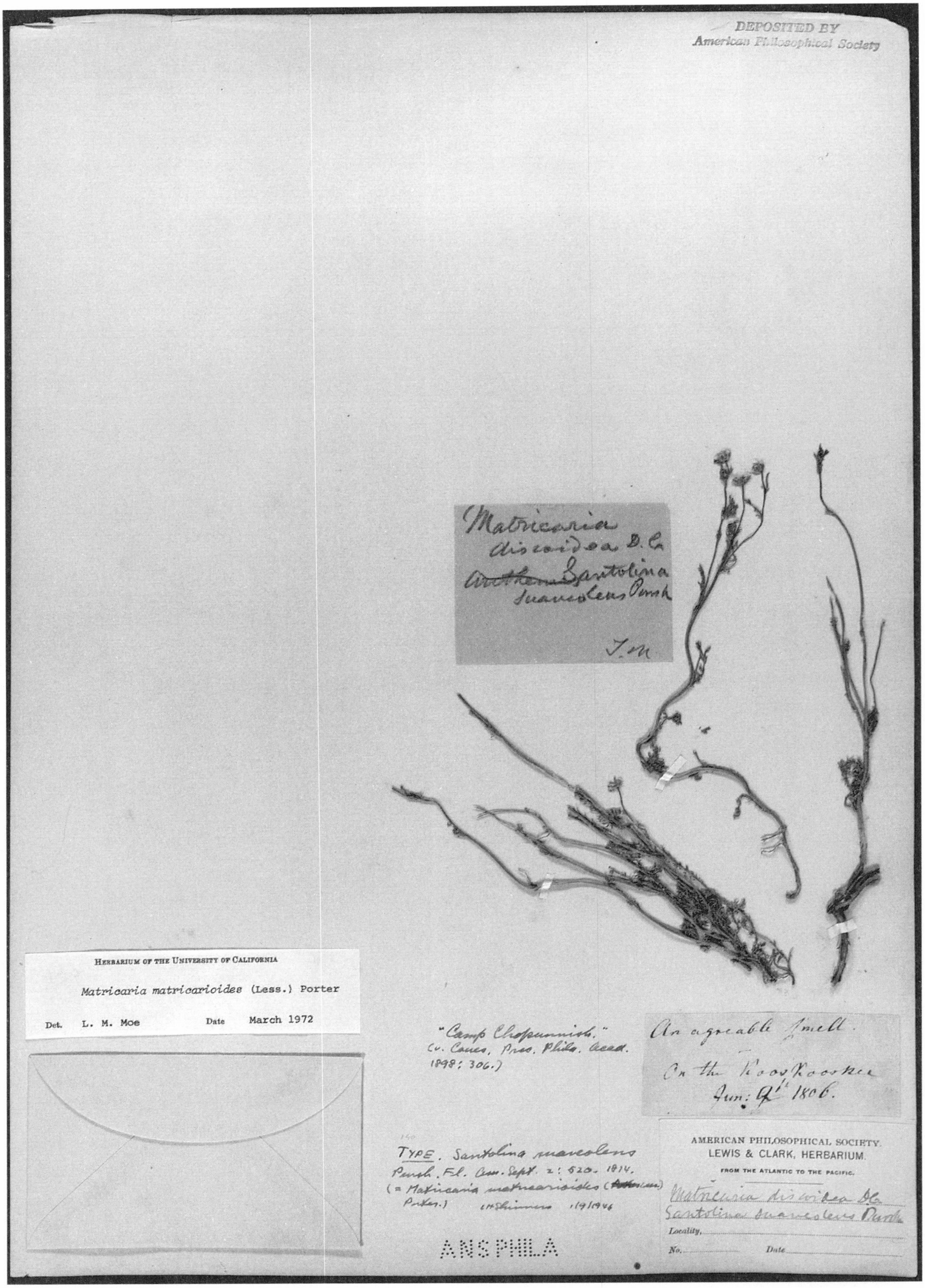

Matricaria
discoidea D. C.
Anthemis Santolina
suaveolens Pursh

J. M.

HERBARIUM OF THE UNIVERSITY OF CALIFORNIA

Matricaria matricarioides (Less.) Porter

Det. L. M. Moe   Date   March 1972

"Camp Chopunnish."
(v. Cones, Proc. Phila. Acad.
1898: 306.)

An agreable smell.

On the Kooskooskie
Jun. 9th 1806.

TYPE. Santolina suaveolens
Pursh. Fl. Am. Sept. 2: 520. 1814.
(= Matricaria matricarioides (Less.)
Porter.)   C.H.Shinners   11/1/1946

AMERICAN PHILOSOPHICAL SOCIETY.
LEWIS & CLARK, HERBARIUM.
FROM THE ATLANTIC TO THE PACIFIC.

Matricaria discoidea D.C.
Santolina suaveolens Pursh

Locality,
No.   Date

ANS PHILA

110a. *Matricaria discoidea* DC., pineapple weed

Santolina suaveolens
Balsamita Koos Kees.
Koos Kooskee Jun. 12. 1806.

EX. HERB. A. B. LAMBERT

Pursh !

Matricaria discoidea DC.,
DC.,

Herb. Lewis & Clarke.

HERBARIUM OF THE UNIVERSITY OF CALIFORNIA

Matricaria matricarioides (Less.) Porter

Det.   L. M. Moe   Date   March 1972

HERBARIUM OF
ACADEMY OF NATURAL SCIENCES, PHILADELPHIA.

Matricaria discoidea DC.

TYPE of *Santolina suaveolens* Pursh

Rickett 2 Mc 1949

ANSPHILA

110b. *Matricaria discoidea* DC., pineapple weed

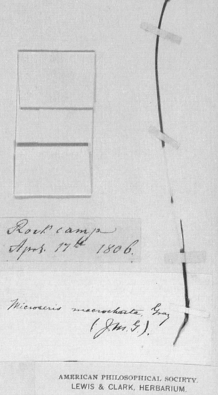

Rock camp
Apr. 17th 1806.

Microseris macrochaeta, Gray
(J.M.G.)

Academy of Natural Sciences
Microseris laciniata var. lindleyi (DC.)Gray
Det: Erica Armstrong   Date: 17 May 1994

111. *Microseris lindleyi* (DC.) Gray, Lindley's microseris

Academy of Natural Sciences
Mimulus guttatus Fisch. ex DC. ssp. *guttatus*
Det: Erica Armstrong Date: 17 May 1994

On the Waters of Clarks
River.
July 4th 1806.

Pursh, Bishop of Lewis & Clark

AMERICAN PHILOSOPHICAL SOCIETY.
LEWIS & CLARK, HERBARIUM.
FROM THE ATLANTIC TO THE PACIFIC.

Mimulus lutens L.

Locality,
No.   Date

A N S P H I L A

112. *Mimulus guttatus* DC., yellow monkey-flower

Open plains. Septbr. 1st 1804.

Oxybophus nyctagineus, Sweet.

Academy of Natural Sciences
Mirabilis nyctaginea (Michx.)MacM.
Det: Erica Armstrong   Date:23 May 1994

AMERICAN PHILOSOPHICAL SOCIETY.
LEWIS & CLARK. HERBARIUM.
FROM THE ATLANTIC TO THE PACIFIC.

Oxybophus nyctagineus Sweet

Locality,

No.   Date

113a. *Mirabilis nyctaginea* (Michx.) MacM., wild four-o'clock

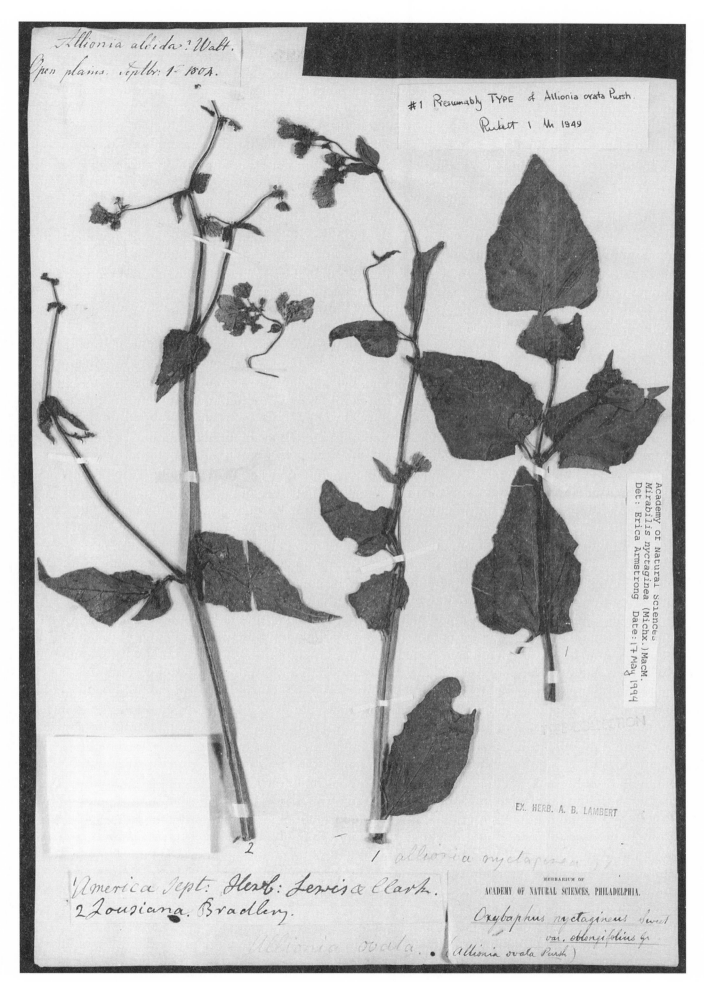

113b. *Mirabilis nyctaginea* (Michx.) MacM., wild four-o'clock

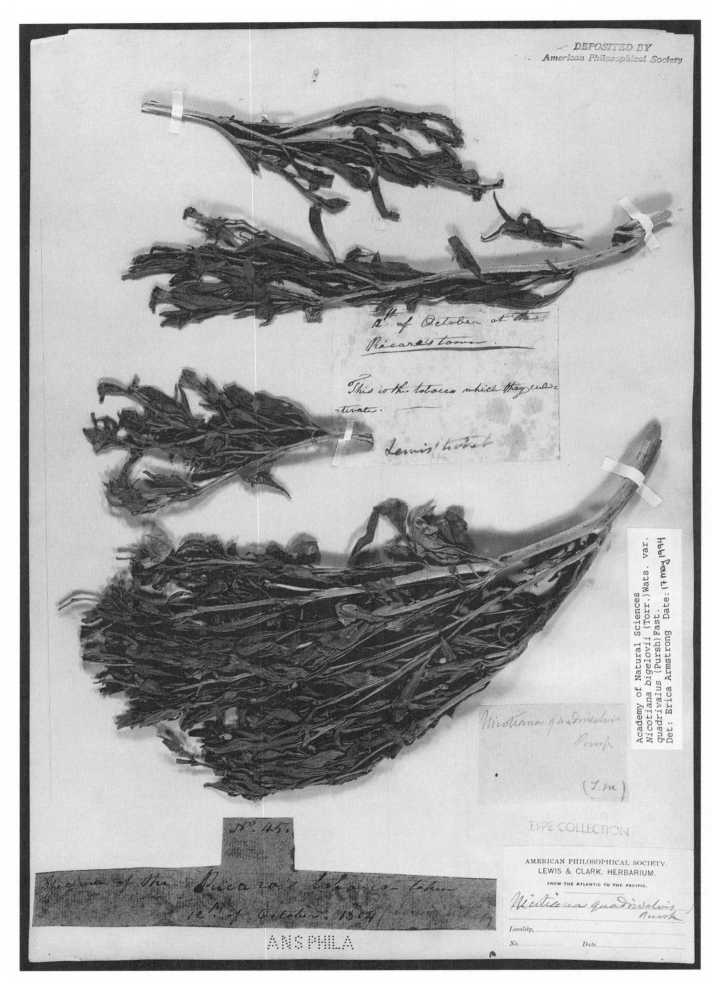

114. *Nicotiana quadrivalvis* Pursh var. *quadrivalvis,* Indian tobacco

Oenothera caespitosa Nutt. subsp.
  caespitosa

ISOLECTOTYPE

Oenothera scapigera Pursh,Fl. Amer. Sept.
  1:263.1814.

Lectotype: PH

Determined by Warren L. Wagner 1980

MISSOURI BOTANICAL GARDEN HERBARIUM (MO)

Near the Falls of
Missouri.
Aug. 17th 1806.

Pursh's copy of Lewis

AMERICAN PHILOSOPHICAL SOCIETY.
LEWIS & CLARK, HERBARIUM.
FROM THE ATLANTIC TO THE PACIFIC.

Oenothera caespitosa Nutt.

Locality,
No.   Date

ANS PHILA

115a. *Oenothera cespitosa* Nutt. ssp. *cespitosa*, gumbo evening primrose

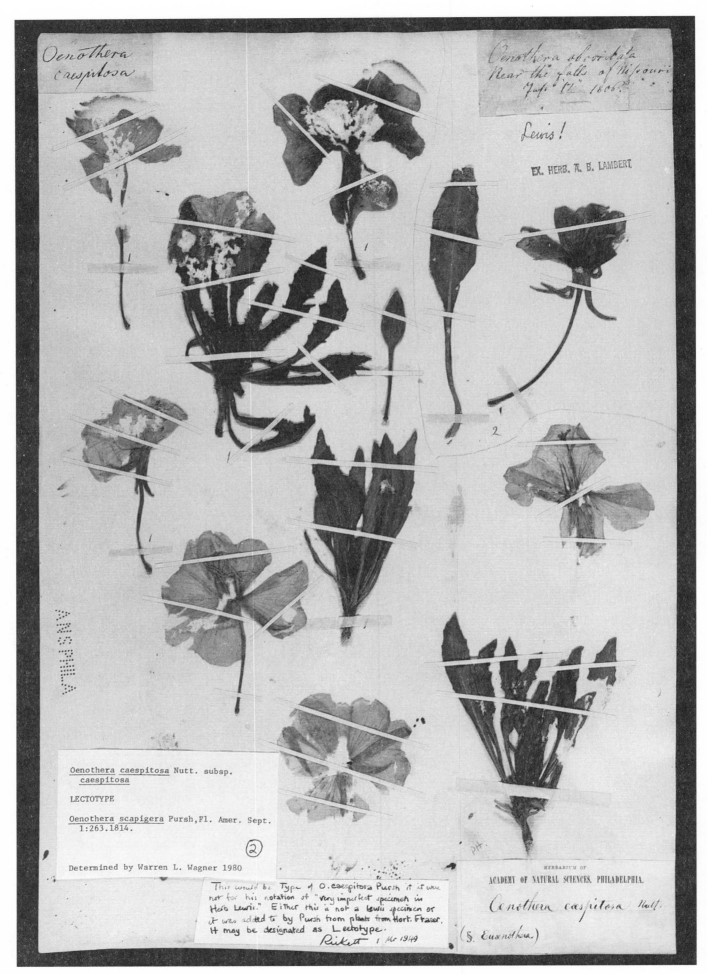

Oenothera
caespitosa

Oenothera obovidata
Near the falls of Missouri
July 14. 1806?

Lewis!

EX. HERB. A. B. LAMBERT

Oenothera caespitosa Nutt. subsp.
    caespitosa

LECTOTYPE

Oenothera scapigera Pursh,Fl. Amer. Sept.
    1:263.1814.

②

Determined by Warren L. Wagner 1980

This would be Type of O. caespitosa Pursh if it were
not for his notation of "very imperfect specimen in
Herb. Lewis." Either this is not a Lewis specimen or
it was added to by Pursh from plants from Hort. Fraser.
It may be designated as Lectotype.
            Rickett 1 Mr 1949

HERBARIUM OF
ACADEMY OF NATURAL SCIENCES, PHILADELPHIA.

Oenothera caespitosa Nutt.

(§ Euœnothera)

115b. *Oenothera cespitosa* Nutt. ssp. *cespitosa*, gumbo evening primrose

l.

*Orthocarpus
tenuifolius* Benth
Bartsia tenuifolius Pursh

(J. m)

Valley of Clarks R.
Jug. 1st 1806

Pursh's copy of Lewis's label.

TYPE COLLECTION

HOLOTYPE
JEPSON HERBARIUM—UNIVERSITY OF CALIFORNIA

Orthocarpus tenuifolius (Pursh) Benth.

T. I. Chuang & L. R. Heckard   1982

AMERICAN PHILOSOPHICAL SOCIETY.
LEWIS & CLARK, HERBARIUM.
FROM THE ATLANTIC TO THE PACIFIC.

Orthocarpus tenuifolius
Benth

Locality.
No.   Date

ANS PHILA

116. *Orthocarpus tenuifolius* (Pursh) Benth., thin-leaved owl-clover

all eaten!

A Species of Fennel root
eaten by the Indians of an
anniseed taste. Flowers
white.

Columbia R.
Aprl. 25th 1806.

117. *Osmorhiza occidentalis* (Nutt. *ex* Torr. & Gray) Torr., western sweet-cicely

571. OXYTROPIS. *Decand. astrag. p.* 24.

1. O. acaulis ; foliolis obovato-lanceolatis sericeo-argenteis,
scapis folia æquantibus, floribus capitatis, bracteis lanceolatis longitudine calycis sericei.— *Pers. syn.* 2.
p. 331.
Astragalus argentatus. *Willd. sp. pl.* 3. *p.* 1310.
Icon. *Pall. astrag. t.* 49.
On the banks of Clarck's river. *M. Lewis.* ⁊. July.
v. s. in Herb. Lewis.

argentata.

*Pursh, Fl. Amer.
Sept. 2 : 473
1814*

As can be plainly seen from Pursh's
words (above), this is not a type-specimen.
Pursh merely misidentified Lewis's plant
from near Missoula as the Oxytropis argentata (Pall.) DC., a morphologically similar
but distinct species native to Siberia.
The footnote from Barneby, Proc. Calif.
Acad. Sci. IV, 27: 232. 1952, is still
relevant (see below).

R. C. BARNEBY
(NY) Jan. 1994

5. This is the plant listed by Pursh, Fl. Amer. Sept. 473—1814, as *O. argentata* (not, however, of DC.),
and according to Coues (Proc. Philad. Acad. 1898, p. 298—1899), who made a special study of Lewis and
Clark's route, it must have been collected on July 1–2 in the Bitterroot valley at the mouth of its Lou-Lou
branch, in the present Missoula County, Montana. This statement is difficult to reconcile with our knowledge
of the range of *O. Besseyi* var. *Besseyi*, to which Lewis's plant unquestionably belongs. July, the month given
also on the label, is late in the season for young flowering material of this species at an altitude not much
exceeding 3,000 feet, and there may be some error in the original data.

This specimen, which I studied at PH circa 1949, is
somewhat ambiguous for lack of leaves or fruit, and could
be a late-flowering example of O. lagopus Nutt. There is
nothing, however, to exclude it from O. besseyi, which I
myself have seen near Missoula, in flower in late June.

*R Barneby
1994*

*Oxytropis argentata
Pursh
[J. Lew]
Oxytropis argentata, Pursh
Graeweana*

*Near the heath of Clarks
River
July 1806*

Academy of Natural Sciences
Oxytropis besseyi (Rydb.)Blank.
Det: Erica Armstrong   Date: 17 May 1994

AMERICAN PHILOSOPHICAL SOCIETY.
LEWIS & CLARK, HERBARIUM.
FROM THE ATLANTIC TO THE PACIFIC.

Oxytropis argentata Pursh

Locality,
No.   Date

118a. *Oxytropis nana* Nutt. var. *besseyi* (Rydb.) Isely, Bessey's crazyweed

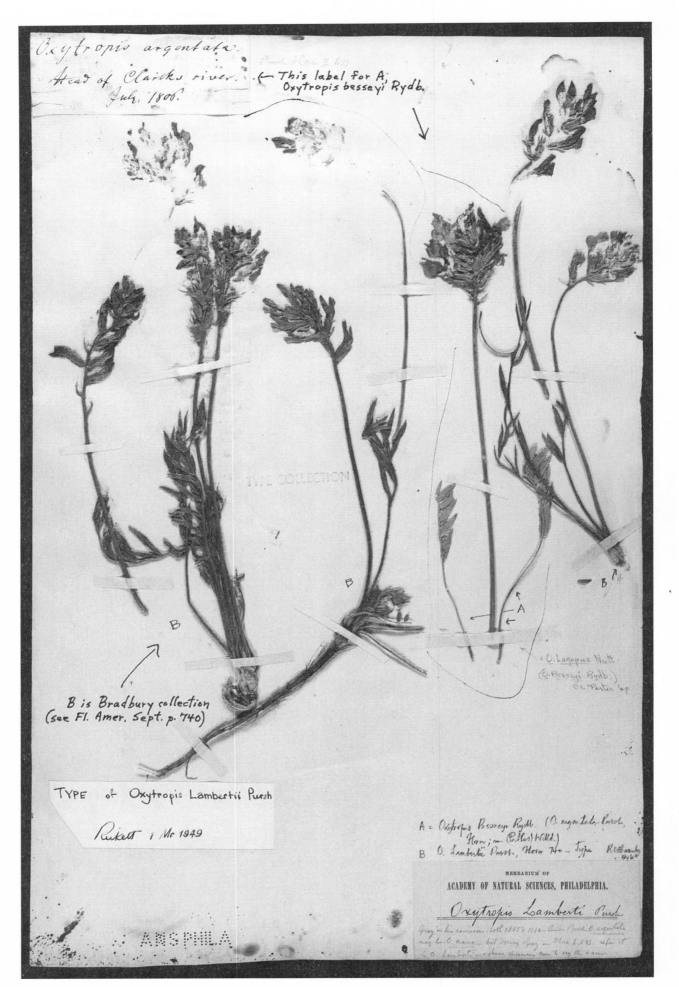

118b. *Oxytropis nana* Nutt. var. *besseyi* (Rydb.) Isely, Bessey's crazyweed

Pachystima myrsinites Raf.
Ilex? myrsinites Pursh

I. M.

A small Shrub about 2 feet high
with a small deep purple
berry, evergreen!
Near the Pacific Ocean
Novbr. 16th 1805.

AMERICAN PHILOSOPHICAL SOCIETY.
LEWIS & CLARK, HERBARIUM.
FROM THE ATLANTIC TO THE PACIFIC.

Locality,
No. .... Date ....

Academy of Natural Sciences
Pachystima myrsinites (Pursh)Raf.
Det: Erica Armstrong   Date: 23May1994

ANS PHILA

119a. *Paxistima myrsinites* (Pursh) Raf., mountain-box

Rhamnus berberidifolius
Near the pacific ocean, Evergreen
about 4. feet high, berry deep purple.
Novbr 16. 1805.

[Pursh scripsit]

2

TYPE *Ilex myrsinites* Pursh !
in Herb. Lambert — his writing at * and
on back of sheet.
Determinavit J. Evans

Herb. Pursh proper
Ilex myrsinites Fl. amer. Ph.

HERBARIUM 1867 HOOKERIANUM

119b. *Paxistima myrsinites* (Pursh) Raf., mountain-box

Pachystima
myrsinites
Raf.
Ilex? myrsinites Pursh

Rocky mountain

June 16th 1806.
Pursh's label by Lewis

AMERICAN PHILOSOPHICAL SOCIETY.
LEWIS & CLARK, HERBARIUM
FROM THE ATLANTIC TO THE PACIFIC.

Locality,

No.   Date

Academy of Natural Sciences
Pachystima myrsinites (Pursh) Raf.
Det: Erica Armstrong Date: 17 May 1994

ANSPHILA

119c. *Paxistima myrsinites* (Pursh) Raf., mountain-box

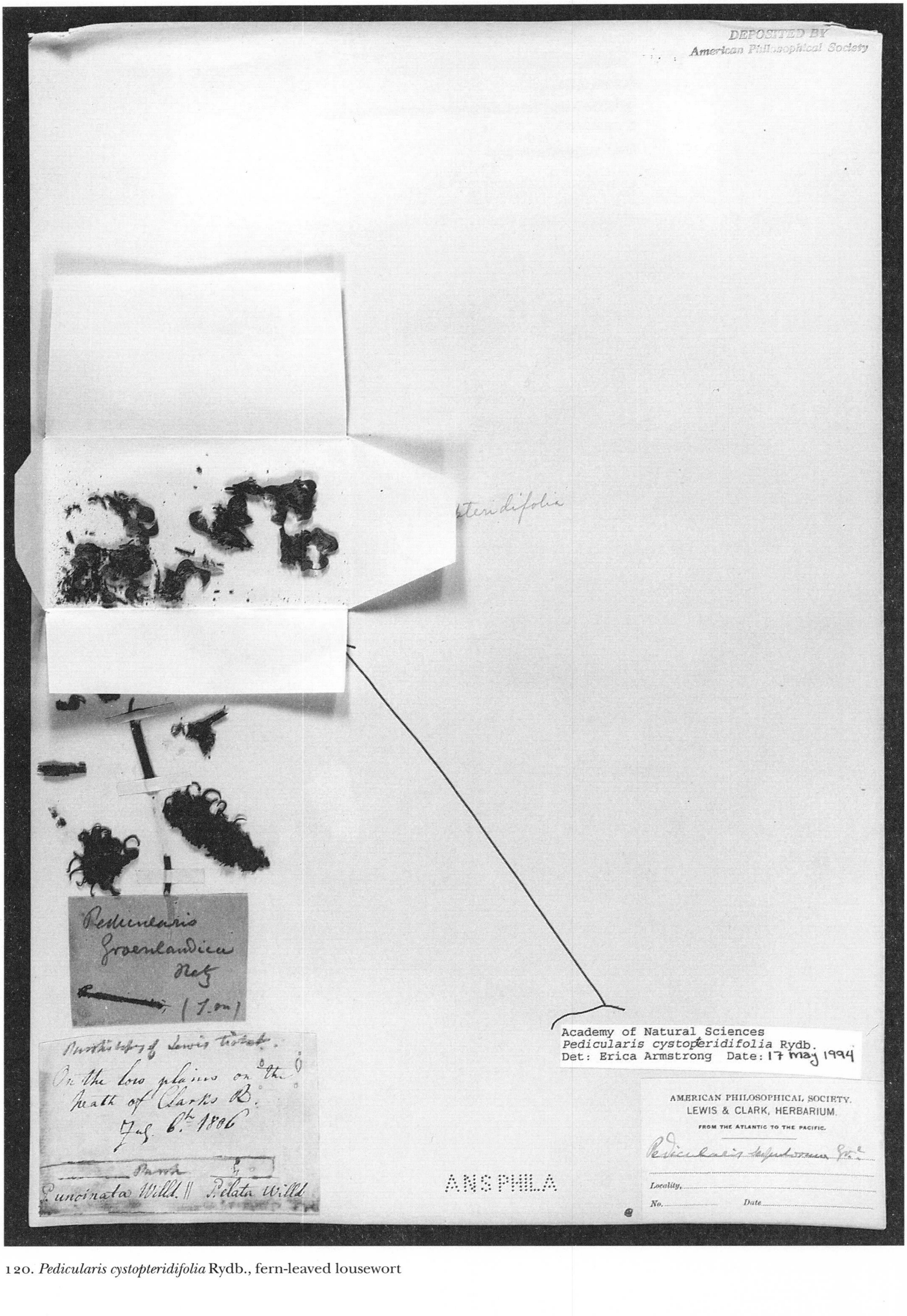

...teridifolia

Pedicularis
Groenlandica
Retz

(1 cm)

North side of Lewis ticket.

On the low plains on the
heath of Clarks R.
Jul. 6th 1806

Punch
Juncinata Willd. // Pelata Willd

ANS PHILA

Academy of Natural Sciences
Pedicularis cystopteridifolia Rydb.
Det: Erica Armstrong   Date: 17 may 1994

AMERICAN PHILOSOPHICAL SOCIETY.
LEWIS & CLARK, HERBARIUM.
FROM THE ATLANTIC TO THE PACIFIC.

Pedicularis ...

Locality,
No.   Date

120. *Pedicularis cystopteridifolia* Rydb., fern-leaved lousewort

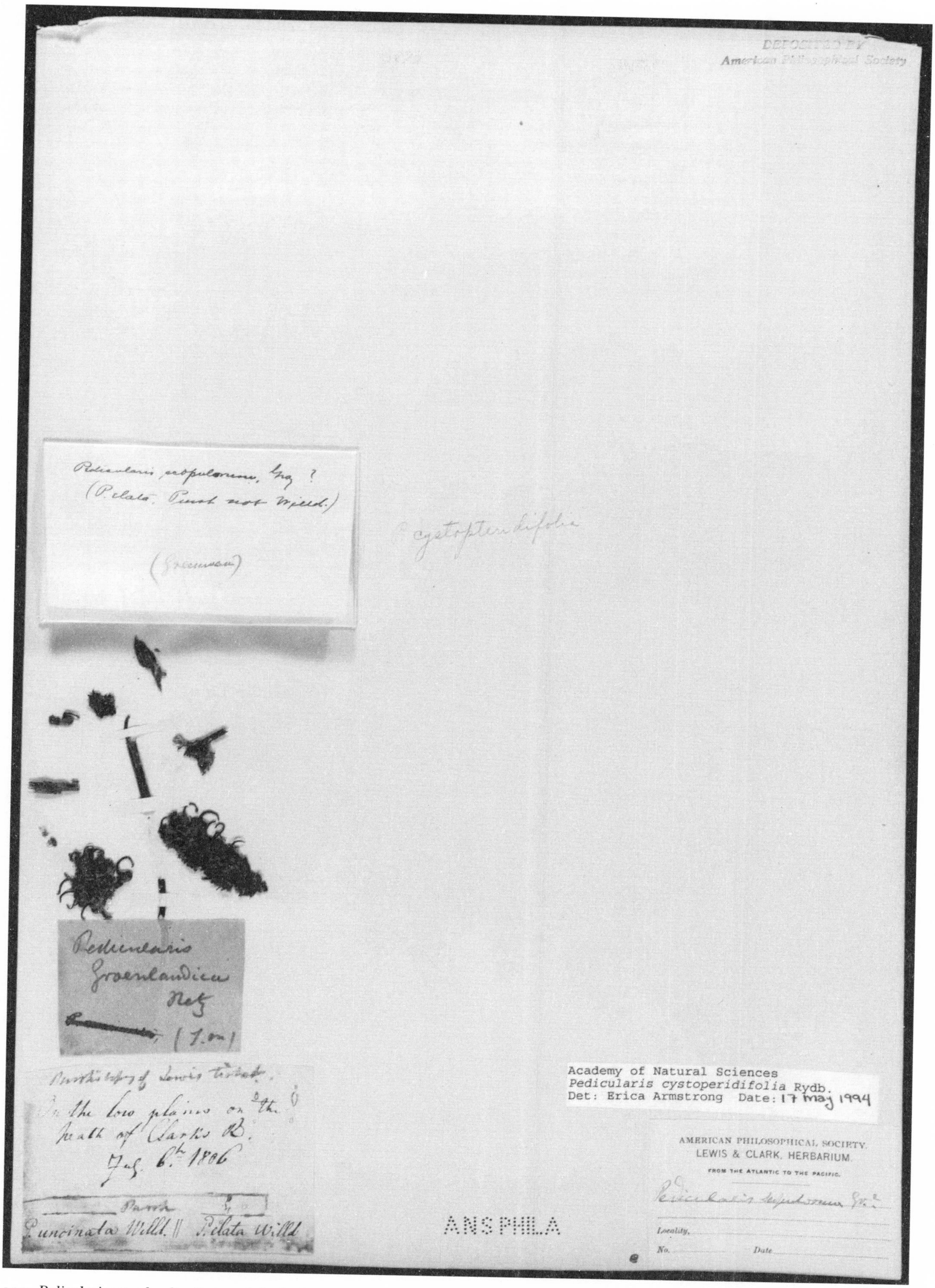

Pedicularis scopulorum, Gray ?
(P. elata. Pursh not Willd.)

(Greenman)

cystopteridifolia

*Pedicularis
groenlandica
Retz*

(1. m)

North history of Lewis ticket.
In the low plains on the
heath of Clark's R.
July 6th 1806

Pursh
uncinata Willd. // *P. elata Willd.*

ANSPHILA

121. *Pedicularis groenlandica* Retz., pink elephants

Psoralea argophylla
Pursh

J. M.

Academy of Natural Sciences
Pediomelum argophylla (Pursh) J. Grimes
Det: Erica Armstrong Date: 17 May 1994

Nº 48.

Nº 103. October 17th 1804.
a decoction of this plant used by the
Indians to wash their wounds

ANSPHILA

AMERICAN PHILOSOPHICAL SOCIETY.
LEWIS & CLARK, HERBARIUM.
FROM THE ATLANTIC TO THE PACIFIC.

Psoralea argophylla
Pursh

Locality,
No.   Date

122a. *Pediomelum argophyllum* (Pursh) J. Grimes, silver-leaf scurf-pea

Psoralea argophylla.
Missouri.

Pursh's specimen !

HOLOTYPUS

Psoralea argophylla Pursh
Fl. Amer. Sept. 475. 1814.

=Pediomelum argophyllum (Pursh) J. Grimes

Det. James Grimes, 1987
THE UNIVERSITY OF TEXAS AT AUSTIN

TYPE of Psoralea argophylla Pursh

Rickett 2 Mr 1949

Psoralea argophylla Pursh

ANSP PHILA

122b. *Pediomelum argophyllum* (Pursh) J. Grimes, silver-leaf scurf-pea

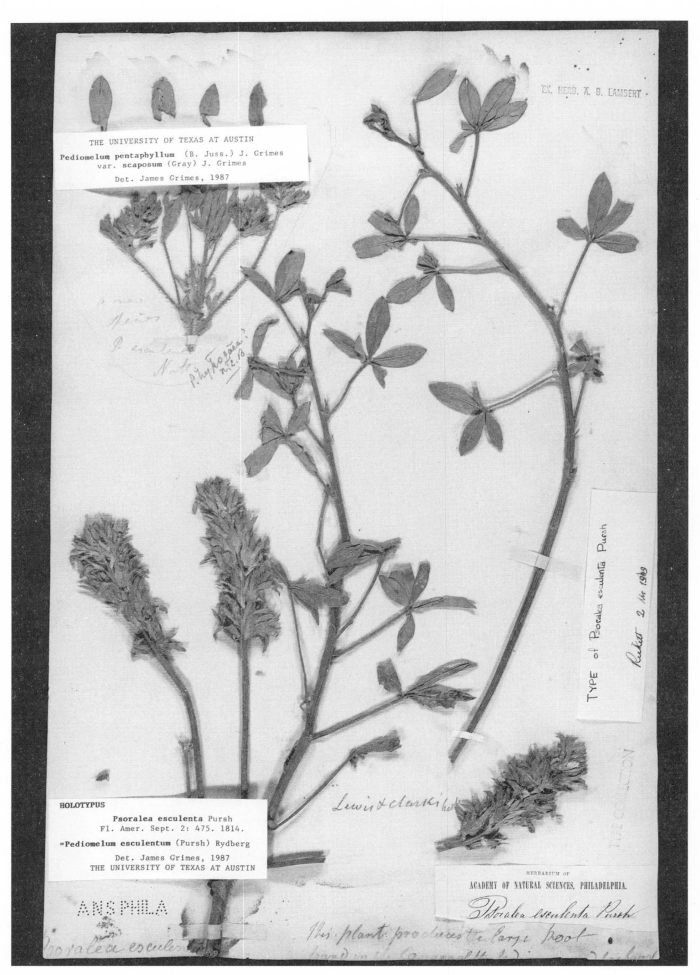

123. *Pediomelum esculentum* (Pursh) Rydb., Indian breadroot

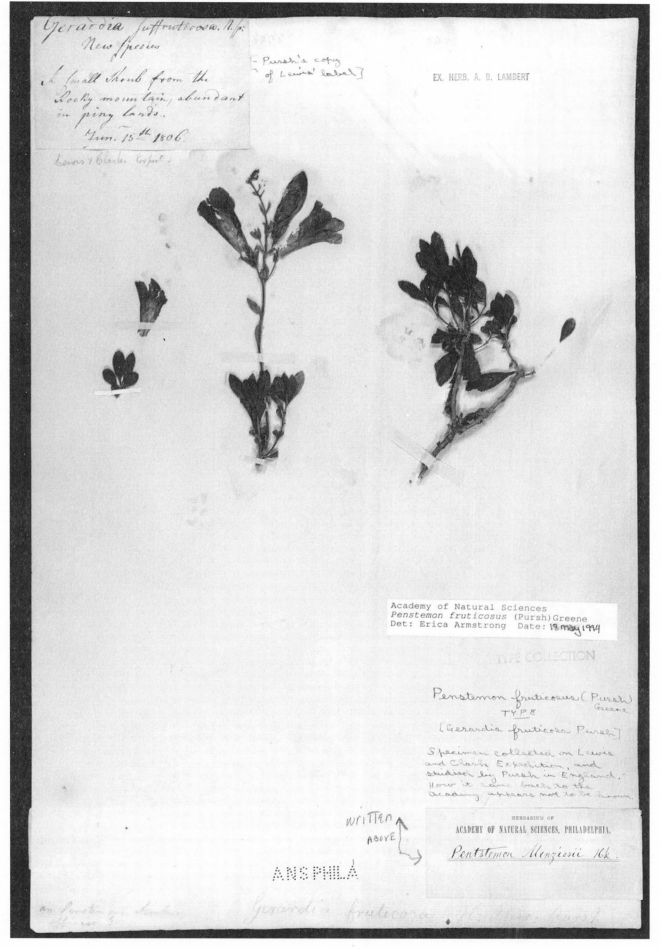

Gerardia suffruticosa. n.s.
New Species

A small Shrub from the
Rocky mountain, abundant
in piny lands.
Jun. 15th 1806.

Lewis & Clarke Exped.

[= Pursh's copy
of Lewis' label]

Academy of Natural Sciences
Penstemon fruticosus (Pursh)Greene
Det: Erica Armstrong   Date: 18 may 1994

TYPE COLLECTION

Penstemon fruticosus (Pursh)
Greene
TYPE
[Gerardia fruticosa Pursh]

Specimen collected on Lewis
and Clarke Expedition, and
studied by Pursh in England.
How it came back to the
Academy appears not to be known.

WRITTEN
ABOVE

HERBARIUM OF
ACADEMY OF NATURAL SCIENCES, PHILADELPHIA.

Penstemon Menziesii Hk.

ANS PHILA

Gerardia fruticosa

124. *Penstemon fruticosus* (Pursh) Greene, shrubby penstemon

Penstemon diffusus Dougl.

J. M

Camp on the Kooskoosky
May 20ᵗ 1806.

Pursh's copy of Lewis' label

Academy of Natural Sciences
Penstemon wilcoxii Rydb.
Det: Erica Armstrong   Date: 17 may 1994

P. wilcoxii Rydb.
FWP, 1942

125. *Penstemon wilcoxii* Rydb., Wilcox's penstemon

Potentilla fruticosa L.

Prairij of the Knobs.
Jug. 5th 1806.

Academy of Natural Sciences
Potentilla fruticosa L.
Det: Erica Armstrong   Date: 17 May 1994

ANSP HLA

126. *Pentaphylloides floribunda* (Pursh) A. L've, shrubby cinquefoil

Phacelia circinata Jacq
P. heterophylla Pursh

J. M.

Root fibrous, plant from 3-4. high.
& dry situation.

On the Kooskooskee
Jun. 9th 1806.

Pursh copy fl 2.

Phacelia circinata Jacq.

Locality,

No.   Date

Academy of Natural Sciences
Phacelia heterophylla Pursh
Det: Erica Armstrong   Date: 17 May 1994

ANSPHILA

127a. *Phacelia heterophylla* Pursh, varileaf phacelia

Phacelia scabiosaefolia
Dry situations on the *hoochoocks*
Jun. 9. 1806?

ANSMILA

TYPE of Phacelia heterophylla Pursh

Rickett 2 Mr 1949

Phacelia heterophylla. fl: am: Sept

rb: Lewes & Clarch

Phacelia circinata Jacq.fl.

127b. *Phacelia heterophylla* Pursh, varileaf phacelia

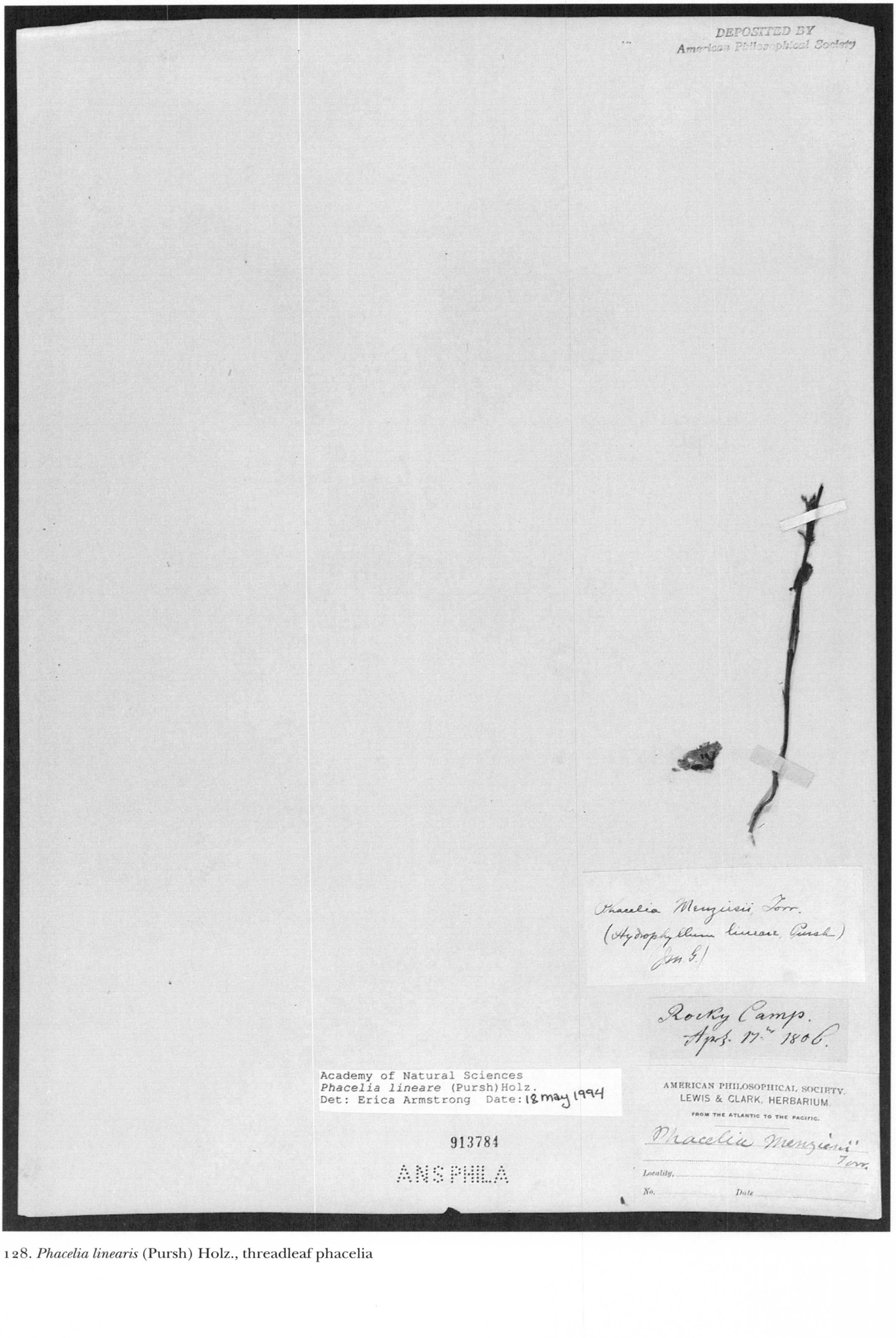
DEPOSITED BY
American Philosophical Society
Phacelia Menziesii, Torr.
(Hydrophyllum lineare, Pursh)
(Jon G.)
Rocky Camps.
Apr. 17th 1806.
Academy of Natural Sciences
Phacelia lineare (Pursh) Holz.
Det: Erica Armstrong Date: 18 May 1994
913784
ANSPHILA
AMERICAN PHILOSOPHICAL SOCIETY.
LEWIS & CLARK, HERBARIUM.
FROM THE ATLANTIC TO THE PACIFIC.
Phacelia Menziesii
Torr.
Locality,
No.
Date

128. *Phacelia linearis* (Pursh) Holz., threadleaf phacelia

Philadelphus Lewisii
Pursh

Philadelphus
Lewisii Pursh

Academy of Natural Sciences
Philadelphus lewisii Pursh
Det: Erica Armstrong Date: 17 May 1994

(7 in)

Purshs copy of Lewis ticket

A Shrub from the
Kooskooky.

May 6th 1806.

An Philadelphus?

[7 in]

On the waters of Clarks R.
Jul. 2nd 1806.

TYPE COLLECTION

ANSP HILA

AMERICAN PHILOSOPHICAL SOCIETY.
LEWIS & CLARK, HERBARIUM.
FROM THE ATLANTIC TO THE PACIFIC.

Philadelphus Lewisii Pursh

Locality,
No.   Date

129. *Philadelphus lewisii* Pursh, Lewis's syringa

This is *Phlox speciosa* but
with narrower leaves than
usual.
A. A. Heller

Rather *P. longifolia* Nutt
C & P

I am unable to locate
this specimen. I have
referred it temporarily
to Philadelphus, from the
appearance of wood and
buds, — the leaves protest
against it!
1897   T. M.

Academy of Natural Sciences
Phlox speciosa Pursh
Det: Erica Armstrong   Date: 17 may 1994

TYPE COLLECTION

Phlox speciosa Pursh

A Shrub about a feet high.
On the plains of Columbia.
May 7th 1806.

AMERICAN PHILOSOPHICAL SOCIETY.
LEWIS & CLARK, HERBARIUM.
FROM THE ATLANTIC TO THE PACIFIC.

Phlox speciosa Pursh

Locality,

No.   Date

ANS PHILA

130a. *Phlox speciosa* Pursh, showy phlox

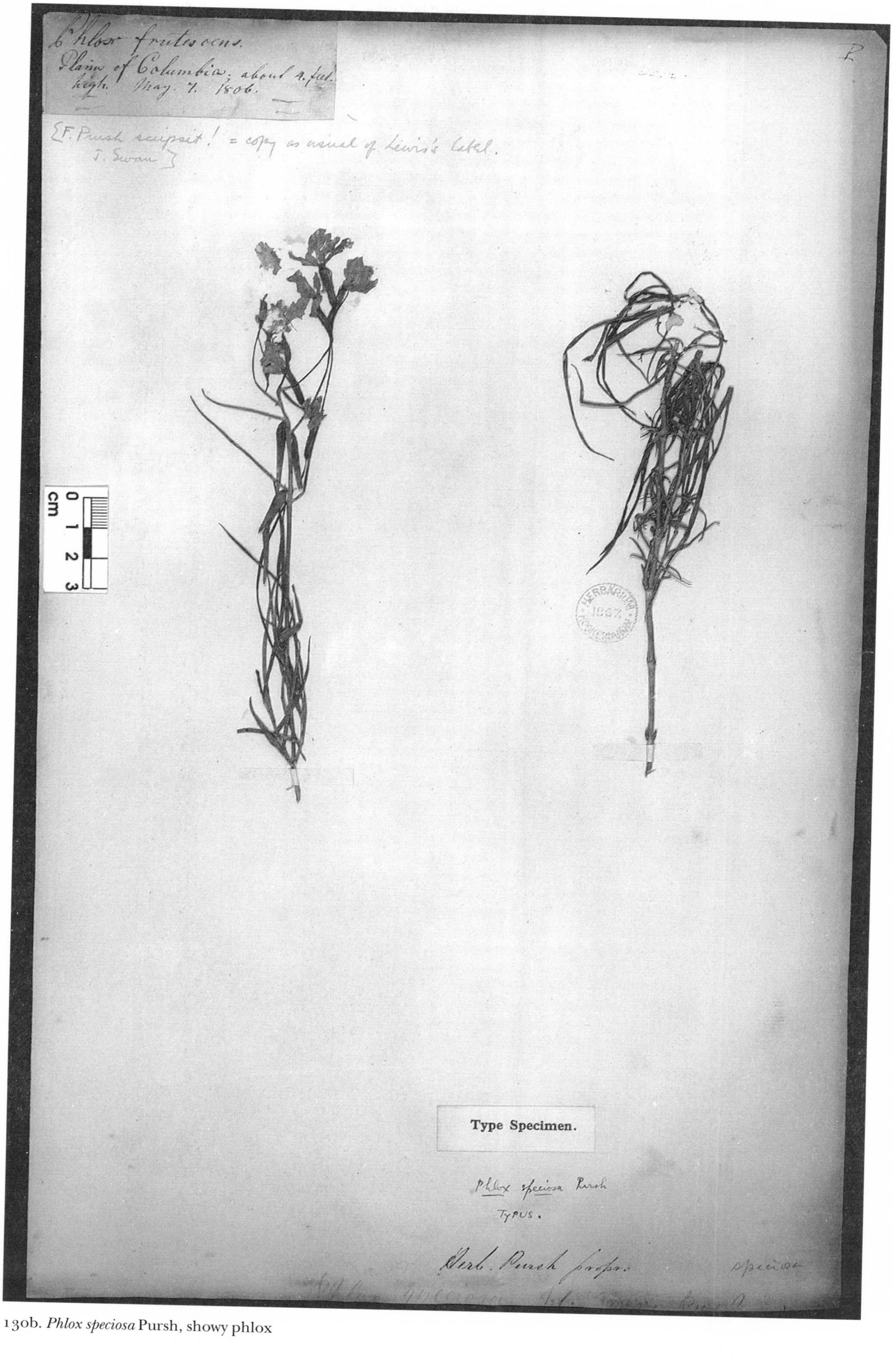

Phlox frutescens.
Plains of Columbia; about 1. ful.
high. May. 7. 1806.

{F. Pursh scripsit! = copy as usual of Lewis's label.
J. Swan}

Type Specimen.

Phlox speciosa Pursh
TYPUS.

Herb. Pursh propr.   species

130b. *Phlox speciosa* Pursh, showy phlox

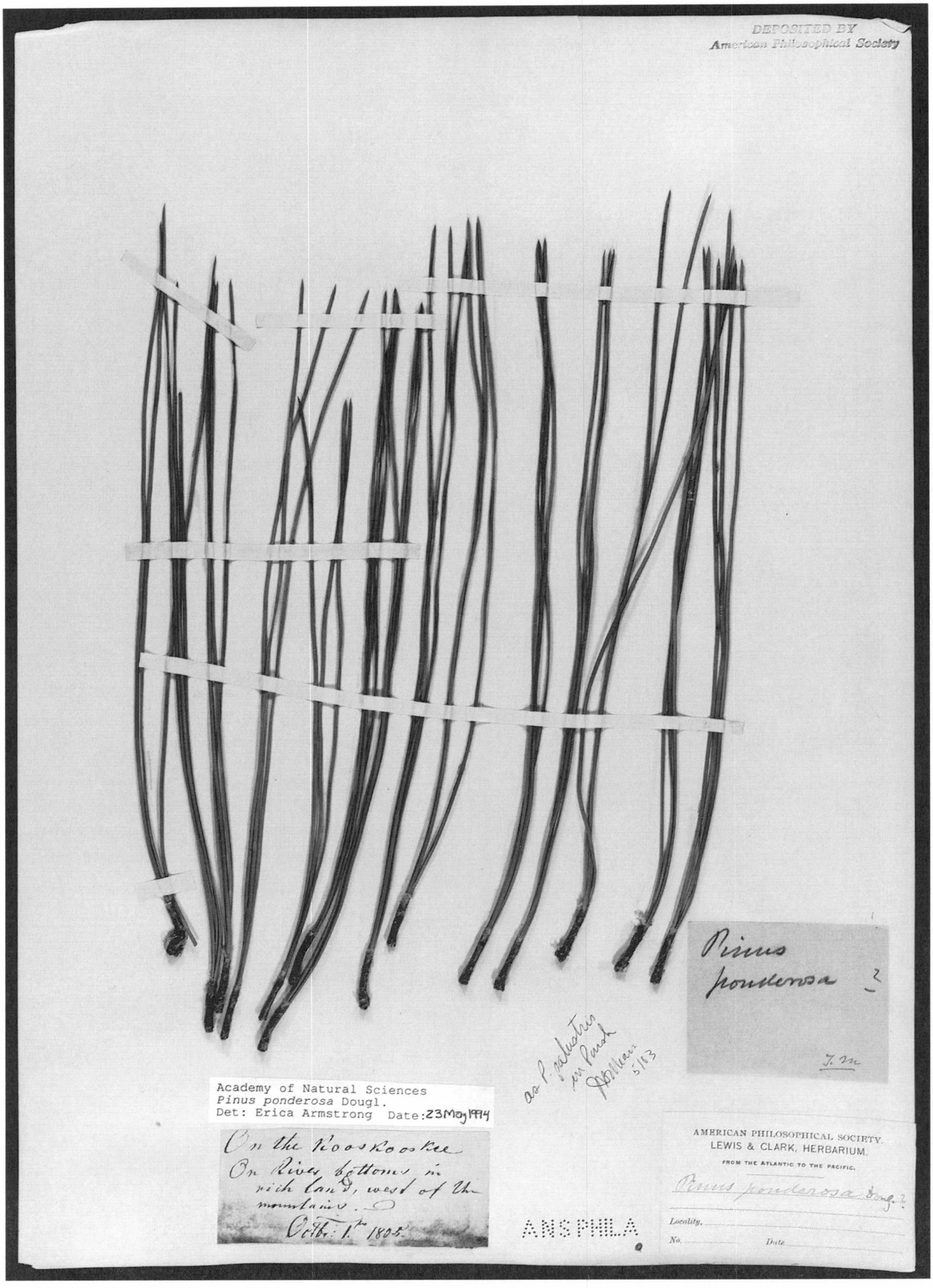

Academy of Natural Sciences
Pinus ponderosa Dougl.
Det: Erica Armstrong   Date: 23 May 1994

On the Kooskooskee
On River bottoms in
rich land, west of the
mountains.
Octbr. 1st 1805.

as P. palustris
in Pursh
McMurrin 5/83

*Pinus
ponderosa* ?

J. M.

AMERICAN PHILOSOPHICAL SOCIETY.
LEWIS & CLARK, HERBARIUM.
FROM THE ATLANTIC TO THE PACIFIC.

Pinus ponderosa Dougl. ?

Locality,
No.   Date

ANS PHILA

131a. *Pinus ponderosa* P. & C. Lawson, ponderosa pine

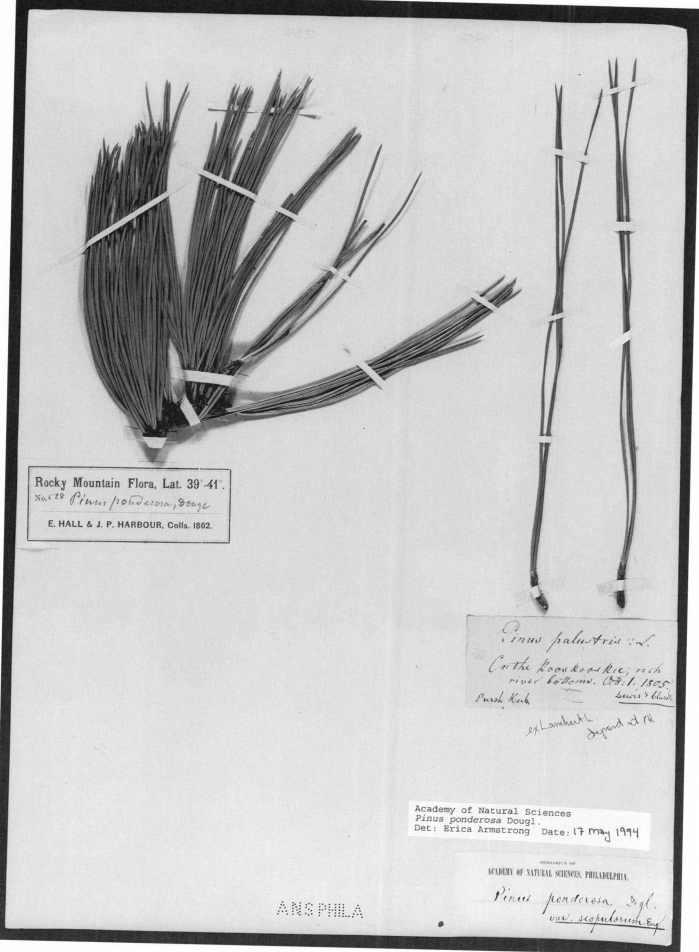

Rocky Mountain Flora, Lat. 39°-41°.
No. 528 *Pinus ponderosa, Dougl*
E. HALL & J. P. HARBOUR, Colls. 1862.

Pinus palustris? L.

On the Kooskooskie; rich
river bottoms. Oct. 1. 1805

Pursh Herb.   Lewis & Clark

ex Lambert's.

Academy of Natural Sciences
Pinus ponderosa Dougl.
Det: Erica Armstrong   Date: 17 May 1994

HERBARIUM OF
ACADEMY OF NATURAL SCIENCES, PHILADELPHIA.

Pinus ponderosa Dgl.
var. scopulorum Eng

ANSP HILA

131b. *Pinus ponderosa* P. & C. Lawson, ponderosa pine

Plagiobothrys tenellus, Gray
(J.M.G.)

Rocky Camp.
Apr. 17th 1806.

Academy of Natural Sciences
Amsinkia intermedia Fisch. & Mey.
Det: Erica Armstrong   Date: 17 may 1994

ANS PHILA

132. *Plagiobothrys tenellus* (Nutt. *ex* Hook.) Gray, slender plagiobothrys

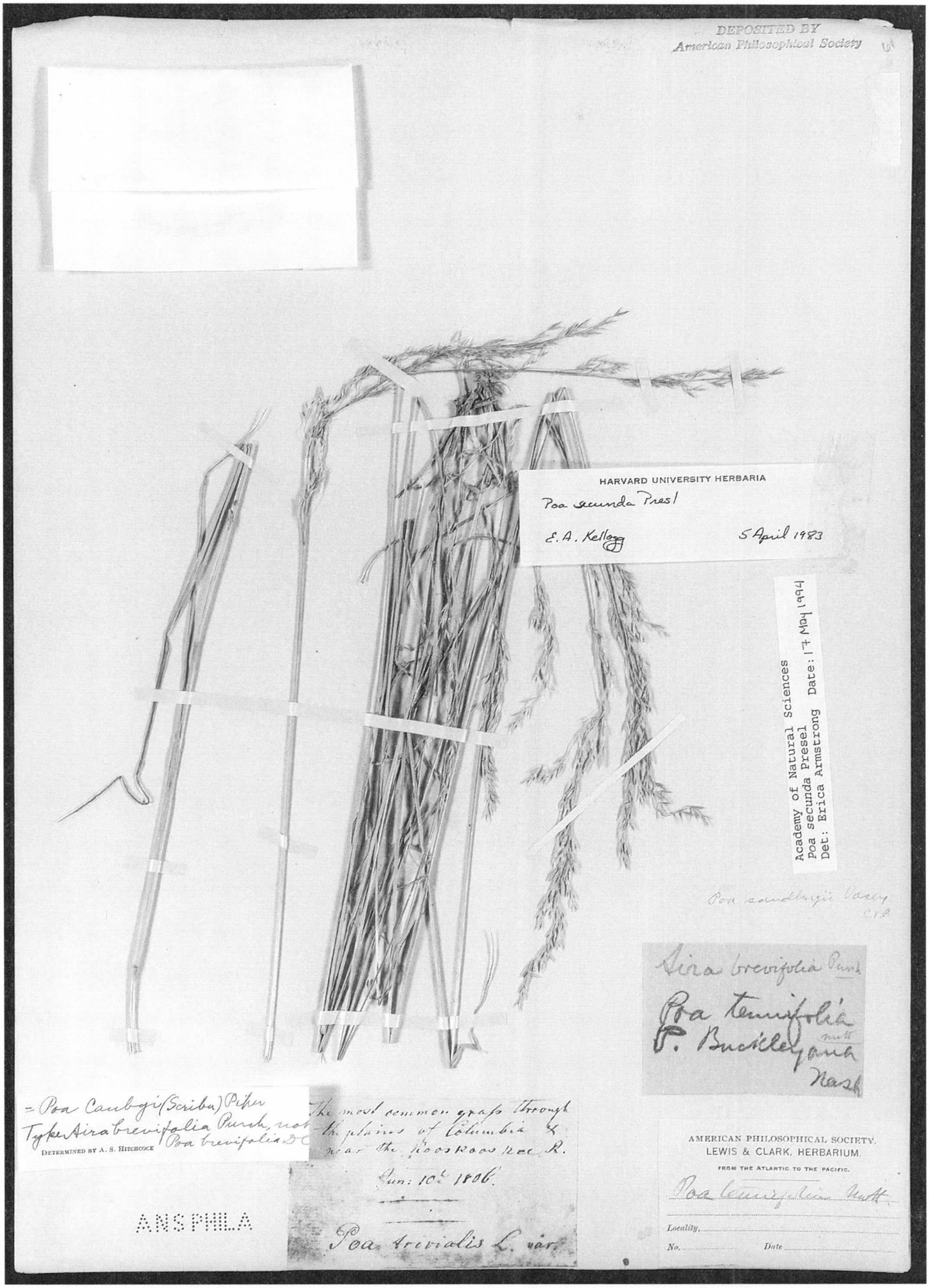

HARVARD UNIVERSITY HERBARIA

Poa secunda Presl

E. A. Kellogg   5 April 1983

Academy of Natural Sciences
Poa secunda Presel   Date: 17 May 1994
Det: Erica Armstrong

Poa sandbergii Vasey
S.D.

Aira brevifolia Pursh

Poa tenuifolia
P. Buckleyana nutt
Nash

= Poa Canbyi (Scribn) Piper
Type Aira brevifolia Pursh, not
Poa brevifolia D
DETERMINED BY A. S. HITCHCOCK

The most common grass through
the plaines of Columbia &
near the Kooskoos nee R.

Jun: 10th 1806.

Poa trivialis L. var.

ANS PHILA

AMERICAN PHILOSOPHICAL SOCIETY.
LEWIS & CLARK, HERBARIUM.
FROM THE ATLANTIC TO THE PACIFIC.

Poa tenuifolia nutt

Locality,

No.   Date

133. *Poa secunda* J. Presl, Sandberg's bluegrass

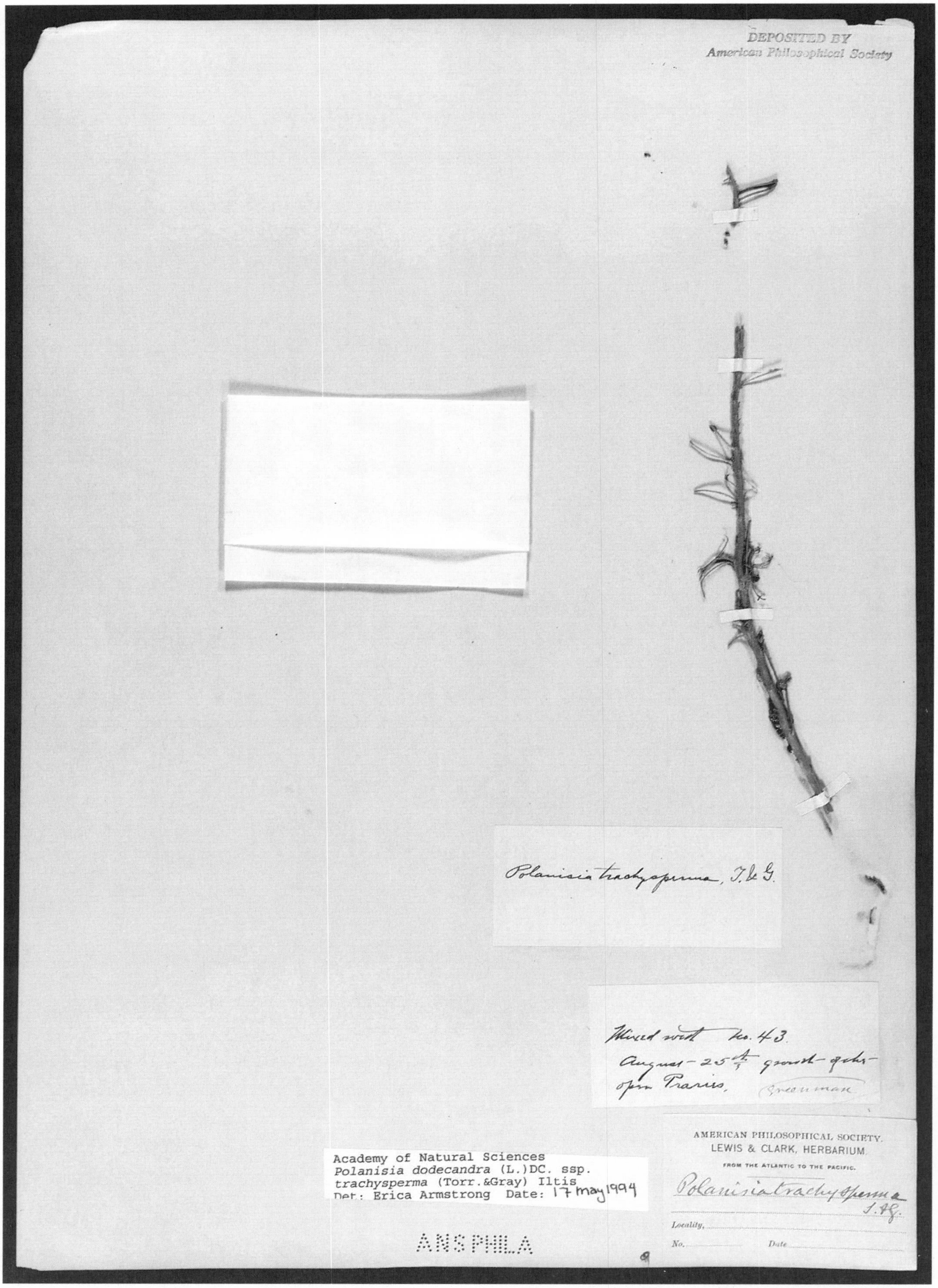

Polanisia trachysperma, T. & G.

Mixed with No. 43.
August 25th, growth of this
open Praries,   (Greenman)

Academy of Natural Sciences
Polanisia dodecandra (L.)DC. ssp.
trachysperma (Torr.&Gray) Iltis
Det: Erica Armstrong Date: 17 May 1994

ANS PHILA

134. *Polanisia dodecandra* (L.) DC. ssp. *trachysperma* (Torr. & Gray) Iltis, clammy-weed

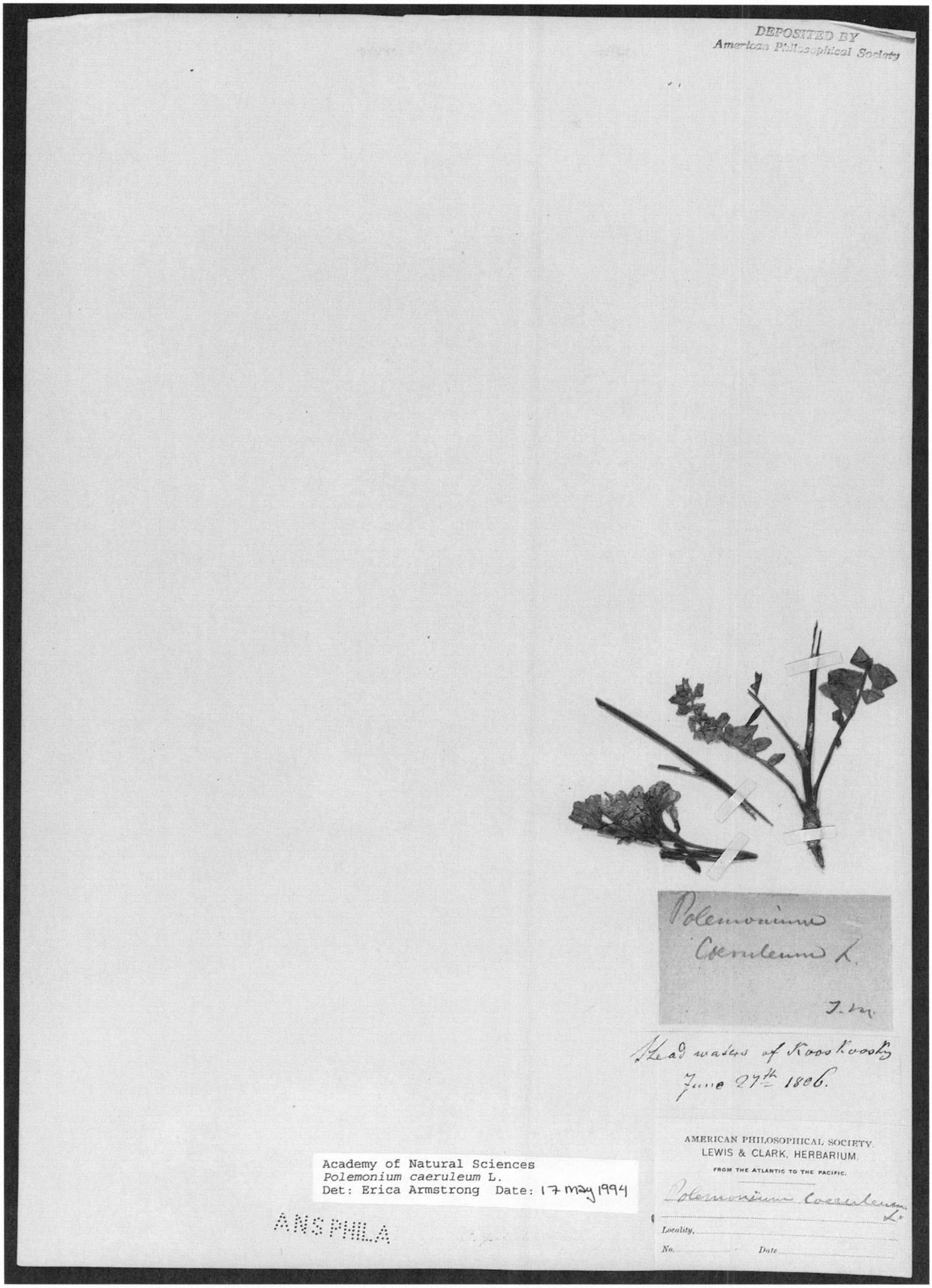

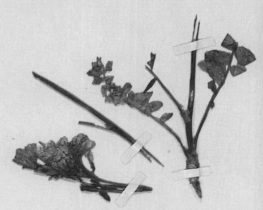

DEPOSITED BY
American Philosophical Society
Polemonium
Coeruleum L.
Head waters of Kooskoosky
June 27th 1806.
AMERICAN PHILOSOPHICAL SOCIETY.
LEWIS & CLARK, HERBARIUM.
FROM THE ATLANTIC TO THE PACIFIC.
Polemonium coeruleum L.
Locality,
No.
Date
Academy of Natural Sciences
Polemonium caeruleum L.
Det: Erica Armstrong Date: 17 May 1994
ANSPHILA

135. *Polemonium caeruleum* L., western polemonium

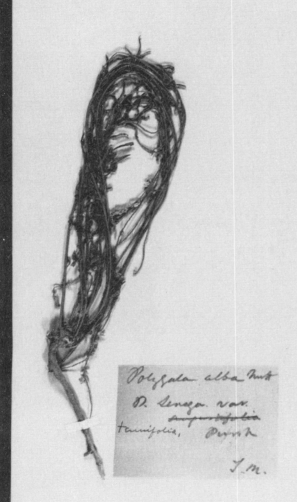

Polygala alba Nutt
P. Senega. var.
~~angustifolia~~
tenuifolia, Pursh

J. M.

Polygala

A kind of Seneca Snake
root.
On the Missouri R.
Yellow Stone River
Augst. 10th 1806.

Leg. M. Lewis

TYPE
Polygala Senega var.
tenuifolia Pursh. Fl.
ed. 2, 2:750. 1816.
= P. alba Nutt 1818.

M.C. Johnston 1958

Academy of Natural Sciences
Polygala alba Nutt.
Det: Erica Armstrong Date: 17 May 1994

136. *Polygala alba* Nutt., white milkwort

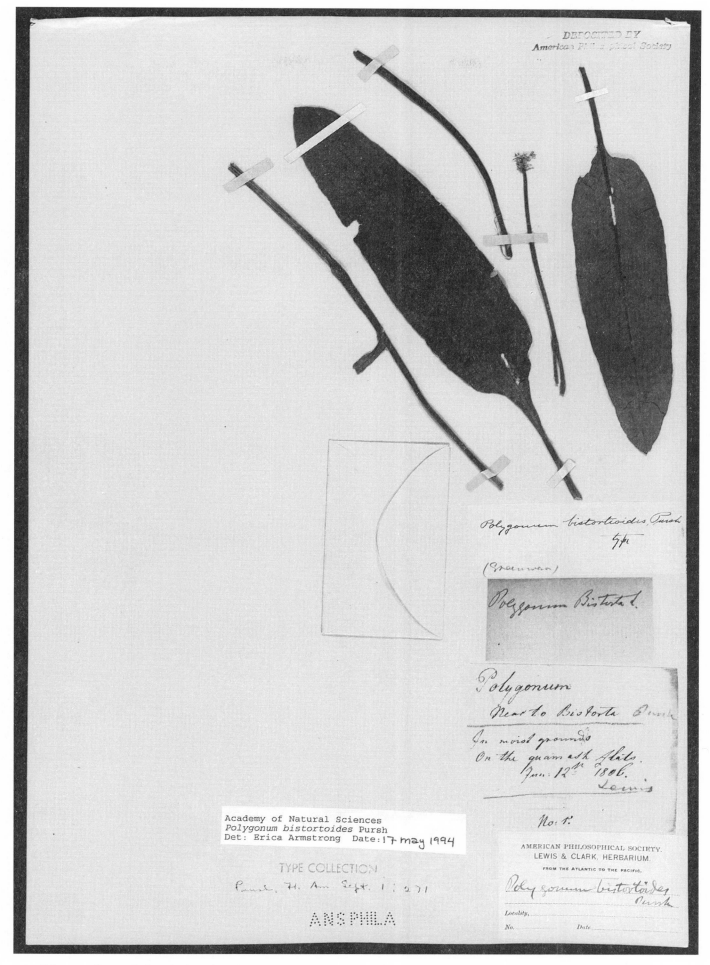

Polygonum bistortoides, Pursh

5/4

(Greenman)

Polygonum Bistorta L.

Polygonum

Near to Bistorta Persh

In moist grounds
On the quamash flats.
Jun. 12th 1806.
Lewis

No. 1.

Academy of Natural Sciences
Polygonum bistortoides Pursh
Det: Erica Armstrong   Date: 17 may 1994

TYPE COLLECTION
Pursh, Fl. Am. Sept. 1 : 271

ANSPHILA

137. *Polygonum bistortoides* Pursh, American bistort

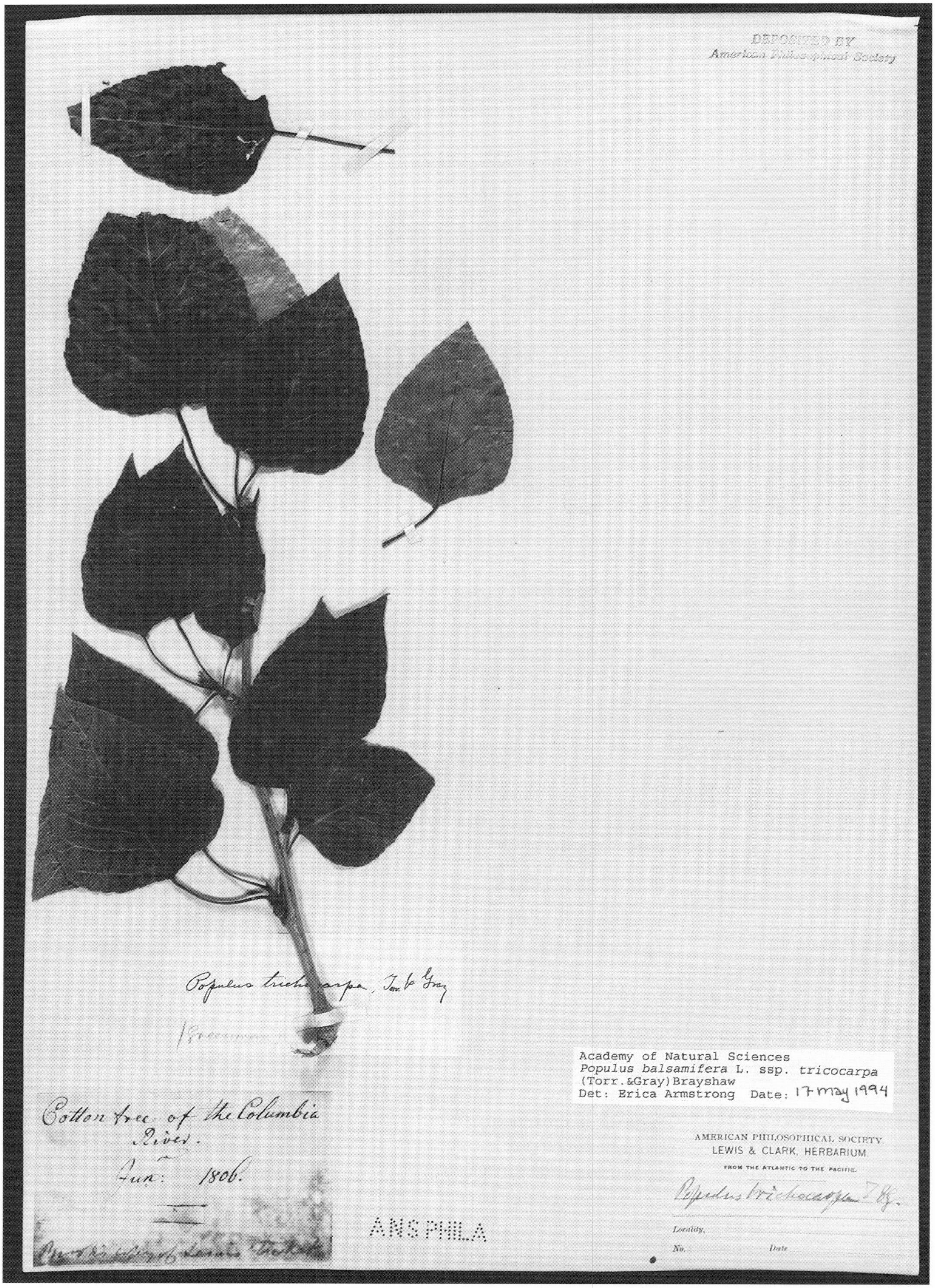

Populus trichocarpa, Torr & Gray

(*Greenman*)

Academy of Natural Sciences
Populus balsamifera L. ssp. *tricocarpa*
(Torr.&Gray)Brayshaw
Det: Erica Armstrong   Date: 17 May 1994

*Cotton tree of the Columbia
River.
Jun: 1806.*

AMERICAN PHILOSOPHICAL SOCIETY.
LEWIS & CLARK, HERBARIUM.
FROM THE ATLANTIC TO THE PACIFIC.

Populus trichocarpa T&G.

Locality,
No.   Date

ANS PHILA

138. *Populus balsamifera* L. ssp. *trichocarpa* (Torr. & Gray *ex* Hook.) Brayshaw, black cottonwood

Populus monilifera Ait
(P. angulata Ait)

(Tru)

Cotton tree of the Mississippi
& Missouri.

Augst. 1806.

Purchased of Lewis...

Academy of Natural Sciences
Populus deltoides Bartr. ex Marsh. ssp.
Monolifera (Ait.)Eckenwalder
Det: Erica Armstrong   Date: 17 may 1994

139. *Populus deltoides* Bartr. *ex* Marsh. ssp. *monilifera* (Ait.) Eckenwalder, cottonwood

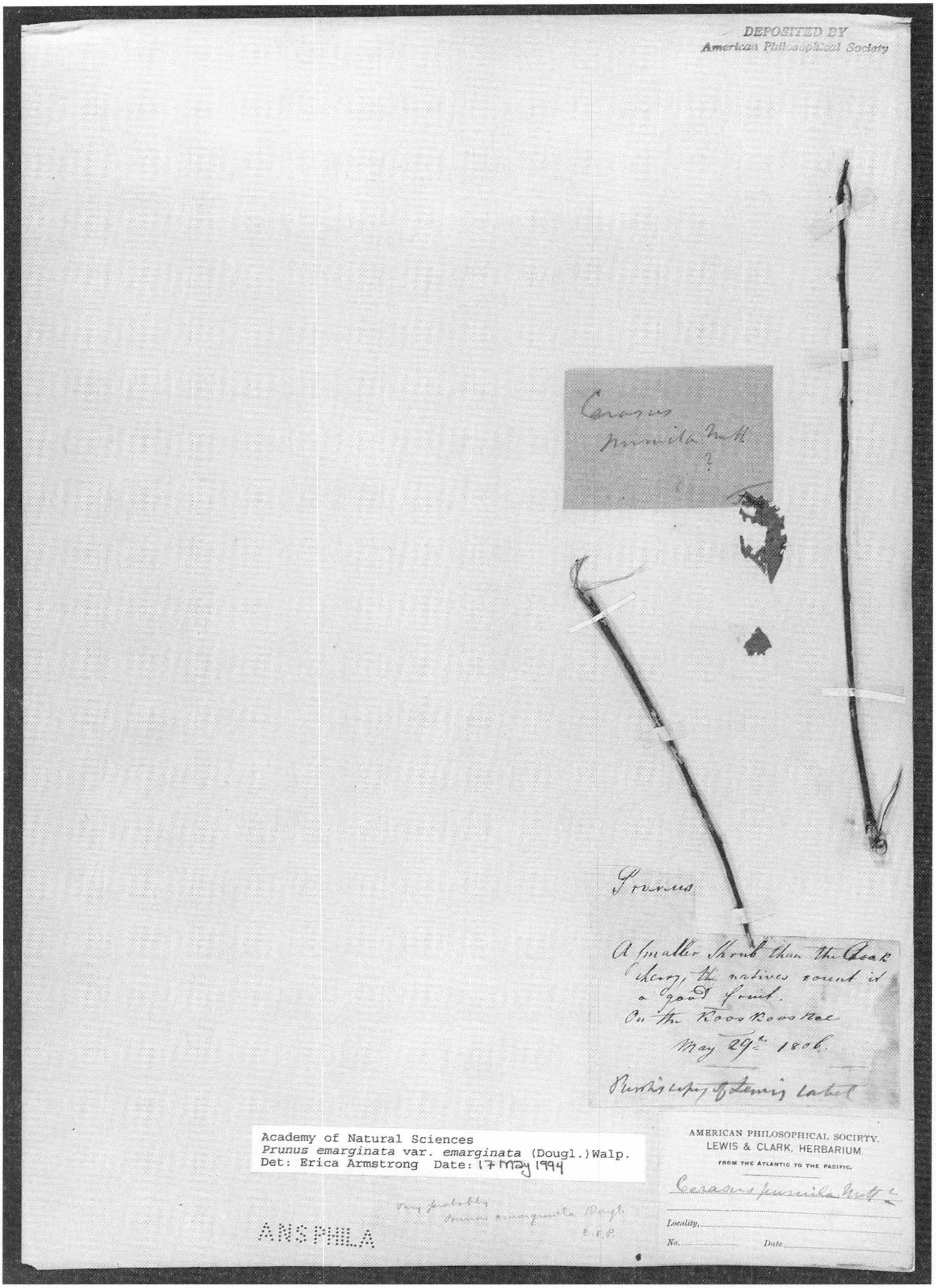

DEPOSITED BY
American Philosophical Society
Cerasus pumila Nutt ?
Prunus
A smaller Shrub than the Choak cherry, the natives count it a good fruit.
On the Koos Koos Kee
May 29th 1806.
Pursh's copy of Lewis's label
Academy of Natural Sciences
Prunus emarginata var. emarginata (Dougl.) Walp.
Det: Erica Armstrong Date: 17 May 1994
AMERICAN PHILOSOPHICAL SOCIETY.
LEWIS & CLARK, HERBARIUM.
FROM THE ATLANTIC TO THE PACIFIC.
Cerasus pumila Nutt
Locality,
No.
Date
ANSPHILA

140. *Prunus emarginata* (Dougl. *ex* Hook.) Walp. var. *emarginata*, bitter cherry

Prunus
Virginiana L.

T. m

Prunus

Choak or Pidgeon Cherry

On th waters of Kooskooshy
May 29th 1806.

Academy of Natural Sciences
Prunus virginiana var. *demissa* (Nutt.)Torr.
Det: Erica Armstrong   Date: 17 May 1994

AMERICAN PHILOSOPHICAL SOCIETY.
LEWIS & CLARK, HERBARIUM.
FROM THE ATLANTIC TO THE PACIFIC.

Prunus Virginiana L.

Locality,

No.   Date

ANS PHILA

141a. *Prunus virginiana* L., choke cherry

Prunus
demissa Nutt

Prunus

A Cherry found near the
beaver bents on the
Missouri

Augst. 10th 1805.

Pursh's copy of Lewis ticket

Academy of Natural Sciences
Prunus virginiana L.
Det: Erica Armstrong   Date: 17 May 1994

ANSPHILA

141b. *Prunus virginiana* L., choke cherry

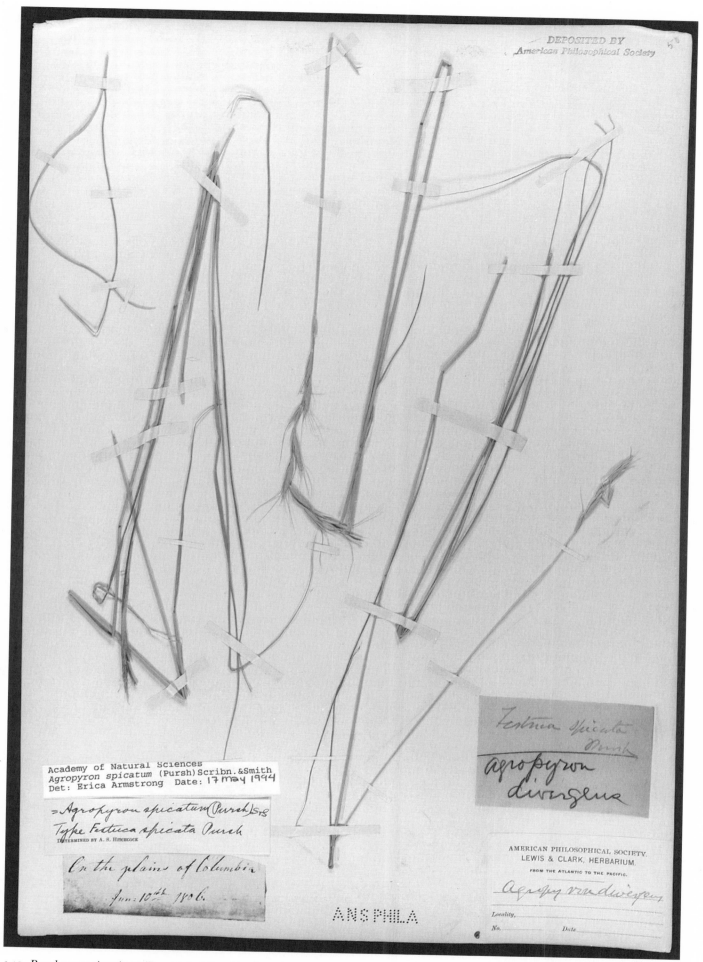

Academy of Natural Sciences
Agropyron spicatum (Pursh) Scribn. &Smith
Det: Erica Armstrong   Date: 17 May 1994

=*Agropyron spicatum* (Pursh) 1878
Type Festuca spicata Pursh
DETERMINED BY A. S. HITCHCOCK

*On the plains of Columbia
Jun. 10th 1806.*

*Festuca spicata
Pursh*

*agropyron
divergens*

AMERICAN PHILOSOPHICAL SOCIETY.
LEWIS & CLARK, HERBARIUM.
FROM THE ATLANTIC TO THE PACIFIC.

agropyron divergens

Locality,

No. _____   Date _____

ANS PHILA

142. *Pseudoroegneria spicata* (Pursh) A. Löve, bluebunch wheatgrass

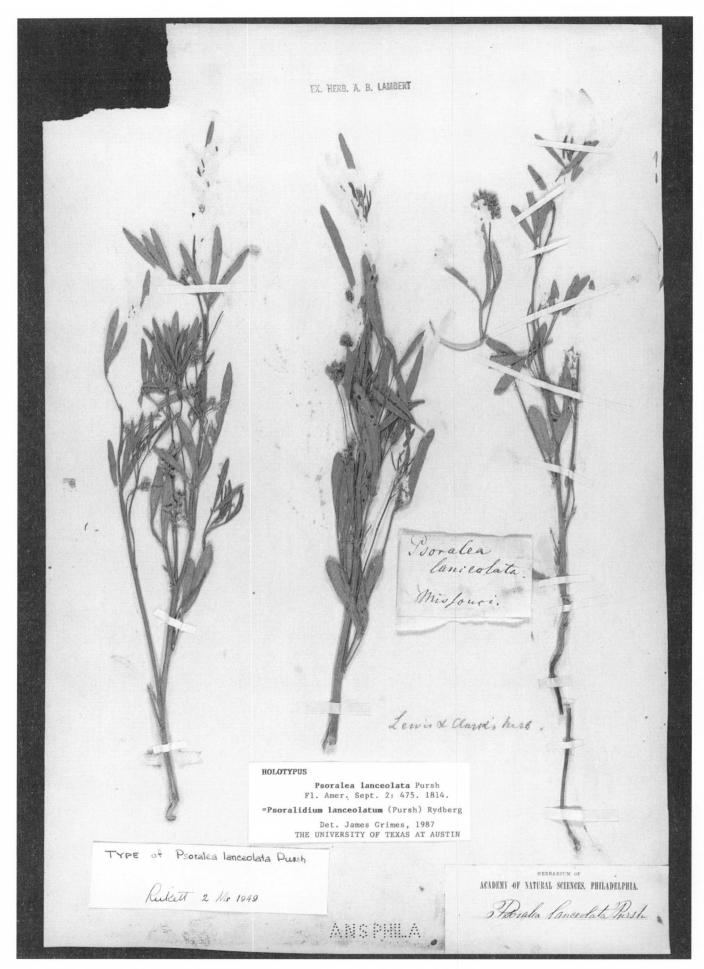

Psoralea lanceolata. Missouri.

Lewis & Clark's herb.

HOLOTYPUS

Psoralea lanceolata Pursh
Fl. Amer. Sept. 2: 475. 1814.

=**Psoralidium lanceolatum** (Pursh) Rydberg

Det. James Grimes, 1987
THE UNIVERSITY OF TEXAS AT AUSTIN

TYPE of Psoralea lanceolata Pursh

Rickett 2 Mr 1949

Psoralea lanceolata Pursh

ANSP HILA

143. *Psoralidium lanceolatum* (Pursh) Rydb., lemon scurf-pea

Psoralea tenuiflora, Pursh
(I.m.g.)

Big bend of the Missouri
Septbr. 21. 1804
Lewis
Pursh, (Id.)

Academy of Natural Sciences
Psoralidium tenuiflorum (Pursh) Rydb.
Det: Erica Armstrong   Date: 17 May 1994

ANS PHILA

144a. *Psoralidium tenuiflorum* (Pursh) Rydb., wild alfalfa

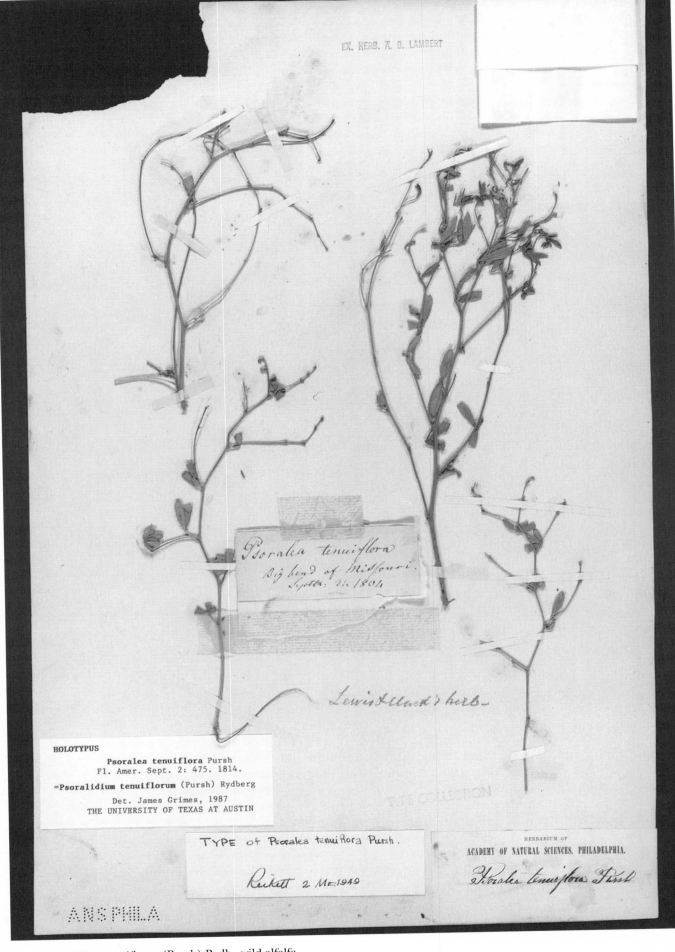

Psoralea tenuiflora
Big bend of Missouri.
Septtr. 24 1804.

Lewis & Clark's herb.

HOLOTYPUS

Psoralea tenuiflora Pursh
Fl. Amer. Sept. 2: 475. 1814.

=Psoralidium tenuiflorum (Pursh) Rydberg

Det. James Grimes, 1987
THE UNIVERSITY OF TEXAS AT AUSTIN

TYPE of Psoralea tenuiflora Pursh.

Reitert 2 Mr 1949

HERBARIUM OF
ACADEMY OF NATURAL SCIENCES, PHILADELPHIA.

Psoralea tenuiflora Pursh

ANS PHILA

144b. *Psoralidium tenuiflorum* (Pursh) Rydb., wild alfalfa

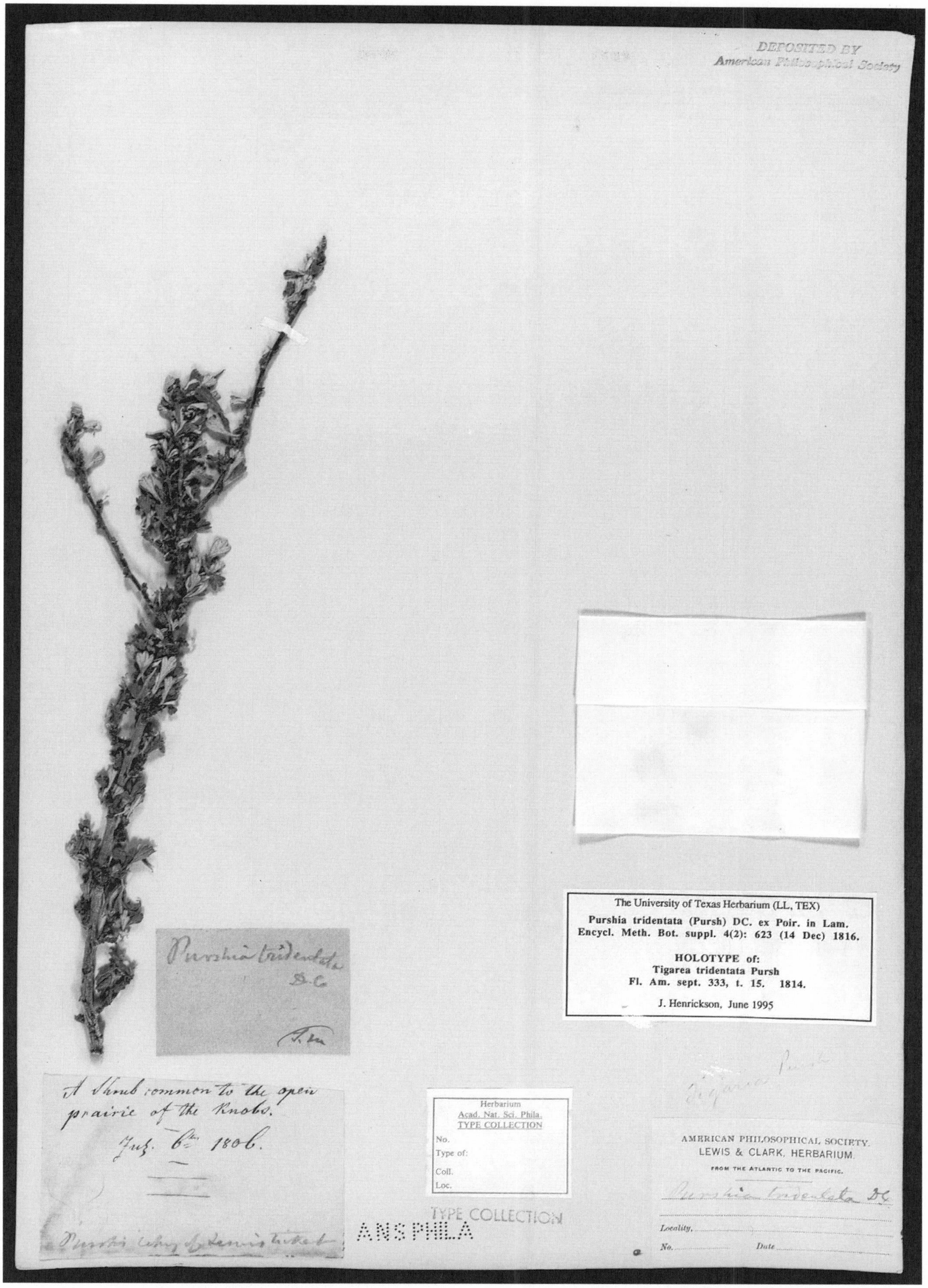

DEPOSITED BY
American Philosophical Society
The University of Texas Herbarium (LL, TEX)
Purshia tridentata (Pursh) DC. ex Poir. in Lam. Encycl. Meth. Bot. suppl. 4(2): 623 (14 Dec) 1816.
HOLOTYPE of:
Tigarea tridentata Pursh
Fl. Am. sept. 333, t. 15. 1814.
J. Henrickson, June 1995
Purshia tridentata D.C.
A Shrub common to the open prairie of the Knobs.
Jul. 6th 1806.
Herbarium
Acad. Nat. Sci. Phila.
TYPE COLLECTION
No.
Type of:
Coll.
Loc.
TYPE COLLECTION
ANSPHILA
AMERICAN PHILOSOPHICAL SOCIETY.
LEWIS & CLARK. HERBARIUM.
FROM THE ATLANTIC TO THE PACIFIC.
Purshia tridentata DC
Locality,
No.
Date

145. *Purshia tridentata* (Pursh) DC., antelope-brush

Academy of Natural Sciences
Quercus garryana Dougl.ex Hook
Det: Erica Armstrong   Date: 17 May 1994

AMERICAN PHILOSOPHICAL SOCIETY.
LEWIS & CLARK, HERBARIUM.
FROM THE ATLANTIC TO THE PACIFIC.

Quercus Garryana Dougl.

Locality,
No.   Date

146a. *Quercus garryana* Dougl. *ex* Hook., Garry oak

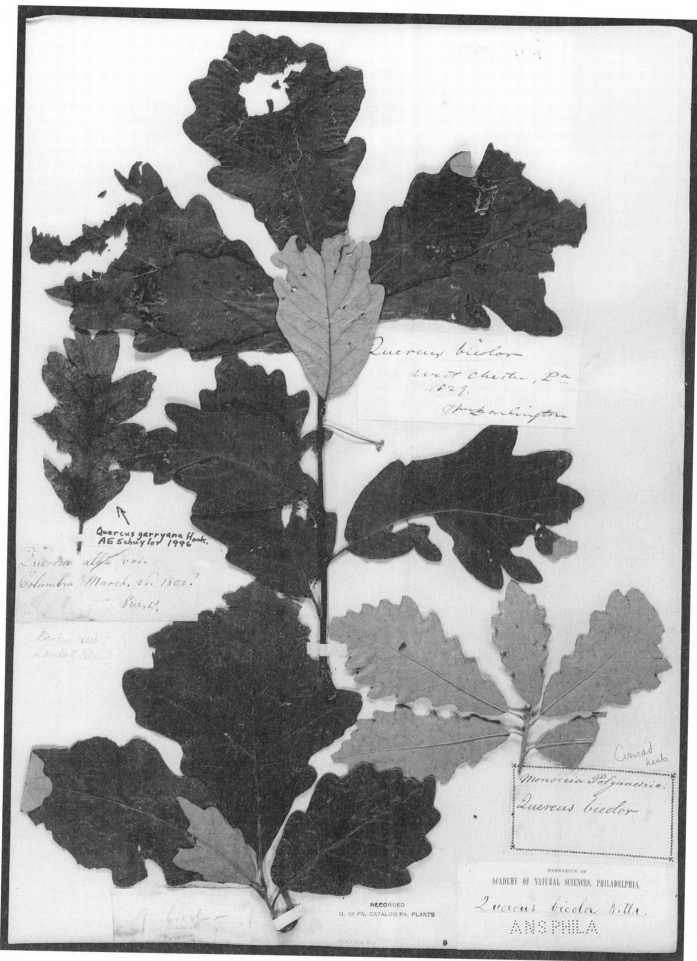

146b. *Quercus garryana* Dougl. *ex* Hook., Garry oak

Academy of Natural Sciences
Quercus macrocarpa Michx.
Det: Erica Armstrong   Date: 17 may 1994

Quercus macrocarpa
Mf
Var. depressa Engel.

T. m   N° 34   Common to the prairies—
Sptb. 5. 1804.

The leaf of oak which is common to the Prairies

5th September 1804

ANS PHILA

147a. *Quercus macrocarpa* Michx., bur oak

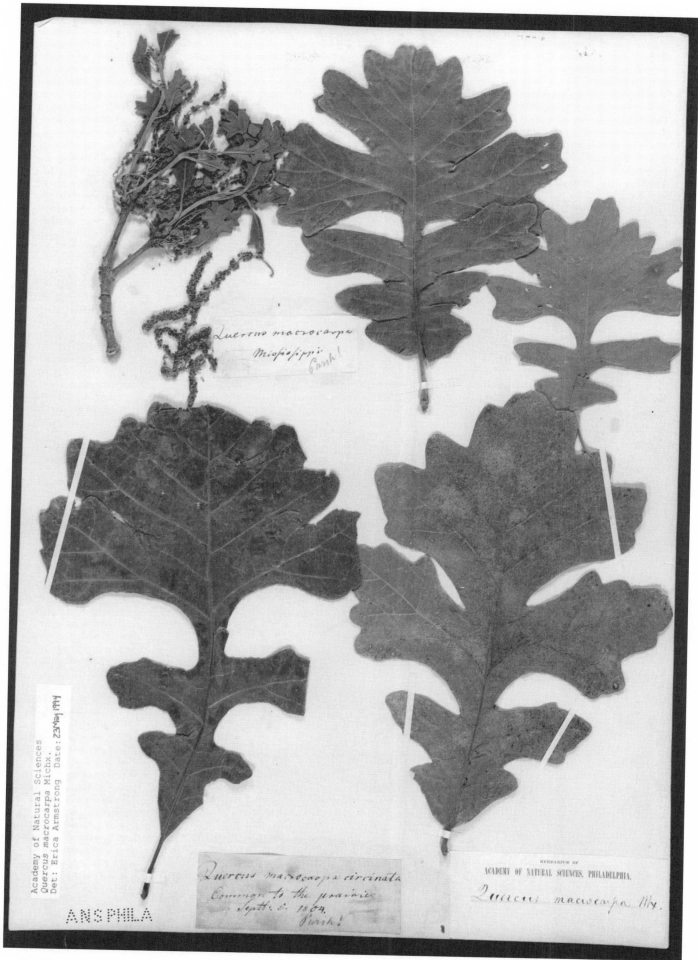

Quercus macrocarpa
Mississippi
Pursh!

Quercus macrocarpa circinata
Common to the prairies
Sept. 5, 1864.
Pursh!

Quercus macrocarpa Mx.

147b. *Quercus macrocarpa* Michx., bur oak

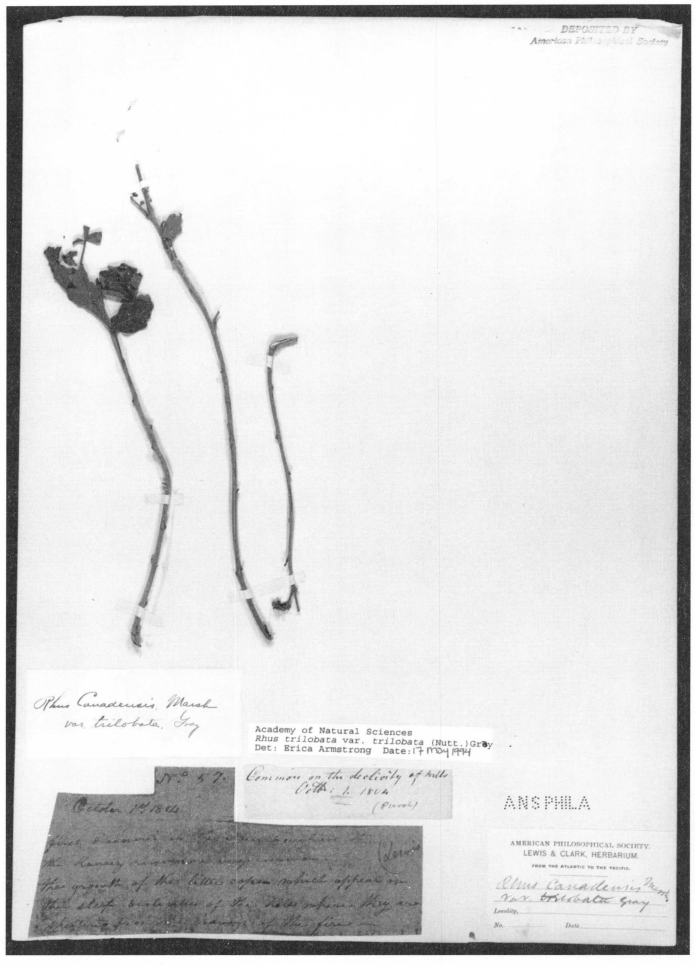

Rhus Canadensis, Marsh
var. *trilobata,* Gray

Academy of Natural Sciences
Rhus trilobata var. trilobata (Nutt.)Gray
Det: Erica Armstrong   Date:17 May 1994

Common on the declivity of hills
Oct: 1. 1804
(Pursh)

N° 57.

October 1st 1804

ANS PHILA

AMERICAN PHILOSOPHICAL SOCIETY.
LEWIS & CLARK, HERBARIUM.
FROM THE ATLANTIC TO THE PACIFIC.

Rhus Canadensis Mch
var. *trilobata* Gray
Locality,
No.   Date

148. *Rhus trilobata* Nutt. var. *trilobata,* fragrant sumac

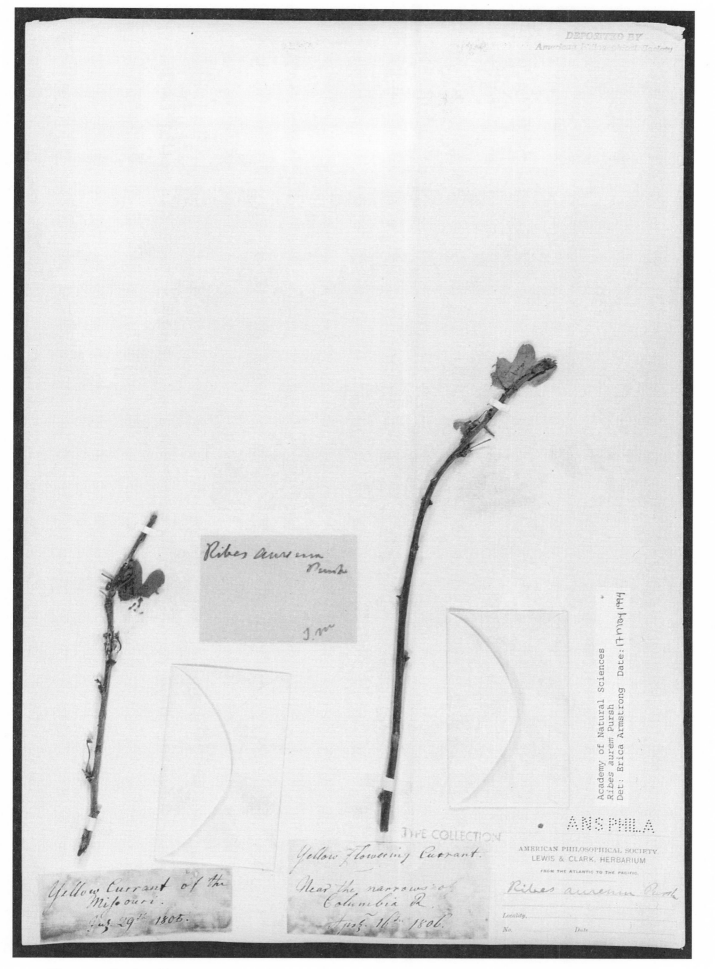

Ribes aureum
Pursh

Academy of Natural Sciences
Ribes aureum Pursh
Det.: Erica Armstrong   Date: 17 May 1994

TYPE COLLECTION

ANS PHILA

AMERICAN PHILOSOPHICAL SOCIETY,
LEWIS & CLARK, HERBARIUM
FROM THE ATLANTIC TO THE PACIFIC.

Ribes aureum Pursh

Locality,
No.   Date

Yellow Currant of the
Missouri.
Aug 29th 1805.

Yellow flowering Currant.
Near the narrows of
Columbia R.
April 16th 1806.

149a. *Ribes aureum* Pursh, golden currant

149b. *Ribes aureum* Pursh, golden currant

Ribes Menziesii
Pursh

(Tm)

Deep purple Gooseberry.

Columbia R.
April 8th 1806.

Pursh's copy of Lewis label

Academy of Natural Sciences
Ribes divaricatum Dougl.
Det: Erica Armstrong   Date:17 May 1994

ANS PHILA   Probably R. divaricatum Dougl.
                                    C.V.P.

150. *Ribes divaricatum* Pursh, straggly gooseberry

Ribes Sanguineum
Pursh

(*Typ*)

Columbia.
March 27. 1806.

Pursh's copy of Lewis' label

151. *Ribes sanguineum* Pursh, red currant

Ribes viscossimum
Pursh

(1 in)

Fruit indifferent & yummy.

The lights of the Rocky
mountain.
Jun: 16th 1806.

Pursh's copy of Lewis label

TYPE COLLECTION

R viscosissimum

Academy of Natural Sciences
Ribes viscossissimum Pursh
Det: Erica Armstrong   Date: 18 May 1994

ANS PHILA

152a. *Ribes viscosissimum* Pursh, sticky currant

152b. *Ribes viscosissimum* Pursh, sticky currant

Rosa

Open prairies Septb. 5. 1804

Purrh who it Lewis totat

Rosa Woodsii Lindl

No. 50
(Lewis)
October 18th

ANS PHILA.

T.m.

The small Rose of the prairies

it rises from 1° to 1½ Inches high does not mere

Academy of Natural Sciences
Rosa arkansana Porter
Det: Erica Armstrong   Date: 18 May 1994

AMERICAN PHILOSOPHICAL SOCIETY.
LEWIS & CLARK, HERBARIUM.
FROM THE ATLANTIC TO THE PACIFIC.

Rosa Woodsii Lindl.

Locality,
No.   Date

153. *Rosa arkansana* Porter, prairie wild rose

Rubus nutkaensis
Moç.
Moç.

J. m.

Rubus nutkanus, Moç.
var. *velutina* Brewer

Greenman

A shrub of which the natives eat the young sprout without Rooting.
On the Columbia.
Apry. 15th 1806.

Provisio copy of Lewis & Clark

Academy of Natural Sciences
Rubus spectabilis Pursh var. *spectabilis*
Det: Erica Armstrong   Date: 18 May 1994

ANS PHILA

154. *Rubus parviflorus* Nutt., thimbleberry

Rubus spectabilis Pursh

Fruit like a Rasberry
Columbia.
March 27th 1806.

AMERICAN PHILOSOPHICAL SOCIETY.
LEWIS & CLARK, HERBARIUM.
FROM THE ATLANTIC TO THE PACIFIC.

Rubus spectabilis Pursh

Locality.
No.   Date

ANS PHILA

155. *Rubus spectabilis* Pursh, salmonberry

Big bend of Missouri
Octbr. 21. 1804.

Salvia Lanceolata, *Willd.*
Pursh
S. trichostemnoides
Pursh

Academy of Natural Sciences
Salvia reflexa Hornem.
Det: Erica Armstrong Date: 18 May 1994

ANS PHILA

156a. *Salvia reflexa* Hornem., lance-leaved sage

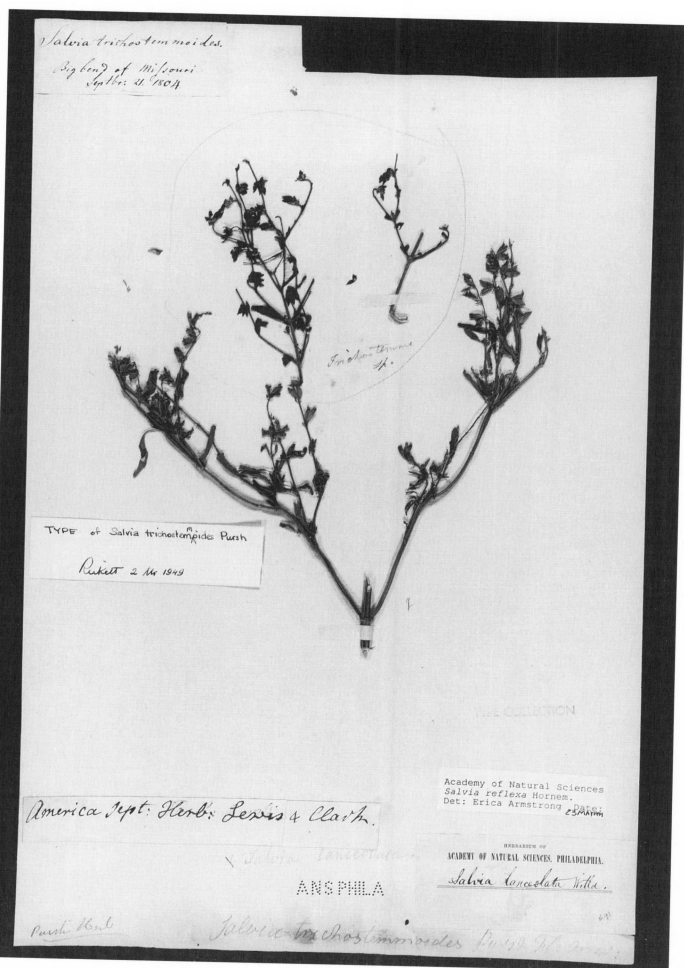

Salvia trichostemmoides.

Big bend of Missouri
Septbr: 21. 1804

Trichenstemme *H.*

TYPE of Salvia trichostem^m^oides Pursh

Rickett 2 Mr 1949

America Sept: Herb: Lewis & Clark.

× *Salvia lanceolata*

ANS PHILA

Salvia lanceolata Willd.

Pursh Herb

Salvia trichostemmoides Pursh

156b. *Salvia reflexa* Hornem., lance-leaved sage

*Sarcobatus
Vermiculatus Torr*

J. m.

A small branchy Shrub
from the plains of
Missouri
July. 20th 1806.

Pursh's copy of Lewis

Academy of Natural Sciences
Sarcobatus vermiculatus (Hook.)Torr.
var. *vermiculatus*
Det: Erica Armstrong   Date: 18 may 1994

AMERICAN PHILOSOPHICAL SOCIETY.
LEWIS & CLARK, HERBARIUM.
FROM THE ATLANTIC TO THE PACIFIC.

Sarcobatus vermiculatus
Torr.

Locality,

No.   Date

157. *Sarcobatus vermiculatus* (Hook.) Torr., greasewood

Scutellaria angustifolia
Pursh

TYPE COLLECTION

On the Kooskooskee
Jun: 5th 1806.

ANS PHILA

Scutellaria angustifolia Pursh HOLOTYPE!
subsp. angustifolia
Det. by: Richard Olmstead 1987
University of Washington

158. *Scutellaria angustifolia* Pursh ssp. *angustifolia*, narrow-leaved skullcap

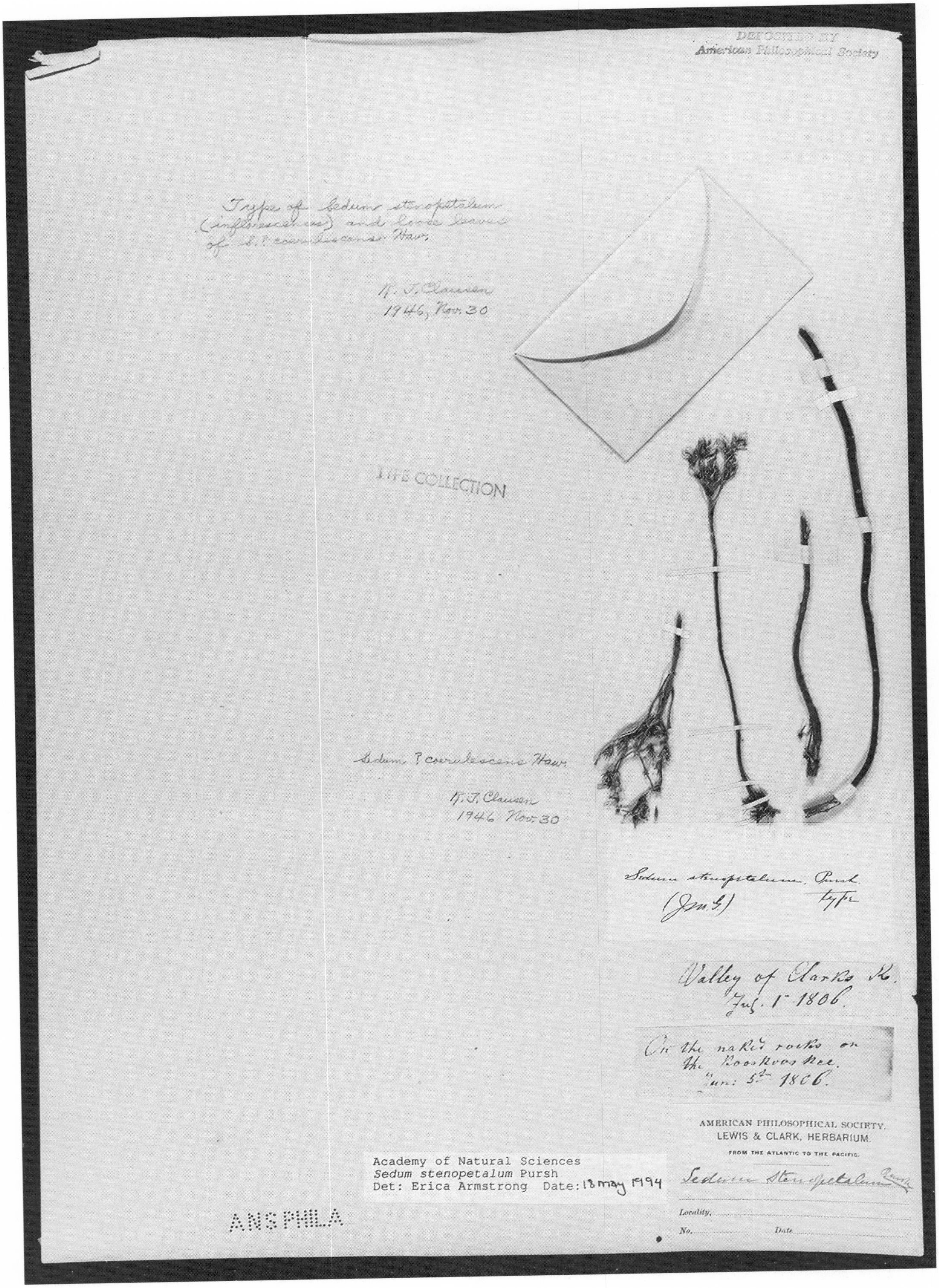

Type of Sedum stenopetalum
(inflorescences) and loose leaves
of S.? coerulescens. Haw.

R. T. Clausen
1946, Nov. 30

TYPE COLLECTION

Sedum ? coerulescens Haw.

R. T. Clausen
1946 Nov. 30

Sedum stenopetalum. Pursh.
(Jm.G)   type

Valley of Clarks R.
July. 1st 1806.

On the naked rocks on
the Rooskoosskee.
"Jun: 5th 1806.

Sedum stenopetalum

Locality,

No.   Date

Academy of Natural Sciences
Sedum stenopetalum Pursh
Det: Erica Armstrong   Date: 18 may 1994

ANS PHILA

159. *Sedum stenopetalum* Pursh, wormleaf stonecrop

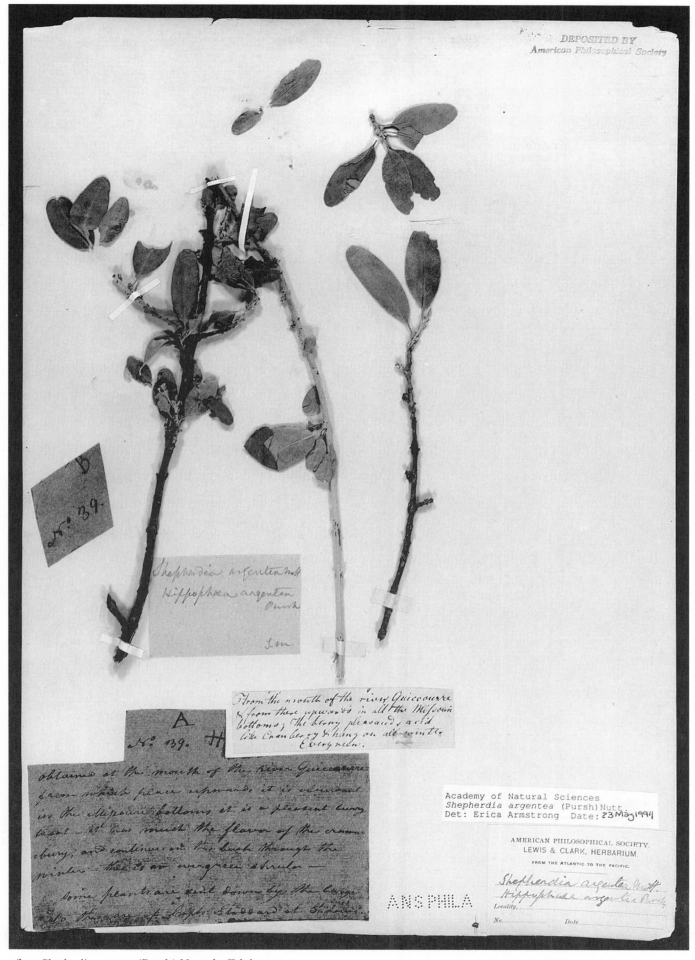

Academy of Natural Sciences
Shepherdia argentea (Pursh) Nutt.
Det: Erica Armstrong   Date: 23 May 1994

AMERICAN PHILOSOPHICAL SOCIETY.
LEWIS & CLARK, HERBARIUM.
FROM THE ATLANTIC TO THE PACIFIC.

ANS PHILA

160a. *Shepherdia argentea* (Pursh) Nutt., buffaloberry

160b. *Shepherdia argentea* (Pursh) Nutt., buffaloberry

Academy of Natural Sciences
Solidago rigida L.
Det: Erica Armstrong Date: 18 may 1994

AMERICAN PHILOSOPHICAL SOCIETY.
LEWIS & CLARK, HERBARIUM.
FROM THE ATLANTIC TO THE PACIFIC.

Solidago rigida L.

Locality,
No.   Date

ANS PHLA

161. *Solidago rigida* L., rigid goldenrod

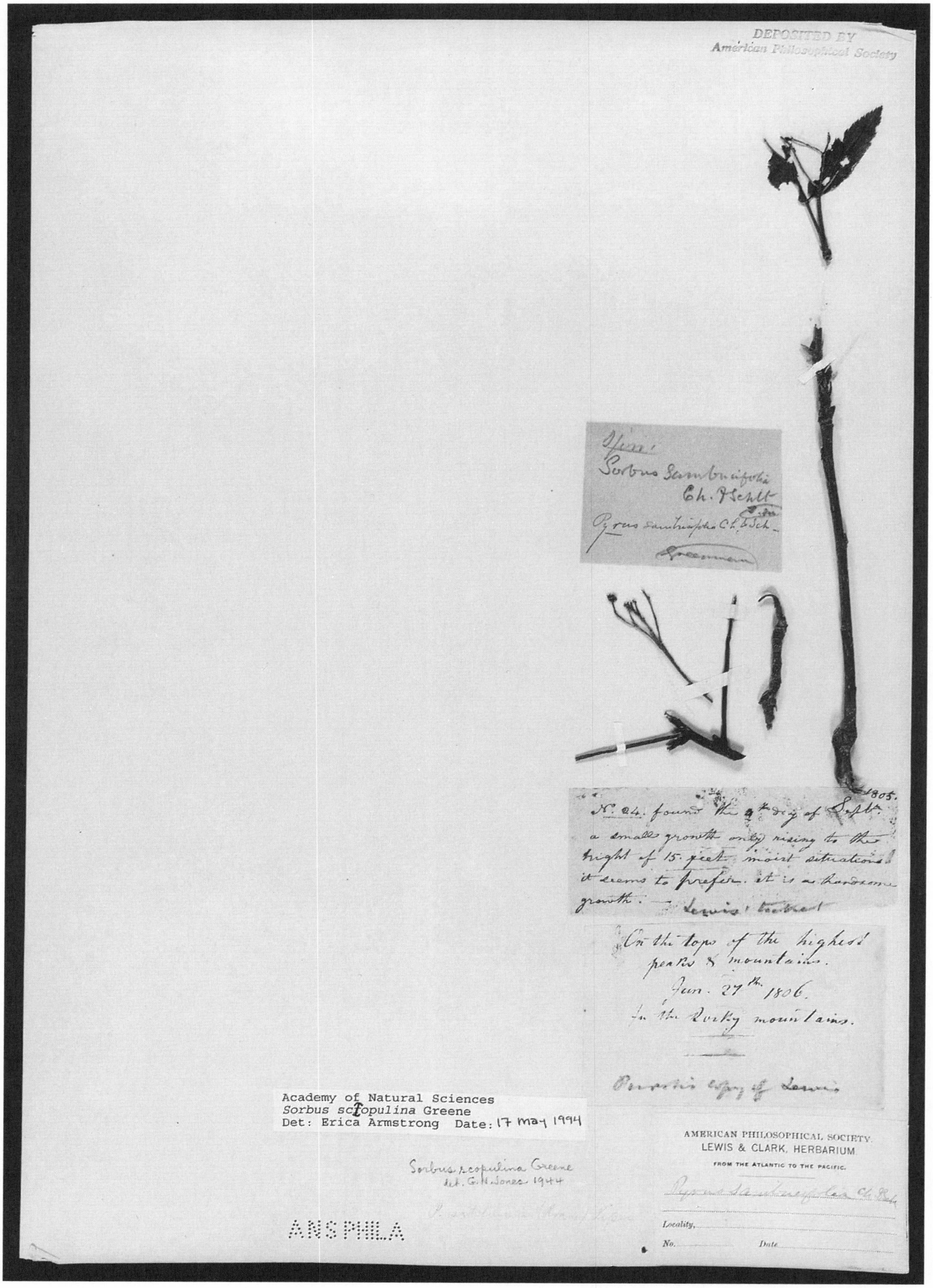

Here!
Sorbus Sambucifolia
Ch. & Schlt
Pyrus sambucifolia Ch. & Sch.
Greenman

N°. 24. found the 4th day of Sept.
a small growth only rising to the
hight of 15 feet. moist situations
it seems to prefer. it is a handsome
growth. — Lewis & tracknot

On the tops of the highest
peaks & mountains.
Jun. 27th 1806.
In the Rocky mountains.

Pursh's copy of Lewis

Academy of Natural Sciences
Sorbus scopulina Greene
Det: Erica Armstrong   Date: 17 May 1994

Sorbus scopulina Greene
det. G. N. Jones 1944

AMERICAN PHILOSOPHICAL SOCIETY.
LEWIS & CLARK, HERBARIUM.
FROM THE ATLANTIC TO THE PACIFIC.

Pyrus sambucifolia Ch. & Sch.

Locality,
No.   Date

162. *Sorbus scopulina* Greene, mountain ash

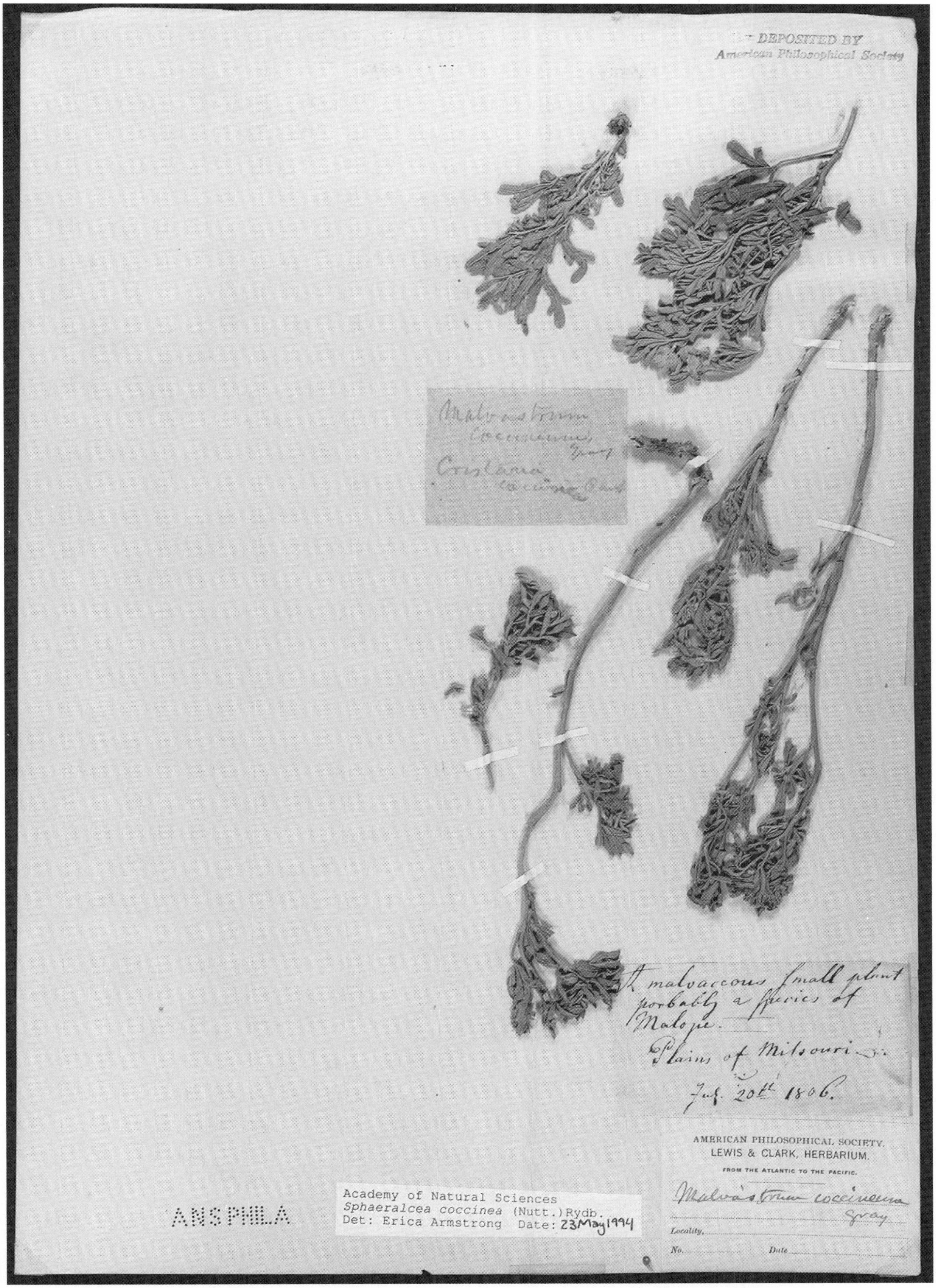

Malvastrum
coccineum,
Gray
Cristaria
coccinia Purs

A malvaccous small plant
porbably a species of
Maloje.
Plains of Missouri
Jul. 20th 1806.

ANS PHILA

Academy of Natural Sciences
Sphaeralcea coccinea (Nutt.) Rydb.
Det: Erica Armstrong   Date: 23 May 1994

163a. *Sphaeralcea coccinea* (Nutt.) Rydb., red false mallow

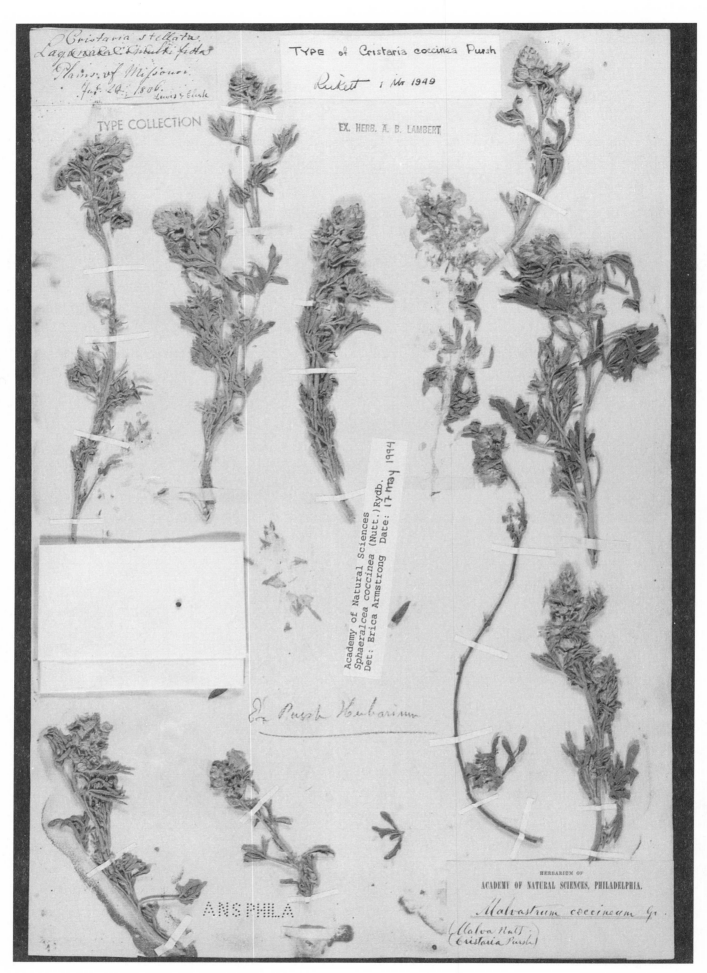

163b. *Sphaeralcea coccinea* (Nutt.) Rydb., red false mallow

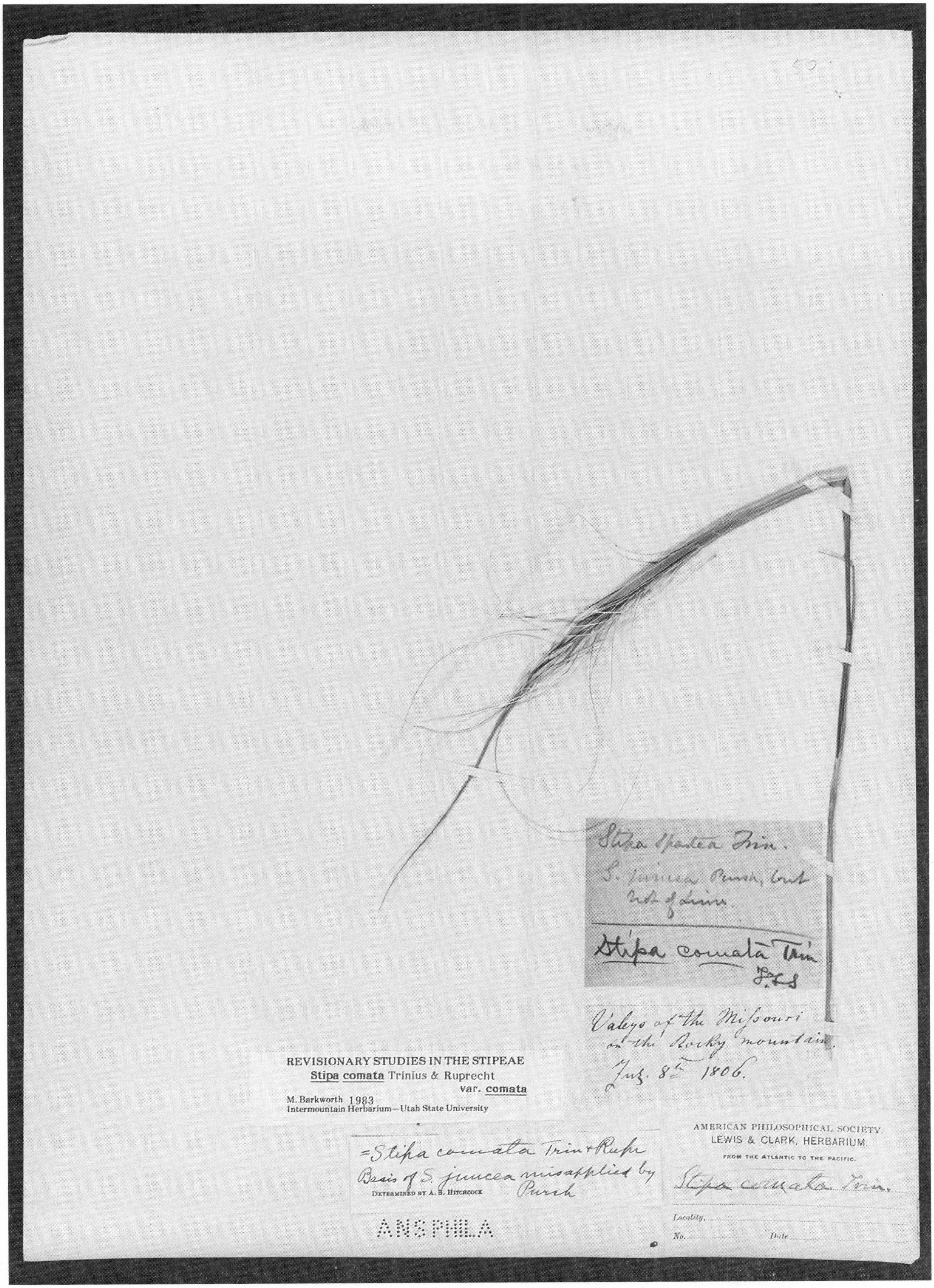

50

REVISIONARY STUDIES IN THE STIPEAE
Stipa comata Trinius & Ruprecht
var. **comata**

M. Barkworth 1983
Intermountain Herbarium—Utah State University

Stipa Spartea Trin.

S. juncea Pursh, but not of Linn.

Stipa comata Trin.
ACS

Valeys of the Missouri on the Rocky mountain.
Jug. 8th 1806.

=Stipa comata Trin & Rupr.
Basis of S. juncea misapplied by Pursh

DETERMINED BY A. S. HITCHCOCK

AMERICAN PHILOSOPHICAL SOCIETY.
LEWIS & CLARK, HERBARIUM.
FROM THE ATLANTIC TO THE PACIFIC.

Stipa comata Trin.

Locality,

No.   Date

164. *Stipa comata* Trin. & Rupr., needle-and-thread

165. *Symphoricarpos albus* (L.) Blake, snowberry

Synthyris reniformis, Benth.
var. major, Hook.

(Greenman)

Synthyris reniformis
Benth

Veronica reniformis
Pursh
??
(J.M.)

Veronica reniformis Pursh

On hungry creek
Jun: 26th 1806.

Pursh's copy of Lewis' label

Academy of Natural Sciences
Synthyris missurica (Raf.) Pennell
Det: Erica Armstrong   Date: 23 May 94

AMERICAN PHILOSOPHICAL SOCIETY.
LEWIS & CLARK, HERBARIUM.
FROM THE ATLANTIC TO THE PACIFIC.

Synthyris reniformis Benth

Locality,
No.   Date

S. missurica (Raf.)
F. P. 1902

166a. *Synthyris missurica* (Raf.) Pennell, mountain kittentails

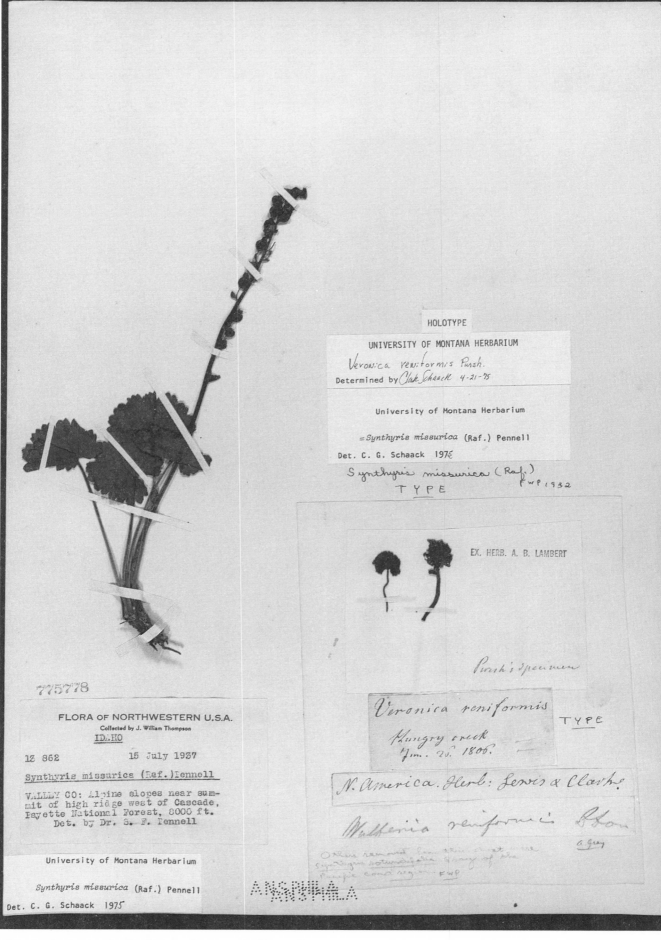

HOLOTYPE

UNIVERSITY OF MONTANA HERBARIUM

Veronica reniformis Pursh.

Determined by *Clark Schaack* 4-21-75

University of Montana Herbarium

=*Synthyris missurica* (Raf.) Pennell

Det. C. G. Schaack 1975

Synthyris missurica (Raf.)

TYPE   FWP 1932

EX. HERB. A. B. LAMBERT

Pursh's specimen

Veronica reniformis

Hungry creek

Jun. W. 1806.   TYPE

N. America. Herb: Lewis & Clark.

Wulfenia reniformis Rom.

A. Gray

775778

FLORA OF NORTHWESTERN U.S.A.

Collected by J. William Thompson

IDAHO

13 862   15 July 1937

Synthyris missurica (Raf.) Pennell

VALLEY CO: Alpine slopes near sum-
mit of high ridge west of Cascade,
Payette National Forest, 8000 ft.
Det. by Dr. S. F. Pennell

University of Montana Herbarium

Synthyris missurica (Raf.) Pennell

Det. C. G. Schaack 1975

166b. *Synthyris missurica* (Raf.) Pennell, mountain kittentails

Holotype of <u>Lupinaster</u> <u>macrocephalus</u> Pursh
Fl. Am. Sept. 2: 479. 1814.
Pursh gave the locality as "Headwaters of
the Missouri, <u>Lewis</u>".
Nuttall merely changed the name of Pursh's
species because he cited Pursh's name in
synonymy. It is therefore based on the
same type. The correct name then is
<u>Trifolium macrocephalum</u> (Pursh) Poir.
Encycl. Suppl. 5: 336. 1817.
This combination is a year earlier than
Nuttall's change anyhow.

J.M.Gillett, 1963

DEPARTMENT OF AGRICULTURE, OTTAWA, CANADA

HOLOTYPE

Lupinaster macrocephalus Pursh

= *Trifolium macrocephalum* (Pursh) Poir.

Michael A. Vincent (MU) 1995

TYPE COLLECTION

Trifolium megacephalum Nutt.

(N.9.)

[Greenman's label
of identification. 189]

A Species of Clover near
Rockford Camp on
high hills.
April 17th 1806.

[Pursh's copy of
Lewis' label]

AMERICAN PHILOSOPHICAL SOCIETY.
LEWIS & CLARK, HERBARIUM.
FROM THE ATLANTIC TO THE PACIFIC.

Trifolium megacephalum
Nutt.

Locality,
No.   Date

["April 17, 1806. Rock Fort (not
'Rockford') Camp at The Dalles
of the Columbia. Ex E. Coues]

ANS PHILA

167a. *Trifolium macrocephalum* (Pursh) Poir., big-head clover

167b. *Trifolium macrocephalum* (Pursh) Poir., big-head clover

ANNOTATION LABEL
Trifolium microcephalum Pursh

James S. Martin   1942

TYPE COLLECTION

Academy of Natural Sciences
Trifolium microcephalum Pursh
Det: Erica Armstrong   Date: 18 May 1994

*Trifolium
microcephalum
Pursh*

J. M.

*Valley of Clarks R.
Jng. 1st 1806.*

For locality see Proc.
Acad. Nat. Sci. Phila. :299. 1898.

AMERICAN PHILOSOPHICAL SOCIETY,
LEWIS & CLARK, HERBARIUM.
FROM THE ATLANTIC TO THE PACIFIC.

*Trifolium microcephalum
Pursh*

Locality,

No.   Date

ANSPHILA

168a. *Trifolium microcephalum* Pursh, small-head clover

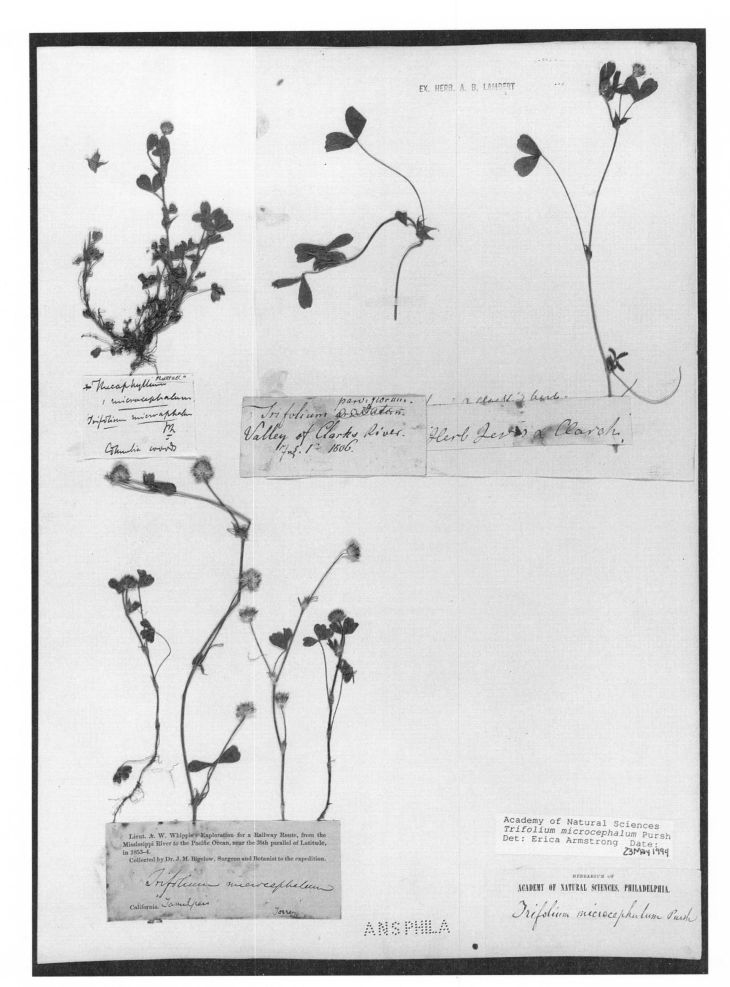

Tricaphyllum *Nuttall.*
, microcephalum,
Trifolium microcephalum
Ph.
Columbia woods

Trifolium parviflorum.
a lotatum.
Valley of Clarks River.
Aug. 1st 1806.

a clearls bank.

Herb. Lewis & Clark.

Lieut. A. W. Whipple's Exploration for a Railway Route, from the
Mississippi River to the Pacific Ocean, near the 35th parallel of Latitude,
in 1853–4.
Collected by Dr. J. M. Bigelow, Surgeon and Botanist to the expedition.

Trifolium microcephalum

California. Tamalpais   Torrey.

Academy of Natural Sciences
Trifolium microcephalum Pursh
Det: Erica Armstrong   Date:
23 May 1994

HERBARIUM OF
ACADEMY OF NATURAL SCIENCES, PHILADELPHIA.

Trifolium microcephalum Pursh

ANSPHILA

168b. *Trifolium microcephalum* Pursh, small-head clover

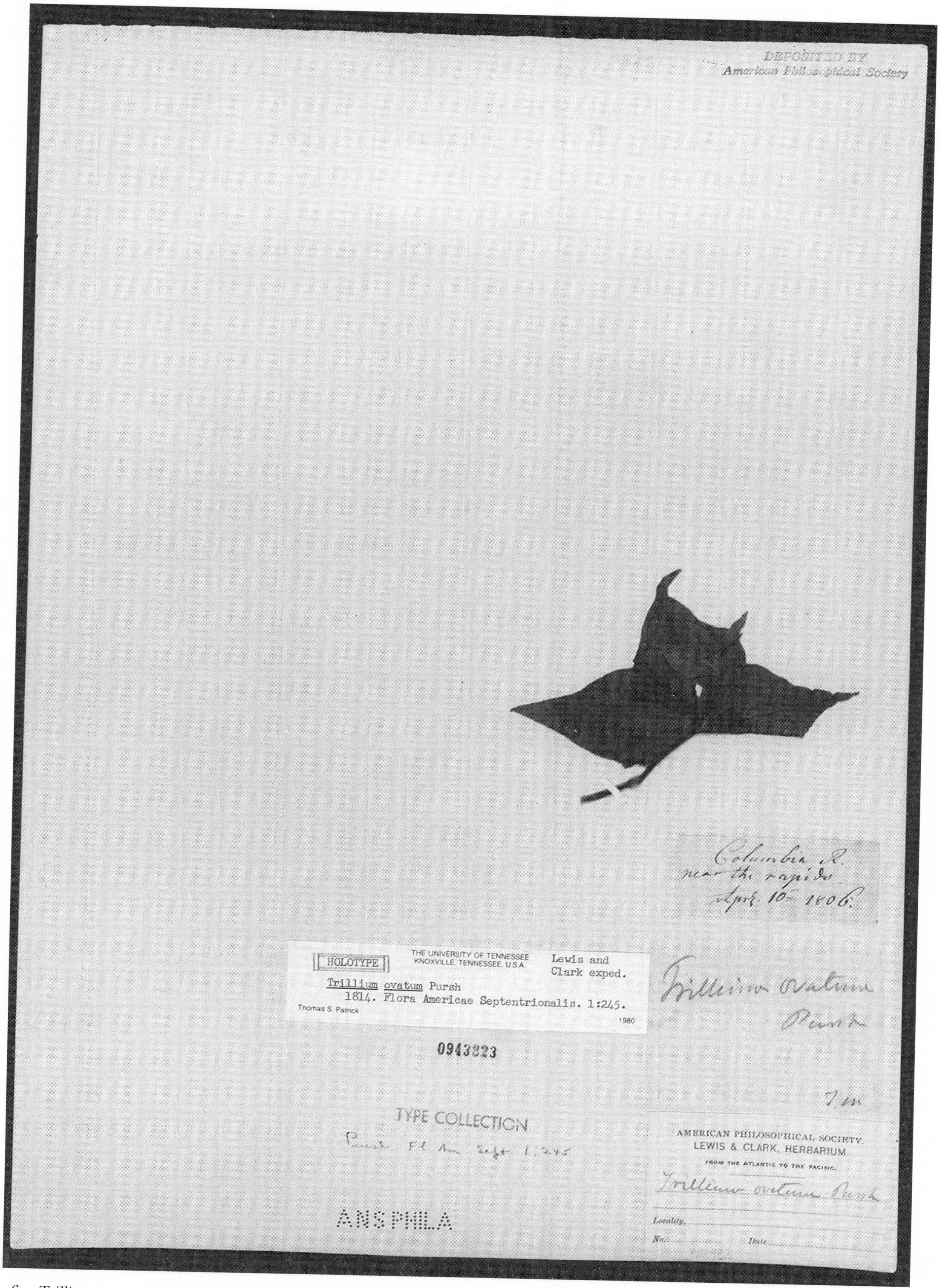

Columbia R.
near the rapids
April 10th 1806.

Trillium ovatum
Pursh

T.m.

HOLOTYPE | THE UNIVERSITY OF TENNESSEE
KNOXVILLE, TENNESSEE, U.S.A | Lewis and
Clark exped.

Trillium ovatum Pursh
1814. Flora Americae Septentrionalis. 1:245.
Thomas S. Patrick   1980

0943823

TYPE COLLECTION

Pursh Fl Am Sept 1:245

AMERICAN PHILOSOPHICAL SOCIETY.
LEWIS & CLARK, HERBARIUM.
FROM THE ATLANTIC TO THE PACIFIC.

Trillium ovatum Pursh

Locality,

No.   Date

ANS PHILA

169. *Trillium ovatum* Pursh, white trillium

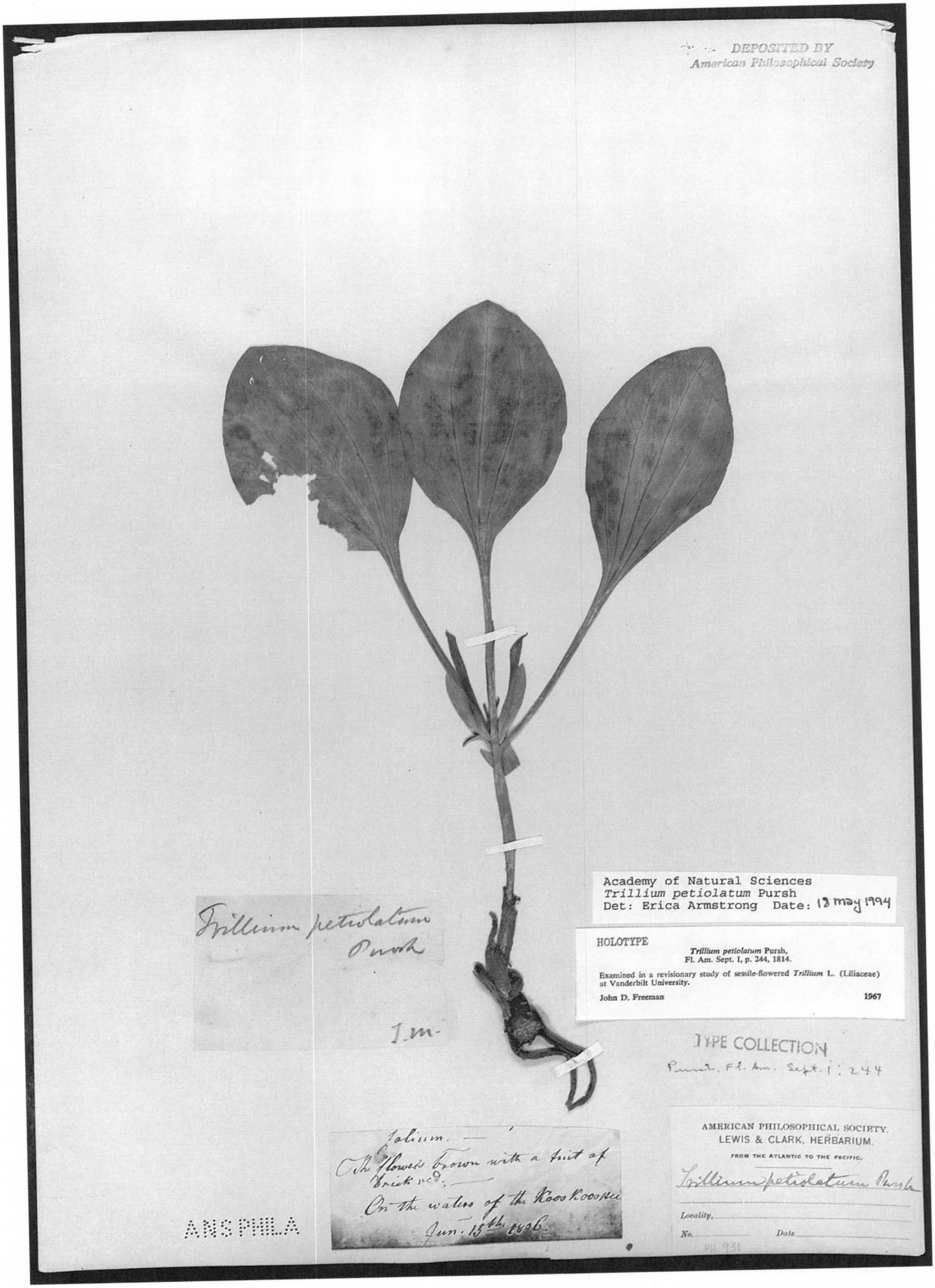

Trillium petiolatum
Pursh

I.m.

Academy of Natural Sciences
Trillium petiolatum Pursh
Det: Erica Armstrong   Date: 13 may 1994

HOLOTYPE

Trillium petiolatum Pursh,
Fl. Am. Sept. I, p. 244, 1814.

Examined in a revisionary study of sessile-flowered *Trillium* L. (Liliaceae)
at Vanderbilt University.

John D. Freeman   1967

TYPE COLLECTION
Pursh, Fl. Am. Sept. i: 244

Solium. —
The flowers brown with a tint of
brick red,
On the waters of the Koos Kooskee
Jun. 15th 1806.

AMERICAN PHILOSOPHICAL SOCIETY.
LEWIS & CLARK, HERBARIUM.

FROM THE ATLANTIC TO THE PACIFIC.

Trillium petiolatum Pursh

Locality,

No.   Date

ANS PHILA

170. *Trillium petiolatum* Pursh, purple trillium

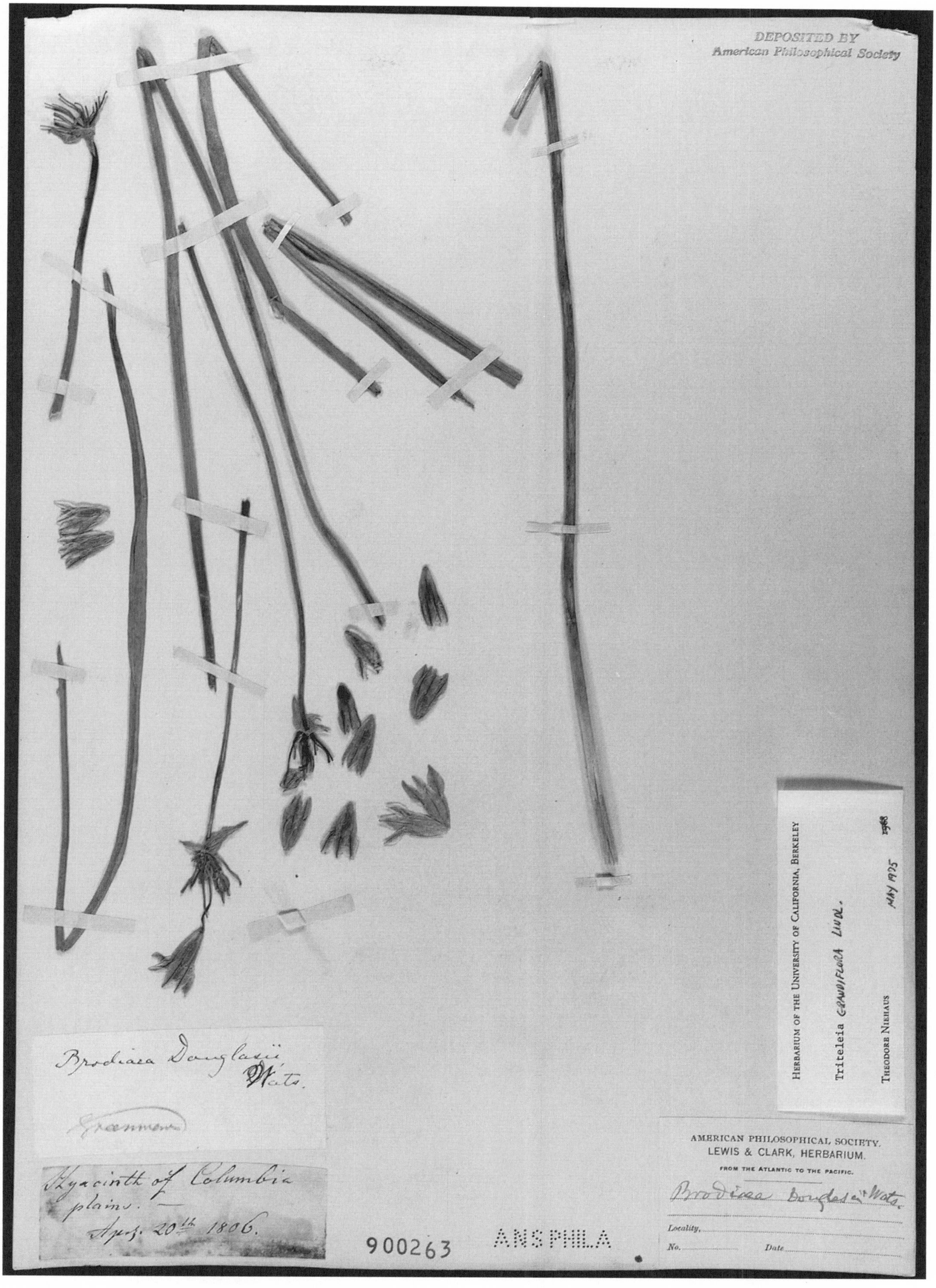

Brodiaea Douglasii
Wats.

Grammon

Hyacinth of Columbia
plains. —
Apr. 20th 1806.

HERBARIUM OF THE UNIVERSITY OF CALIFORNIA, BERKELEY

Triteleia GRANDIFLORA Lindl.

MAY 1975

THEODORE NIEHAUS

AMERICAN PHILOSOPHICAL SOCIETY.
LEWIS & CLARK, HERBARIUM.
FROM THE ATLANTIC TO THE PACIFIC.

Brodiaea Douglasii Wats.

Locality,
No.   Date

900263   ANSPHILA

171a. *Triteleia grandiflora* Lindl., Douglas' brodiaea

171b. *Triteleia grandiflora* Lindl., Douglas' brodiaea

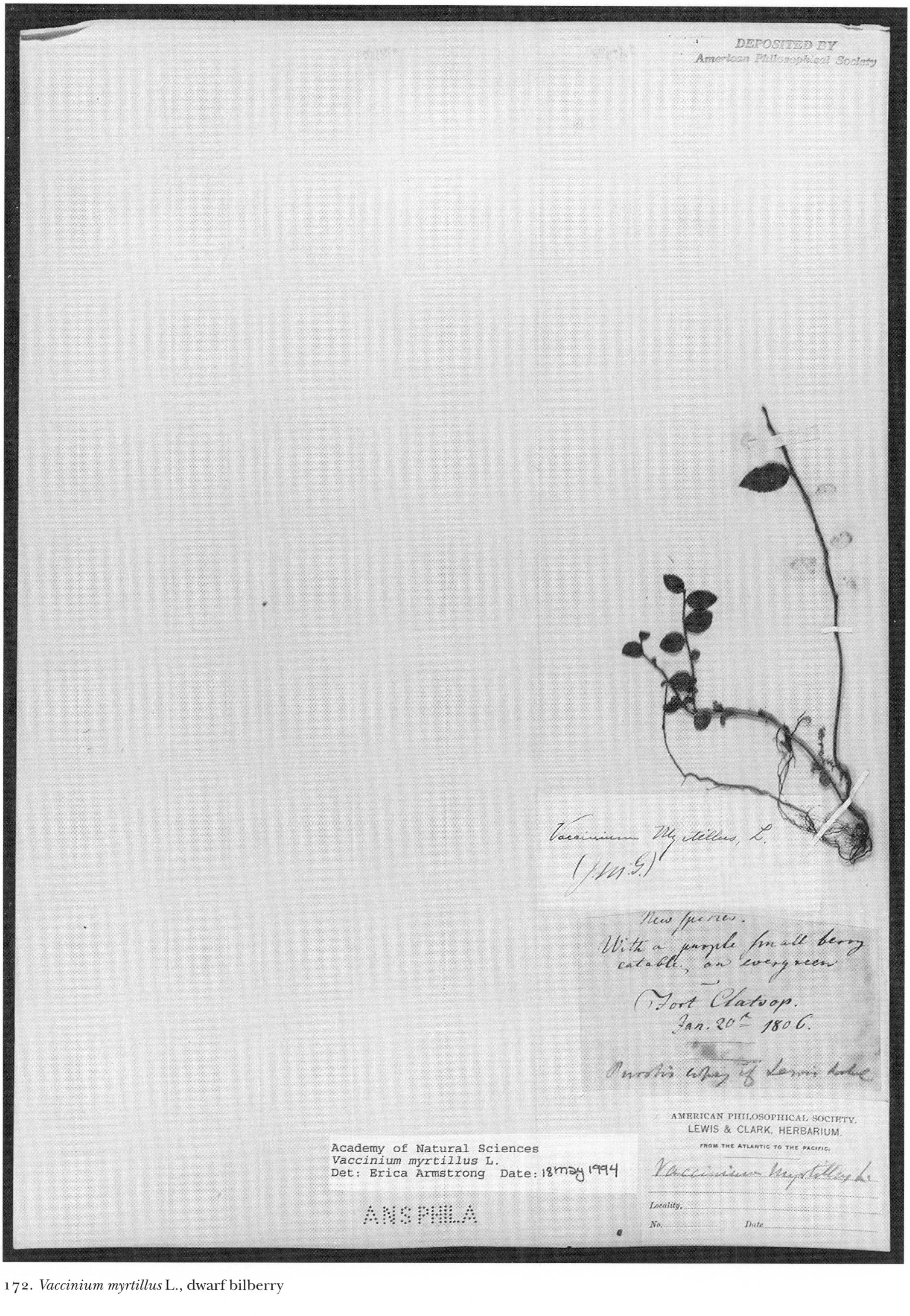

Vaccinium Myrtillus, L.
(*her G.*)

New species.
With a purple small berry
eatable, an evergreen

Fort Clatsop.
Jan. 20th 1806.

Pursh's copy of Lewis label.

Academy of Natural Sciences
Vaccinium myrtillus L.
Det: Erica Armstrong   Date: 18 May 1994

ANSPHILA

172. *Vaccinium myrtillus* L., dwarf bilberry

Vaccinium
ovatum Pursh

(7.m)

A shrub of 7 or 8 feet high,
Supposed to be a species of
Vaccinium; the berries are
eaten by the natives.

On the Pacific Ocean
Fort Clatsop.
Jan: 27th 1806.

Pursh copy of Lewis herbal

ANS PHILA

Academy of Natural Sciences
Vaccinium ovatum Pursh
Det: Erica Armstrong   Date: 19 May 1994

AMERICAN PHILOSOPHICAL SOCIETY.
LEWIS & CLARK, HERBARIUM.
FROM THE ATLANTIC TO THE PACIFIC.

Vaccinium ovatum Pursh

Locality,

No.   Date

173. *Vaccinium ovatum* Pursh, evergreen huckleberry

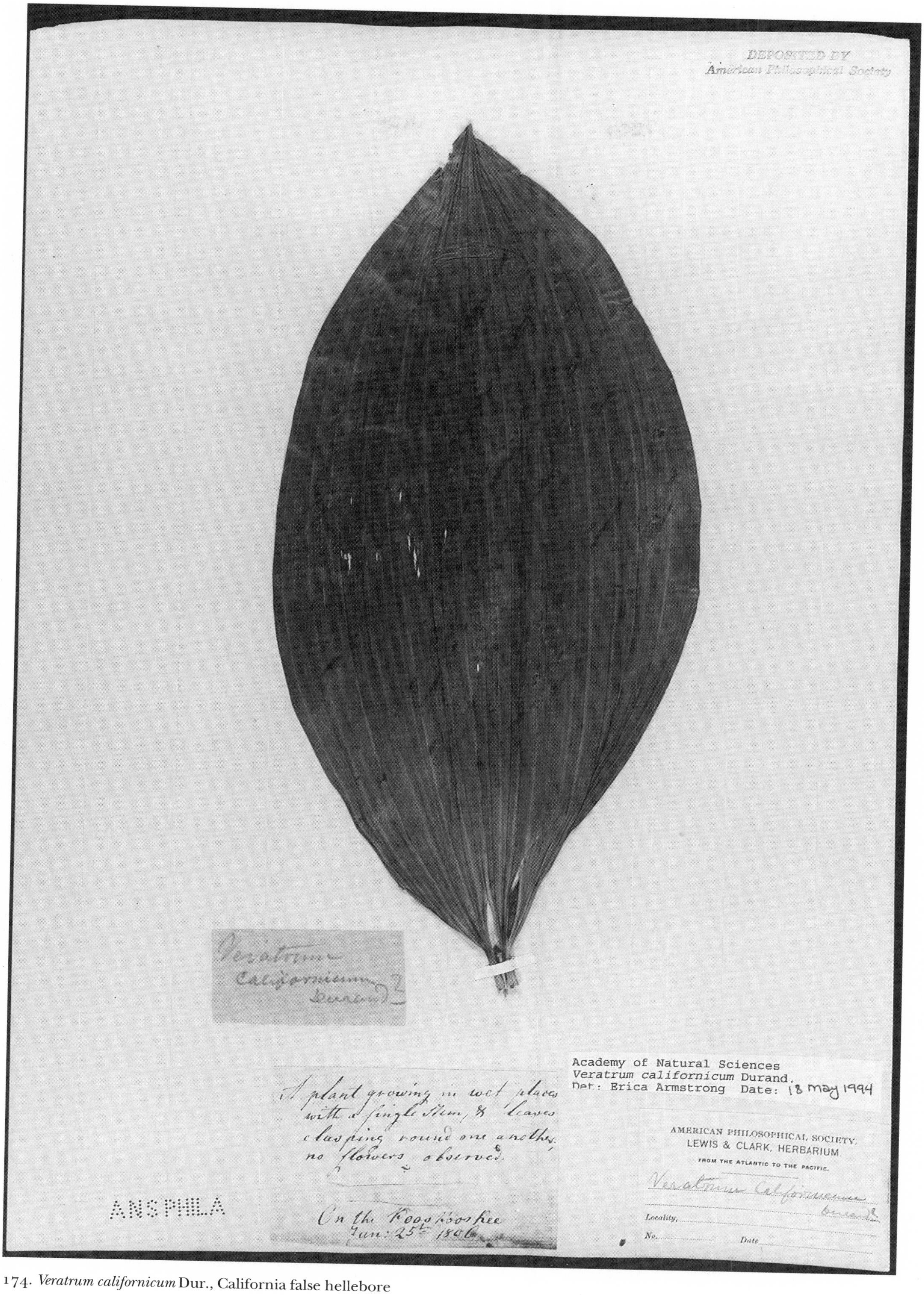
DEPOSITED BY
American Philosophical Society
Veratrum
Californicum
Durand?
A plant growing in wet places
with a single stem, & leaves
clasping round one another,
no flowers observed.
On the Koos koos kee
Jun: 25th 1806
Academy of Natural Sciences
Veratrum californicum Durand.
Det: Erica Armstrong Date: 18 May 1994
AMERICAN PHILOSOPHICAL SOCIETY.
LEWIS & CLARK, HERBARIUM.
FROM THE ATLANTIC TO THE PACIFIC.
Veratrum Californicum
Durand?
Locality,
No.
Date
ANSPHILA

174. *Veratrum californicum* Dur., California false hellebore

*Xerophyllum
Asphodeloides Nutt.
Helonias tenax
Pursh*

Xerophyllum tenax, Nutt.

(genuinum)

*The leaves are made use of by
the natives, to make baskets
& other ornaments.
On high land, Rocky mountains
Jan. 15th 1806.*

Academy of Natural Sciences
Xerophyllum tenax (Pursh) Nutt.
Det: Erica Armstrong   Date: 18 May 1994

TYPE COLLECTION

Pursh, H. Am. Sept. 1 : 243.

Helonias tenax Pursh

ANSPHILA

AMERICAN PHILOSOPHICAL SOCIETY.
LEWIS & CLARK, HERBARIUM.
FROM THE ATLANTIC TO THE PACIFIC.

Xerophyllum tenax Nutt.

Locality.
No.   Date.

175a. *Xerophyllum tenax* (Pursh) Nutt., Indian basket-grass

Helonias tenax.
Rocky mountain; high lands.
* Jun. 15. 1806.
Leaves used to make baskets.

p

* F. Pursh scripsit
** A.B. Lambert scripsit
J. Sowan

Melanthaceae

** Helonias tenax. Pursh. Fl. Amer.

Herb. Pursh propr.

175b. *Xerophyllum tenax* (Pursh) Nutt., Indian basket-grass

Zigadenus
elegans Pursh

J.M

On the Cokahlaishkit. 2
Js. 7th 1806.

ANS PHILA

Academy of Natural Sciences
Zigadenus elegans Pursh
Det: Erica Armstrong   Date: 18 May 1994

TYPE COLLECTION

ANNOTATION LABEL

Zigadenus elegans PURSH

DET: O. S. WALSH   T Y P E   MAY 1940

AMERICAN PHILOSOPHICAL SOCIETY.
LEWIS & CLARK, HERBARIUM.
FROM THE ATLANTIC TO THE PACIFIC.

T Y P E   *Zygadenus elegans Pursh*

Locality,

No.   Date

176. *Zigadenus elegans* Pursh, white camass

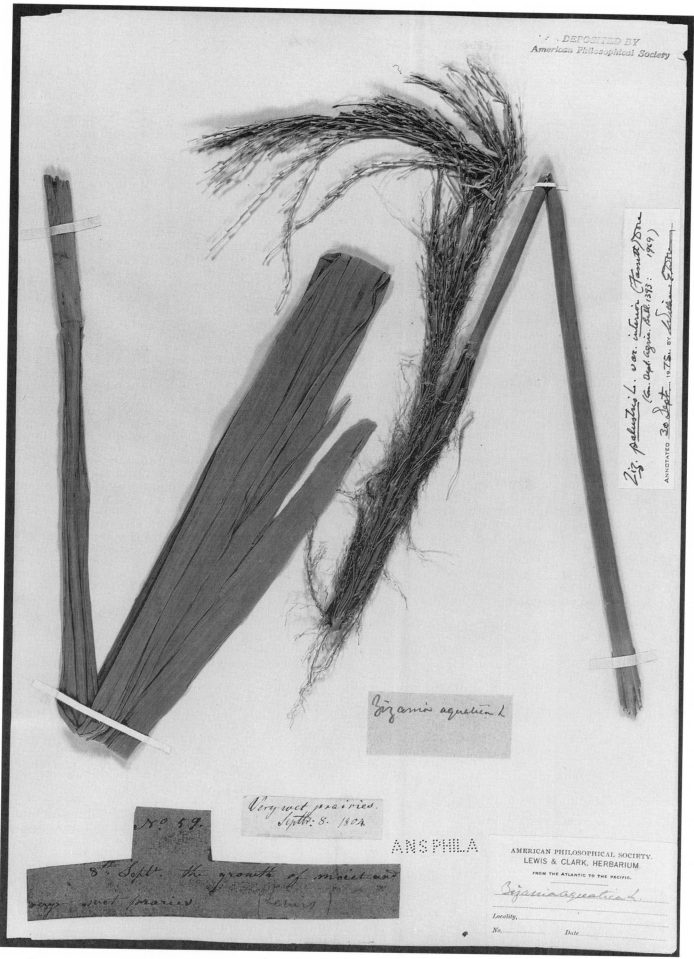

177. *Zizania palustris* L. var. *interior* (Fassett) Dore, wild rice

Table of the Herbarium of the Lewis and Clark Expedition

ID	Scientific name	Common name	Place collected	Date collected	Archive	Pursh	Meehan	Cutright	Barkley	H & C	Kartesz
1	Acer circinatum Pursh	vine maple	Cascades of the Columbia River, WA-OR	Oct. [31?], 1805	ANS-A, ANS-L	E-57, 267	21	244, 400	—	289	1:30, 2:4
2	Acer macrophyllum Pursh	big-leaf maple	Cascades of the Columbia River, WA-OR	Apr. 10, 1806	ANS-A, ANS-L	E-57, 267	22	289, 401	—	289	1:30, 2:4
3	Achillea millefolium L.	yarrow	Camp Chopunnish, Idaho County, ID	May 20, 1806	ANS-A, ANS-L	563	30	307	854	478	1:59, 2:6
4	Allium textile A. Nels. & J. F. Macbr.	textile onion	Walla Walla River, WA	Apr. 30, 1806	ANS-A	223	42	289	1246	681	1:359, 2:23
5	Alnus rubra Bong.	red alder	Cowlitz County, WA, or Columbia County, OR	Mar. 26, 1806	ANS-A	41	—	289, 401	—	72	1:144, 2:25
6	Amelanchier alnifolia (Nutt.) Nutt. ex M. Roemer	western serviceberry	The Dalles of the Columbia River, WA-OR	Apr. 15, 1806	ANS-A	—	24	289, 402	368	208	1:514, 2:29
7	Amelanchier sp.?	serviceberry	Clearwater River, Nez Perce County, ID; Lolo Trail, ID	May 7, 1806; June 27, 1806	ANS-A	—	25	290, 308	—	—	—
8	Amorpha fruticosa L.	false indigo	Big Bend of the Missouri River, Lyman County, SD	Aug. 27, 1806	ANS-A, Kew	E-59, 466	22	348	419	—	1:269, 2:31
9	Ampelopsis cordata Michx.	raccoon grape	Council Bluff, Washington County, NE; Leavenworth County, KS	Sept. 8, 1806; Sept. 14, 1806	ANS-A	—	21	348	557	—	1:609, 2:31
10	Amsinckia intermedia Fisch. & C. A. Mey.	ranchers fiddleneck	Rock Fort Camp, Wasco County, OR	Apr. 17, 1806	ANS-A	—	37	289	687	386	1:147, 2:32
11	Anemone canadensis L.	meadow anemone	Tonwontonga village, Dakota County, NE	Aug. 17, 1804	ANS-A	—	17	75	87	126	1:500, 2:37
12	Anemone quinquefolia L.	wood anemone	Lolo Trail, ID	June 15, 1806	ANS-A	—	17	307	88	—	1:500, 2:38
13	Angelica sp.?	angelica	Lost Trail Pass, MT-ID; Lolo Trail, ID	Sept. 3, 1805; June 25, 1806	ANS-A	—	28	196, 307, 402	—	—	—
14	Arbutus menziesii Pursh	Pacific madrone	Cascades of the Columbia River, WA-OR	Nov. 1, 1805	ANS-A	—	35	244, 402	—	342	1:252, 2:51
15	Arctostaphylos uva-ursi (L.) Spreng.	bearberry	Fort Mandan, McLean County, ND	winter 1804-1805	ANS-A	—	35	122	334	342	1:254, 2:55

16	*Argentina anserina* (L.) Rydb.	silverweed	Fort Clatsop, Clatsop County, OR	Mar. 13, 1806	ANS-A	—	25	274	383	216	1:514, 2:59
17	*Artemisia cana* Pursh	dwarf sagebrush	Dewey, Sully, or Stanley County, SD; Dewey or Sully County, SD	Oct. 1, 1804; Oct. 2, 1804	ANS-A (3), ANS-L	E-61, 521	31	105, 403	869	488	1:68, 2:64
18	*Artemisia dracunculus* L.	silky wormwood	Lyman or Brule County, SD	Sept. 15, 1804	ANS-A	521	31	88, 403	869	487	1:68, 2:64
19	*Artemisia frigida* Willd.	pasture sagewort	Bon Homme County, SD, or Knox County, NE; Potter-Sully county line, SD	Sept. 2, 1804; Oct. 3, 1804	ANS-A (2), ANS-L	521	31	75, 105	870	487	1:68, 2:65
20	*Artemisia longifolia* Nutt.	long-leaved sage	Potter-Sully county line, SD	Oct. 3, 1804	ANS-A	—	31	105, 403	870	487	1:68, 2:65
21	*Artemisia ludoviciana* Nutt.	white sage	Dewey, Sully, or Stanley County, SD; Skamania County, WA, or Multnomah County, OR, or Rock Fort Camp, Wasco County, OR	Oct. 1, 1804; [Apr. 10, 1806?]	ANS-A, ANS-L	520	32	289, 403	870	486	1:68, 2:65
22	*Aster oblongifolius* Nutt.	aromatic aster	Big Bend of the Missouri River, Lyman County, SD	Sept. 21, 1804	ANS-A	—	32	88, 403	880	—	1:73, 2:77
23	*Aster oregonensis* (Nutt.) Cronq.	Oregon white-topped aster	Snake River, WA	Oct. 1805	ANS-A	—	32	226, 403	876	491	1:73, 2:77
24	*Astragalus canadensis* L. var. *mortonii* (Nutt.) S. Wats.	Canada milk-vetch	Lyman or Brule County, SD	Sept. 15, 1804	ANS-A	—	22	88	426	231, 254	1:271, 2:82
25	*Astragalus missouriensis* Nutt.	Missouri milk-vetch	Lyman or Brule County, SD	Sept. 18, 1804	ANS-A	—	22	88, 404	430	232, 249	1:275, 2:87
26	*Atriplex canescens* (Pursh) Nutt.	four-wing saltbush	Big Bend of the Missouri River, Lyman County, SD	Sept. 21, 1804	ANS-A	E-65, 370	39	88, 404	162	95	1:208, 2:92
27	*Atriplex gardneri* (Moq.) D. Dietr.	moundscale	Marias River, Toole County, MT	July 20, 1806	ANS-A	—	39	326, 404	164	95	1:208, 2:92
28	*Balsamorhiza sagittata* (Pursh) Nutt.	arrowleaf balsamroot	Skamania or Klickitat County, WA, or Hood River or Wasco County, OR; Lewis and Clark Pass, Lewis and Clark County, MT	Apr. 14, 1806; July 7, 1806	ANS-A	E-65, 564	32	289, 326, 405	889	495	1:76, 2:97

(continued)

ID	Scientific name	Common name	Place collected	Date collected	Archive	Pursh	Meehan	Cutright	Barkley	H & C	Kartesz
29	Bazzania trilobata (L.) S. F. Gray	liverwort	Travelers' Rest, Missoula County, MT	July 1, 1806	ANS-A	—	47	307	—	—	—
30	Blechnum spicant (L.) Roth	deer-fern	Fort Clatsop, Clatsop County, OR; Fort Clatsop, Clatsop County, OR?	Jan. 20, 1806; [Jan. 20, 1806?]	ANS-A, ANS-C	669	47	274	—	49	1:5, 2:105
31	Calochortus elegans Pursh	northwest mariposa	Camp Chopunnish, Idaho County, ID	May 17, 1806	ANS-A	E-65, 240	43	307, 405	1270	688	1:360, 2:124
32	Calypso bulbosa (L.) Oakes	fairy-slipper	Lolo Trail, ID	June 16, 1806	ANS-A	593	42	307	—	700	1:405, 2:127
33	Camassia quamash (Pursh) Greene	camas	Weippe Prairie, Clearwater County, ID	June 23, 1806	ANS-A	E-90, 226	43	307, 405	—	688	1:361, 2:128
34	Camissonia subacaulis (Pursh) Raven	long-leaf evening primrose	Weippe Prairie, Clearwater County, ID	June 14, 1806	ANS-A	E-82, 304	28, 49	308, 412	—	311	1:397, 2:130
35	Cardamine nuttallii Greene var. nuttallii	slender toothwort	Sandy River, Multnomah County, OR	Apr. 1, 1806	ANS-A, ANS-L	E-73, 439	18	289, 408	—	159	1:160, 2:133
36	Ceanothus sanguineus Pursh	redstem ceanothus	Lolo Trail, ID	June 27, 1806	ANS-L	E-67, 167	48	307, 405	—	290	1:511, 2:158
37	Ceanothus velutinus Dougl. ex Hook.	mountain balm	Clearwater River, ID	unknown	ANS-A	—		307, 406	555	290	1:511, 2:158
38	Cerastium arvense L.	field chickweed	Klickitat County, WA, or Wasco or Sherman County, OR	Apr. 22, 1806	ANS-A	E-67, 321	18	289	197	113	1:196, 2:160
39	Chrysothamnus nauseosus (Pallas ex Pursh) Britt. ssp. graveolens (Nutt.) Piper	rabbit brush	Big Bend of the Missouri River, Lyman County, SD; Dewey or Sully County, SD	Sept. 21, 1804; Oct. 2, 1804	ANS-A (2), ANS-L (2)	E-68, 517	32, 34	75, 105, 405	906	502	1:83, 2:181
40	Chrysothamnus nauseosus (Pallas ex Pursh) Britt. ssp. nauseosus	rabbit brush	Missouri River; [Missouri River?]	Oct. 1804; [Oct. 1804?]	ANS-L, ANS-A	517	33	—	906	502	1:83, 2:181
41	Chrysothamnus viscidiflorus (Hook.) Nutt. ssp. viscidiflorus	green rabbit brush	Clearwater River, Nez Perce County, ID	May 6, 1806	ANS-A	—	32	289, 404	907	502	1:84, 2:182

42	*Cirsium edule* Nutt.	edible thistle	Fort Clatsop, Clatsop County, OR	Mar. 13, 1806	ANS-A	—	33	274, 406	—	505	1:85, 2:184
43	*Clarkia pulchella* Pursh	ragged robin	Camp Chopunnish, Idaho County, ID	June 1, 1806	ANS-A	E-69, 260	28	307, 406	—	305	1:398, 2:188
44	*Claytonia lanceolata* Pursh	western springbeauty	Lolo Trail, ID	June 27, 1806	ANS-A	E-69, 175	19	308, 406	—	105	1:491, 2:189
45	*Claytonia parviflora* Dougl. *ex* Hook.	littleleaf montia	Cowlitz County, WA, or Columbia County, OR	Mar. 26, 1806	ANS-A	—	20	—	—	107	1:492, 2:189
46	*Claytonia perfoliata* Donn *ex* Willd. ssp. *perfoliata*	miner's lettuce	Rock Fort Camp, Wasco County, OR	Apr. 17, 1806	ANS-A	176	20	289	—	108	1:492, 2:189
47	*Claytonia sibirica* L.	Siberian montia	Multnomah County, OR, or Skamania County, WA	Apr. 8, 1806	ANS-A	175	20	289	—	108	1:492, 2:189
48	*Clematis hirsutissima* Pursh	Douglas's clematis	Camp Chopunnish, Idaho County, ID	May 27, 1806	ANS-A	E-69, 385	17, 34	289, 407	90	129	1:502, 2:190
49	*Cleome serrulata* Pursh	Rocky Mountain bee plant	Clay County, SD, or Cedar or Dixon County, NE	Aug. 25, 1804	ANS-A (2), ANS-L	E-69, 441	18	75, 348, 407	292	180	1:192, 2:191
50	*Collinsia parviflora* Lindl. var. *grandiflora* (Lindl.) Ganders & Krause	small-flowered blue-eyed Mary	Rock Fort Camp, Wasco County, OR	Apr. 17, 1806	ANS-A	E-60, 421	38	289, 402	763	422	1:574, 2:195
51	*Collomia linearis* Nutt.	narrow-leaf collomia	Rock Fort Camp, Wasco County, OR	Apr. 17, 1806	ANS-A	—	36	289, 407	667	368	1:467, 2:196
52	*Coreopsis tinctoria* Nutt. var. *atkinsoniana* (Dougl. *ex* Lindl.) H. M. Parker	calliopsis	Snake River, WA	Oct. 1805	ANS-A	—	32	226	916	506	1:88, 2:203
53	*Cornus canadensis* L.	bunchberry	Lolo Trail, ID	June 16, 1806	ANS-A	—	30	—	528	339	1:222, 2:204
54	*Crataegus douglasii* Lindl.	black hawthorn	Walla Walla River, WA	Apr. 29, 1806	ANS-A	—	24	289, 407	370	210	1:517, 2:210

(continued)

ID	Scientific name	Common name	Place collected	Date collected	Archive	Pursh	Meehan	Cutright	Barkley	H & C	Kartesz
55	Dalea purpurea Vent.	purple prairie clover	Bon Homme County, SD, or Knox County, NE; Camp Disappointment, Glacier County, MT	Sept. 2, 1804; July 22, 1806	ANS-A	—	23	75, 326	444	272	1:283, 2:237
56	Delphinium menziesii DC.	Menzies' larkspur	Skamania or Klickitat County, WA, or Hood River or Wasco County, OR	Apr. 14, 1806	ANS-A	—	18	289, 407	93	132	1:503, 2:241
57	Dodecatheon jeffreyi Van Houtte	Jeffrey's shooting star	The Dalles of the Columbia River, WA-OR	Apr. 16, 1806	ANS-A	—	36	289	—	352	1:496, 2:255
58	Dryopteris expansa (K. Presl) Fraser-Jenkins & Jermy	mountain wood-fern	Fort Clatsop, Clatsop County, OR	Jan. 20, 1806	ANS-A	—	47	274	—	51	1:8, 2:262
59	Egregia menziesii (Turn.) Aresch.	Menzies' rockweed	Pacific County, WA	Nov. 17, 1805	ANS-A	—	47	244	—	—	—
60	Elaeagnus commutata Bernh. ex Rydb.	silverberry	Nevada Valley, Powell County, MT	July 6, 1806	ANS-A, Kew	E-74, 114	40	326, 408	491	302	1:251, 2:272
61	Equisetum arvense L.	field horsetail	Burt County, NE, or Monona County, IA	Aug. 10, 1804	ANS-A, ANS-L	—	47	75	43	44	1:11, 2:284
62	Erigeron compositus Pursh	cut-leaved daisy	Clearwater River, ID	unknown	ANS-L	E-75, 535	49	308, 408	928	516	1:94, 2:289
63	Eriophyllum lanatum (Pursh) Forbes var. lanatum	common eriophyllum	Camp Chopunnish, Idaho County, ID	June 6, 1806	ANS-A, ANS-L	E-58, 560	33	307, 401	—	520	1:97, 2:305
64	Erysimum asperum (Nutt.) DC.	rough wallflower	Camp Chopunnish, Idaho County, ID	June 1, 1806	ANS-A	—	18	308, 408	314	168	1:165, 2:306
65	Erythronium grandiflorum Pursh	pale fawn-lily	Clearwater River, Nez Perce or Clearwater County, ID; Lolo Trail, ID	May 8, 1806; June 15, 1806	ANS-A (2)	E-75, 231	43	289, 308, 408	—	690	1:363, 2:308
66	Euphorbia cyathophora Murr.	fire-on-the-mountain	Dewey or Potter County, SD Sioux or Emmons County, ND	Oct. 4, 1804; Oct. [15?], 1804	ANS-A	—	40	105	544	—	1:265, 2:315
67	Euphorbia marginata Pursh	snow-on-the-mountain	Rosebud County, MT	July 28, 1806	ANS-A	E-75, 607	40	326, 408	547	—	1:266, 2:316

68	*Festuca idahoensis* Elmer	Idaho fescue	Camp Chopunnish, Idaho County, ID	June 10, 1806	ANS-A	—	45	—	—	642	1:445, 2:323
69	*Frangula purshiana* (DC.) Cooper	cascara	Camp Chopunnish, Idaho County, ID	May 29, 1806	ANS-A, ANS-L	E-94, 166	21	308, 416	—	290	1:512, 2:328
70	*Frasera fastigiata* (Pursh) Heller	clustered frasera	Weippe Prairie, Clearwater County, ID	June 14, 1806	ANS-A	E-106, 101	36	308, 420	—	358	1:319, 2:328
71	*Fritillaria lanceolata* Pursh	checker lily	Bradford Island, Multnomah County, OR	Apr. 10, 1806	ANS-A, ANS-L	E-76, 230	44	289, 409	—	691	1:363, 2:330
72	*Fritillaria pudica* (Pursh) Spreng.	yellow bell	Clearwater River, Nez Perce or Clearwater County, ID	May 8, 1806	ANS-A, ANS-L	E-83, 228	44	289, 409	1250	691	1:363, 2:330
73	*Gaillardia aristata* Pursh	blanket flower	Lewis and Clark Pass, Lewis and Clark County, MT	July 7, 1806	ANS-A	E-76, 573	33	326, 409	938	521	1:100, 2:331
74	*Gaultheria shallon* Pursh	salal	Fort Clatsop, Clatsop County, OR	Jan. 20, 1806	ANS-A	E-77, 283	35	274, 409	—	344	1:254, 2:338
75	*Geum triflorum* Pursh	old man's whiskers	Weippe Prairie, Clearwater County, ID	June 12, 1806	ANS-A	E-77, 352, 736	24	308, 409	379	212	1:522, 2:346
76	*Grindelia squarrosa* (Pursh) Dunal	curly-top gumweed	Tonwontonga village, Dakota County, NE	Aug. 17, 1804	ANS-A, ANS-L (2)	559	33	75, 409	944	523	1:102, 2:357
77	*Gutierrezia sarothrae* (Pursh) Britt. & Rusby	snakeweed	Big Bend of the Missouri River, Lyman or Buffalo County, SD	Sept. 19, 1804	ANS-A, Kew	E-105, 540	34	88, 420	945	524	1:102, 2:359
78	*Holodiscus discolor* (Pursh) Maxim.	creambush ocean-spray	Camp Chopunnish, Idaho County, ID	May 29, 1806	ANS-A, ANS-L	E-106, 342	26	308, 420	—	213	1:523, 2:385
79	*Hordeum jubatum* L.	foxtail barley	Fort Clatsop, Clatsop County, OR; White Bear Islands, Cascade County, MT	Mar. 13, 1806; July 12, 1806	ANS-A (2)	89	45	274, 326	1185	646	1:447, 2:386
80	*Hypnum oreganum* Sull.	moss	Fort Clatsop, Clatsop County, OR	Jan. 20, 1806	ANS-A	—	47	274	—	—	—
81	*Ipomopsis aggregata* (Pursh) V. Grant ssp. *aggregata*	scarlet gilia	Lolo Trail, ID	June 26, 1806	ANS-A	E-66, 147	37	307, 405	—	369	1:469, 2:399

(continued)

ID	Scientific name	Common name	Place collected	Date collected	Archive	Pursh	Meehan	Cutright	Barkley	H & C	Kartesz
82	Iris missouriensis Nutt.	western blue flag	Nevada Valley, Powell County, MT	July 5, 1806	ANS-A	—	42	326, 410	1260	697	1:337, 2:401
83	Juniperus communis L. var. depressa Pursh	common juniper	Sioux or Emmons County, ND; Lewis and Clark Pass, Lewis and Clark County, MT	Oct. 17, 1804; July 7, 1806	ANS-A (2), ANS-L (2)	—	46	105, 326	72	58	1:23, 2:410
84	Juniperus horizontalis Moench	creeping juniper	Sioux or Emmons County, ND	Oct. 16, 1804	ANS-A, ANS-L	647	46	105	72	58	1:23, 2:410
85	Juniperus scopulorum Sarg.	Rocky Mountain juniper	Dewey or Sully County, SD	Oct. 2, 1804	ANS-A	647	46	105	73	58	1:23, 2:410
86	Koeleria macrantha (Ledeb.) J. A. Schultes	prairie Junegrass	Camp Chopunnish, Idaho County, ID	June 10, 1806	ANS-A	85	45	308	1186	647	1:448, 2:413
87	Lewisia rediviva Pursh	bitterroot	Travelers' Rest, Missoula County, MT	July 1, 1806	ANS-A	E-83, 368	19	308, 410	—	106	1:493, 2:433
88	Lewisia triphylla (S. Wats.) B. L. Robins.	threeleaved lewisia	Lolo Trail, ID	June 27, 1806	ANS-A	—	19	308, 406	—	106	1:493, 2:433
89	Leymus arenarius (L.) Hochst.	dune wildrye	unknown	unknown	ANS-A	—	46	420	—	637	1:449, 2:433
90	Liatris aspera Michx.	gay-feather	Brule County, SD	Sept. 12, 1804	ANS-A	—	34	88	972	—	1:113, 2:434
91	Liatris pycnostachya Michx.	blazing star	Lyman or Brule County, SD	Sept. 18, 1804	ANS-A	—	34	88	973	—	1:113, 2:434
92	Linum lewisii Pursh var. lewisii	blue flax	Lewis and Clark, Teton, or Cascade County, MT	July 9, 1806	ANS-A, ANS-L	E-83, 210	19	326, 410	562	282	1:371, 2:440
93	Lomatium cous (S. Wats.) Coult. & Rose	cous	Walla Walla River, WA	Apr. 29, 1806	ANS-A	—	29	289, 410	—	329, 331	1:43, 2:446
94	Lomatium dissectum (Nutt.) Mathias & Constance	fern-leaved lomatium	Camp Chopunnish, Idaho County, ID	June 10, 1806	ANS-A	195	29	308, 413	—	330	1:44, 2:446
95	Lomatium grayi (Coult. & Rose) Coult. & Rose	Gray's lomatium	Klickitat County, WA, or Wasco County, OR	Apr. 14, 1806	ANS-A	—	28	—	—	333	1:44, 2:446

No.	Scientific name	Common name	Location	Date	Herbaria						
96	*Lomatium nudicaule* (Pursh) Coult. & Rose	barestem lomatium	The Dalles of the Columbia River, WA-OR	Apr. 15, 1806	ANS-A	E-104, 196	28	290, 420	—	328	1:44, 2:447
97	*Lomatium triternatum* (Pursh) Coult. & Rose	nine-leaf lomatium	Clearwater River, Nez Perce County, ID	May 6, 1806	ANS-A	E-102, 197	29	289, 413	—	327	1:45, 2:447
98	*Lomatium* sp.?	lomatium	Skamania or Klickitat County, WA, or Hood River or Wasco County, OR	Apr. 14, 1806	ANS-A	—	29, 48	—	—	—	—
99	*Lomatium* sp.?	lomatium	The Dalles of the Columbia River, WA-OR	Apr. 15, 1806	ANS-A	—	29	289	—	—	—
100	*Lonicera ciliosa* (Pursh) Poir. *ex* DC.	trumpet honeysuckle	North Fork Salmon River, Lemhi County, ID; Camp Chopunnish, Idaho County, ID; Lolo Trail, ID	Sept. 2, 1805; June 5, 1806; June 16, 1806	ANS-A (2)	E-66, 160	30	308, 410	—	452	1:193, 2:448
101	*Lonicera involucrata* Banks *ex* Spreng.	bearberry honeysuckle	Lewis and Clark Pass, Lewis and Clark County, MT	July 7, 1806	ANS-A	—	30	196, 326, 410	—	451	1:193, 2:448
102	*Lupinus argenteus* Pursh	silvery lupine	Blackfoot River, Lewis and Clark County, MT; Clearwater River, ID?	July 7, 1806; July 1806	ANS-A, Kew	E-84, 468	22	326, 411	462	267	1:292, 2:452
103	*Lupinus pusillus* Pursh	rusty lupine	Missouri River?	unknown	Kew	E-84, 468	—	—	464	265	1:297, 2:461
104	*Lupinus sericeus* Pursh	silky lupine	Camp Chopunnish, Idaho County, ID; Blackfoot River, Lewis and Clark County, MT	June 5, 1806; July 7, 1806	ANS-A, Kew	E-84, 468	23	308, 411	464	266	1:298, 2:462
105	*Machaeranthera canescens* (Pursh) Gray	hoary aster	Columbia River	Oct. 1805	ANS-A	—	31	88, 402	—	538	1:115, 2:471
106	*Machaeranthera pinnatifida* (Hook.) Shinners ssp. *pinnatifida* var. *pinnatifida*	spiny goldenweed	Lyman or Brule County, SD	Sept. 15, 1804	ANS-A	E-59, 564	30	88, 244, 402	950	525	1:117, 2:472
107	*Maclura pomifera* (Raf.) Schneid.	Osage orange	unknown	unknown	ANS-A	—	41	61, 411	126	75	1:385, 2:473

(continued)

ID	Scientific name	Common name	Place collected	Date collected	Archive	Pursh	Meehan	Cutright	Barkley	H & C	Kartesz
108	Mahonia aquifolium (Pursh) Nutt.	Oregon grape	Cascades of the Columbia River, WA-OR	Apr. 11, 1806	ANS-L	E-64, 219	48	289, 404	—	142	1:144, 2:474
109	Mahonia nervosa (Pursh) Nutt.	dull Oregon grape	Cascades of the Columbia River, WA-OR	Oct. [31?], 1805	ANS-L	E-64, 219	48	244, 404	—	142	1:144, 2:474
110	Matricaria discoidea DC.	pineapple weed	Weippe Prairie, Clearwater County, ID	June 12, 1806	ANS-A, ANS-L	E-100, 520	34	308, 419	978	540	1:118, 2:482
111	Microseris lindleyi (DC.) Gray	Lindley's microseris	Rock Fort Camp, Wasco County, OR	Apr. 17, 1806	ANS-A	—	34	289, 411	—	540	1:119, 2:493
112	Mimulus guttatus DC.	yellow monkey-flower	Blackfoot River, Missoula County, MT	July 4, 1806	ANS-A	426	38	326, 411	771	427	1:579, 2:496
113	Mirabilis nyctaginea (Michx.) MacM.	wild four-o'clock	Bon Homme County, SD, or Knox County, NE	Sept. 1, 1804	ANS-A, ANS-L	E-59, 97	39	75	150	103	1:391, 2:500
114	Nicotiana quadrivalvis Pursh var. quadrivalvis	Indian tobacco	Campbell or Corson County, SD	Oct. 12, 1804	ANS-A	E-87, 141	37	105, 411	637	—	1:592, 2:514
115	Oenothera cespitosa Nutt. ssp. cespitosa	gumbo evening primrose	Great Falls of the Missouri River, Cascade County, MT	July 17, 1806	ANS-A, ANS-L	E-87, 263, 735	28	326, 411	518	310	1:402, 2:520
116	Orthocarpus tenuifolius (Pursh) Benth.	thin-leaved owl-clover	Travelers' Rest, Missoula County, MT	July 1, 1806	ANS-A	E-64, 429	38	308, 412	—	429	1:581, 2:535
117	Osmorhiza occidentalis (Nutt. ex Torr. & Gray) Torr.	western sweet-cicely	Klickitat or Benton County, WA, or Gilliam or Morrow County, OR	Apr. 25, 1806	ANS-A	—	29	289, 413	—	335	1:45, 2:536
118	Oxytropis nana Nutt. var. besseyi (Rydb.) Isely	Bessey's crazyweed	Travelers' Rest, Missoula County, MT	July [1?], 1806	ANS-A, ANS-L	E-88, 473	23	308, 412	467	271	1:302, 2:540
119	Paxistima myrsinites (Pursh) Raf.	mountain-box	Pacific County, WA; Lolo Trail, ID	Nov. 16, 1805; June 16, 1806	ANS-A (2), Kew	E-81, 119	20	244, 308, 412	—	288	1:207, 2:556
120	Pedicularis cystopteridifolia Rydb.	fern-leaved lousewort	Blackfoot River, Powell County, MT	July 6, 1806	ANS-A	425	38	326, 413	—	431	1:581, 2:557
121	Pedicularis groenlandica Retz.	pink elephants	Blackfoot River, Powell County, MT	July 6, 1806	ANS-A	426	38	326	—	432	1:581, 2:557

#	Scientific name	Common name	Locality	Date								
122	*Pediomelum argophyllum* (Pursh) J. Grimes	silver-leaf scurf-pea	Sioux or Emmons County, ND	Oct. 17, 1804	ANS-A, ANS-L	E-93, 475	23	105, 415	472	273	1:303, 2:559
123	*Pediomelum esculentum* (Pursh) Rydb.	Indian breadroot	Missouri River?	unknown	ANS-L	E-93, 475	48	105, 416	473	273	1:303, 2:559
124	*Penstemon fruticosus* (Pursh) Greene	shrubby penstemon	Lolo Trail, ID	June 15, 1806	ANS-L	E-77, 423	49	308, 409	—	433	1:584, 2:566
125	*Penstemon wilcoxii* Rydb.	Wilcox's penstemon	Camp Chopunnish, Idaho County, ID	May 20, 1806	ANS-A	—	39	308, 413	—	440	1:587, 2:569
126	*Pentaphylloides floribunda* (Pursh) A. Löve	shrubby cinquefoil	Nevada Valley, Powell County, MT	July 6, 1806	ANS-A	355	25	326	385	216	1:525, 2:570
127	*Phacelia heterophylla* Pursh	varileaf phacelia	Camp Chopunnish, Idaho County, ID	June 9, 1806	ANS-A, ANS-L	E-90, 140	37	308, 413	—	381	1:334, 2:577
128	*Phacelia linearis* (Pursh) Holz.	threadleaf phacelia	Rock Fort Camp, Wasco County, OR	Apr. 17, 1806	ANS-A	E-80, 134	37	289, 410	682	382	1:334, 2:577
129	*Philadelphus lewisii* Pursh	Lewis's syringa	Clearwater River, Nez Perce County, ID; Blackfoot River, Missoula County, MT	May 6, 1806; July 4, 1806	ANS-A	E-90, 329	27	326, 413	—	204	1:330, 2:580
130	*Phlox speciosa* Pursh	showy phlox	Nez Perce County, ID	May 7, 1806	ANS-A, Kew	E-90, 149	48	290, 414	—	374	1:474, 2:585
131	*Pinus ponderosa* P. & C. Lawson	ponderosa pine	Canoe Camp, Clearwater County, ID	Oct. 1, 1805	ANS-A, ANS-L	—	46	226, 414	76	62	1:26, 2:594
132	*Plagiobothrys tenellus* (Nutt. ex Hook.) Gray	slender plagiobothrys	Rock Fort Camp, Wasco County, OR	Apr. 17, 1806	ANS-A	—	37	290, 414	—	397	1:154, 2:598
133	*Poa secunda* J. Presl	Sandberg's bluegrass	Camp Chopunnish, Idaho County, ID	June 10, 1806	ANS-A	E-58, 76	45	401	1214	663	1:458, 2:606
134	*Polanisia dodecandra* (L.) DC. ssp. *trachysperma* (Torr. & Gray) Iltis	clammy-weed	unknown	unknown	ANS-A	—	18	75, 415	292	181	1:192, 2:607
135	*Polemonium caeruleum* L.	western polemonium	Lolo Trail, ID	June 27, 1806	ANS-A	—	37	308, 415	—	376	1:474, 2:607
136	*Polygala alba* Nutt.	white milkwort	Williams or McKenzie County, ND	Aug. 10, 1806	ANS-A	750	22	326, 415	565	—	1:475, 2:609

(continued)

ID	Scientific name	Common name	Place collected	Date collected	Archive	Pursh	Meehan	Cutright	Barkley	H & C	Kartesz
137	Polygonum bistortoides Pursh	American bistort	Weippe Prairie, Clearwater County, ID	June 12, 1806	ANS-A	E-91, 271	40	308, 415	—	86	1:486, 2:611
138	Populus balsamifera L. ssp. trichocarpa (Torr. & Gray ex Hook.) Brayshaw	black cottonwood	unknown	June 1806	ANS-A	—	42	290, 415	—	65	1:550, 2:617
139	Populus deltoides Bartr. ex Marsh. ssp. monilifera (Ait.) Eckenwalder	cottonwood	unknown	Aug. 1806	ANS-A	—	42	415	278	—	1:550, 2:617
140	Prunus emarginata (Dougl. ex Hook.) Walp. var. emarginata	bitter cherry	Camp Chopunnish, Idaho County, ID	May 29, 1806	ANS-A	—	25	307	—	221	1:528, 2:629
141	Prunus virginiana L.	choke cherry	Camp Chopunnish, Idaho County, ID; Williams or McKenzie County, ND	May 29, 1806; Aug. 10, 1806	ANS-A (2)	—	25	308, 326	395	221	1:529, 2:630
142	Pseudoroegneria spicata (Pursh) A. Löve	bluebunch wheatgrass	Camp Chopunnish, Idaho County, ID	June 10, 1806	ANS-A	E-76, 83	45	408	1126	614	1:459, 2:630
143	Psoralidium lanceolatum (Pursh) Rydb.	lemon scurf-pea	Missouri River?	unknown	ANS-L	E-93, 475	—	416	474	273	1:304, 2:633
144	Psoralidium tenuiflorum (Pursh) Rydb.	wild alfalfa	Big Bend of the Missouri River, Lyman County, SD	Sept. 21, 1804	ANS-A, ANS-L	E-93, 475	23	88, 416	475	273	1:304, 2:633
145	Purshia tridentata (Pursh) DC.	antelope-brush	Nevada Valley, Powell County, MT	July 6, 1806	ANS-A	E-107, 333	26	326, 416	—	222	1:529, 2:637
146	Quercus garryana Dougl. ex Hook.	Garry oak	Cowlitz County, WA, or Columbia County, OR	Mar. 26, 1806	ANS-A, ANS-L	—	41	290, 416	—	74	1:314, 2:641
147	Quercus macrocarpa Michx.	bur oak	Knox County, NE, or Charles Mix County, SD	Sept. 5, 1804	ANS-A, ANS-L	—	41	88	138	—	1:315, 2:642
148	Rhus trilobata Nutt. var. trilobata	fragrant sumac	Dewey, Sully, or Stanley County, SD	Oct. 1, 1804	ANS-A	—	21	105, 417	572	287	1:39, 2:655
149	Ribes aureum Pursh	golden currant	Three Forks of the Missouri River, Gallatin County, MT; The Dalles of the Columbia River, WA-OR	July 29, 1805; Apr. 16, 1806	ANS-A, Kew	E-95, 164	27	183, 290, 417	—	202	1:326, 2:657

No.	Species	Common name	Location	Date	Herbarium						Reference
150	*Ribes divaricatum* Pursh	straggly gooseberry	Multnomah County, OR, or Skamania County, WA	Apr. 8, 1806	ANS-A	—	27	290, 417	—	201	1:326, 2:658
151	*Ribes sanguineum* Pursh	red currant	Cowlitz County, WA, or Columbia County, OR	Mar. 27, 1806	ANS-A	E-96, 164	27	290, 418	—	203	1:327, 2:659
152	*Ribes viscosissimum* Pursh	sticky currant	Lolo Trail, ID	June 16, 1806	ANS-A, Kew	E-96, 163	27	308, 418	—	202	1:328, 2:660
153	*Rosa arkansana* Porter	prairie wild rose	Knox County, NE, or Charles Mix County, SD; Morton, Sioux, or Emmons County, ND	Sept. 5, 1804; Oct. 18, 1804	ANS-A	—	26	88, 418	398	223	1:529, 2:663
154	*Rubus parviflorus* Nutt.	thimbleberry	The Dalles of the Columbia River, WA-OR	Apr. 15, 1806	ANS-A	—	26	290, 418	403	224	1:534, 2:669
155	*Rubus spectabilis* Pursh	salmonberry	Cowlitz County, WA, or Columbia County, OR	Mar. 27, 1806	ANS-A	E-97, 348	26	290, 418	—	224	1:535, 2:670
156	*Salvia reflexa* Hornem.	lance-leaved sage	Big Bend of the Missouri River, Lyman County, SD	Sept. 21, 1804	ANS-A, ANS-L	E-99, 19	39	88	732	—	1:352, 2:691
157	*Sarcobatus vermiculatus* (Hook.) Torr.	greasewood	Marias River, Toole County, MT	July 20, 1806	ANS-A	—	40	326, 419	177	101	1:212, 2:694
158	*Scutellaria angustifolia* Pursh ssp. *angustifolia*	narrow-leaved skullcap	Camp Chopunnish, Idaho County, ID	June 5, 1806	ANS-A	E-101, 412	39	308, 419	—	408	1:352, 2:707
159	*Sedum stenopetalum* Pursh	wormleaf stonecrop	Camp Chopunnish, Idaho County, ID; Travelers' Rest, Missoula County, MT	June 5, 1806; July 1, 1806	ANS-A	E-101, 324	28	308, 419	—	183	1:225, 2:709
160	*Shepherdia argentea* (Pursh) Nutt.	buffaloberry	Niobrara River, Knox County, NE, or Bon Homme County, SD	Sept. 4, 1804	ANS-A, ANS-L	E-80, 115	40	75, 419	491	302	1:251, 2:717
161	*Solidago rigida* L.	rigid goldenrod	Doniphan or Atchison County, KS, or Buchanan County, MO	Sept. 12, 1806	ANS-A	—	34	88	1006	551	1:133, 2:733
162	*Sorbus scopulina* Greene	mountain ash	North Fork Salmon River, Lemhi County, ID; Lolo Trail, ID	Sept. 2, 1805; June 27, 1806	ANS-A	—	24, 47	196, 308, 416	405	227	1:536, 2:736
163	*Sphaeralcea coccinea* (Nutt.) Rydb.	red false mallow	Marias River, Toole County, MT	July 20, 1806	ANS-A, ANS-L	E-71, 453	19	326, 407	251	294	1:381, 2:739

(continued)

ID	Scientific name	Common name	Place collected	Date collected	Archive	Pursh	Meehan	Cutright	Barkley	H & C	Kartesz
164	Stipa comata Trin. & Rupr.	needle-and-thread	Lewis and Clark or Teton County, MT	July 8, 1806	ANS-A	72	45	183, 420	1229	671	1:464, 2:749
165	Symphoricarpos albus (L.) Blake	snowberry	Missouri River?	unknown	CM	E-106, 162	49	212, 420	827	453	1:194, 2:754
166	Synthyris missurica (Raf.) Pennell	mountain kittentails	Lolo Trail, ID	June 26, 1806	ANS-A, ANS-L	10	39	308, 421	—	441	1:558, 2:756
167	Trifolium macrocephalum (Pursh) Poir.	big-head clover	Rock Fort Camp, Wasco County, OR	Apr. 17, 1806	ANS-A, ANS-L	E-84, 479	24	290, 421	—	275	1:311, 2:781
168	Trifolium microcephalum Pursh	small-head clover	Travelers' Rest, Missoula County, MT	July 1, 1806	ANS-A, ANS-L	E-108, 478	24	308, 421	—	275	1:311, 2:781
169	Trillium ovatum Pursh	white trillium	Cascades of the Columbia River, WA-OR	Apr. 10, 1806	ANS-A	E-108, 245	44	290, 421	—	695	1:368, 2:783
170	Trillium petiolatum Pursh	purple trillium	Lolo Trail, ID	June 15, 1806	ANS-A	E-108, 244	44	308, 422	—	695	1:368, 2:783
171	Triteleia grandiflora Lindl.	Douglas' brodiaea	The Dalles of the Columbia River, Klickitat County, WA, or Wasco County, OR	Apr. 20 1806	ANS-A, ANS-L	223	42	289, 405	—	686	1:368, 2:785
172	Vaccinium myrtillus L.	dwarf bilberry	Fort Clatsop, Clatsop County, OR	Jan. 20, 1806	ANS-A	—	36	275	—	349	1:257, 2:790
173	Vaccinium ovatum Pursh	evergreen huckleberry	Fort Clatsop, Clatsop County, OR	Jan. 27, 1806	ANS-A	E-109, 290	36	275, 422	—	349	1:257, 2:791
174	Veratrum californicum Dur.	California false hellebore	Lolo Trail, ID	June 25, 1806	ANS-A	—	44	308, 422	—	695	1:369, 2:793
175	Xerophyllum tenax (Pursh) Nutt.	Indian basket-grass	Lolo Trail, ID	June 15, 1806	ANS-A, Kew	E-80, 243	44	308, 422	—	696	1:369, 2:811
176	Zigadenus elegans Pursh	white camass	Blackfoot River, Lewis and Clark County, MT	July 7, 1806	ANS-A	E-112, 241	45	326, 423	1258	696	1:369, 2:815
177	Zizania palustris L. var. interior (Fassett) Dore	wild rice	Charles Mix or Gregory County, SD, or Boyd County, NE	Sept. 8, 1804	ANS-A	—	46	88	1234	674	1:467, 2:816

Table of the Herbarium of the Lewis and Clark Expedition, Sorted by Date Collected

ID	Scientific name	Common name	Place collected	Date collected	Archive	Pursh
61	*Equisetum arvense* L.	field horsetail	Burt County, NE, or Monona County, IA	Aug 10, 1804	ANS-A, ANS-L	——
11	*Anemone canadensis* L.	meadow anemone	Tonwontonga village, Dakota County, NE	Aug 17, 1804	ANS-A	——
76	*Grindelia squarrosa* (Pursh) Dunal	curly-top gumweed	Tonwontonga village, Dakota County, NE	Aug 17, 1804	ANS-A, ANS-L (2)	559
49	*Cleome serrulata* Pursh	Rocky Mountain bee plant	Clay County, SD, or Cedar or Dixon County, NE	Aug 25, 1804	ANS-A (2), ANS-L	E-69, 441
113	*Mirabilis nyctaginea* (Michx.) MacM.	wild four-o'clock	Bon Homme County, SD, or Knox County, NE	Sept. 1, 1804	ANS-A, ANS-L	E-59, 97
19	*Artemisia frigida* Willd.	pasture sagewort	Bon Homme County, SD, or Knox County, NE; Potter-Sully county line, SD	Sept. 2, 1804; Oct. 3, 1804	ANS-A (2), ANS-L	521
55	*Dalea purpurea* Vent.	purple prairie clover	Bon Homme County, SD, or Knox County, NE; Camp Disappointment, Glacier County, MT	Sept. 2, 1804; July 22, 1806	ANS-A	——
160	*Shepherdia argentea* (Pursh) Nutt.	buffaloberry	Niobrara River, Knox County, NE, or Bon Homme County, SD	Sept. 4, 1804	ANS-A, ANS-L	E-80, 115
147	*Quercus macrocarpa* Michx.	bur oak	Knox County, NE, or Charles Mix County, SD	Sept. 5, 1804	ANS-A, ANS-L	——
153	*Rosa arkansana* Porter	prairie wild rose	Knox County, NE, or Charles Mix County, SD; Morton, Sioux, or Emmons County, ND	Sept. 5, 1804; Oct. 18, 1804	ANS-A	——
177	*Zizania palustris* L. var. *interior* (Fassett) Dore	wild rice	Charles Mix or Gregory County, SD, or Boyd County, NE	Sept. 8, 1804	ANS-A	——
90	*Liatris aspera* Michx.	gay-feather	Brule County, SD	Sept. 12, 1804	ANS-A	——
18	*Artemisia dracunculus* L.	silky wormwood	Lyman or Brule County, SD	Sept. 15, 1804	ANS-A	521
24	*Astragalus canadensis* L. var. *mortonii* (Nutt.) S. Wats.	Canada milk-vetch	Lyman or Brule County, SD	Sept. 15, 1804	ANS-A	——
106	*Machaeranthera pinnatifida* (Hook.) Shinners ssp. *pinnatifida* var. *pinnatifida*	spiny goldenweed	Lyman or Brule County, SD	Sept. 15, 1804	ANS-A	E-59, 564
25	*Astragalus missouriensis* Nutt.	Missouri milk-vetch	Lyman or Brule County, SD	Sept. 18, 1804	ANS-A	——
91	*Liatris pycnostachya* Michx.	blazing star	Lyman or Brule County, SD	Sept. 18, 1804	ANS-A	——
77	*Gutierrezia sarothrae* (Pursh) Britt. & Rusby	snakeweed	Big Bend of the Missouri River, Lyman or Buffalo County, SD	Sept. 19, 1804	ANS-A, Kew	E-105, 540
22	*Aster oblongifolius* Nutt.	aromatic aster	Big Bend of the Missouri River, Lyman County, SD	Sept. 21, 1804	ANS-A	——
26	*Atriplex canescens* (Pursh) Nutt.	four-wing saltbush	Big Bend of the Missouri River, Lyman County, SD	Sept. 21, 1804	ANS-A	E-65, 370
144	*Psoralidium tenuiflorum* (Pursh) Rydb.	wild alfalfa	Big Bend of the Missouri River, Lyman County, SD	Sept. 21, 1804	ANS-A, ANS-L	E-93, 475

ID	Scientific name	Common name	Place collected	Date collected	Archive	Pursh
156	*Salvia reflexa* Hornem.	lance-leaved sage	Big Bend of the Missouri River, Lyman County, SD	Sept. 21, 1804	ANS-A, ANS-L	E-99, 19
39	*Chrysothamnus nauseosus* (Pallas *ex* Pursh) Britt. ssp. *graveolens* (Nutt.) Piper	rabbit brush	Big Bend of the Missouri River, Lyman County, SD; Dewey or Sully County, SD	Sept. 21, 1804; Oct. 2, 1804	ANS-A (2), ANS-L (2)	E-68, 517
148	*Rhus trilobata* Nutt. var. *trilobata*	fragrant sumac	Dewey, Sully, or Stanley County, SD	Oct. 1, 1804	ANS-A	——
17	*Artemisia cana* Pursh	dwarf sagebrush	Dewey, Sully, or Stanley County, SD; Dewey or Sully County, SD	Oct. 1, 1804; Oct. 2, 1804	ANS-A (3), ANS-L	E-61, 521
21	*Artemisia ludoviciana* Nutt.	white sage	Dewey, Sully, or Stanley County, SD; Skamania County, WA, or Multnomah County, OR, or Rock Fort Camp, Wasco County, OR	Oct. 1, 1804; [Apr 10, 1806?]	ANS-A, ANS-L	520
85	*Juniperus scopulorum* Sarg.	Rocky Mountain juniper	Dewey or Sully County, SD	Oct. 2, 1804	ANS-A	647
20	*Artemisia longifolia* Nutt.	long-leaved sage	Potter-Sully county line, SD	Oct. 3, 1804	ANS-A	——
66	*Euphorbia cyathophora* Murr.	fire-on-the-mountain	Dewey or Potter County, SD Sioux or Emmons County, ND	Oct. 4, 1804 Oct. [15?], 1804	ANS-A	——
114	*Nicotiana quadrivalvis* Pursh var. *quadrivalvis*	Indian tobacco	Campbell or Corson County, SD	Oct. 12, 1804	ANS-A	E-87, 141
84	*Juniperus horizontalis* Moench	creeping juniper	Sioux or Emmons County, ND	Oct. 16, 1804	ANS-A, ANS-L	647
122	*Pediomelum argophyllum* (Pursh) J. Grimes	silver-leaf scurf-pea	Sioux or Emmons County, ND	Oct. 17, 1804	ANS-A, ANS-L	E-93, 475
83	*Juniperus communis* L. var. *depressa* Pursh	common juniper	Sioux or Emmons County, ND; Lewis and Clark Pass, Lewis and Clark County, MT	Oct. 17, 1804; July 7, 1806	ANS-A (2), ANS-L (2)	——
40	*Chrysothamnus nauseosus* (Pallas *ex* Pursh) Britt. ssp. *nauseosus*	rabbit brush	Missouri River; [Missouri River?]	Oct. 1804; [Oct. 1804?]	ANS-L, ANS-A	517
15	*Arctostaphylos uva-ursi* (L.) Spreng.	bearberry	Fort Mandan, McLean County, ND	winter 1804–1805	ANS-A	——
149	*Ribes aureum* Pursh	golden currant	Three Forks of the Missouri River, Gallatin County, MT; The Dalles of the Columbia River, WA-OR	July 29, 1805; Apr. 16, 1806	ANS-A, Kew	E-95, 164
100	*Lonicera ciliosa* (Pursh) Poir. *ex* DC.	trumpet honeysuckle	North Fork Salmon River, Lemhi County, ID; Camp Chopunnish, Idaho County, ID; Lolo Trail, ID	Sept. 2, 1805; June 5, 1806; June 16, 1806	ANS-A (2)	E-66, 160
162	*Sorbus scopulina* Greene	mountain ash	North Fork Salmon River, Lemhi County, ID; Lolo Trail, ID	Sept. 2, 1805; June 27, 1806	ANS-A	——
13	*Angelica* sp.?	angelica	Lost Trail Pass, MT-ID; Lolo Trail, ID	Sept. 3, 1805; June 25, 1806	ANS-A	——

(*continued*)

ID	Scientific name	Common name	Place collected	Date collected	Archive	Pursh
131	*Pinus ponderosa* P. & C. Lawson	ponderosa pine	Canoe Camp, Clearwater County, ID	Oct. 1, 1805	ANS-A, ANS-L	——
23	*Aster oregonensis* (Nutt.) Cronq.	Oregon white-topped aster	Snake River, WA	Oct. 1805	ANS-A	——
52	*Coreopsis tinctoria* Nutt. var. *atkinsoniana* (Dougl. *ex* Lindl.) H. M. Parker	calliopsis	Snake River, WA	Oct. 1805	ANS-A	——
1	*Acer circinatum* Pursh	vine maple	Cascades of the Columbia River, WA-OR	Oct. [31?], 1805	ANS-A, ANS-L	E-57, 267
109	*Mahonia nervosa* (Pursh) Nutt.	dull Oregon grape	Cascades of the Columbia River, WA-OR	Oct. [31?], 1805	ANS-L	E-64, 219
105	*Machaeranthera canescens* (Pursh) Gray	hoary aster	Columbia River	Oct. 1805	ANS-A	——
14	*Arbutus menziesii* Pursh	Pacific madrone	Cascades of the Columbia River, WA-OR	Nov. 1, 1805	ANS-A	——
119	*Paxistima myrsinites* (Pursh) Raf.	mountain-box	Pacific County, WA; Lolo Trail, ID	Nov. 16, 1805; June 16, 1806	ANS-A (2), Kew	E-81, 119
59	*Egregia menziesii* (Turn.) Aresch.	Menzies' rockweed	Pacific County, WA	Nov. 17, 1805	ANS-A	——
30	*Blechnum spicant* (L.) Roth	deer-fern	Fort Clatsop, Clatsop County, OR; Fort Clatsop, Clatsop County, OR?	Jan. 20, 1806; [Jan. 20 1806?]	ANS-A, ANS-C	669
58	*Dryopteris expansa* (K. Presl) Fraser-Jenkins & Jermy	mountain wood-fern	Fort Clatsop, Clatsop County, OR	Jan. 20, 1806	ANS-A	——
74	*Gaultheria shallon* Pursh	salal	Fort Clatsop, Clatsop County, OR	Jan. 20, 1806	ANS-A	E-77, 283
80	*Hypnum oreganum* Sull.	moss	Fort Clatsop, Clatsop County, OR	Jan. 20, 1806	ANS-A	——
172	*Vaccinium myrtillus* L.	dwarf bilberry	Fort Clatsop, Clatsop County, OR	Jan. 20, 1806	ANS-A	——
173	*Vaccinium ovatum* Pursh	evergreen huckleberry	Fort Clatsop, Clatsop County, OR	Jan. 27, 1806	ANS-A	E-109, 290
16	*Argentina anserina* (L.) Rydb.	silverweed	Fort Clatsop, Clatsop County, OR	Mar. 13, 1806	ANS-A	——
42	*Cirsium edule* Nutt.	edible thistle	Fort Clatsop, Clatsop County, OR	Mar. 13, 1806	ANS-A	——
79	*Hordeum jubatum* L.	foxtail barley	Fort Clatsop, Clatsop County, OR; White Bear Islands, Cascade County, MT	Mar 13, 1806; July 12, 1806	ANS-A (2)	89
5	*Alnus rubra* Bong.	red alder	Cowlitz County, WA, or Columbia County, OR	Mar 26, 1806	ANS-A	——
45	*Claytonia parviflora* Dougl. *ex* Hook.	littleleaf montia	Cowlitz County, WA, or Columbia County, OR	Mar 26, 1806	ANS-A	——
146	*Quercus garryana* Dougl. *ex* Hook.	Garry oak	Cowlitz County, WA, or Columbia County, OR	Mar 26, 1806	ANS-A, ANS-L	——

ID	Scientific name	Common name	Place collected	Date collected	Archive	Pursh
151	*Ribes sanguineum* Pursh	red currant	Cowlitz County, WA, or Columbia County, OR	Mar 27, 1806	ANS-A	E-96, 164
155	*Rubus spectabilis* Pursh	salmonberry	Cowlitz County, WA, or Columbia County, OR	Mar 27, 1806	ANS-A	E-97, 348
35	*Cardamine nuttallii* Greene var. *nuttallii*	slender toothwort	Sandy River, Multnomah County, OR	Apr. 1, 1806	ANS-A, ANS-L	E-73, 439
47	*Claytonia sibirica* L.	Siberian montia	Multnomah County, OR, or Skamania County, WA	Apr. 8, 1806	ANS-A	175
150	*Ribes divaricatum* Pursh	straggly gooseberry	Multnomah County, OR, or Skamania County, WA	Apr. 8, 1806	ANS-A	——
71	*Fritillaria lanceolata* Pursh	checker lily	Bradford Island, Multnomah County, OR	Apr. 10, 1806	ANS-A, ANS-L	E-76, 230
2	*Acer macrophyllum* Pursh	big-leaf maple	Cascades of the Columbia River, WA-OR	Apr. 10, 1806	ANS-A, ANS-L	E-57, 267
169	*Trillium ovatum* Pursh	white trillium	Cascades of the Columbia River, WA-OR	Apr. 10, 1806	ANS-A	E-108, 245
108	*Mahonia aquifolium* (Pursh) Nutt.	Oregon grape	Cascades of the Columbia River, WA-OR	Apr. 11, 1806	ANS-L	E-64, 219
56	*Delphinium menziesii* DC.	Menzies' larkspur	Skamania or Klickitat County, WA, or Hood River or Wasco County, OR	Apr. 14, 1806	ANS-A	——
95	*Lomatium grayi* (Coult. & Rose) Coult. & Rose Gray's	lomatium	Klickitat County, WA, or Wasco County, OR	Apr. 14, 1806	ANS-A	——
98	*Lomatium* sp.?	lomatium	Skamania or Klickitat County, WA, or Hood River or Wasco County, OR	Apr. 14, 1806	ANS-A	——
28	*Balsamorrhiza sagittata* (Pursh) Nutt.	arrowleaf balsamroot	Skamania or Klickitat County, WA, or Hood River or Wasco County, OR; Lewis and Clark Pass, Lewis and Clark County, MT	Apr. 14, 1806; July 7, 1806	ANS-A	E-65, 564
6	*Amelanchier alnifolia* (Nutt.) Nutt. *ex* M. Roemer western	serviceberry	The Dalles of the Columbia River, WA-OR	Apr. 15, 1806	ANS-A	——
96	*Lomatium nudicaule* (Pursh) Coult. & Rose	barestem lomatium	The Dalles of the Columbia River, WA-OR	Apr. 15, 1806	ANS-A	E-104, 196
99	*Lomatium* sp.?	lomatium	The Dalles of the Columbia River, WA-OR	Apr. 15, 1806	ANS-A	——
154	*Rubus parviflorus* Nutt.	thimbleberry	The Dalles of the Columbia River, WA-OR	Apr. 15, 1806	ANS-A	——
57	*Dodecatheon jeffreyi* Van Houtte	Jeffrey's shooting star	The Dalles of the Columbia River, WA-OR	Apr. 16, 1806	ANS-A	——
10	*Amsinckia intermedia* Fisch. & C. A. Mey.	ranchers fiddleneck	Rock Fort Camp, Wasco County, OR	Apr. 17, 1806	ANS-A	——
46	*Claytonia perfoliata* Donn *ex* Willd. ssp. *perfoliata*	miner's lettuce	Rock Fort Camp, Wasco County, OR	Apr. 17, 1806	ANS-A	176

(*continued*)

ID	Scientific name	Common name	Place collected	Date collected	Archive	Pursh
50	Collinsia parviflora Lindl. var. grandiflora (Lindl.) Ganders & Krause	small-flowered blue-eyed Mary	Rock Fort Camp, Wasco County, OR	Apr. 17, 1806	ANS-A	E-60, 421
51	Collomia linearis Nutt.	narrow-leaf collomia	Rock Fort Camp, Wasco County, OR	Apr. 17, 1806	ANS-A	——
111	Microseris lindleyi (DC.) Gray	Lindley's microseris	Rock Fort Camp, Wasco County, OR	Apr. 17, 1806	ANS-A	——
128	Phacelia linearis (Pursh) Holz.	threadleaf phacelia	Rock Fort Camp, Wasco County, OR	Apr. 17, 1806	ANS-A	E-80, 134
132	Plagiobothrys tenellus (Nutt. ex Hook.) Gray	slender plagiobothrys	Rock Fort Camp, Wasco County, OR	Apr. 17, 1806	ANS-A	——
167	Trifolium macrocephalum (Pursh) Poir.	big-head clover	Rock Fort Camp, Wasco County, OR	Apr. 17, 1806	ANS-A, ANS-L	E-84, 479
171	Triteleia grandiflora Lindl.	Douglas' brodiaea	The Dalles of the Columbia River, Klickitat County, WA, or Wasco County, OR	Apr. 20, 1806	ANS-A, ANS-L	223
38	Cerastium arvense L.	field chickweed	Klickitat County, WA, or Wasco or Sherman County, OR	Apr. 22, 1806	ANS-A	E-67, 321
117	Osmorhiza occidentalis (Nutt. ex Torr. & Gray) Torr.	western sweet-cicely	Klickitat or Benton County, WA, or Gilliam or Morrow County, OR	Apr. 25, 1806	ANS-A	——
54	Crataegus douglasii Lindl.	black hawthorn	Walla Walla River, WA	Apr. 29, 1806	ANS-A	——
93	Lomatium cous (S. Wats.) Coult. & Rose	cous	Walla Walla River, WA	Apr. 29, 1806	ANS-A	——
4	Allium textile A. Nels. & J. F. Macbr.	textile onion	Walla Walla River, WA	Apr. 30, 1806	ANS-A	223
41	Chrysothamnus viscidiflorus (Hook.) Nutt. ssp. viscidiflorus	green rabbit brush	Clearwater River, Nez Perce County, ID	May 6, 1806	ANS-A	——
97	Lomatium triternatum (Pursh) Coult. & Rose	nine-leaf lomatium	Clearwater River, Nez Perce County, ID	May 6, 1806	ANS-A	E-102, 197
129	Philadelphus lewisii Pursh	Lewis's syringa	Clearwater River, Nez Perce County, ID; Blackfoot River, Missoula County, MT	May 6, 1806; July 4, 1806	ANS-A	E-90, 329
130	Phlox speciosa Pursh	showy phlox	Nez Perce County, ID	May 7, 1806	ANS-A, Kew	E-90, 149
7	Amelanchier sp.?	serviceberry	Clearwater River, Nez Perce County, ID; Lolo Trail, ID	May 7, 1806; June 27, 1806	ANS-A	——
72	Fritillaria pudica (Pursh) Spreng.	yellow bell	Clearwater River, Nez Perce or Clearwater County, ID	May 8, 1806	ANS-A, ANS-L	E-83, 228
65	Erythronium grandiflorum Pursh	pale fawn-lily	Clearwater River, Nez Perce or Clearwater County, ID; Lolo Trail, ID	May 8, 1806; June 15, 1806	ANS-A (2)	E-75, 231
31	Calochortus elegans Pursh	northwest mariposa	Camp Chopunnish, Idaho County, ID	May 17, 1806	ANS-A	E-65, 240

ID	Scientific name	Common name	Place collected	Date collected	Archive	Pursh
3	*Achillea millefolium* L.	yarrow	Camp Chopunnish, Idaho County, ID	May 20, 1806	ANS-A, ANS-L	563
125	*Penstemon wilcoxii* Rydb.	Wilcox's penstemon	Camp Chopunnish, Idaho County, ID	May 20, 1806	ANS-A	——
48	*Clematis hirsutissima* Pursh	Douglas's clematis	Camp Chopunnish, Idaho County, ID	May 27, 1806	ANS-A	E-69, 385
69	*Frangula purshiana* (DC.) Cooper	cascara	Camp Chopunnish, Idaho County, ID	May 29, 1806	ANS-A, ANS-L	E-94, 166
78	*Holodiscus discolor* (Pursh) Maxim.	creambush ocean-spray	Camp Chopunnish, Idaho County, ID	May 29, 1806	ANS-A, ANS-L	E-106, 342
140	*Prunus emarginata* (Dougl. *ex* Hook.) Walp. var. *emarginata*	bitter cherry	Camp Chopunnish, Idaho County, ID	May 29, 1806	ANS-A	——
141	*Prunus virginiana* L.	choke cherry	Camp Chopunnish, Idaho County, ID; Williams or McKenzie County, ND	May 29, 1806; Aug 10, 1806	ANS-A (2)	——
43	*Clarkia pulchella* Pursh	ragged robin	Camp Chopunnish, Idaho County, ID	June 1, 1806	ANS-A	E-69, 260
64	*Erysimum asperum* (Nutt.) DC.	rough wallflower	Camp Chopunnish, Idaho County, ID	June 1, 1806	ANS-A	——
158	*Scutellaria angustifolia* Pursh ssp. *angustifolia*	narrow-leaved skullcap	Camp Chopunnish, Idaho County, ID	June 5, 1806	ANS-A	E-101, 412
159	*Sedum stenopetalum* Pursh	wormleaf stonecrop	Camp Chopunnish, Idaho County, ID; Travelers' Rest, Missoula County, MT	June 5, 1806; July 1, 1806	ANS-A	E-101, 324
104	*Lupinus sericeus* Pursh	silky lupine	Camp Chopunnish, Idaho County, ID; Lewis and Clark Pass, Lewis and Clark County, MT	June 5, 1806; July 7, 1806	ANS-A, Kew	E-84, 468
63	*Eriophyllum lanatum* (Pursh) Forbes var. *lanatum*	common eriophyllum	Camp Chopunnish, Idaho County, ID	June 6, 1806	ANS-A, ANS-L	E-58, 560
127	*Phacelia heterophylla* Pursh	varileaf phacelia	Camp Chopunnish, Idaho County, ID	June 9, 1806	ANS-A, ANS-L	E-90, 140
68	*Festuca idahoensis* Elmer	Idaho fescue	Camp Chopunnish, Idaho County, ID	June 10, 1806	ANS-A	——
86	*Koeleria macrantha* (Ledeb.) J. A. Schultes	prairie Junegrass	Camp Chopunnish, Idaho County, ID	June 10, 1806	ANS-A	85
94	*Lomatium dissectum* (Nutt.) Mathias & Constance	fern-leaved lomatium	Camp Chopunnish, Idaho County, ID	June 10, 1806	ANS-A	195
133	*Poa secunda* J. Presl	Sandberg's bluegrass	Camp Chopunnish, Idaho County, ID	June 10, 1806	ANS-A	E-58, 76
142	*Pseudoroegneria spicata* (Pursh) A. Löve	bluebunch wheatgrass	Camp Chopunnish, Idaho County, ID	June 10, 1806	ANS-A	E-76, 83
75	*Geum triflorum* Pursh	old man's whiskers	Weippe Prairie, Clearwater County, ID	June 12, 1806	ANS-A	E-77, 352, 736

(*continued*)

ID	Scientific name	Common name	Place collected	Date collected	Archive	Pursh
110	*Matricaria discoidea* DC.	pineapple weed	Weippe Prairie, Clearwater County, ID	June 12, 1806	ANS-A, ANS-L	E-100, 520
137	*Polygonum bistortoides* Pursh	American bistort	Weippe Prairie, Clearwater County, ID	June 12, 1806	ANS-A	E-91, 271
34	*Camissonia subacaulis* (Pursh) Raven	long-leaf evening primrose	Weippe Prairie, Clearwater County, ID	June 14, 1806	ANS-A	E-82, 304
70	*Frasera fastigiata* (Pursh) Heller	clustered frasera	Weippe Prairie, Clearwater County, ID	June 14, 1806	ANS-A	E-106, 101
12	*Anemone quinquefolia* L.	wood anemone	Lolo Trail, ID	June 15, 1806	ANS-A	——
124	*Penstemon fruticosus* (Pursh) Greene	shrubby penstemon	Lolo Trail, ID	June 15, 1806	ANS-L	E-77, 423
170	*Trillium petiolatum* Pursh	purple trillium	Lolo Trail, ID	June 15, 1806	ANS-A	E-108, 244
175	*Xerophyllum tenax* (Pursh) Nutt.	Indian basket-grass	Lolo Trail, ID	June 15, 1806	ANS-A, Kew	E-80, 243
32	*Calypso bulbosa* (L.) Oakes	fairy-slipper	Lolo Trail, ID	June 16, 1806	ANS-A	593
53	*Cornus canadensis* L.	bunchberry	Lolo Trail, ID	June 16, 1806	ANS-A	——
152	*Ribes viscosissimum* Pursh	sticky currant	Lolo Trail, ID	June 16, 1806	ANS-A, Kew	E-96, 163
33	*Camassia quamash* (Pursh) Greene	camas	Weippe Prairie, Clearwater County, ID	June 23, 1806	ANS-A	E-90, 226
174	*Veratrum californicum* Dur.	California false hellebore	Lolo Trail, ID	June 25, 1806	ANS-A	——
81	*Ipomopsis aggregata* (Pursh) V. Grant ssp. *aggregata*	scarlet gilia	Lolo Trail, ID	June 26, 1806	ANS-A	E-66, 147
166	*Synthyris missurica* (Raf.) Pennell	mountain kittentails	Lolo Trail, ID	June 26, 1806	ANS-A, ANS-L	10
36	*Ceanothus sanguineus* Pursh	redstem ceanothus	Lolo Trail, ID	June 27, 1806	ANS-L	E-67, 167
44	*Claytonia lanceolata* Pursh	western springbeauty	Lolo Trail, ID	June 27, 1806	ANS-A	E-69, 175
88	*Lewisia triphylla* (S. Wats.) B. L. Robins.	threeleaved lewisia	Lolo Trail, ID	June 27, 1806	ANS-A	——
135	*Polemonium caeruleum* L.	western polemonium	Lolo Trail, ID	June 27, 1806	ANS-A	——
138	*Populus balsamifera* L. ssp. *trichocarpa* (Torr. & Gray *ex* Hook.) Brayshaw	black cottonwood	unknown	June 1806	ANS-A	——
29	*Bazzania trilobata* (L.) S. F. Gray	liverwort	Travelers' Rest, Missoula County, MT	July 1, 1806	ANS-A	——
87	*Lewisia rediviva* Pursh	bitterroot	Travelers' Rest, Missoula County, MT	July 1, 1806	ANS-A	E-83, 368
116	*Orthocarpus tenuifolius* (Pursh) Benth.	thin-leaved owl-clover	Travelers' Rest, Missoula County, MT	July 1, 1806	ANS-A	E-64, 429

ID	Scientific name	Common name	Place collected	Date collected	Archive	Pursh
168	*Trifolium microcephalum* Pursh	small-head clover	Travelers' Rest, Missoula County, MT	July 1, 1806	ANS-A, ANS-L	E-108, 478
118	*Oxytropis nana* Nutt. var. *besseyi* (Rydb.) Isely	Bessey's crazyweed	Travelers' Rest, Missoula County, MT	July [1?], 1806	ANS-A, ANS-L	E-88, 473
112	*Mimulus guttatus* DC.	yellow monkey-flower	Blackfoot River, Missoula County, MT	July 4, 1806	ANS-A	426
82	*Iris missouriensis* Nutt.	western blue flag	Nevada Valley, Powell County, MT	July 5, 1806	ANS-A	——
60	*Elaeagnus commutata* Bernh. *ex* Rydb.	silverberry	Nevada Valley, Powell County, MT	July 6, 1806	ANS-A, Kew	E-74, 114
120	*Pedicularis cystoperidifolia* Rydb.	fern-leaved lousewort	Blackfoot River, Powell County, MT	July 6, 1806	ANS-A	425
121	*Pedicularis groenlandica* Retz.	pink elephants	Blackfoot River, Powell County, MT	July 6, 1806	ANS-A	426
126	*Pentaphylloides floribunda* (Pursh) A. Löve	shrubby cinquefoil	Nevada Valley, Powell County, MT	July 6, 1806	ANS-A	355
145	*Purshia tridentata* (Pursh) DC.	antelope-brush	Nevada Valley, Powell County, MT	July 6, 1806	ANS-A	E-107, 333
73	*Gaillardia aristata* Pursh	blanket flower	Lewis and Clark Pass, Lewis and Clark County, MT	July 7, 1806	ANS-A	E-76, 573
101	*Lonicera involucrata* Banks *ex* Spreng.	bearberry honeysuckle	Lewis and Clark Pass, Lewis and Clark County, MT	July 7, 1806	ANS-A	——
176	*Zigadenus elegans* Pursh	white camass	Blackfoot River, Lewis and Clark County, MT	July 7, 1806	ANS-A	E-112, 241
102	*Lupinus argenteus* Pursh	silvery lupine	Blackfoot River, Lewis and Clark County, MT; Clearwater River, ID?	July 7, 1806; July 1806	ANS-A, Kew	E-84, 468
164	*Stipa comata* Trin. & Rupr.	needle-and-thread	Lewis and Clark or Teton County, MT	July 8, 1806	ANS-A	72
92	*Linum lewisii* Pursh var. *lewisii*	blue flax	Lewis and Clark, Teton, or Cascade County, MT	July 9, 1806	ANS-A, ANS-L	E-83, 210
115	*Oenothera cespitosa* Nutt. ssp. *cespitosa*	gumbo evening primrose	Great Falls of the Missouri River, Cascade County, MT	July 17, 1806	ANS-A, ANS-L	E-87, 263, 735
27	*Atriplex gardneri* (Moq.) D. Dietr.	moundscale	Marias River, Toole County, MT	July 20, 1806	ANS-A	——
157	*Sarcobatus vermiculatus* (Hook.) Torr.	greasewood	Marias River, Toole County, MT	July 20, 1806	ANS-A	——
163	*Sphaeralcea coccinea* (Nutt.) Rydb.	red false mallow	Marias River, Toole County, MT	July 20, 1806	ANS-A, ANS-L	E-71, 453
67	*Euphorbia marginata* Pursh	snow-on-the-mountain	Rosebud County, MT	July 28, 1806	ANS-A	E-75, 607
136	*Polygala alba* Nutt.	white milkwort	Williams or McKenzie County, ND	Aug. 10, 1806	ANS-A	750

(continued)

ID	Scientific name	Common name	Place collected	Date collected	Archive	Pursh
8	*Amorpha fruticosa* L.	false indigo	Big Bend of the Missouri River, Lyman County, SD	Aug. 27, 1806	ANS-A, Kew	E-59, 466
139	*Populus deltoides* Bartr. *ex* Marsh. ssp. *monilifera* (Ait.) Eckenwalder	cottonwood	unknown	Aug. 1806	ANS-A	——
9	*Ampelopsis cordata* Michx.	raccoon grape	Council Bluff, Washington County, NE; Leavenworth County, KS	Sept. 8, 1806; Sept. 14, 1806	ANS-A	——
161	*Solidago rigida* L.	rigid goldenrod	Doniphan or Atchison County, KS, or Buchanan County, MO	Sept. 12, 1806	ANS-A	——
103	*Lupinus pusillus* Pursh	rusty lupine	Missouri River?	unknown	Kew	E-84, 468
123	*Pediomelum esculentum* (Pursh) Rydb.	Indian breadroot	Missouri River?	unknown	ANS-L	E-93, 475
143	*Psoralidium lanceolatum* (Pursh) Rydb.	lemon scurf-pea	Missouri River?	unknown	ANS-L	E-93, 475
165	*Symphoricarpos albus* (L.) Blake	snowberry	Missouri River?	unknown	CM	E-106, 162
37	*Ceanothus velutinus* Dougl. *ex* Hook.	mountain balm	Clearwater River, ID	unknown	ANS-A	——
62	*Erigeron compositus* Pursh	cut-leaved daisy	Clearwater River, ID	unknown	ANS-L	E-75, 535
89	*Leymus arenarius* (L.) Hochst.	dune wildrye	unknown	unknown	ANS-A	——
107	*Maclura pomifera* (Raf.) Schneid.	Osage orange	unknown	unknown	ANS-A	——
134	*Polanisia dodecandra* (L.) DC. ssp. *trachysperma* (Torr. & Gray) Iltis	clammy-weed	unknown	unknown	ANS-A	——

Lewis's Plants Illustrated in Pursh's *Flora Americae Septentrionalis;* and Pursh's Unpublished Illustrations of Lewis's Plants

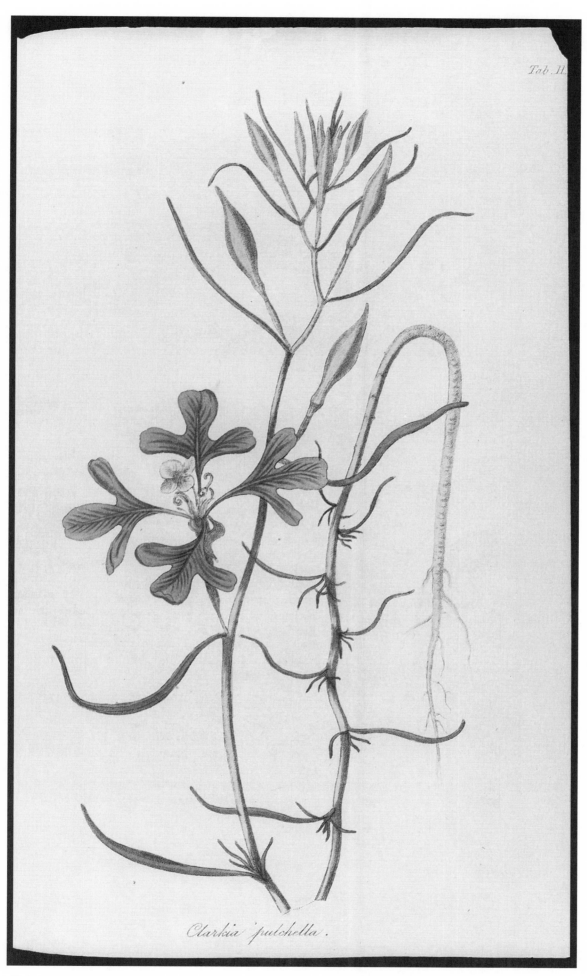

Tab. II.

Clarkia pulchella.

Clarkia pulchella Pursch [43]

Tab. 3. p. 175.

Claytonia lanceolata.

Claytonia lanceolata Pursh [44]

Tab. 3. p.

Lilium pudicum.

1   2

Fritillaria pudica (Pursh) Spreng. [72]

Tab. 12. p. 283.

Gualtheria shallon.

Gaultheria shallon Pursh [74]

Berberis aquifolium.

Mahonia aquifolium (Pursh) Nutt. [108]

Tab. 5. p. 219.

Berberis nervosa.

Drawn & Engraved by W. Hooker.

Mahonia nervosa (Pursh) Nutt. [109]

Tab. 20. p. 427.

Mimulus Lewisii.

Drawn & Engraved by W.H.

Mimulus lewisii Pursh [missing]

Tab. 22. p. 475.

Psoralea esculenta.

Pediomelum esculentum (Pursh) Rydb. [123]

Tab. 18. p. 423.

Gerardia fruticosa.

Drawn & Engraved by W. Hooker.

Penstemon fruticosus (Pursh) Greene [124]

Tab. 15

p. 262.

Tigarea tridentata.

1   2   3

Oenothera   minima.

Purshia tridentata (Pursh) DC. [145]

Tab. 16.

Rubus spectabilis.

Drawn & Engraved by B.

Rubus spectabilis Pursh [155]

Tab. 23. p. 47

Lupinaster macrocephalus.

Trifolium macrocephalum (Pursh) Poir. [167]

Tab. 9. p. 243.

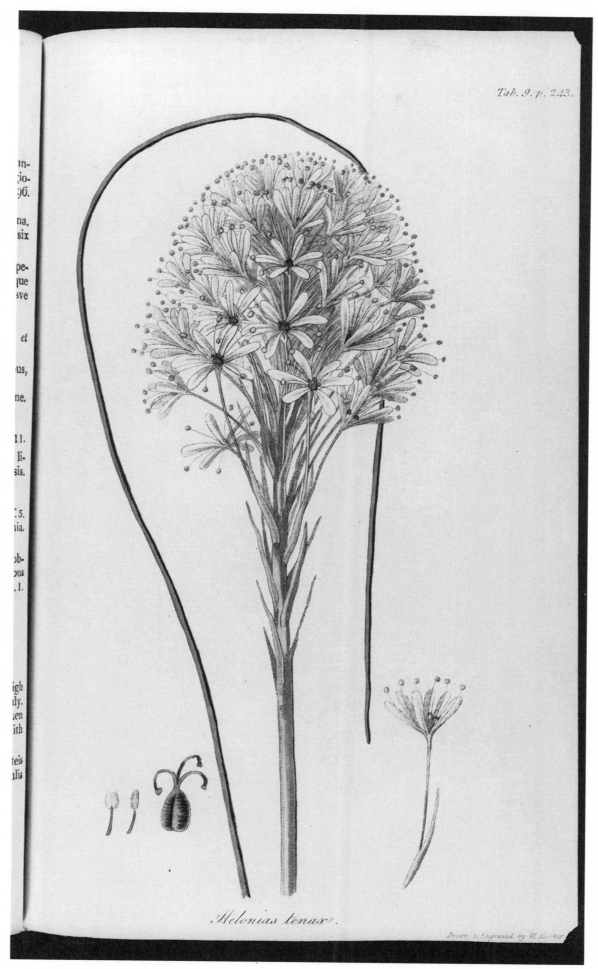

Helonias tenax.

Drawn & Engraved by W. Hooker

Xerophyllum tenax (Pursh) Nutt. [175]

Calochortus elegans Pursh [31]; unpublished

F. Pursh del.

Epipactis unifolia.

A. A side view of the flower. B & C. A front view.

1. The beard on the opening of the lower lip.

2. The upper lip, connected with the column of the fructification

3. The lower lip, which is with its inner sides connected.

4. The five petals (or leaves of the calyx.)

Calypso bulbosa (L.) Oakes [32]; unpublished

Fritillaria lanceolata Pursh [71]; *Fritillaria pudica* (Pursh) Spreng. [72]; unpublished

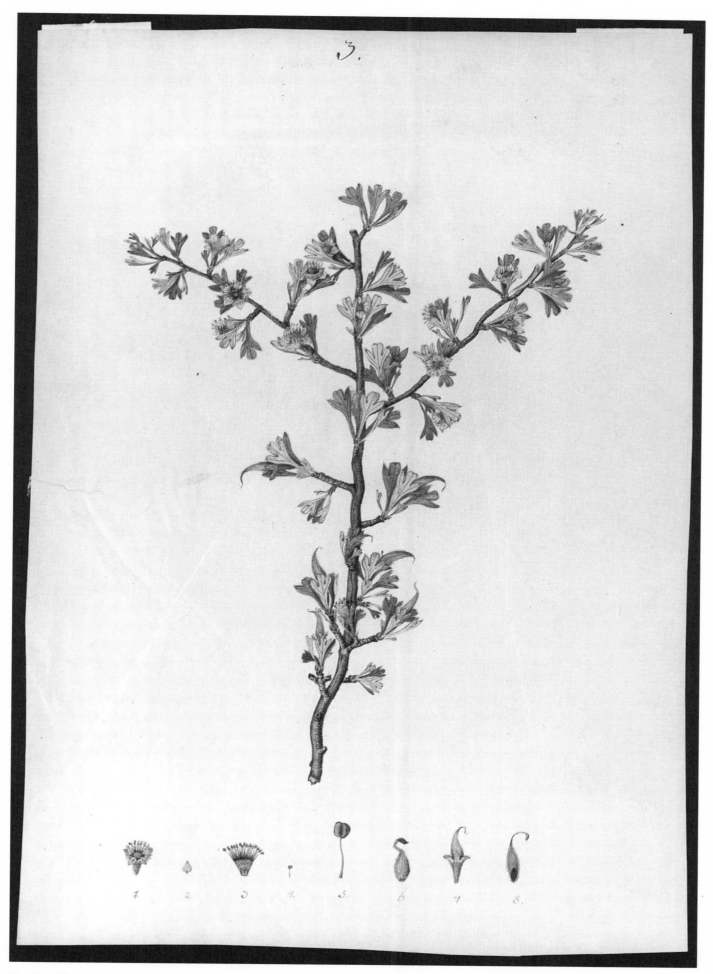

Purshia tridentata (Pursh) DC. [145]; unpublished

Ribes aureum Pursh [149]; unpublished

Table of Lewis's Plants in Pursh's *Flora Americae Septentrionalis*

ID	Current name	Pursh name	Archive	Pursh	Meehan	Cutright	Barkley	H & C	Kartesz
1	*Acer circinatum* Pursh, vine maple	*Acer circinatum*	ANS-A, ANS-L	E-57, 267	21	244, 400	——	289	1:30, 2:4
2	*Acer macrophyllum* Pursh, big-leaf maple	*Acer macrophyllum*	ANS-A, ANS-L	E-57, 267	22	289, 401	——	289	1:30, 2:4
3	*Achillea millefolium* L., yarrow	*Achillea tomentosa*	ANS-A, ANS-L	563	30	307	854	478	1:59, 2:6
4	*Allium textile* A. Nels. & J. F. Macbr., textile onion	*Allium angulosum*	ANS-A	223	42	289	1246	681	1:359, 2:23
8	*Amorpha fruticosa* L., false indigo	*Amorpha fruticosa* var. *angustifolia*	ANS-A, Kew	E-59, 466	22	348	419	——	1:269, 2:31
	Amorpha nana Nutt., dwarf wild indigo	*Amorpha microphylla*	missing	E-59, 466	——	——	419	——	1:270, 2:31
	Anemone caroliniana Walt., Carolina anemone	*Anemone tenella*	missing	E-60, 386	——	——	87	——	1:500, 2:37
	Artemisia campestris L., western sagewort	*Artemisia campestris*	missing	521	——	——	868	488	1:67, 2:64
17	*Artemisia cana* Pursh, dwarf sagebrush	*Artemisia cana*	ANS-A (3), ANS-L	E-61, 521	31	105, 403	869	488	1:68, 2:64
18	*Artemisia dracunculus* L., silky wormwood	*Artemisia Dracunculus*	ANS-A	521	31	88, 403	869	487	1:68, 2:64
19	*Artemisia frigida* Willd., pasture sagewort	*Artemisia frigida*	ANS-A (2), ANS-L	521	31	75, 105	870	487	1:68, 2:65
21	*Artemisia ludoviciana* Nutt., white sage	*Artemisia integrifolia*	ANS-A, ANS-L	520	32	289, 403	870	486	1:68, 2:65
	unknown	*Artemisia Santonica*	missing	521	——	——	——	——	——
	Astragalus tennellus Pursh, pulse milk-vetch	*Astragalus tenellus; Ervum multiflorum*	missing	E-63, E-75, 473, 739	——	——	435	237, 258	1:277, 2:89
26	*Atriplex canescens* (Pursh) Nutt., four-wing saltbush	*Calligonum canescens*	ANS-A	E-65, 370	39	88, 404	162	95	1:208, 2:92
	Baccharis angustifolia Michx., unnamed baccharis	*Baccharis angustifolia*	missing	523	——	——	——	——	1:75, 2:96
28	*Balsamorhiza sagittata* (Pursh) Nutt., arrowleaf balsamroot	*Buphthalmum sagittatum*	ANS-A	E-65, 564	32	289, 326, 405	889	495	1:76, 2:97
	Besseya ruba (Dougl.) Rydb., red besseya	*Bartsia Gymnandra*	missing	430	49	——	——	415	1:570, 2:101
30	*Blechnum spicant* (L.) Roth, deer-fern	*Blechnum boreale*	ANS-A, ANS-C	669	47	274	——	49	1:5, 2:105
31	*Calochortus elegans* Pursh, northwest mariposa	*Calochortus elegans*	ANS-A	E-65, 240	43	307, 405	——	688	1:360, 2:124
32	*Calypso bulbosa* (L.) Oakes, fairy-slipper	*Calypso borealis*	ANS-A	593	42	307	1270	700	1:405, 2:127
33	*Camassia quamash* (Pursh) Greene, camas	*Phalangium Quamash*	ANS-A	E-90, 226	43	307, 405	——	688	1:361, 2:128
34	*Camissonia subacaulis* (Pursh) Raven, long-leaf evening primrose	*Jussieua subacaulis*	ANS-A	E-82, 304	28, 49	308, 412	——	311	1:397, 2:130
35	*Cardamine nuttallii* Greene var. *nuttallii*, slender toothwort	*Dentaria tenella*	ANS-A, ANS-L	E-73, 439	18	289, 408	——	159	1:160, 2:133

ID	Current name	Pursh name	Archive	Pursh	Meehan	Cutright	Barkley	H & C	Kartesz
36	*Ceanothus sanguineus* Pursh, redstem ceanothus	*Ceanothus sanguineus*	ANS-L	E-67, 167	48	307, 405	——	290	1:511, 2:158
38	*Cerastium arvense* L., field chickweed	*Cerastium elongatum*	ANS-A	E-67, 321	18	289	197	113	1:196, 2:160
39	*Chrysothamnus nauseosus* (Pallas *ex* Pursh) Britt. ssp. *graveolens* (Nutt.) Piper, rabbit brush	*Chrysocoma dracunculoides*	ANS-A (2), ANS-L (2)	E-68, 517	32, 34	75, 105, 405	906	502	1:83, 2:181
40	*Chrysothamnus nauseosus* (Pallas *ex* Pursh) Britt. ssp. *nauseosus*, rabbit brush	*Chrysocoma nauseosa*	ANS-A, ANS-L	517	33	——	906	502	1:83, 2:181
43	*Clarkia pulchella* Pursh, ragged robin	*Clarckia pulchella*	ANS-A	E-69, 260	28	307, 406	——	305	1:398, 2:188
44	*Claytonia lanceolata* Pursh, western springbeauty	*Claytonia lanceolata*	ANS-A	E-69, 175	19	308, 406	——	105	1:491, 2:189
46	*Claytonia perfoliata* Donn *ex* Willd. ssp. *perfoliata*, miner's lettuce	*Claytonia perfoliata*	ANS-A	176	20	289	——	108	1:492, 2:189
47	*Claytonia sibirica* L., Siberian montia	*Claytonia alsinoides*	ANS-A	175	20	289	——	108	1:492, 2:189
48	*Clematis hirsutissima* Pursh, Douglas's clematis	*Clematis hirsutissima*	ANS-A	E-69, 385	17, 34	289, 407	90	129	1:502, 2:190
49	*Cleome serrulata* Pursh, Rocky Mountain bee plant	*Cleome serrulata*	ANS-A (2), ANS-L	E-69, 441	18	75, 348, 407	292	180	1:192, 2:191
50	*Collinsia parviflora* Lindl. var. *grandiflora* (Lindl.) Ganders & Krause, small-flowered blue-eyed Mary	*Antirrhinum tenellum*	ANS-A	E-60, 421	38	289, 402	763	422	1:574, 2:195
	Corispermum hyssopifolium L., hyssopleaf tickseed	*Corispermum hyssopifolium*	missing	4	——	——	173	99	1:211, 2:204
	perhaps *Crataegus columbiana* T. J. Howell, Columbia hawthorn	*Crataegus glandulosa*	missing	337	——	——	——	210	1:516, 2:210
	Dalea candida Willd., white prairie-clover	*Petalostemum candidum*	missing	461	——	——	440	272	1:282, 2:236
60	*Elaeagnus commutata* Bernh. *ex* Rydb., silverberry	*Elaeagrus argentea*	ANS-A, Kew	E-74, 114	40	326, 408	491	302	1:251, 2:272
62	*Erigeron compositus* Pursh, cut-leaved daisy	*Erigeron compositum*	ANS-L	E-75, 535	49	308, 408	928	516	1:94, 2:289
63	*Eriophyllum lanatum* (Pursh) Forbes var. *lanatum*, common eriophyllum	*Actinella lanata*	ANS-A, ANS-L	E-58, 560	33	307, 401	——	520	1:97, 2:305
65	*Erythronium grandiflorum* Pursh, pale fawn-lily	*Erythronium grandiflorum*	ANS-A (2)	E-75, 231	43	289, 308, 408	——	690	1:363, 2:308
67	*Euphorbia marginata* Pursh, snow-on-the-mountain	*Euphorbia marginata*	ANS-A	E-75, 607	40	326, 408	547	——	1:266, 2:316

(continued)

ID	Current name	Pursh name	Archive	Pursh	Meehan	Cutright	Barkley	H & C	Kartesz
69	*Frangula purshiana* (DC.) Cooper, cascara	*Rhamnus alnifolius*	ANS-A, ANS-L	E-94, 166	21	308, 416	——	290	1:512, 2:328
70	*Frasera fastigiata* (Pursh) Heller, clustered frasera	*Swertia fastigiata*	ANS-A	E-106, 101	36	308, 420	——	358	1:319, 2:328
71	*Fritillaria lanceolata* Pursh, checker lily	*Fritillaria lanceolata*	ANS-A, ANS-L	E-76, 230	44	289, 409	——	691	1:363, 2:330
72	*Fritillaria pudica* (Pursh) Spreng., yellow bell	*Lilium pudicum*	ANS-A, ANS-L	E-83, 228	44	289, 409	1250	691	1:363, 2:330
73	*Gaillardia aristata* Pursh, blanket flower	*Galardia aristata*	ANS-A	E-76, 573	33	326, 409	938	521	1:100, 2:331
74	*Gaultheria shallon* Pursh, salal	*Gaultheria Shallon*	ANS-A	E-77, 283	35	274, 409	——	344	1:254, 2:338
75	*Geum triflorum* Pursh, old man's whiskers	*Geum ciliatum*	ANS-A	E-77, 352, 736	24	308, 409	379	212	1:522, 2:346
76	*Grindelia squarrosa* (Pursh) Dunal, curly-top gumweed	*Donia squarrosa*	ANS-A, ANS-L (2)	559	33	75, 409	——	——	1:102, 2:357
77	*Gutierrezia sarothrae* (Pursh) Britt. & Rusby, snakeweed	*Solidago Sarothrae*	ANS-A, Kew	E-105, 540	34	88, 420	945	——	1:102, 2:359
78	*Holodiscus discolor* (Pursh) Maxim., creambush ocean-spray	*Spiraea discolor*	ANS-A, ANS-L	E-106, 342	26	308, 420	——	213	1:523, 2:385
79	*Hordeum jubatum* L., foxtail barley	*Hordeum jubatum*	ANS-A (2)	89	45	274, 326	1185	646	1:447, 2:386
81	*Ipomopsis aggregata* (Pursh) V. Grant ssp. *aggregata*, scarlet gilia	*Cantua aggregata*	ANS-A	E-66, 147	37	307, 405	——	369	1:469, 2:399
	Iris sibirica L., unnamed flag or iris	*Iris sibirica*	missing	30	——	——	——	——	1:337, 2:401
84	*Juniperus horizontalis* Moench, creeping juniper	*Juniperus Sabina* var. *procumbens*	ANS-A, ANS-L	647	46	105	72	58	1:23, 2:410
85	*Juniperus scopulorum* Sarg., Rocky Mountain juniper	*Juniperus excelsa*	ANS-A	647	46	105	73	58	1:24, 2:410
86	*Koeleria macrantha* (Ledeb.) J. A. Schultes, prairie Junegrass	*Koeleria cristata*	ANS-A	85	45	308	1186	647	1:448, 2:413
	Krascheninnikovia lanata (Pursh) Guldenstaedt, white sage	*Diotis lanata*	missing	E-73, 602	49	——	166	99	1:212, 2:414
87	*Lewisia rediviva* Pursh, bitterroot	*Lewisia rediviva*	ANS-A	E-83, 368	19	308, 410	——	106	1:493, 2:433
	Lilium philadelphicum L. var. *andinum* (Nutt.) Ker-Gawl, red lily	*Lilium umbellatum*	missing	E-83, 229	49	——	1252	692	1:365, 2:436
92	*Linum lewisii* Pursh var. *lewisii*, blue flax	*Linum Lewisii*	ANS-A, ANS-L	E-83, 210	19	326, 410	562	282	1:371, 2:440
94	*Lomatium dissectum* (Nutt.) Mathias & Constance, fern-leaved lomatium	*Phellandrium aquaticum*	ANS-A	195	29	308, 413	——	330	1:44, 2:446
96	*Lomatium nudicaule* (Pursh) Coult. & Rose, barestem lomatium	*Smyrnium nudicaule*	ANS-A	E-104, 196	28	290, 420	——	328	1:44, 2:447

ID	Current name	Pursh name	Archive	Pursh	Meehan	Cutright	Barkley	H & C	Kartesz
97	*Lomatium triternatum* (Pursh) Coult. & Rose, nine-leaf lomatium	*Seseli triternatum*	ANS-A	E-102, 197	29	289, 413	——	327	1:45, 2:447
100	*Lonicera ciliosa* (Pursh) Poir. *ex* DC., trumpet honeysuckle	*Caprifolium ciliosum*	ANS-A (2)	E-66, 160	30	308, 410	——	452	1:193, 2:448
102	*Lupinus argenteus* Pursh, silvery lupine	*Lupinus argenteus*	ANS-A, Kew	E-84, 468	22	326, 411	462	267	1:292, 2:452
103	*Lupinus pusillus* Pursh, rusty lupine	*Lupinus pusillus*	Kew	E-84, 468	——	——	464	265	1:297, 2:461
104	*Lupinus sericeus* Pursh, silky lupine	*Lupinus sericeus*	ANS-A, Kew	E-84, 468	23	308, 411	464	266	1:298, 2:462
106	*Machaeranthera pinnatifida* (Hook.) Shinners ssp. *pinnatifida* var. *pinnatifida*, spiny goldenweed	*Amellus spinulosus*	ANS-A	E-59, 564	30	88, 244, 402	950	525	1:117, 2:472
108	*Mahonia aquifolium* (Pursh) Nutt., Oregon grape	*Berberis Aquifolium*	ANS-L	E-64, 219	48	289, 404	——	142	1:144, 2:474
109	*Mahonia nervosa* (Pursh) Nutt., dull Oregon grape	*Berberis nervosa*	ANS-L	E-64, 219	48	244, 404	——	142	1:144, 2:474
110	*Matricaria discoidea* DC., pineapple weed	*Santolina suaveolens*	ANS-A, ANS-L	E-100, 520	34	308, 419	978	540	1:118, 2:482
	Mentzelia decapetala (Pursh) Urban & Gilg, sand lily	*Bartonia ornata*	missing	E-63, 327	——	——	271	300	1:372, 2:488
	Menziesia ferruginea Smith, fool's huckleberry	*Menziesia ferruginea*	missing	264	49	——	——	345	1:256, 2:489
112	*Mimulus guttatus* DC., yellow monkey-flower	*Mimulus luteus*	ANS-A	426	38	326, 411	771	427	1:579, 2:496
	Mimulus lewisii Pursh, Lewis's monkey-flower	*Mimulus Lewisii*	missing	E-85, 427	49	——	——	426	1:579, 2:497
113	*Mirabilis nyctaginea* (Michx.) MacM., wild four-o'clock	*Allionia ovata*	ANS-A, ANS-L	E-59, 97	39	75	150	103	1:391, 2:500
114	*Nicotiana quadrivalvis* Pursh var. *quadrivalvis*, Indian tobacco	*Nicotiana quadrivalvis*	ANS-A	E-87, 141	37	105, 411	637	——	1:592, 2:514
115	*Oenothera cespitosa* Nutt. ssp. *cespitosa*, gumbo evening primrose	*Oenothera scapigeraOenothera caespitosa*	ANS-A, ANS-L	E-87, 263, 735	28	326, 411	518	310	1:402, 2:520
116	*Orthocarpus tenuifolius* (Pursh) Benth., thin-leaved owl-clover	*Bartsia tenuifolia*	ANS-A	E-64, 429	38	308, 412	——	429	1:581, 2:535
118	*Oxytropis nana* Nutt. var. *besseyi* (Rydb.) Isely, Bessey's crazyweed	*Oxytropis argentata*	ANS-A, ANS-L	E-88, 473	23	308, 412	467	271	1:302, 2:540
119	*Paxistima myrsinites* (Pursh) Raf., mountain-box	*Ilex myrsinites*	ANS-A (2), Kew	E-81, 119	20	244, 308, 412	——	288	1:207, 2:556
120	*Pedicularis cystopteridifolia* Rydb., fern-leaved lousewort	*Pedicularis elata*	ANS-A	425	38	326, 413	——	431	1:581, 2:557

(*continued*)

ID	Current name	Pursh name	Archive	Pursh	Meehan	Cutright	Barkley	H&C	Kartesz
121	*Pedicularis groenlandica* Retz., pink elephants	*Pedicularis groenlandica*	ANS-A	426	38	326	——	432	1:581, 2:557
122	*Pediomelum argophyllum* (Pursh) J. Grimes, silver-leaf scurf-pea	*Psoralea argophylla*	ANS-A, ANS-L	E-93, 475	23	105, 415	472	273	1:303, 2:559
123	*Pediomelum esculentum* (Pursh) Rydb., Indian breadroot	*Psoralea esculenta*	ANS-L	E-93, 475	48	105, 416	473	273	1:303, 2:559
	Pennelianthus frutescens (Lamb.) Crosswh., beardtongue	*Pentstemon frutescens*	missing	E-89, 428	49	——	——	——	——
124	*Penstemon fruticosus* (Pursh) Greene, shrubby penstemon	*Gerardia fruticosa*	ANS-L	E-77, 423	49	308, 409	——	433	1:584, 2:566
126	*Pentaphylloides floribunda* (Pursh) A. Löve, shrubby cinquefoil	*Potentilla fruticosa*	ANS-A	355	25	326	385	216	1:525, 2:570
127	*Phacelia heterophylla* Pursh, varileaf phacelia	*Phacelia heterophylla*	ANS-A, ANS-L	E-90, 140	37	308, 413	——	381	1:334, 2:577
128	*Phacelia linearis* (Pursh) Holz., threadleaf phacelia	*Hydrophyllum lineare*	ANS-A	E-80, 134	37	289, 410	682	382	1:334, 2:577
129	*Philadelphus lewisii* Pursh, Lewis's syringa	*Philadelphus Lewisii*	ANS-A	E-90, 329	27	326, 413	——	204	1:330, 2:580
130	*Phlox speciosa* Pursh, showy phlox	*Phlox speciosa*	ANS-A, Kew	E-90, 149	48	290, 414	——	374	1:474, 2:585
	Phyllodoce empetriformis (Sw.) D. Don, pink mountain heather	*Menziesia empetriformis*	missing	264	49	——	——	346	1:256, 2:588
	Physocarpus capitatus (Pursh) Kuntze, Pacific ninebark	*Spiraea capitata*	missing	E-106, 342	49	——	——	216	1:525, 2:591
133	*Poa secunda* J. Presl, Sandberg's bluegrass	*Aira brevifolia*	ANS-A	E-58, 76	45	401	1214	663	1:458, 2:606
136	*Polygala alba* Nutt., white milkwort	*Polygala Seneca* var. *tenuifolia*	ANS-A	750	22	326, 415	565	——	1:475, 2:609
137	*Polygonum bistortoides* Pursh, American bistort	*Polygonum bistortoides*	ANS-A	E-91, 271	40	308, 415	——	86	1:486, 2:611
	Potentilla pensylvanica L. var. *strigosa* Pallas *ex* Pursh, prairie cinquefoil	*Potentilla pensylvanica* var. *strigosa*	missing	E-92, 356	——	——	387	218	1:527, 2:625
142	*Pseudoroegneria spicata* (Pursh) A. Löve, bluebunch wheatgrass	*Festuca spicata*	ANS-A	E-76, 83	45	408	1126	614	1:459, 2:630
	Pseudotsuga menziesii (Mirbel) Franco, Douglas fir	*Pinus taxifolia*	missing	640	49	203	——	63	1:26, 2:630
143	*Psoralidium lanceolatum* (Pursh) Rydb., lemon scurf-pea	*Psoralea lanceolata*	ANS-L	E-93, 475	——	416	474	273	1:304, 2:633
144	*Psoralidium tenuiflorum* (Pursh) Rydb., wild alfalfa	*Psoralea tenuiflora*	ANS-A, ANS-L	E-93, 475	23	88, 416	475	273	1:304, 2:633
145	*Purshia tridentata* (Pursh) DC., antelope-brush	*Tigarea tridentata*	ANS-A	E-107, 333	26	326, 416	——	222	1:529, 2:637

ID	Current name	Pursh name	Archive	Pursh	Meehan	Cutright	Barkley	H & C	Kartesz
149	*Ribes aureum* Pursh, golden currant	*Ribes aureum*	ANS-A, Kew	E-95, 164	27	183, 290, 417	——	202	1:326, 2:657
151	*Ribes sanguineum* Pursh, red currant	*Ribes sanguineum*	ANS-A	E-96, 164	27	290, 418	——	203	1:327, 2:659
152	*Ribes viscosissimum* Pursh, sticky currant	*Ribes viscosissimum*	ANS-A, Kew	E-96, 163	27	308, 418	——	202	1:328, 2:660
155	*Rubus spectabilis* Pursh, salmonberry	*Rubus spectabilis*	ANS-A	E-97, 348	26	290, 418	——	224	1:535, 2:670
156	*Salvia reflexa* Hornem., lance-leaved sage	*Salvia trichostemoides*	ANS-A, ANS-L	E-99, 19	39	88	732	——	1:352, 2:691
158	*Scutellaria angustifolia* Pursh ssp. *angustifolia*, narrow-leaved skullcap	*Scutellaria angustifolia*	ANS-A	E-101, 412	39	308, 419	——	408	1:352, 2:707
159	*Sedum stenopetalum* Pursh, wormleaf stonecrop	*Sedum stenopetalum*	ANS-A	E-101, 324	28	308, 419	——	183	1:225, 2:709
	Senecio canus Hook., gray ragwort	*Cineraria integrifolia* var. *minor*	missing	E-69, 528	——	——	994	549	1:128, 2:711
	unknown	*Siegesbeckia flosculosa*	missing	E-69, 561	——	——	——	——	——
160	*Shepherdia argentea* (Pursh) Nutt., buffaloberry	*Hippophae argentea*	ANS-A, ANS-L	E-80, 115	40	75, 419	491	302	1:251, 2:717
163	*Sphaeralcea coccinea* (Nutt.) Rydb., red false mallow	*Cristaria coccinea*	ANS-A, ANS-L	E-71, 453	19	326, 407	251	294	1:381, 2:739
164	*Stipa comata* Trin. & Rupr., needle-and-thread	*Stipa juncea*	ANS-A	72	45	183, 420	1229	671	1:464, 2:749
165	*Symphoricarpos albus* (L.) Blake, snowberry	*Symphoria racemosa*	CM	E-106, 162	49	212, 420	827	453	1:194, 2:754
166	*Synthyris missurica* (Raf.) Pennell, mountain kittentails	*Veronica reniformis*	ANS-A, ANS-L	10	39	308, 421	——	441	1:558, 2:756
167	*Trifolium macrocephalum* (Pursh) Poir., big-head clover	*Lupinaster macrocephalus*	ANS-A, ANS-L	E-84, 479	24	290, 421	——	275	1:311, 2:781
168	*Trifolium microcephalum* Pursh, small-head clover	*Trifolium microcephalum*	ANS-A, ANS-L	E-108, 478	24	308, 421	——	275	1:311, 2:781
169	*Trillium ovatum* Pursh, white trillium	*Trillium ovatum*	ANS-A	E-108, 245	44	290, 421	——	695	1:368, 2:783
170	*Trillium petiolatum* Pursh, purple trillium	*Trillium petiolatum*	ANS-A	E-108, 244	44	308, 422	——	695	1:368, 2:783
171	*Triteleia grandiflora* Lindl., Douglas' brodiaea	*Brodiaea grandiflora*	ANS-A, ANS-L	223	42	289, 405	——	686	1:368, 2:785
173	*Vaccinium ovatum* Pursh, evergreen huckleberry	*Vaccinium ovatum*	ANS-A	E-109, 290	36	275, 422	——	348	1:257, 2:791
175	*Xerophyllum tenax* (Pursh) Nutt., Indian basket-grass	*Helonias tenax*	ANS-A, Kew	E-80, 243	44	308, 422	——	696	1:369, 2:811
176	*Zigadenus elegans* Pursh, white camass	*Zigadenus elegans*	ANS-A	E-112, 241	45	326, 423	1258	696	1:369, 2:815

Authors of Botanical Annotation

Anderson, Loran C. (1936–), 39b, 39c, 39d, 40a, 40b, 41

Armstrong, Erica (1970–) [author of ANS 1994 labels], 1a, 1b, 2a, 2b, 3a, 4, 5, 6, 8a, 9, 10, 11, 12, 14, 15, 16, 17a, 17c, 17d, 18, 19a, 19b, 19c, 20, 21a, 21b, 23, 24, 25, 28, 30a, 30b, 31, 32, 33, 34, 35a, 35b, 37, 38, 42, 43, 48, 49a, 49b, 49c, 50, 51, 52, 53, 54, 55, 56, 57, 58, 59, 60a, 61a, 61b, 62, 63a, 63b, 64, 65a, 65b, 66, 67, 68, 69a, 69b, 70, 71a, 71b, 72a, 72b, 73, 74, 75, 76a, 76b, 76c, 79a, 79b, 81, 82, 83a, 83b, 83c, 83d, 84a, 84b, 85, 86, 87, 89, 90, 91, 92a, 92b, 93, 94, 95, 96, 97, 100a, 100b, 101, 102a, 104a, 105, 106, 107, 108, 109, 111, 112, 113a, 113b, 114, 118a, 119a, 119c, 120, 121, 122a, 124, 125, 126, 127a, 127b, 128, 129, 130a, 131a, 131b, 132, 133, 134, 135, 136, 137, 138, 139, 140, 141a, 141b, 142, 144a, 146a, 147a, 147b, 148, 149a, 150, 151, 152a, 153, 154, 155, 156a, 156b, 157, 159, 160a, 160b, 161, 162, 163a, 163b, 166a, 168a, 168b, 170, 172, 173, 174, 175a, 176, 177

Barkworth, Mary Elizabeth (1941–), 164

Barneby, Rupert Charles (1911–), 118a, 118b

Beaman, John Homer (1929–), 62

Bessey, Ernst Athearn (1877–1957), 152b

Bigelow, John Milton (1804–78), 168b

Braxton, John Worth (1948–), 100b

Britton, Nathaniel Lord (1859–1934), 123

Brown, Stewardson (1867–1921), 78b

Chambers, Kenton L. (1929–), 23, 44

Chuang, Tsan Iang (1933–), 116

Clausen, Robert Theodore (1911–81), 159

Coile, Nancy Craft (1940–), 36

Collins, Zaccheus (1764–1831), 165

Crovello, Theodore J. (1940–), 35b

Darlington, William (1782–1863), 146b

Dore, William G. (1912–), 177

Dunn, David Baxter (1917–), 102a, 104a

Eastwood, Alice (1859–1953), 104b

Elliott, Stephen (1771–1830), 165

Engelmann, George (1809–84), 83d

Erickson, Ralph Orlando (1914–), 48

Ewan, Joseph Andorfer (1909–), 8b, 60b, 77b, 102b, 103, 104b, 119b, 130b, 149b, 152b, 175b

Farlow, William Gilson (1844–1919), 59

Freeman, John D. (1941–), 170

Gillett, John Montague (1918–), 167a

Gould, Frank Walton (1913–81), 33

Gray, Asa (1810–88), 17d, 21b, 39b, 102b, 104b, 110b

Greenman, Jesse More (1867–1951), 10, 11, 12, 15, 17a, 17c, 20, 22, 23, 30a, 32, 34, 39a, 39c, 45, 46, 47, 49a, 50, 52, 55, 56, 58, 60a, 64, 69a, 70, 73, 75, 77a, 85, 88, 91, 94, 96, 97, 100a, 105, 106, 111, 113a, 118a, 120, 121, 128, 132, 134, 137, 138, 144a, 148, 154, 159, 162, 166a, 167a, 171a, 172, 175a

Grimes, James W. (1953–), 122b, 123, 143, 144b

Hall, Elihu (1822–82), 131b

Hall, Harvey Monroe (1874–1932), 39a, 39b, 41

Harbour, J. P. (unknown), 131b

Harrison, A. T. (1942–), 39a

Heckard, Lawrence Ray (1923–91), 116

Heller, Amos Arthur (1867–1944), 130a

Henrickson, James (1940–), 145

Hitchcock, Albert Spear (1865–1935), 133, 142, 164

Jackson, Raymond C. (1928–), 106

Johnson, Dale E. (1949–), 63a, 63b

Johnston, Marshall Conring (1930–), 106, 136

Jones, George Neville (1904–70), 162

Kellogg, Albert (1813–87), 83d

Kellogg, Elizabeth Anne (1951–), 133

Lambert, Aylmer Bourke (1761–1842), 1b, 2b, 3b, 8b, 17d, 19b, 21b, 35b, 36, 39b, 39d, 40a, 49c, 60b, 62, 63b, 69b, 71b, 72b, 76b, 76c, 77b, 92b, 102b, 103, 104b, 108, 109, 110b, 113b, 115b, 118b, 119b, 122b, 123, 124, 127b, 130b, 143, 144b, 149b, 152b, 156b, 160b, 163b, 166b, 167b, 168b, 171b, 175b

Lane, Meredith A. (1951–), 77a

Lewis, Meriwether (1774–1809), 3a, 15, 17a, 17b, 18, 19a, 19c, 20, 24, 25, 26, 39a, 39c, 40b, 49a, 55, 61a, 66, 71a, 76a, 77a, 83a, 85, 90, 91, 100a, 114, 122a, 147a, 148, 153, 160a, 162, 177

Martin, James S. (1914–), 168a

Mathias, Mildred Esther (1906–), 93, 94, 95, 96, 97

McNeill, John (1933–), 26

Mears, James A. (1944–), 30b, 34, 61b, 65a, 69b, 76c, 78b, 108, 131a, 146b

Meehan, Thomas (1826–1901) [annotation on all sheets except the following], 5, 8b, 13, 17d, 21b, 29, 30b, 38, 39b, 47, 49a, 60a, 60b, 65a, 70, 77b, 78b, 80, 91, 95, 102b, 103, 104b, 111, 113b, 115b, 117, 119b, 124, 127b, 128, 130b, 132, 149b, 152b, 159, 160b, 165, 167a, 171b, 175b

Miller, John M. (1952–), 44, 45, 46, 47, 88

Moe, L. Maynard (1944–), 110a, 110b

Murray, A. Edward (1935–), 1a

Niehaus, Theodore F. (1937–), 171a, 171b

Nuttall, Thomas (1786–1859), 3b, 30b, 35b, 168b

Olmstead, Richard G. (1951–), 158

Pamphlin, William (1806–99), 8b, 60b, 77b, 102b, 103, 104b, 119b, 130b, 149b, 152b, 175b

Patrick, Thomas S. (1944–), 169

Pennell, Francis Whittier (1886–1952), 31, 39c, 44, 50, 63, 65b, 71b, 81, 85, 124, 125, 166a, 166b, 167a, 168a, 169, 170, 175a

Perino, Charles H. (1940–), 100b

Piper, Charles Vancouver (1867–1926), 4, 7, 10, 48, 52, 54, 57, 68, 93, 94, 100a, 105, 130a, 133, 135, 140, 150

Porter, Cedric Lambert (1905–), 118b

Pursh, Frederick Traugott (1774–1820) [annotation on all sheets except the following], 3a, 17b, 19c, 25, 30b, 40b, 60b, 76c, 92b, 107, 114, 122a, 123, 134, 165

Raven, Peter Hamilton (1936–), 34

Redfield, John H. (1815–1895), 84b

Rickett, Harold W. (1896–1989), 110b, 113b, 115b, 118b, 122b, 123, 127b, 143, 144b, 156b, 160b, 163b

Robinson, Benjamin Lincoln (1864–1935), 65a

Rothrock, Joseph Trimble (1839–1922), 78b

Rudd, Velva E. (1910–), 40a, 49b

Rydberg, Per Axel (1860–1931), 48, 129, 152b

Santana, Donald O. (1943–), 71a

Sargent, Charles Sprague (1841–1927), 83d

Additional Nomenclature

The following nomenclatural modifications (those given after the equal sign) of names used in this volume (those preceding the equal sign) were provided by James L. Reveal of the University of Maryland and Alfred E. Schuyler of the Academy of Natural Sciences, based on their examination of the Lewis and Clark herbarium at the academy. Completed just as this volume was going to press, they are added as an appendix.

3 *Achillea millefolium* L. = *A. millefolium* var. *lanulosa* (Nutt.) Piper

4 *Allium textile* A. Nels. & J. F. Macbr. = *A. geyeri* S. Watson

6 *Amelanchier alnifolia* (Nutt.) Nutt. *ex* M. Roemer = *A. alnifolia* var. *semiintegrifolia* (Hook.) C. L. Hitchc.

10 *Amsinckia intermedia* Fisch. & C. A. Mey. = *A. menziesii* (Lehm.) A. Nelson & J. F. Macr. var. retrorsa (Suskd.) Reveal & Schuyler

12 *Anemone quinquefolia* L. = *A. piperi* Britton *ex* Rydb.

16 *Argentina anserina* (L.) Rydb. = *A. anserina* var. *grandis* (Torr. & A. Gray) Rydb.

21a *Artemisia ludoviciana* Nutt. = *A. ludoviciana* var. *latiloba* Nutt.

21b *Artemisia ludoviciana* Nutt. = *A. longifolia*

23 *Aster oregonensis* (Nutt.) Cronq. = *A. eatonii* (A. Gray) Howell

27 *Atriplex gardneri* (Moq.) D. Dietr. = *A. nuttalli* S. Watson

30 *Blechnum spicant* (L.) Roth = *B. spicant* (L.) Sm.

32 *Calypso bulbosa* (L.) Oakes = *C. bulbosa* (L.) Oakes var. *occidentalis* (Holz.) B. Boivin

39 *Chrysothamnus nauseosus* (Pallas *ex* Pursh) Britt. ssp. *graveolens* (Nutt.) Piper = *Ericameria nauseosa* (Pall. *ex* Pursh) G. L. Nesom & Baird var. *graveolens* (Nutt.) Reveal & Schuyler

40 *Chrysothamnus nauseosus* (Pallas *ex* Pursh) Britt. ssp. *nauseosus* = *Ericameria nauseosa* (Pallas *ex* Pursh) G. L. Nesom & Baird var. *nauseosa*

44 *Claytonia lanceolata* Pursh = *C. lanceolata* Pall. *ex* Pursh

52 *Coreopsis tinctoria* Nutt. var. *atkinsoniana* (Dougl. *ex* Lindl.) H. Parker = *C. tinctoria* Nutt. var. *atkinsoniana* (Douglas *ex* Lindl.) H. Parker *ex* E. B. Sm.

56 *Delphinium menziesii* DC. = *D. menziesii* var. *pyramidale* (Ewan) C. L. Hitchc.

57 *Dodecatheon jeffreyi* Van Houtte = *D. poeticum* L. F. Hend.

58 *Dryopteris expansa* (K. Presl) Fraser-Jenkins & Jermy = *D. carthusiana* (Vill.) H. P. Fuchs

64 *Erysimum asperum* (Nutt.) DC. = *E. capitatum* Douglas *ex* Hook. var. *purshii* (Durand) Rollins

71 *Fritillaria lanceolata* Pursh = *F. affinis* (Schultes & Schultes f.) Sealy

75 *Geum triflorum* Pursh = *G. triflorum* var. *ciliatum* (Pursh) Fassett

80 *Hypnum oreganum* Sull. = *Stokesiella oregana* (Sull.) H. Rob.

89 *Leymus arenarius* (L.) Hochst. = *L. mollis* (Trin.) Pilger

94 *Lomatium dissectum* (Nutt.) Mathias & Constance = *L. dissectum* var. *multifidum* (Nutt.) Mathias & Const.

95 *Lomatium grayi* (Coult. & Rose) Coult. & Rose = *L. cuspidatum* Mathias & Const.

100a *Lonicera ciliosa* (Pursh) Poir. *ex* DC. = *L. utahensis* S. Watson

101 *Lonicera involucrata* Banks *ex* Spreng. = *L. involucrata* (Richardson) Banks *ex* Spreng.

105 *Machaeranthera canescens* (Pursh) Gray = *M. canescens* var. *incana* (Lindl.) A. Gray

108 *Mahonia aquifolium* (Pursh) Nutt. = *Berberis aquifolium* Pursh

109 *Mahonia nervosa* (Pursh) Nutt. = *Berberis nervosa* Pursh

110 *Matricaria discoidea* DC. = *M. matricarioides* (Less.) Porter

111 *Microseris lindeyi* (DC.) Gray = *Uropappus lindleyi* (DC.) Nutt.

112 *Mimulus guttatus* DC. = *M. guttatus* Fisch. *ex* DC.

115 *Oenothera cespitosa* Nutt. ssp. *cespitosa* = *O. cespitosa* Fraser f. & J. T. Fraser

118 *Oxytropis nana* Nutt. var. *besseyi* (Rydb.) Isely = *O. besseyi* (Rydb.) Blank.

126 *Pentaphylloides floribunda* (Pursh) A. Löve = *Dasiphora fruticosa* (L.) Rydb.

131 *Pinus ponderosa* P. & C. Lawson = *P. ponderosa* Douglas *ex* Lawson and C. Lawson

133 *Poa secunda* J. Presl = *P. canbyi* (Scribn.) Howell

135 *Polemonium caeruleum* L. = *P. pulcherrimum* Hook.

141a *Prunus virginiana* L. = *P. virginiana* var. *melanocarpa* (A. Nelson) Sarg.

145 *Purshia tridentata* (Pursh) DC. = *P. tridentata* (Pursh) DC. *ex* Poir.

149b *Ribes aureum* Pursh = *R. aureum* var. *aureum* [flowering specimen on right]; *R. aureum* var. *villosum* Berland. [two sterile specimens on left]

159 *Sedum stenopetalum* Pursh = *S. stenopetalum* Pursh [packet]; *S. lanceolatum* Torr. [stems]

161 *Solidago rigida* L. = *S. rigida* L. var. *humilis* Porter

163 *Sphaeralcea coccinea* (Nutt.) Rydb. = *S. coccinea* (Fraser f. & J. T. Fraser) Rydb.

164 *Stipa comata* Trin. & Rupr. = *Hesperostipa comata* (Trin. & Rupr.) Barkworth

165 *Symphoricarpos albus* (L.) Blake = *S. albus* var. *laevigatus* (Fernald) Blake

Sources Cited

BARKLEY: Barkley, T. M., ed. *Flora of the Great Plains.* Lawrence: University Press of Kansas, 1986.

CUTRIGHT: Cutright, Paul Russell. *Lewis and Clark: Pioneering Naturalists.* Urbana: University of Illinois Press, 1969.

E [Ewan]: [Separately paged introduction to Pursh; listed in Pursh column of appendixes with E preceding the page number.]

H & C: Hitchcock, C. Leo, and Arthur Cronquist. *Flora of the Pacific Northwest: An Illustrated Manual.* Seattle: University of Washington Press, 1973.

KARTESZ: Kartesz, John T. *A Synonymized Checklist of the Vascular Flora of the United States, Canada, and Greenland.* 2d ed. 2 vols. Portland, Oreg.: Timber Press, 1994.

MEEHAN: Meehan, Thomas. "The Plants of Lewis and Clark's Expedition Across the Continent, 1804–1806." *Proceedings of the Academy of Natural Sciences of Philadelphia* 50 (1898): 12–49.

PURSH: Pursh, Frederick. *Flora Americae Septentrionalis.* 1814. Reprint. Edited by Joseph Ewan. Braunschweig, Germany: Strauss and Cramer, 1979.

Alexander, Edward P. *Museum Masters: Their Museums and Their Influence.* Nashville, Tenn.: American Association for State and Local History, 1983.

Betts, Edwin Morris. *Thomas Jefferson's Garden Book.* Philadelphia: American Philosophical Society, 1944.

Conservatoire et Jardin botaniques de la Ville de Genève, Geneva, Switzerland. Personal communications, June 5 and 14, 1996.

Coues, Elliott. "Notes on Mr. Thomas Meehan's Paper on the Plants of Lewis and Clark's Expedition Across the Continent, 1804–06." *Proceedings of the Academy of Natural Sciences of Philadelphia* 50 (1898): 291–315.

Cutright, Paul Russell. "*Cleome integrifolia* the Third." *We Proceeded On* 9 (May-June 1983): 4–7.

———. "Contributions of Philadelphia to Lewis and Clark History: Part II, Postlude (1807–1814)." *WPO Publication No. 6* (Portland, Oreg., 1982), 21–39.

———. "Meriwether Lewis: Botanist." *Oregon Historical Quarterly* 69 (June 1968): 148–70.

———. "Meriwether Lewis Prepares for a Trip West." *Bulletin of the Missouri Historical Society* 23 (October 1966): 3–20.

———. "Well-traveled Plants of Lewis and Clark." *We Proceeded On* 4 (February 1978): 6–9.

de Condolle, A. P. "Remarks on two Genera of Plants. . . ."

Transactions of the Linnaean Society of London 12 (1818): 152–58.

Ewan, Joseph. "Frederick Pursh, 1774–1820, and His Botanical Associates." *Proceedings of the American Philosophical Society* 96 (October 1952): 599–628.

———. "Publication of the *Flora,*" "Chronology," and "Sertum Purshianum," in Pursh, *Flora,* 33–36, 40–47, 55–112.

Greene, John C. *American Science in the Age of Jefferson.* Ames: Iowa State University Press, 1984.

Harrison, A. T. Personal communication, October 8, 1984.

Hu, Shiu-ying. "A Monograph of the Genus *Philadelphus.*" *Journal of the Arnold Arboretum* 35 (October 1954): 275–333, 36 (January 1955): 52–109, 37 (January 1956): 15–90.

Jackson, Donald D. "Some Books Carried by Lewis and Clark." *Bulletin of the Missouri Historical Society* 16 (October 1959): 3–13.

Jackson, Donald, ed. *Letters of the Lewis and Clark Expedition with Related Documents, 1783–1854.* 2d ed., 2 vols. Urbana: University of Illinois Press, 1978.

Mears, James A. "Some Sources of the Herbarium of Henry Muhlenberg (1753–1815)." *Proceedings of the American Philosophical Society* 122 (June 1978): 155–74.

Miller, Hortense S. "The Herbarium of Aylmer Bourke Lambert: Notes on Its Acquisition, Dispersal, and Present Whereabouts." *Taxon* 19 (August 1970): 489–656.

Pennell, Francis W. "Historic Botanical Collections of the American Philosophical Society and the Academy of Natural Sciences of Philadelphia." *Proceedings of the American Philosophical Society* 94 (April 1950): 137–51.

Rogers, George A. Personal communications, June 27 and 28, 1997.

Rogers, George A., and Albert E. Sanders. "Stephen Elliott's Northward Journey, June–November 1808," unpublished MS (private collection), 1995.

Rossi, Linda, and Alfred E. Schuyler. "The Iconography of Plants Collected on the Lewis and Clark Expedition." *Great Plains Research* 3 (February 1993): 39–60.

Sanders, Albert E. Personal communications, September 25, 1996, and September 8, 1997.

Silverstein, Michael. Personal communications, August 30 and September 16, 1996.

True, Rodney H. "Some Neglected Botanical Results of the Lewis and Clark Expedition," *Proceedings of the American Philosophical Society* 67 (1928): 1–19.